WOMEN IN STATE POLITICS IN INDIA

The dynamics of Indian politics is reflected in the flexible and fluctuating relations between the centre and the states as well as in the equations within the multiparty political system. This book is one of the first to explore the participation of women in state politics in India and how women navigate the dynamic spaces and hierarchies of the Indian political system.

With the help of in-depth studies of 16 states in India, it analyses the gender profile of political parties and legislative bodies in these states; the question of women's representation which is miniscule in legislative assemblies and women voters and their voting choices. It also explores the roadblocks and barriers they face, along with a study of women's participation in informal politics. The chapters in this book underline the need for women's active participation both inside and outside the party system to make democracy more robust and meaningful.

Topical, rich in empirical data, this book will be an essential read for scholars and researchers of Indian politics, gender studies, political science, sociology, public administration, and South Asia studies.

Pam Rajput is Professor Emeritus at Panjab University, Chandigarh; Former Dean, Faculty of Arts, Chair and Professor of Political Science, and Founder Director of the Centre for Women's Studies and Development, Chandigarh. She has been a Visiting Professor at Hiroshima University, Japan; Rand Afrikaans University (now University of Johannesburg) South Africa; and a number of Canadian universities under the Shastri Indo-Canadian Institute's visiting professor programme. Her publications (co-authored/co-edited) include *Women and Globalisation, Narratives of Women's Studies*. In addition to her academic profile, Rajput chaired the Government of India High-Level Committee on the Status of Women.

Usha Thakkar is President of the Mani Bhavan Gandhi Sangrahalaya, Mumbai. She retired as Professor and Head at the Department of Political Science, SNDT Women's University, Mumbai.

She has done her post-doctoral research at the University of Chicago and at Cornell University on Fulbright fellowships and at York University,

Canada, on a WID fellowship from the Shastri Indo-Canadian Institute. The Asiatic Society of Mumbai has conferred her with an Honorary Fellowship. Her publications (authored/co-authored/co-edited) include *Congress Radio: Usha Mehta and the Underground Radio Station of 1942*, *Gandhi in Bombay: Towards Swaraj*, *Women in Indian Society*, and *Culture and the Making of Identity in Contemporary India*.

WOMEN IN STATE POLITICS IN INDIA

Missing in the Corridors of Power

Edited by Pam Rajput and Usha Thakkar

LONDON AND NEW YORK

First published 2023
by Routledge
4 Park Square, Milton Park, Abingdon, Oxon OX14 4RN

and by Routledge
605 Third Avenue, New York, NY 10158

Routledge is an imprint of the Taylor & Francis Group, an informa business

© 2023 selection and editorial matter, Pam Rajput and Usha Thakkar;
individual chapters, the contributors

The right of Pam Rajput and Usha Thakkar to be identified as the
authors of the editorial material, and of the authors for their individual
chapters, has been asserted in accordance with sections 77 and 78 of
the Copyright, Designs and Patents Act 1988.

All rights reserved. No part of this book may be reprinted or
reproduced or utilised in any form or by any electronic, mechanical, or
other means, now known or hereafter invented, including photocopying
and recording, or in any information storage or retrieval system,
without permission in writing from the publishers.

Trademark notice: Product or corporate names may be trademarks
or registered trademarks, and are used only for identification and
explanation without intent to infringe.

British Library Cataloguing-in-Publication Data
A catalogue record for this book is available from the British Library

Library of Congress Cataloging-in-Publication Data
A catalog record has been requested for this book

ISBN: 978-1-032-32833-1 (hbk)
ISBN: 978-1-032-44996-8 (pbk)
ISBN: 978-1-003-37486-2 (ebk)

DOI: 10.4324/9781003374862

Typeset in Sabon
by Deanta Global Publishing Services, Chennai, India

IN THE 75TH YEAR OF INDIA'S INDEPENDENCE,
DEDICATED TO ALL UNKNOWN AND KNOWN
WOMEN FREEDOM FIGHTERS OF INDIA AND
HON'BLE DROUPADI MURMU, THE FIRST TRIBAL
WOMAN PRESIDENT OF INDIA

CONTENTS

List of Figures	ix
List of Tables	x
List of Contributors	xiii
Foreword	xv
Preface	xviii
List of Acronyms	xix

	Introduction	1
1	Women and politics in Jammu and Kashmir	53
	REKHA CHOWDHARY AND VIBHUTI UBBOTT	
2	Women in Haryana's politics: Myth of empowerment	71
	RANBIR SINGH AND KUSHAL PAL	
3	Women in Punjab politics: Missing, voiceless, inactive	83
	SIMRIT KAHLON AND SEEMA THAKUR	
4	Political participation of women in politics of Uttar Pradesh	101
	MANUKA KHANNA	
5	Women in politics in Himachal Pradesh	116
	BHAWANA JHARTA	
6	Women and state politics in Haryana	133
	REICHA TANWAR	
7	Kerala: Beyond the politicking of gender politics	141
	MEENA T. PILLAI	

vii

CONTENTS

8 Women in Telangana state politics and their struggles 160
REKHA PANDE

9 Women in Goa's politics: The need for fast tracking to
achieve gender equality 176
ALAKNANDA SHRINGARE

10 Maharashtra: Engendering the dilemmas of democratic politics 191
CHAITRA REDKAR

11 Women and politics in Gujarat 211
KALPANA SHAH

12 Women and politics in Maharashtra 228
BHARATI PATIL

13 Women in Madhya Pradesh state politics: An analysis 244
RASHMI SHRIVASTAVA

14 Women legislators in Rajasthan: A paradoxical scenario 257
ASHA KAUSHIK

15 Women in state politics in West Bengal 273
KABERI CHAKRABARTI

16 Engendering Bihar politics: Myth or Reality? 289
SHEFALI ROY

17 Women's representation in state politics in Sikkim 305
NANCY CHODEN LHASUNGPA

18 The landscape of inadequate assertion: Women in Bihar politics 318
NARENDRA KUMAR ARYA

19 Gender dynamics in electoral politics in Assam 335
PALLABI MEDHI AND SANDHYA GOSWAMI

Epilogue: Glimpses of perspectives/experiences of four women
active in politics and movements 354

Index 363

LIST OF FIGURES

11.1	Gross enrolment ratio	213
11.2	Voting patterns in the state assembly (1962–2017)	216
11.3	Male and female candidates in state assembly elections (1962–2017)	217
11.4	Number of male and female members in the Gujarat assembly	218
11.5	Number of male and female Lok Sabha members from Gujarat	220
16.1	Male versus female voting behaviour in assembly elections (percentage)	293
16.2	Percentage of female contestants in assembly elections	294

LIST OF TABLES

1.1	Women voters in the assembly elections (1972–87)	58
1.2	Women voters in the assembly elections (1996–2014)	58
1.3	Women contestants in the assembly elections (1972–2014)	59
3.1	Punjab: Socioeconomic profile	87
3.2	Punjab: Women voter turnout during successive assembly elections	92
3.3	Representation of women from Punjab in the Lok Sabha (1952–2019)	93
3.4	Women members of the Rajya Sabha (1952–2003)	93
3.5	Representation of women in Punjab's assembly (1952–2017)	94
3.6	Performance of women candidates in successive assembly polls in Punjab (1967–2022)	96
4.1	UP women's representation in the Lok Sabha (1952–2019)	107
4.2	Women's representation in the UP state assembly (1952–2022)	108
5.1	Women voters in different legislative assembly elections (1972–2017)	120
5.2	Representation of women in the HP assembly (1972–2007)	122
5.3	Women in party hierarchies	125
6.1	Number of elected members in the Lok Sabha from Haryana	134
6.2	Number of Rajya Sabha members from Haryana	135
6.3	Women's representation in the legislative assembly (1967–2019)	136
6.4	Contestants in Lok Sabha elections from Haryana (1971, 2014, and 2019)	137

LIST OF TABLES

7.1	State-wise women voter turnout for general elections (2019)	142
7.2	State-wise women's participation in the 17th Lok Sabha elections	144
7.3	Participation of women in the state assembly	146
7.4	Women's representatives in Panchayati Raj Institutions	148
9.1	Gender-wise data of candidates contesting the Goa assembly elections	179
9.2	Voting percentage in the Goa assembly elections	181
9.3	Party tickets given to women candidates	183
9.4	Women candidates in the 2022 assembly elections	183
10.1	Women members in the Rajya Sabha from Maharashtra	193
10.2	Women in the Lok Sabha from Maharashtra	194
10.3	Women candidates in the legislative assembly elections	195
10.4	Women members of the Maharashtra legislative council	197
10.5	No-confidence motions against women sarpanches (1999–2001)	199
11.1	Major crimes against women under the Indian Penal Code (IPC)	214
12.1	Women from Maharashtra in the Rajya Sabha	231
12.2	Voting percentage of women voters	234
12.3	Number of women in the state legislative assembly	234
13.1	Women in various institutions (2018)	246
13.2	Number of women MLAs in the state assembly	247
13.3	Party-wise number of women candidates who contested in the last three assembly elections in Madhya Pradesh	248
13.4	Women candidates who won the elections out of the total number of women candidates who contested the elections	248
14.1	Voting patterns in Rajasthan's Vidhan Sabha elections	263
14.2	Contestants in the Vidhan Sabha elections	266
14.3	Women legislators in the Rajasthan assembly	267
14.4	Women in the council of ministers and in other high positions in the assembly	269
15.1	Performance of women candidates in the 2016 assembly elections	278
16.1	Bihar's demographic status	290
16.2	Elected women representatives in the Bihar assembly	295
16.3	Women members in the Rajya Sabha from Bihar since 1952	295

LIST OF TABLES

16.4	Number of women voters in the Lok Sabha elections in Bihar	296
16.5	Women representatives in the Lok Sabha from Bihar	297
16.6	Elected women representatives in PRIs	298
17.1	Female representation in Sikkim's legislative assembly (1974–2019)	311
18.1	Women in assembly elections in Bihar (1952–2015)	320
18.2	Women candidates in state assembly elections (2000–10)	323
18.3	Dynastic trends in Bihar politics	328
18.4	Dynastic trends in state politics	329
19.1	(A) Women candidates nominated by major national political parties assembly elections (1952–2021)	341
19.1	(B) Women candidates nominated by major state political parties assembly elections (1985–2021)	342
19.2	Voter turnout in assembly elections (1962–2021)	344
19.3	Assembly elections, Assam (gender-wise) (1952–2021)	346
19.4	Women contestants for the Lok Sabha (1952–2019)	347
19.5	Winnability percentage in the assembly elections (1952–2021)	349

LIST OF CONTRIBUTORS

Narendra Kumar Arya is Associate Professor at the Department of Political Science, Mahatma Gandhi Central University, Bihar, India.

Kaberi Chakrabarti is Associate Professor of the Department of Political Science, University of Calcutta, Kolkata, West Bengal, India.

Rekha Chowdhary is former Professor of Political Science at the University of Jammu, Jammu, India.

Sandhya Goswami is Former Professor at the Department of Political Science, Gauhati University, Assam, India.

Bhawana Jharta is Professor at the Department of Political Science, International Center for Distance Education and Open Learning, Himachal Pradesh University, Shimla, Himachal Pradesh, India.

Simrit Kahlon is Professor of Geography at the Panjab University, Chandigarh, India.

Asha Kaushik is Former Dean of Social Sciences, Professor of Political Science, and Director at the Centre for Women's Studies, University of Rajasthan, Jaipur, Rajasthan, India.

Manuka Khanna is Head of Department of Political Science at the University of Lucknow, Lucknow, Uttar Pradesh, India.

Nancy Choden Lhasungpa is Assistant Professor at the Department of Sociology, Nar Bahadur Bhandari Government College, Tadong, Gangtok, Sikkim, India.

Pallabi Medhi is Assistant Professor at the Department of Political Science, Guwahati College, Guwahati, Assam, India.

Kushal Pal is Associate Professor and Head of Department of Political Science at the Dyal Singh College, Karnal, Haryana, India.

Rekha Pande is Professor of History and Women's Studies at the University of Hyderabad, Hyderabad, Telangana, India.

LIST OF CONTRIBUTORS

Bharati Patil is Professor of the Department of Political Science at Shivaji University, Kolhapur, Maharashtra, India.

Meena T Pillai is Professor and Director at the Centre for Cultural Studies, University of Kerala, Thiruvananthapuram, Kerala, India.

Chaitra Redkar is Associate Professor in Humanities and Social Sciences at the Indian Institute of Science Education & Research (IISER), Pune, Maharashtra, India.

Shefali Roy is Professor and Head at the Department of Political Science, Patna University, Patna, Bihar, India.

Kalpana Shah is Professor of Sociology (Retired) at the Veer Narmad South Gujarat University, Surat, Gujarat, India.

Alaknanda Shringare is Assistant Professor at the Department of Political Science, Goa University, Taleigao Plateau, Panaji, Goa, India.

Rashmi Shrivastava is Professor (Retired) at the School of Studies in Political Science, Public Administration and Human Rights, Vikram University, Ujjain, Madhya Pradesh, India.

Ranbir Singh is Senior Fellow at the Institute of Social Sciences, New Delhi, India, and Former Dean Social Sciences and Academic Affairs, Kurukshetra University, Kurukshetra, Haryana, India.

Reicha Tanwar is Former Director of Women's Studies Research Center at the Kurukshetra University, Kurukshetra, Haryana, India.

Seema Thakur is Guest Faculty at the Department of Gandhian and Peace Studies and Masters' Programme in Governance and Leadership, Panjab University, Chandigarh, India.

Vibhuti Ubbott is Assistant Professor of Political Science at the Department of Higher Education, Government of Jammu and Kashmir, India.

FOREWORD

Today, only one-fourth of the members of the world's parliaments are women. Despite the many gains in the decades following the UN World Conference on Women, Beijing, 1995, politics is still grossly male dominated. This implies that three-fourth of the world's parliamentarians are men, still far from the stated goal of parity, which is normally defined as 50–50 or at least 45–55. Under 10 per cent of the world's heads of states and under 10 per cent of the world's prime ministers are women. Yet, in 13 countries, women are holding 50 per cent or more of the ministerial positions, including in Nicaragua, Austria, Belgium, and Sweden.

For centuries, women were blamed for their under-representation in simplistic terms, 'women do not understand politics' or 'women are not interested in politics' or 'women are not qualified for leadership positions'. The Platform for Action, adopted at the Beijing Conference 1995, turned the argument around. The declaration directed attention towards those cultural and institutional mechanisms which tend to exclude women from political decision-making. Thus, the focus of the discussion changed from an individual woman or women as a group to the responsibility of the political institutions themselves, including political parties, who are the real gatekeepers to elected positions, since in most political systems the political parties control the nomination of candidates for elections.

With its focus on women in the state assemblies, this excellent book fills a gap in research on women in politics in India. Till now, such research has predominantly focused on the globally renowned 33 per cent reservation for women in the panchayats and on the lack of progress in women's representation at the national level. In general, we need more research on why women are under-represented at all levels of political decision-making.

This book argues rightly that women do not constitute a unified political group as they are divided, socially and politically, just as men are. Women's parties, which have emerged in many countries throughout history, as also in India as this book shows, usually have short political careers. Yet, women are undoubtedly an emerging and important political factor in India, as in many other countries in the world. Increasing gender

FOREWORD

gap is discussed in many countries today. Even if all women do not vote the same (just like all men do not), political parties have to pay attention to the gender gap, that is, statistical differences in women's and men's support for different political issues and gendered differences in party preferences. The gender gap becomes especially important when there is fierce competition between two large parties with only marginal differences in their voter support.

Research has found a considerable gender gap among voters and politicians when it comes to gender equality politics. Not all women are advocates for women's rights and the empowerment of women though many men are, yet in all parliaments there are more feminists among women politicians than among their male colleagues. Today, a gender gap is also found in attitudes concerning issues other than just equality policies, like policies concerning military spending or climate politics.

Writing this foreword made me speculate, if perhaps we should stop labelling all the strategies for women and gender equality for 'affirmative action'. Instead, we could begin to talk about what is truly at stake, 'democratic adjustments strategies'. When, for instance, a country lowers the voting age in order to include younger people in politics, we would not call such a move 'affirmative action for youth'.

With one-third reservation for women in local panchayats and municipalities, India has placed itself in the forefront globally. It is remarkable for the world that following the 1993 amendment to the Constitution reserving one-third of the seats for women more than a million Indian women are a part of the third tier of electoral politics in India. Moreover, since these reservations for women are built into the existing reservations for Scheduled Castes, including for council heads, we see the principle of intersectionality in praxis. This book tells us that more than 20 Indian states have raised the percentage of local reservations for women from 33 to 50 per cent. With this book, our knowledge about gender politics at the state level will increase hugely.

So much more striking is the repeated rejection of gender quotas by the national Parliament in India for its own elections. The gender quota provisions adopted at the local level in India, together with other types of electoral gender quotas adopted in other countries, have shown that there are ways to overcome the difficulties of combining a quota system with the single member constituency electoral system. The proposal of double representation – one woman and one man to be elected from each constituency – is one such solution, even if this model without changing the constituency structure means doubling the number of Parliament members. Another option is the so-called 'horizontal candidate quotas', known from Mexico and France. This model implies that each political party is obliged to nominate an equal number of male and female candidates, calculated for a whole region or state.

xvi

FOREWORD

This book, based on comprehensive research on women in state politics in India, fills a gap in literature, since most research looks at either the national or the local level. The 28 state governments in India are important arenas for policymaking, and yet, the representation of women is only 9 per cent on average varying from 0 to 14 per cent as the book shows.

Reading the book from a comparative perspective is an eye-opener, since the variations between women's representation in different state assemblies challenge traditional theories, which tend to focus on larger cultural and socioeconomic trends. A comparative perspective will inevitably point to the importance of institutional changes and variations, not least in party structures, when trying to explain variations in women's under-representation. As an example, the differences presented in this book between women's relatively higher representation in Rajasthan despite the state's strong patriarchal traditions compared to Kerala's remarkably lower representation of women, show that institutional factors and party culture can be just as important for women's participation and representation in politics as socioeconomic factors.

Drude Dahlerup
Professor Emerita of Political Science, Stockholm University

PREFACE

It is an irony of fate that as India celebrates its 75th anniversary of independence, as the largest democracy of the world, we need to ask: 'Where are the women' in the federal polity at the state level. We feel honoured and privileged to have the second woman to be elected as the President of India in Hon'ble Droupadi Murmu and who is the first Tribal woman to be elected to the highest office, yet the fact remains that women seem to be lost in the vortex of masculine politics. They seem to be lost in the vortex of masculine politics. This edited book is the first of its kind on women in state politics which presents this irony, covering 16 states and all regions. The framework of the book goes beyond the narrative of numbers by relating women's political participation to the larger context of the politics of the state. We do hope that this book will be of added value not only to academics but also to policymakers.

We wish to put on record our gratitude to all the contributors to this book. We thank the support provided by the libraries, in particular, 'Dosti House: Your American Space' at the US Consulate General, Mumbai, and Panjab University, Chandigarh. We are indebted to Professor Drude Dahlerup for sparing her valuable time to go through our manuscript and writing the foreword to this book. We thank Dr Seema Thakur, Lakshmi Vivek, and Rajesh Shinde for their support. Last but not the least we are grateful to our friend Punam Thakur for scanning through the book professionally and giving us valuable suggestions. The team at Routledge has been cooperative and efficient. Our special thanks to them all.

Pam Rajput
Usha Thakkar
August 1, 2022

LIST OF ACRONYMS

AAP	Aam Aadmi Party
ABVP	Akhil Bharatiya Vidyarthi Parishad
ADR	Association for Democratic Reforms
AGP	Assam Gana Parishad
AIADMK	All India Anna Dravida Munnetra Kazhagam
AICC	All India Congress Committee
AICCTU	All India Central Council of Trade Union
AIDWA	All India Democratic Women's Association
AIFB	All India Forward Bloc
AIMC	All India Mahila Congress
AIPWA	All India Progressive Women's Association
AISHE	All India Survey of Higher Education
AITMC	All India Trinamool Congress
AITUC	All India Trade Union Congress
AIUDF	All India United Democratic Front
AJP	Assam Jatiya Parishad
AMS	Andhra Mahasabha
AMS	Assam Mahila Samiti
APRCC	The Revolutionary Communist Centre of Andhra Pradesh
ASHA	Accredited Social Health Activist
AWAG	Ahmedabad Women's Action Group
BBGP	Bhausaheb Bandodkar Gomantak Party
BBMP	Bruhat Bengaluru Mahanagara Palike
BEW	Bihar Election Watch
BIMARU	Bihar, Madhya Pradesh, Rajasthan, and Uttar Pradesh
BJD	Biju Janata Dal
BJP	Bharatiya Janata Party
BL	Bhutia Lepcha
BMC	Brihanmumbai Municipal Corporation
BMJ	British Medical Journal
BMM	Bharatiya Mahila Morcha
BPF	Bodoland People's Front

LIST OF ACRONYMS

BPFA	Beijing Declaration and Platform for Action
BPPF	Bodo Peoples Progressive Front
BSP	Bahujan Samaj Party
C3	Centre for Catalyzing Change
CAA	Citizenship Amendment Act, 2019
CEC	Central Election Committee
CEDAW	Convention on the Elimination of All Forms of Discrimination Against Women
CITU	Centre of Indian Trade Union
Cong-I	Congress (Indira)
CPI	Communist Party of India
CPI(M)	The Communist Party of India (Marxist)
CSAG	Civil Society Advisory Groups
CSDS	Centre for the Study of Developing Societies
CSW	Commission on the Status of Women
CSWI	Committee on Status of Women in India
DCC	District Congress Committee
DEM	Dukhtaran-E-Millat
DESM&E	Directorate of Economics, Statistics, Monitoring and Evaluation
DMK	Dravida Munnetra Kazhagam
ECI	Election Commission of India
ECOSOC	Economic and Social Council
EGM	Expert Group Meeting
FAOW	Forum Against Oppression of Women
GA	General Assembly
GBA	Goa Bachao Abhiyan
GEF	Global Environment Facility
GER	Gross Enrolment Ratio
GID-DB	Gender, Institutions and Development Database
GII	Global Innovation Index
GNP	Gross National Product
GP HDI	Gram Panchayat Human Development Index
GPRA	Goa Panchayati Raj Act
GPU	Gram Panchayat Unit
GSDP	Gross State Domestic Product
HAM	Hindustani Awam Party
HDI	Human Development Index
HJC	Haryana Janhit Congress
HLCSW	High Level Committee on Status of Women
HMS	Hind Mazdoor Sabha
HVP	Haryana Vikas Party
IMR	Infant Mortality Rate
INC	Indian National Congress

LIST OF ACRONYMS

INLD	Indian National Lok Dal
INTUC	Indian National Union Congress
IPC	Indian Penal Code
IPS	Indian Police Service
IPU	Inter Parliamentarian Union
IRS	Indian Revenue Service
IUML	The Indian Union Muslim League
IWWAGE	Initiative for What Works to Advance Women and Girls in the Economy
J&K	Jammu and Kashmir
JAP	Jan Adhikar Party
JD	Janata Dal
JD(S)	Janata Dal (Secular)
JD(U)	Janata Dal (United)
JJP	Jannayak Janta Party
KCR	K Chandrashekar Rao
KOL	Kiss of Love
LDF	Left Democratic Front
LFPR	Labour Force Participation Rate
LGBT	Lesbian, Gay, Bisexual, and Transgender
LJP	Lok Janshakti Party
MC	Mahila Congress
MCP	Mother and Child Protection
MGP	Maharashtrawadi Gomantak Party
MISA	Maintenance of Internal Security Act
MKP	Mahila Kalyan Parishad
MMR	Maternal Mortality Ratio
MNM	Makkal Needhi Maiam
MNREGA	Mahatma Gandhi National Rural Employment Guarantee Act 2005
MNS	Maharashtra Navnirman Sena
MoPR	Ministry of Panchayat Raj
MoPSI	Ministry of Statistics and Programme Implementation
MP	Madhya Pradesh
MP	Member of Parliament
MP	Mukhiya Pati
MRA	Mahila Rajsatta Andolan
MY	Muslim-Yadav
NABARD	National Bank of Agricultural and Rural Development
NAWO	National Alliance of Women
NBA	Narmada Bachao Andolan
NC	National Conference
NCAS	National Centre for Advocacy Studies
NCP	Nationalist Congress Party

xxi

LIST OF ACRONYMS

NCRB	National Crime Record Bureau
NDA	National Democratic Alliance
NEC	North Eastern Council
NEN	North East Network
NFDW	National Federation of Dalit Women
NFHS	National Family Health Survey
NIOS	National Institute of Open Schooling
NITI	National Institution for Transforming India
NLM	National Literacy Mission
NPPW	National Perspective Plan for Women
NSO	National Statistical Office
NSSO	National Sample Survey Office
NTSZC	North Telangana Special Zone Committee
OBC	Other Backward Caste
OECD	The Organisation for Economic Co-operation and Development
PBET	Purva Bharati Educational Trust
PBGMS	Paschim Banga Ganatantrik Mahila Samiti
PDF	Progressive Democratic Front
PDP	People's Democratic Party
PLFS	Periodic Labour Force Survey
PRC	Permanent Residence Certificate
PRI	Panchayat Raj Institutions
PT	Primitive Tribe
PVMT	PV Mandlik Trust
PWG	Peoples War Group
PWP	Peasants and Workers Party of India
RBI	Reserve Bank of India
RIS	Rising Sun Party
RJD	Rashtriya Janata Dal
RLD	Rashtriya Lok Dal
RLSP	Rashtriya Lok Samta Party
RPI	Republican Party of India
RSS	Rashtriya Swayamsevak Sangh
SAD	Shiromani Akali Dal
SC	Scheduled Caste
SDF	Sikkim Democratic Front
SDG	Sustainable Development Goal
SEWA	Self-Employed Women's Association
SEWA MP	Self-Employed Women's Association Madhya Pradesh
SGRGY	Sampoorna Grameen Rozgar Guarantee Yojana
SHG	Self-Help Group
SKM	Sikkim Krantikari Morcha
SLL	Special and Local Laws

LIST OF ACRONYMS

SNDP	Sree Narayana Dharma Paripalana
SP	Samajwadi Party
SPSC	State Public Service Commission
SPSDC	A Non-Governmental Organization in Bihar
SSCW	Sikkim State Commission for Women
SSP	Sikkim Sangram Parishad
ST	Scheduled Tribe
SUCI	Socialist Unity Centre of India
SVD	Samyukta Vidhayak Dal
SVEEP	Systematic Voters Education and Electoral Participation
TAR	Tibet Autonomous Region
TDP	Telugu Desam Party
TMC	The All India Trinamool Congress
TPS	Telangana Praja Samithi
TRS	Telangana Rashtra Samithi
TUCC	Trade Union Coordination Centre
UDF	United Democratic Front
UDHR	Universal Declaration of Human Rights
UGP	United Goans Party
ULB	Urban Local Bodies
UNDP	United Nations Development Program
UNGA	United Nations General Assembly
UNGASS	United Nations General Assembly Special Session
UNU-WIDER	United Nations University World Institute for Development Economics Research
UP	Uttar Pradesh
UPA	United Progressive Alliance
UPSC	Union Public Services of India
UWF	United Women's Front
VAWP	Violence Against Women in Politics
VIP	Vikassheel Insaan Party
W20	Women 20
WID	Women in Development
WinG	Women in Governance
WLTC	Women's Leadership Training Centre
WPR	Work Participation Rate
WRB	Women's Reservation Bill
YASHADA	Yashwantrao Chavan Academy of Development Administration
YSR CP	Yuvajana Sramika Rythu Congress Party
ZP	Zila Panchayat

INTRODUCTION

Introduction

Pam Rajput and Usha Thakkar

'She has proved herself as a leader in politics, just like a man'. 'She is efficient in political work, just like a man'. 'She can cope with the challenges in elections, just like a man'. 'She is good at organizing political meetings, just like a man'. 'She can take tough decisions, just like a man'.

Comments and remarks like these do not make a rainbow of different shades reflecting women politicians' successes and failures; they also do not catch the nuances of their struggles in politics. Rather they appear to be a medley of prejudices and biases inherent in the social milieu and entrenched in the political arena. Perspectives of women in politics are far from such preconceived notions, opinions, and casual remarks. In fact, women are members of society and citizens of the state, just as men are. In a democratic state they have the rights and obligations just as male citizens. Women have been involved in women's movements and people's struggles. It seems strange, in this context, to find that women are still not equal to men in politics; they lag behind, like in many other nations in India too both at the central and state levels.

The dynamics of Indian politics is reflected in the flexible and fluctuating relations between the Centre and the states as much as the equations within the multi-party (at times with one party dominance) system and the federating political parties. In this dynamics the study of state politics assumes significance. Though earlier called an 'uncultivated' area of study, it has come a long way from the times Myron Weiner (1968) and Iqbal Narain (1967) initiated studies on state politics. Over the years there have been attempts at building theoretical frameworks to study state politics (Kumar, 2011; Pai, 1989; Yadav and Palshikar, 2008). The emphasis is now on autonomy of state politics and the states are emerging as an effective arena of 'political choice' with regional/ local political parties assuming, or rather asserting, their pronounced roles in the contestations taking place at the state level.

DOI: 10.4324/9781003374862-1

INTRODUCTION

Drawn in this analysis are issues of the sociology of power, structure, and control of power, politics of caste, politics of corporate influence, politics of violence, politics of ideology, and other political configurations in the context of diversities and complexities of governance. But in most of the studies in this emerging area, missing or even invisible are women. Where are the women in state politics and its governance? Are they treated as citizens or as mere proxies for men?

A study of women in politics need not be a dull or routine exercise yielding predictable results. In fact, it offers exciting opportunities to analyse women politicians' journeys to leadership and the challenges that they faced on the way. It unravels their struggles and victories, as well as their failures and frustrations in the political arena. A probe into their strategies and styles can uncover huge obstacles in their way and their grit and determination to survive and thrive in the public domain.

Women in national politics in India have of late been engaging the attention of scholars but there are hardly any studies on women in state politics reflecting the gender dynamics and perspectives in the broader context of the assertion of the states in national politics. The present volume addresses this gap. The 19 chapters in this volume cover 16 states representing all regions of the country. Women's political participation at the state level is discussed in the context of the social composition and economic development of the states, movement politics, major issues of governance, and the question of gender. The critical questions posed are as follows:

- Where are women in state politics?
- Have women succeeded in shattering the glass ceiling?
- Is there a correlation between socioeconomic variables and women's political participation?
- Does identity politics overshadow women's political participation?
- Is there a connect between women political elites and women's movement(s)?
- What are the systemic and other barriers faced by women in politics?
- Do women evolve special strategies or follow the norms of 'malestream'/ mainstream politics?
- Is feminization of politics in terms of transformative politics taking place?
- Has democracy failed women or have women failed democracy?

It is not that answers to such questions are easy or even possible at this juncture; very often serious efforts are not made to understand them and seek answers to them. Some critical observations on these issues are highlighted by the authors in this volume. One issue that is addressed by most of the authors is an obvious one: women's minuscule representation in legislative assemblies. Intertwined with this are the issues of women's voting,

2

INTRODUCTION

a kaleidoscope of elected women, women's movements, their participation in informal politics, barriers faced by women in formal politics, the issue of reservations, and the UN framework. Another significant issue on which there is general agreement among women's organizations pertains to the need for women's reservation. The demand for the passage of the pending women's reservation bill is gaining momentum.

Women's votes/are women a political constituency?

A heartening feature of contemporary Indian politics is the narrowing of the gender gap in voting. Till recently it was believed that women were not interested in politics and were even apathetic to it. However, the emerging political scenario shows a surging rise in the number of women voters. Various chapters in this volume mention increased ratio of voting by women in state assemblies. According to Asha Kaushik, in Rajasthan this ratio went up from 50.02 per cent in 1972 to 74.66 per cent in 2018 and according to Alaknanda Shringare, in Goa it went up from 67.42 per cent in 1967 to 83.94 per cent in 2017. This increase can be seen across India. Rekha Chowdhary and Vibhuti Ubbott point out that in Jammu and Kashmir the ratio of voting by women voters went up from 53.92 per cent in 1972 to 66.27 per cent in 2014. Narendra Kumar Arya notices that in Bihar from 32.47 per cent in 1962 it increased to 60.48 per cent in 2015 and Shefali Roy points out that in 2020 it was 59.7 per cent in Bihar. Simrit Kahlon and Seema Thakur point out that in Punjab the number of women voters increased from 59.09 per cent in 1952 to 77.90 per cent in 2017 assembly elections.

All the chapters in the volume report higher number of women voting as compared to men in the last assembly elections. However, Kalpana Shah and Bharati Patil find women voters still trailing behind male voters in Gujarat and Maharashtra, respectively.

Women's movements, autonomous organizations, and reservation of seats for women at the local level have motivated women to vote in large numbers. Moreover, the Election Commission of India (ECI) has played a proactive role in increasing the number of women voters. In addition to steps like arranging separate queues for women at polling stations and a mandatory woman polling official, ECI has worked hard to address gender-specific hurdles like lack of security and the absence of toilet facilities at polling stations. S.Y. Quraishi (2020), former Chief Election Commissioner, states, 'Making women count in the political agenda is a singular achievement of the ECI'. An increase in women's voter turnout in elections to the state assemblies is visible in elections held from 1962 to 2012 (Kapoor and Ravi, 2014) and is noticed in the assembly polls held in various states since 2014 (Kumar, 2021a). The chapters in this volume validate this trend.

Political leaders and their parties have now realized that women's votes can help them get positions of power. In the 2015 assembly elections in

INTRODUCTION

Bihar, women voters helped Nitish Kumar win. They liked his promises for women's safety and education as well as the scheme of providing free bicycles to girls for attending high school. Women voters had contributed to AIADMK's victory in Tamil Nadu earlier and TMC's in West Bengal in the 2016 and 2021 assembly elections. Their influence was also visible in the Delhi elections in 2020 (Sardesai, 2020) and now in Uttar Pradesh, Punjab, Goa, Manipur, and Uttarakhand in the 2022 assembly elections.

The connection between Mamata Banerjee and women voters has been unambiguous. Her government's initiatives such as *Duare Sarkar* (government at the doorstep) and *Didi Ke Bolo* (Tell Didi) and promises of universal basic income for women guardians of every household, working women's hostels, and widow pensions in her party's manifesto deepened women's support for her party (Ray Chaudhury, 2021). An editorial in the *Indian Express* on May 10, 2021, noted that women have been a mainstay of Mamata Banerjee's support base in past elections. Further, an analysis of the 2021 verdict suggested that 50 per cent women voted for Trinamool Congress compared to 37 per cent support among the women for the BJP (Kumar, 2021b).

Political parties have also started recognizing the importance of women homemakers as can be seen in their promises in the recently held elections for state assemblies. Such promises ranged from support for education and marriage to cash incentives and gifts of household appliances. However, condescending attitude of the leaders and emphasis on the traditional image of the woman as the homemaker seemed to be dominating.

Bihar's JD(U), Odisha's BJD, and Delhi's AAP attracted women voters with various schemes. Schemes like Ujjwala offering free LPG cylinders to poor households have also helped the BJP. In the 2021 Tamil Nadu assembly elections there were abundant promises to women voters. DMK promised 33 per cent reservations for women in legislative and parliamentary elections. Viduthalai Siruthai also initially declared 33 per cent reservations for women that was later increased to 50 per cent. These two and AIADMK agreed to provide marriage assistance to women. Homemakers were wooed with a fixed amount every month – DMK promised Rs 1,000 and AIDMK Rs 1,500. Parties like DMK, AIADMK, Viduthalai Siruthai, Congress, MNM, and Naam Tamilar made attractive promises of financial assistance, jobs, pregnancy leave and related benefits, and special SHG benefits for women. The manifesto of Makkal Needhi Maiam, the party founded by film star Kamal Haasan, also promised Rs 3,000 every month as 'value rights assistance'.

In Assam too political parties made winsome promises to women and tea workers. BJP promised to implement the Orunodoi scheme for deserving households from Rs 830 to Rs 3,000 per month, with 30 lakh families brought under it to help pregnant women, and other schemes for women's well-being. The Congress announced the Grihini Samman scheme of Rs

4

2,000 per month for homemakers. Both the parties promised schemes for women's education, health, jobs, and also for women tea garden workers. Regional parties like Assam Gana Parishad and Assam Jatiya Parishad also had their schemes for women.

The same trend of attracting women voters with promises and schemes was noticeable in the elections to the five state assemblies in 2022.

Now women increasingly exercise their right to vote guided by their own choices. A 2014 CSDS survey debunked a fallacious theory that women voters were guided by men when it came to voting in elections in India. As many as 70 per cent of the women surveyed said that they never consulted their husbands on who to vote for (Poojari, 2021).

Due to such encouraging trends, it is felt by some observers that recognizing women as a vote bank has emerged as an important facet of Indian politics. According to S.Y. Quraishi, an enthusiastic response of women voters creates an impression that women have become a predominant 'vote bank'. Every political party's campaigns and policies seek to address women's needs, be it the BJP's Swachh Bharat Abhiyan, AAP's free bus travel for women, or the JDU's alcohol ban and bicycles for schoolgirls in Bihar (Quraishi, 2020). Prannoy Roy and Dorab R. Sopariwala (2019, p. 43) also found that women were a distinct and independent 'vote bank', on which political parties have started focusing for winning elections.

Gender is undoubtedly emerging as an important factor in Indian politics. However, despite women voters' enthusiasm, women are still not a constituency of their own. Deshpande finds in her analysis of the 2009 Lok Sabha elections that Indian women do not always vote as women – as gendered beings independent of social and regional level politics (Deshpande, 2009). Recently, Sanjay Kumar also argued that an increased turnout among women voters does not indicate that women are emerging as a vote bank in Indian elections with their votes still divided between various political parties. Women voters tend not to vote en bloc like voters belonging to other social blocs often do, though some political parties do get more women's votes. A series of surveys done during various assembly polls in different states by Lokniti-CSDS suggests that women's votes have remained more or less equally divided between different parties in different states with a few exceptions. Voting patterns among women do not suggest that, except for Tamil Nadu and West Bengal, women are emerging as a new social voting bloc in the rest of India (Kumar, 2021a).

Women's voting remains intertwined with issues of caste, class, economy, region, religion, and ethnicity. Wider political and socioeconomic issues are important for women voters as they are for men voters. The increase in the number of women voting by itself cannot be a reason to believe that women's constituency has evolved. In the drab routine daily life going out to vote can be a break; getting an opportunity to be out with other women or family members can even lead to a little festivity. Voting is the beginning of assimilation in the political system, and that process has certainly started. However, the contours of the women's constituency are yet to emerge clearly.

With the upsurge of women's movements and the rise of autonomous organizations, women have been voicing their concerns especially since the late 1980s. Concerned with the attitude of the political parties, women's organizations such as Vimochana, Forum for Women's Rights in Bengaluru, Stree Mukti Andolan Sampark Samiti in Pune, and SEWA in Ahmedabad have come out with special appeals for voting. In 1996, the National Alliance of Women presented a women's manifesto. Women's organizations continue to voice their demands. Before the recent assembly elections in Assam five organizations working in the field of gender equality (NEN, Purva Bharati Educational Trust (PBET), Women in Governance (WinG), Women's Leadership Training Centre (WLTC), and Xobdo, Assam) prepared the 'Women's Manifesto-2021' which included demands for increased reservation for women in elected bodies, adequate security for them to earn their livelihoods, equitable economic participation, and better health and education facilities (*The Hindu*, March 18, 2021). Ahead of the 17th Lok Sabha elections, a group of Muslim women activists had also rolled out a 39-point manifesto demanding restoring the rights of all minorities. Unfortunately, none of the political parties paid heed to it (Jolliffe, 2019).

While celebrating the increasing percentage of voting by women voters, it should not be forgotten that there are a large number of women who are missing from voters' lists. According to Roy and Sopariwala (2019, pp. 50–56), despite huge efforts by the Election Commission, 21 million women are denied their constitutional right to vote simply because their names are not registered in the voters' lists around the country. Uttar Pradesh, Maharashtra, and Rajasthan are the top three states that have the largest number of women who are not registered despite being eligible voters. This is a result of a combination of social and political factors.

Women politicians

Elected women members

If the increasing number of women voters is a heartening fact in contemporary Indian politics, the presence of very few women in the state assemblies is a hard-hitting reality. The chapters in this volume bring out very clearly that political parties like to get women's votes and they have no hesitation in declaring generous promises for women voters before the elections. But such promises do not convert into tickets for women in adequate numbers. The issue of giving tickets is often entangled with various negotiations and compromises leading to an evaporation of assurances of equality. Women find it difficult to enter seemingly impregnable structures of political parties.

INTRODUCTION

At times they fight elections as independents but have rare chances of winning. Very few get elected, but each one of them can be viewed as a special case. The trend of women contesting as independent candidates is increasing in the Lok Sabha as well as the state assembly elections. There are references to independent candidates in some chapters in this volume. According to Alaknanda Shringare, many women in Goa have contested as independent candidates and Rashmi Shrivastava points out that 124 women contested as independent candidates in the 2018 assembly elections in Madhya Pradesh.

Pallabi Medhi and Sandhya Goswami also refer to independent women candidates in the 2021 state assembly elections in Assam. Interestingly, there were quite a few Muslim women among the independent candidates. In the 2022 Punjab assembly elections, 29 (31 per cent) women candidates contested the elections as independent candidates.

The chapters in this volume give a glimpse of the harsh political reality that ignores women. There are six studies of states from the northern region. A study by Ranbir Singh and Kushal Pal shows that women from Haryana have had a nominal representation in the Lok Sabha and the Rajya Sabha. Women's representation in the Haryana legislature has remained inadequate as it has varied between 4.44 and 14.44 per cent. So far no Muslim or Sikh woman has become a member of the state assembly.

A gender analysis of women's political participation in Haryana by Reicha Tanwar also reveals the absence of women at the decision-making level in political life. In the 2019 Vidhan Sabha elections, out of the 105 women candidates in the fray, only nine succeeded in making it to the assembly as against 13 in 2014. A discussion of the position of women in the politics of Uttar Pradesh by Manuka Khanna states that women are still kept away from power and there is more 'symbolism' than substance in giving them representation. The number of women elected to the Uttar Pradesh assembly was 11 in 1952 which reached 42 in 2017 and 46 in 2022. Even the BSP led by Mayawati and INC led by Sonia Gandhi could not get more women in politics.

Bhawana Jharta found that women are still marginal in Himachal Pradesh's politics and state politics is dominated by men. There were five women in 2017 in the House of 68 members. Simrit Kahlon and Seema Thakur in their chapter draw attention to the abysmally low representation of women in the Punjab assembly. From eight women contestants in the 1967 elections, the year of reorganization of the state, the number increased to 93 in 2012, which came down to 81 in 2017. Only once did the share of women among the legislators touch double digits – 11.97 per cent in 2012. In the 2017 elections, only six women got elected in a House of 117 members (5.1 per cent). However, in 2022, once again the percentage of women in the assembly touched double digits (11.1 per cent). Women from AAP increased their strength in the House from 3 in 2017 to 11 in 2022.

INTRODUCTION

Case studies of Madhya Pradesh and Rajasthan are from the central part of the country. Rashmi Shrivastava observes that in Madhya Pradesh only 18 women were elected to the assembly in 2018 and only four to the Lok Sabha in 2019. Despite women candidates' high winnability, when it comes to giving tickets to women, parties have barely given 10 per cent tickets to them. Asha Kaushik underscores the fact that the total number of women legislators spanning 15 legislative assemblies in Rajasthan has been merely 202; after the 2018 polls this number is 24. The state has had the distinction of having a woman Chief Minister twice (Vasundhara Raje), but women's position in the power hierarchy has not changed.

There are four studies on the states in the western India. Alaknanda Shringare found that in Goa not more than three women have been elected to the assembly except in 1994. In 2017, 19 women contested, but only two won. In 2022, there were 26 women candidates, but only three won. Having Shashikala Kakodkar as the first woman Chief Minister of Goa also did not promote more women in politics in the state. After analysing women's position in the politics of Gujarat, Kalpana Shah finds that women's representation in the state legislative assembly and Parliament over the years has increased but it is still minuscule. These representatives are not effective in raising their voices for women. However, it is important to note that during the tenure of Anandiben Patel, the first and the only woman Chief Minister of the state so far, the 'gender budget' was introduced for the first time and 33 per cent reservation for women in the police force was provided.

Though Maharashtra is regarded as a progressive state, Bharati Patil points out that women have not succeeded in making a big dent in Maharashtra politics. Politics is still a male domain. The number of women elected to the assembly increased from 13 in 1962 to 24 in 2019. Women's representation in the assembly has remained below 7 per cent with exceptions of 7.4 per cent in 1972 and 8.3 per cent in 2019. This state, of course, is credited with giving the first and the only woman President of India.

According to Chaitra Redkar, women in Maharashtra have long been in public life and there is a vibrant tradition of non-party democratic activism in the state. However, this has not been reflected in the statistics of women's participation in electoral politics in the state. Only a few women have been elected to the assembly and the Lok Sabha. Though seats are reserved for women in local bodies, the path is not smooth for them. Redkar draws attention to the use of no-confidence motions against the women sarpanches.

The situation in the states in eastern India is not very different. Shefali Roy shows that the number of women in the assembly in Bihar has been low; it increased insignificantly from 13 in 1952 to 26 in 2020. Roy found that in the 2020 assembly elections, almost all the political parties were reluctant to give tickets to women candidates. Poor representation of women in Bihar's decision-making bodies is also highlighted by Narendra Kumar Arya. He further draws attention to the adverse impact of money and criminalization of politics

8

INTRODUCTION

and women being tainted by these. In his opinion, women are neglected in this complex mess. The political networks of dynastic families and the patronage of a leader as a protégé also help women to enter the political arena.

Nancy Choden Lhasungpa states that in Sikkim, only one woman was elected to the assembly in 1974 and in 2019 the number reached three. In 1979 and 1985, no woman was elected to the assembly. Kaberi Chakrabarti adds that West Bengal, a site for various movements, remains a state with an unsatisfactory record of women's political representation. Data shows a discouraging trend of a small number of women candidates being given tickets by most major political parties and their low rate of success in the elections. The number of women elected in the last assembly elections is 40. Mamata Banerjee, the first woman Chief Minister of the state, is, of course, a powerful leader.

Turning to southern states, Meena T. Pillai found that commendable indices like high levels of female literacy, employment, sex ratio, and health achievements together with 50 per cent reservation of seats in local governance bodies for women do not seem to find a positive echo when it comes to women in politics in Kerala. In the 2021 state assembly elections, 11 women got elected to a House of 140 members for the first time. Even though Karnataka has high education levels and scores well on human development parameters, it falls way short of the national average of 9 per cent representation for women in politics.

Internal disturbances in some states have affected women's political participation. Women have failed to become a significant political constituency in Jammu and Kashmir according to Rekha Chowdhary and Vibhuti Ubbott. The number of elected women in the legislature in the 2008 elections was three while it was two in the 2014 elections. In the Jammu and Kashmir region, the discourse on issues related to women has been articulated within the limits of community identity.

Pallabi Medhi and Sandhya Goswami find that political parties in Assam do not field women candidates in sufficient numbers. Women representatives in the assembly since the first elections till 2016 are only 90 as against 1,600 for men. In the 2021 assembly elections only six women got elected (4.8 per cent). According to Rekha Pande though women participated very actively in all the agitations and movements for the formation of the separate state of Telangana, they got a raw deal at the hands of the male politicians and there are very few women representatives in the assembly. In the 119-member Telangana assembly, only five women could get elected in 2018.

A recent report by NITI Aayog points out that average women's representation in state legislative assemblies is 8.46 per cent. The legislative assembly of Chhattisgarh has the highest representation of women at 14.44 per cent followed by West Bengal at 13.61 per cent, and Nagaland and Mizoram have no women's representation (NITI Aayog, 2021, p. 104).

INTRODUCTION

The chapters in this volume situate an analysis of women in state politics in the broader socioeconomic situation and other informal processes in the states. It is interesting to note that there is neither any definite emerging pattern nor necessarily a connect of women's political participation with socioeconomic parameters in the states. The most glaring example is that of Kerala with high socioeconomic indicators but being rather low in terms of women's participation in the state other than at the local level. This is also affirmed by the SDG Index (2021). The Index on SDG 5 on gender equality and empowerment of women ranks the states on a scale of 100 points. Chhattisgarh is the only state that has a corresponding ranking on women's representation. This state has the highest SDG 5 score as a performing state at 64 and is also the state with the highest percentage of women in the state assembly at 14.4 per cent. Kerala, however, which is next with a score of 63, has only 5.71 per cent women's representation (NITI Aayog, 2021, p. 104). There was a slight increase to 7.8 per cent in the 2021 elections.

On the other hand, West Bengal with 13.61 per cent representation of women, Rajasthan with 12 per cent, and Bihar with 11.52 per cent women's representation in their assemblies are non-performing states and score very low on the index. Rajasthan's score is only 39, fourth from the bottom among the 28 states and that of Bihar is 48 (Annexure 1). This once again stimulates our thinking about India, the land where modernity mingles with traditions, where opposites co-exist, and where democracy survives despite the barriers of socioeconomic inequalities.

While the number of elected women in the local bodies in 2020 was 1.37 million, the presence of only a few women in state assemblies and the Parliament is a sad commentary on the working of democracy. Women are found mostly in the lowest rung of politics; they still have to climb many steps in the ladder of power. Political parties continue to deny tickets to women candidates despite their 'winnability'.

Diversity among women political leaders

The makers of the Constitution had visualized a society of diverse people based on mutual respect and mutual cooperation transcending barriers of religion, region, caste, class, and gender. It has been a matter of concern that women from the minorities and suppressed classes find it difficult to enter the political arena. However, the other side of the argument is that they do not want to enter politics.

Among prominent names of Dalit women politicians are Meira Kumar and Mayawati.

However, SC/ST women have had a fair share of representation at different levels. Because of reservations, they have a one-third share of seats in local bodies including chair positions under the 73rd and 74th Constitutional Amendments. In the state assemblies, of the 4,300 constituencies,

INTRODUCTION

650 constituencies for SCs and 300 for STs are reserved. In state assembly elections held between 2004 and 2014, SC men constituted 21.7 per cent of all male candidates, whereas SC women constituted 26.3 per cent of all female candidates and in terms of winning the seats also they performed better. SC women constituted 23.7 per cent of all female elected members of the legislative assemblies (Jensenius, 2016). It is observed that from the 1990s, SC/ST women have actually fared better than general category women in terms of both party nominations and winning seats (Jensenius, 2019).

Mayawati's political prominence has been a boost to Dalit women's struggles. Though there are not many prominent Dalit women in formal politics, their contribution to informal politics, particularly to Dalit women's movement, is very strong.

The under-representation of Muslim women in elected bodies is also a matter of concern. Muslim women form 6.9 per cent of the population, but have just 0.7 per cent representation in the Lok Sabha (Bhandare, 2019).

It may be noted here that Begum Qudsia Aizaz Rasool, representing the Muslim League, was the only Muslim woman member of the Constituent Assembly. There have been Muslim women politicians like Mohsina Kidwai, Begum Mofida Ahmed, and Begum Abida Ahmed in post-independence India. Nilofer Khan in her analysis of the role of women in the politics of Jammu and Kashmir provides interesting details. According to her, Begum Akbar Jehan and Zainab Begum who rose to some sort of political stature were helped by their strong political backgrounds. Akbar Jehan Abdullah, the wife of Sheikh Abdulla, former Chief Minister of Jammu and Kashmir, the mother of Farooq Abdullah, the former Chief Minister of Jammu and Kashmir, and the grandmother of Omar Abdullah, former Chief Minister of Jammu and Kashmir, served as a member of the Lok Sabha. Mehbooba Mufti, who was the first woman Chief Minister of Jammu and Kashmir and daughter of Mufti Mohammad Sayeed, former Chief Minister of Jammu and Kashmir, is the president of the Jammu and Kashmir People's Democratic Party (PDP). She was also a member of the Lok Sabha. Mehmooda Ahmed Ali Shah has been active at the state level (Khan, 2020). There have been some Muslim women politicians in states like Uttar Pradesh as well as Jammu and Kashmir.

Syeda Anwara Taimur was the first and the only woman Chief Minister of Assam, who was in office for nearly six months. Mehbooba Mufti is another Muslim woman to occupy the chair of the Chief Minister.

The Indian Union of Muslim League (IUML) in Kerala created history by fielding its first-ever woman candidate Qamarunnisa Anwar in the 1996 assembly elections, but she lost. This defeat was interpreted as the poor 'winnability' of women candidates. In four subsequent assembly elections and an equal number of Parliament elections, IUML did not field any women leaders, even though it had a string of them who had proven their mettle in local governments. It took 25 years for the party to consider

Noorbina Rashid for a seat to the state assembly. She has also been a member of IUML's state secretariat (Ramachandran, 2021).

Despite working with grit and determination, women politicians are successful sometimes and at times not. However, ultimately, almost every political profile of women politicians contains a chronicle of impressive achievements and bitter disappointments.

Prominent women political leaders

Even if women in politics are few and far between, one is fascinated by the profiles of women politicians in India. Only a few of them are like stars emitting their own light. A few are also like shooting stars that shine, but only for a while. However, many are lost in oblivion even before their presence is noted. Each of them has a story of varied experiences brimming with hope, despair, and challenges.

Indira Gandhi was one of the most powerful politicians in India. Pratibha Patil was the first woman President of India. Sumitra Mahajan and Meira Kumar have been respected Speakers of the Lok Sabha and Najma Heptulla, the deputy Chairperson of the Rajya Sabha and later Governor of Manipur. Women like Sarojini Naidu, Anandiben Patel, and Margaret Alva have been governors. Laxmi Menon, Amrit Kaur, Sushila Nayar, Tarkeshwari Sinha, Kumari Selja, Sushma Swaraj, and Nirmala Sitharaman have been ministers at the Centre. Though it is assumed that women generally get 'soft' portfolios like health, education, or women and child development, now women are getting portfolios like finance, defence, and foreign affairs. Women like Sonia Gandhi in the Congress, Jayawantiben Mehta in the BJP, and Geeta Mukherjee in the CPI have held positions in decision-making bodies in their respective parties.

Some women political leaders like Hansa Mehta, Amrit Kaur, Sucheta Kriplani, and Maniben Patel had strong ties with the freedom movement. Members like Geeta Mukherjee, Pramila Dandavate, Ahilya Rangnekar, Parvati Krishnan, and Sushila Gopalan were deeply concerned with people's lives. Uma Bharati and Pragya Singh Thakur attract attention due to their saffron ideology. There are some women whom people have elected time and again, like Geeta Mukherjee and Sumitra Mahajan to the Lok Sabha, Sumitra Singh to the assembly in Rajasthan, and K.R. Gouri to the assembly in Kerala. Now members like Nusrat Jahan and Mimi Chakraborty bring the enthusiasm of the youth to the Lok Sabha.

Apart from being legislators, a few women have had the opportunity to head governments of their respective states as chief ministers and also hold gubernatorial posts. The accounts of their journeys are engaging and each case demands a separate study; however, that is beyond the scope of this book. At the time of publication of this volume, there was only one woman Chief Minister, Mamata Banerjee of TMC, holding the fort for the third

INTRODUCTION

time as Chief Minister of West Bengal. Earlier Sheila Dikshit had the distinction of being the Chief Minister of Delhi for 15 years without a break. Overall, there have been 16 women chief ministers, covering the states of Uttar Pradesh, Goa, Odisha, Assam, Rajasthan, Tamil Nadu, Madhya Pradesh, Bihar, Punjab, Gujarat, West Bengal, Jammu and Kashmir (earlier a state), and Delhi (UT). Five women chief ministers were from the Congress Party, four from the BJP, and the remaining have represented regional/local parties like MGP, RJD, AIADMK, BSP, PDP, and TMC. Two chief ministers have been from the Muslim community, one from the Sikh community and one from the Dalit community.

Since independence India has had 24 women governors of states and five lieutenant governors of the Union Territory of Puducherry. Currently, there are three women governors in Uttar Pradesh, Chhattisgarh, and Telangana. For the first time diversity is well reflected as women from the Scheduled Castes, Scheduled Tribes, OBCs, and minorities have been appointed as governors.

Many women politicians are educated and come from middle- or upper-class backgrounds. Connections with elites and political families certainly help them. Women like Vyjayanthimala, Rekha, Hema Malini, Jaya Prada, and Jaya Bachchan have brought glamour to the House. Film stars and celebrities are becoming political parties' choice at the central and state levels to attract voters. However, there are women who have come to the limelight from modest backgrounds like Mamata Banerjee, Mayawati, Sahodrabai, and Laxmi Kanta Chawla. Equally interesting is the life story of Phoolan Devi who moved from being an abused woman turned into a dacoit and then one of the policymakers by entering the Lok Sabha.

Some women members have been members of the Lok Sabha, the Rajya Sabha, as well as the state assembly. Some examples are Sushma Swaraj, Jamuna Devi, Vidyawati Chaturvedi, and Mayawati. Some women have followed the principle of upward mobility in politics. Pratibha Patil and Sumitra Mahajan started their political careers in urban local bodies. Mrinal Gore, Pramila Dandavate, Ahilya Rangnekar, and Jayawantiben Mehta also began their political journeys at the local level. Rita Bahuguna Joshi was the Mayor of the Municipal Corporation of Allahabad, and thereafter she became a member of the Uttar Pradesh state assembly and a minister. Now she has been elected to the 17th Lok Sabha from Allahabad. Sampatiya Uikey in Madhya Pradesh started her political career as a sarpanch of Tikarwadagram panchayat and has now been elected to the Rajya Sabha as a BJP candidate. Riti Pathak, a member of the 16th and the 17th Lok Sabhas from Madhya Pradesh, was introduced to politics when she contested elections for the zila panchayat adhyaksh.

Some women have attained positions of eminence at the state level and are creating waves. Neelam Gorhe has been elected to the legislative council of Maharashtra consecutively for four times and is its deputy Chairperson.

INTRODUCTION

Kalawati Subba was selected as the first and only woman speaker of the legislative assembly in Sikkim. Women like Supriya Sule in Maharashtra, Kiran Chaudhary in Haryana, Sumitra Singh and Kamla Beniwal in Rajasthan, and Renu Devi in Bihar have been important in state politics.

Women members are not silent spectators in the deliberations in the House. They do express their views on women's as well as other issues. But it goes without saying that while raising issues they have to follow their party's line and its ideology. Women members' concern for women is a double-edged sword. The chapters in this volume do not tell us much about the performance of the members in the deliberations in the House. That would require a separate study.

Women politicians and dynasties

Dynasties help some women reach positions of power. Women leaders in South Asia like Indira Gandhi, Sirimavo Bandaranaike, Chandrika Kumaratunga, Benazir Bhutto, Khaleda Zia, and Sheikh Hasina Wajed have been trailblazers and have left their mark in history. Interestingly, in India, we observe women leaders from dynasties not only at the national level but also at the state and local levels.

It is often argued that dynastic politics is against democratic norms; it favours only a few because of family ties and not necessarily because of abilities. It also tends to emphasize the identity of women leaders as members of their families rather than their own identity.

However, there is a counter-argument that in a situation that presents many barriers to women's entry into politics, dynastic ties can promote more women in legislatures. Women can rely on family connections when they otherwise lack access to resources. Dynastic women politicians are also protected to an extent from increasing violence and criminalization of politics (Basu, 2016). However, it is important to remember that numbers alone cannot change the unequal power structure. What needs to be watched is what kind of women and men enter decision-making bodies.

For India, a country seeped in the tradition of rule by dynasties, which in fact does affect the circulation of elites, the concept of political dynasties is not alien. It is often observed that when the issue of succession to a seat of power comes up, members of the inner circle in the family (mostly wife, son, and daughter) stake their claim for the seat, and the seat meant for a democratically elected candidate slips into the hands of a family member rather smoothly, of course through the democratic electoral process. This happens in many democracies. In India traditions and cultural norms add a touch of acceptability to such elections.

Politics in the period soon after independence witnessed the entry of persons who had participated in the freedom struggle and also from some royal or elite families. Slowly and quietly the practice of favouring an immediate

INTRODUCTION

family member for a seat falling vacant by the death or retirement of the patriarch, at times matriarch, made way to the circles of political parties and found approval of the political leadership. It is not difficult to locate the dynastic leaders in Indian politics.

In the Indian patriarchal society, the son gets precedence over the daughter not only in social and economic spheres but also in the political sphere. However, some women are capitulated to the public sphere by circumstances and/or personal choice of the patriarch. Very few have in-built potential to become strong leaders. Not many frowned at Indira Gandhi emerging as a powerful leader after her illustrious father once she proved her mettle. It is interesting to see some mother–daughter pairs also in the public sphere. Sarojini Naidu was the Governor of Uttar Pradesh, the first woman Governor in India, and her daughter Padmaja Naidu was the Governor of West Bengal. Moreover, there have been some power couples like Sucheta Kriplani and J.B. Kriplani, Pramila Dandavate and Madhu Dandavate, K.R. Gouri Amma and T.V. Thomas, Rabri Devi and Lalu Prasad, Preneet Kaur and Amarinder Singh, Navjot Kaur Sidhu and Navjot Singh Sidhu, Harsimrat Kaur and Sukhbir Singh Badal, and Dimple Yadav and Akhilesh Yadav.

The chapters in this volume cite some examples of dynastic women leaders. Manuka Khanna in her chapter on Uttar Pradesh states that Meira Kumar, the first woman Speaker of the Lok Sabha, is the daughter of an important political leader and freedom fighter Jagjivan Ram. Sonia Gandhi and Maneka Gandhi are directly related to the Nehru family. Rita Bahuguna Joshi is the daughter of H.N. Bahuguna, a former Chief Minister of Uttar Pradesh and Kamala Bahuguna. Other examples include Begum Abida Ahmed, wife of the former President of India, Fakhruddin Ali Ahmed and Ratna Singh, the daughter of Dinesh Singh.

Bhawana Jharta's study of women in politics in Himachal Pradesh also includes examples of women from political dynasties. After the death of Congress MLA, Lal Chand Stokes, his wife Vidya Stokes was elected to the assembly. Pratibha Singh, wife of the then Chief Minister Virbhadra Singh, was elected as a member of the Lok Sabha.

Haryana too has had its share of dynastic women politicians. Ranbir Singh and Kushal Pal in their chapter refer to some women in the politics of Haryana. Kumari Selja is the daughter of former union minister Chaudhary Dalbir Singh. Savitri Jindal is widow of Haryana minister, O.P. Jindal; Kiran Chaudhary, widow of another Haryana minister Surinder Singh; Shruti Chaudhary, the daughter of Surender Singh and Kiran Choudhry, and granddaughter of former Chief Minister Bansi Lal; and Naina Devi, wife of Ajay Chautala and daughter-in-law of O.P. Chautala. In Punjab, Harsimrat Kaur Badal, daughter-in-law of Prakash Singh Badal, and Preneet Kaur, wife of Amarinder Singh, the former Chief Minister of Punjab, are members of the Lok Sabha.

15

In their chapter, Rekha Chowdhary and Vibhuti Ubbott state that in Jammu and Kashmir, Begum Abdullah, Sheikh Abdullah's wife, played a prominent role in the politics of the state. Mehbooba Mufti, Mufti Mohammad Sayeed's daughter, evolved into a powerful political leader and was the first woman Chief Minister of Jammu and Kashmir.

Rashmi Shrivastava's study on Madhya Pradesh throws light on the political legacy of Vijaya Raje Scindia from the royal family of Gwalior. Veena Singh had staked her claim to the legacy of her father, Arjun Singh. A royal scion among the tribals in the Vindhya region, Himadri Singh is the daughter of seasoned politician and former union minister Dalbir Singh and Rajesh Nandini Singh, once elected to the Lok Sabha. It is important to note that Vijaya Raje Scindia's daughters have followed their mother and are active in politics in Rajasthan. Vasundhara Raje was the Chief Minister of Rajasthan twice and Yashodhara Raje is a member of the assembly.

Though opposed to reservations for women, Mulayam Singh Yadav and Lalu Prasad Yadav did not hesitate to promote women of their own families. Shefali Roy and Narendra Arya in their respective chapters note that in Bihar, Rabri Devi became the first woman Chief Minister of the state after her husband Lalu Yadav had to resign. Misa Bharti, Lalu Prasad Yadav's daughter, is a member of the Rajya Sabha.

Kaberi Chakrabarti points out that in West Bengal, Deepa Dasmunshi entered politics after a critical illness of her husband, Priyaranjan Dasmunshi, and Swati Khandoker entered politics after the death of her husband, Akbar Ali Khandoker. Pallabi Medhi and Sandhya Goswami refer to some women politicians in Assam. Sushmita Dev hails from a political family. Her father Santosh Mohan Dev was a veteran politician and her mother Bithika Dev was a member of the assembly. Ranee Narah's husband Bharat Narah has been a politician in the state for many years. In the small state of Sikkim, Nancy Choden Lhasungpa mentions that Dil Kumari Bhandari is the wife of the then Chief Minister Nar Bahadur Bhandari.

Bharati Patil and Chaitra Redkar in their respective chapters show the presence of a good number of women politicians from political dynasties in Maharashtra. Some of them are Shalinitai Patil, wife of Chief Minister Vasantdada Patil; Premalabai Chavan, wife of Dajisaheb Chavan and mother of Prithviraj Chauhan who has been the Chief Minister of the state; Supriya Sule, Sharad Pawar's daughter; Priya Dutt, Sunil Dutt's daughter; Varsha Gaikwad, Eknath Gaikwad's daughter; Poonam Mahajan, Pramod Mahajan's daughter; and Pankaja Munde-Palwe and Pritam Munde, Gopinath Munde's daughters. Alaknanda Shringare discusses the ascent of Shashikala Kakodkar as the first woman Chief Minister of Goa after her father Dayanand Bandodkar's death. Kalpana Shah points out that Nisha Amarsinh Choudhary, a three-time member of the Lok Sabha from Gujarat, was the wife of Amarsinh Choudhary, a former Chief Minister of the state.

INTRODUCTION

Rekha Pande in her analysis of women in Telangana politics and struggles points out that K. Kavitha is the daughter of K. Chandrashekar Rao, the first Chief Minister of Telangana. The latest entry in Telangana politics is by Y.S. Sharmila, daughter of Y.S. Rajasekhara Reddy, former Chief Minister of Andhra Pradesh and sister of Y.S. Jaganmohan Reddy, the current Chief Minister of Andhra Pradesh. Nandamuri Suhasini, N.T. Rama Rao's granddaughter, tried to enter the political arena but lost the elections. In Karnataka, Margaret Alva, Violet's Alva's daughter-in-law, emerged as a powerful politician. Kanimozhi, daughter of M. Karunanidhi, former Chief Minister of Tamil Nadu and sister of M.K. Stalin, the Chief Minister of Tamil Nadu, is now elected to the Lok Sabha after two terms in the Rajya Sabha.

It is interesting to note that at times a wife occupies her husband's seat of power as a guardian of his constituency when he is busy somewhere. In Bihar, Rabri Devi started her political career only to keep the seat of power safe for her husband when he had to vacate it. In Uttar Pradesh when Akhilesh Yadav vacated his seat in the Lok Sabha to enter state politics, his wife Dimple Yadav was elected to the Lok Sabha from the same constituency. In Haryana, when Bhajan Lal went to the Centre, his wife Jasma Devi became his substitute at the state level. In Madhya Pradesh, when Kamal Nath could not contest the elections, his wife Alka Nath contested and was elected. Later she resigned to make way for Kamal Nath's re-entry from the same constituency.

Women and political parties

Political parties play a vital role in shaping the government and influencing women's political participation. They select the candidates and the political aspirants turn to them because contesting independently is very difficult and more so for women.

Political parties' approach towards women is an indication of their intentions for a just and strong democracy. They can use their platforms to propagate the ideals of democracy and gender equality. Their policies differ when it comes to promoting women to leadership positions, selecting women as party candidates, and including women's issues in their agendas. They may take special steps to improve women's numbers in politics by promoting them in large numbers in elections and providing them help and resources and their women's wings may contribute to women's political advancement. However, it is observed that, in practice, political parties are male dominated and women get pushed to the margins. Women's wings also play an ancillary role.

In India, over the years, many parties have emerged, split, merged, and disappeared. In the 2019 Lok Sabha elections, there were 673 parties (7 national parties, 43 recognized state parties, and 623 registered unrecognized

INTRODUCTION

parties). However, women do not get adequate representation in the decision-making bodies of their own parties. In the BJP national executive of the 12 vice presidents, five are women. Out of eight national general secretaries one is a woman and out of 13 national secretaries three are women. Just one woman is a member of BJP's CEC (*The Tribune*, September 26, 2020). In the national executive of 80 nominated members (plus the president), 13 are women (*The Tribune*, October 7, 2021). In the Congress Working Committee (CWC), out of 53 members (including members and permanent and special invitees) there are only six women. Among the 12 members of the Central Election Committee of the Congress Party, four are women. CPI(M) has just one woman member in the politburo. CPI also has one woman member in the NEC.

Most of the parties, national and regional/ local, have mahila wings (women's wings) though differently christened. The All India Mahila Congress (AIMC) of the Congress Party and the Mahila Morcha of BJP have their presence in all the states up to the block level. The All India Democratic Women's Association (CPI(M)) and the National Federation of Indian Women (CPI) have a presence in the states of their influence. The influence of mahila wings of regional/local parties like AITMC in West Bengal, AIADMK and DMK in Tamil Nadu, Istri Akali Dal in Punjab, and SP and BSP in Uttar Pradesh is limited to their states.

These mahila wings provide support to their respective parties in enrolling and mobilizing women supporters for the parties, take the party's programmes to the voters and take out protests as and when necessary but they are 'peripheral' in terms of shaping the policies and programmes of their parties or securing more tickets for women. They have not been able to function as pressure groups within the parties and have been ineffective in securing tickets for women candidates.

Of late, the voices for more tickets to women are being heard from leaders of mahila wings. Prior to the last Madhya Pradesh assembly elections, the State Mahila Morcha President (Lata Elkar) of the BJP had asked the party to consider giving at least 25 per cent tickets to women. (*The Times of India*, August 14, 2018). A similar demand came from the then president of the Haryana Pradesh Mahila Congress, Sumitra Chauhan, who demanded 50 per cent tickets for women from her party in the Lok Sabha and assembly elections in the state (*The Tribune*, February 14, 2019). Interestingly, soon thereafter she left the Congress Party and joined the BJP (*The Tribune*, September 8, 2019). It is important to note here that the Congress had announced 40 per cent tickets for women in the 2022 Uttar Pradesh assembly elections. Political parties are crucial in bringing women to the legislatures. Advocating the gender quota, Drude Dahlerup argues for demanding 50 per cent women in candidate selection committees as political parties are the real gatekeepers (Dahlerup, 2021).

INTRODUCTION

It is interesting to note that there are some political parties headed by women in India (Sonia Gandhi – Congress, earlier Indira Gandhi headed it; Jayalalitha – AIADMK; Mayawati – BSP; and Mehbooba Mufti – PDP). However, they have not made much difference in terms of providing more space to women in electoral politics. There have also been a few women who have attempted to set up political parties. The most successful is Mamata Banerjee who started TMC, a party that has been successful in winning the West Bengal elections for three consecutive terms. Before the Bihar assembly elections in 2020, a new woman-led party called Plurals was floated by Pushpam Priya Choudhary, an alumna of the London School of Economics and Political Science. It put up many candidates in the elections but all including Pushpam lost.

Disgusted with meagre women's representation in the state assemblies and Parliament, some women have ventured to set up all-women parties. The first such political party came up in 1998, called the All India Mahila Dal. There are around 15 women's political parties, the latest being Mohilar Dal in Assam. Uttar Pradesh alone has nine such parties. A few notable ones are National Women's Party (also called the Mothers' Party), All Women's Party, Womanist Party of India, United Women's Front (UWF), and Swabhiman Party. The main aim of these parties is to remove gender disparities in politics. To quote the founder leader of UWF, Suman Krishan Kant, 'Women have simply not been getting the kind of governance they deserve ... and all this is because we do not have enough women in decision-making and in political processes. A few women here and there cannot make a difference' (WOMEN'S eNews, 2008). Despite laudable efforts, none of these parties have been able to make a debut in electoral politics. A few of them attempted to put up some candidates but with no success. In fact, all the candidates lost their security deposits (Chaturvedi, 2015). It is obvious that ultimately in politics winning is of crucial importance and women's political aspirations get entangled in the web of politics.

Competent women politicians work hard with sincerity and without much hype. However, when they get name and fame, their own parties adopt an approach of aloofness. K.K. Shailaja, the health minister in Kerala's last ministry, had won praise at the national and international levels because of her handling of the Covid-19 pandemic. She got the highest number of votes in the 2021 elections but was not given a place in the ministry formed thereafter. This brings to memory the political fate of K.R. Gouri (popularly known as Gouri Amma). Though once projected as CPI(M)'s chief ministerial candidate and one of the longest-serving politicians in the state, she had to face many obstacles. A rift developed between her and the party, and her energy was diverted to fighting consequent battles. Such cases are not merely regional experiences but reverberate beyond the geographical boundaries of a state.

It seems that while women can stay at the periphery or the first stage of political participation, the ladder of power is only for the chosen ones, mostly men. Political parties become closefisted when faced with the issue of giving tickets to women. Whether only carrots of promises will be accepted by women voters for a long time is a moot question. While women's contribution to formal politics is limited, their contribution to informal politics through participation in movements in India is notable. They have given the unambiguous message that women are not silent and submissive persons but responsible citizens striving for an egalitarian society.

Women in informal politics

The border line between formal and informal politics is thin; at times they seem to be near and at times even parallel. However, there is no sustained connect and dialogue between women in movements and women political leaders. The ties between them have been fragile. Powerful and respected leaders of women's movements are generally not inclined to enter the area of formal politics. They are often wary of the procedures of formal politics, compulsions of party politics, and the ways of working in government structures. Spontaneity of working in movements gets lost in the labyrinth of the institutions, their hierarchies, and their mechanisms. Strategists in formal politics are also not keen to field women activists. For political parties, electoral victory is important rather than pursuing the ideal of gender equality. Women's movements are hardly nurseries for emerging political leaders. There are very few examples of women entering formal politics with a background in various movements. Women like Mrinal Gore and Pramila Dandavate were capable members of the Lok Sabha but could not have a sustained time in formal politics. Winning an election is an altogether different game, which is certainly not easy. Thousands of women had participated in the freedom movement but only a handful could enter decision-making bodies.

Women's participation in large numbers in the freedom struggle and formation of their own organizations, however, gave a new dimension to Indian politics and changed their own perspective of life. Though this did not secure equal share for women in political power, optimism generated by the principle of equality enshrined in the Constitution prevailed during the first two decades after independence. Complacency about women's issues was shattered in the 1970s by the rising political and social restlessness and the report *Towards Equality* that brought the women's question centre stage. Voices of dissent started being heard and protests against injustices started becoming louder. Women got involved in such movements making some of them their own movements.

It became increasingly evident that committed to a cause with conviction, women preferred to evolve their own perceptions about politics and their

INTRODUCTION

own methods to protest against injustices and discrimination. Women's movements very often have their roots in their spontaneous and determined responses to a particular issue or situation. While discussing women in formal politics, the chapters in this volume refer to important contributions by women to informal politics in various states. Some movements became widespread, some remained local. Some had strong leaders and some preferred to work as a group. Some made headlines in the national and international media, some remained limited to regional news. Some maintained their ties to parties while some preferred non-party ways. The tone and tenor of each one of them was distinct. Each of them continues to be a milestone in the women's journey towards equality and justice.

The reverberations of cases like the Mathura rape case, the Roopkunwar Sati case, the Shah Bano case, the Bhanwari Devi case, and the Nirbhaya case were felt beyond the places where these incidents happened. They ignited nation-wide protests, rallies, and meetings and also led to the enactment of some pieces of legislation. A movement like the Chipko movement in Uttarakhand (earlier in Uttar Pradesh) emerged from environmental degradation and widened its scope covering issues that touched women's lives like wife-beating and alcoholism among men. Women's participation in the Bodh Gaya land movement in Bihar and their work with the Chhatra Yuva Sangharsh Vahini attracted the attention of many. A strong women's movement in Maharashtra has brought women's issues to the forefront. Here women had been active in the movement for a separate state of Maharashtra and were on the forefront in the anti-price movement in the state. Women in Goa played a significant role in the Goa liberation movement and were at the forefront mobilizing people.

Women in Karnataka have been active in the Dalit movement and have organized women in the informal sector. In Kerala the issue of women's entry into the Sabarimala temple created a furore and *Pembilai Orumai*, the non-party-affiliated spontaneous agitation of over 5,000 women workers, shocked the establishment. Very recently, women farmers, mainly from rural areas of Punjab, Haryana, and Uttar Pradesh, were in the news for their participation in protests against the new agriculture laws.

Women have not hesitated to take a plunge into combative politics. They participated in the Naxal movement and peasant agitations in West Bengal, Telangana, and Bihar. They participated very actively in all the agitations and movements for the formation of the separate state of Telangana. Likewise, their participation in the Assam movement was intense. At many crucial times when male leaders were either in jail or being hunted by the armed forces, women came to the forefront of the movement. In Jammu and Kashmir, women were active during the Amarnath agitation politics and also during the period of separatism and militancy.

Some movements, though important, remain limited to a particular region. These include a naked protest by Manipur mothers against the

INTRODUCTION

alleged rape and murder of a woman by the members of Assam Rifles, the anti-liquor movement in Haryana, the anti-arrack movement in Andhra Pradesh, the work of 'Gulabi Gang' (a women's group wearing pink saris, fighting against gendered social evils and other wrongdoings) in Uttar Pradesh, and Kinkri Devi's protest against illegal mining and quarrying in Himachal Pradesh.

Women's movements are affected by developments at the macro level and changing economic and social scenarios and policies. Women are also influenced by the cultural norms and traditions of the place or state of their origin. They have brought issues like rape, dowry, domestic violence, sexual exploitation, amniocentesis, women's health, women's work and women's legal status, atrocities on Dalit and tribal women, portrayal of women in the media, and land rights and environment to the public domain and have given impetus to the enactment of laws and policies and also the emergence of women's studies as an academic discipline. There have also been issue-based groups like women in peace and security, feminist economists, women with disabilities, widows and older women, and women for land rights.

Women's movements have become diverse, multi-layered, and multi-pronged. They take into their fold women from different regions, religions, belief systems, and ideas. Issues of caste, class, and gender are getting increasingly intertwined giving rise to intersectional feminism. More vulnerable women because of their identities as Adivasis, Dalits, religious minorities, marginalized groups, LGBTs, and transgenders are finding their voice.

However, robust participation of women in the movements in all the states has not been converted into their active engagement in politics and getting space in decision-making bodies. Unfortunately, in all the states irrespective of the party in power, women are left at the periphery of the 'main' politics. They have not succeeded in entering the citadels of power. Activists like Ruth Manorama and Nina Nayak contested the 2014 Lok Sabha elections but lost. By and large, politics still remains a male domain. It is acutely felt by women when they are ignored at the crucial moments of decision-making, though they have played an active role in the process. For instance, women in Assam were marginalized when the peace table was set, though women were very visible at the community level managing survival and building peace. Gender justice remained undermined by identity politics of ethnicity and religion in the state. In Jammu and Kashmir what remained important was the primacy of 'political identity' and 'political questions' over socioeconomic questions. All gender issues are debated within the realm of this community identity. Women in the Naxal movement also cannot claim to be free from the control of patriarchy. Women are conspicuous by their absence in any negotiations in disturbed areas and in peace negotiations and accords. The only exception is that of the inclusion of a woman (Radha Kumar) among the three interlocutors appointed by the then central government for Jammu and Kashmir in 2010.

The role of women's movements and the operating organizations cannot be underestimated in the context of their informed critical role in advocacy, policy influencing, and independent assessment of the performance of not only women legislators but of overall gender-responsive governance. There is a need for an effective caucus of women in informal politics which should not only mediate for an effective caucus of women legislators but also interact with them frequently to assimilate a gender perspective in legislation and policies, if possible with feminist research and data from the grassroots. It is an effective mechanism to negotiate and sharpen a gender perspective in the public domain.

Barriers in women's ways

It is a paradox that women are celebrated in India as queens of the homes and makers of the nation's destiny, but the number of women in politics is dismal. The reasons are not far to seek. Obstacles in the way of women's political journeys permeate every sphere of their lives, from personal to political, from structural to social.

In between all the promises for equal share of power and in the midst of the thudding and slamming of slogans, women are pushed to the margin, at times subtly but often glaringly. Politically motivated women face formidable barriers in their way. With a poor support system and overpowering forces they lose verve and vigour to confront the challenges.

Structures of power, built over time, are mostly erected by men. They are not women friendly. Women's contribution is acknowledged but only figuratively, limited to flowery words and glowing tributes to their sacrifices in preserving the traditions of the family and society. Structural obstacles – political, economic, and social – hamper women's way to power. In the male-dominated sphere of politics, by and large, political structures neither provide easy entry to women nor initiate any change. The prevailing model of politics is masculine. Politics is viewed as a game of winning; combating and confronting are the accepted rules. Manoeuvrings and manipulations are seen as effective techniques. Politics itself is considered murky or 'a dirty game'. Such an environment is hostile to women and many women like to keep away from it.

This often leads to the argument that women themselves do not like to enter politics. However, in practice, women realize that there are two standards before them if they decide to join politics. In her personal world a woman is feminine – home oriented, emotional, nurturing, and not confronting men. However, there is another standard if she enters the public sphere that wants her to be rational, ambitious, professional, goal oriented, and even combative. If she joins politics and is on her way to success, there is every possibility that she will invite criticism and jibes. A goal-driven woman in politics is often branded as 'non-feminine' or even 'masculine' – aggressive, practical, stone hearted, and calculating. When a woman becomes a successful politician, she is seen as 'not feminine' and 'more like a man'.

Some women survive this challenge, but their number is very small. A woman aspirant gets a clear message that she will be a strange entrant to the world of politics that will not welcome her and it will be arduous for her to bring a 'woman's perspective' to politics.

Politics is not regarded as a place for women and there is lack of serious political will to change this idea and its practice. Political parties, often called 'gatekeepers of democracy', are apathetic to give tickets for elections to women candidates. They present a huge institutional barrier for women. Right from the selection of a candidate to supporting her, parties have their own norms, written or unwritten procedures that do not view women as politically inclined citizens. We often hear women aspirants talking about how they feel that the party office is a 'men's club' and important decisions like giving tickets are taken by men.

Women participate effectively in people's and women's movements. They are also used for organizing fund drives, rallies, processions, managing male politicians' campaigns, and for mobilizing people for meetings but are not given political positions/posts. But very few are given tickets; often they are brushed aside as losers or not winnable candidates. This despite the fact that the 'winnability' of women is higher than that of men. This is reflected in most of the chapters in this volume.

Even after selecting women candidates, the parties provide very little or no support to them. A woman politician in Maharashtra shared that it was not unusual that women candidates got tickets for constituencies where the chances of their party winning were not bright. Thus, women suffer an indifferent approach within their parties and an unfriendly atmosphere outside the parties; the combined effect is effective enough to dampen women's political ambitions. This despite the fact that elected women are capable, they take part in the proceedings of the House, and take care of their constituencies.

There is an interesting study that presents significant findings regarding the performance of women legislators in India. This research is based on data for 4,265 state assembly constituencies for 1992–2012 which, in most states, spans four elections. According to this study, women legislators in India raised economic performance in their constituencies by about 1.8 percentage points per year more than male legislators. The findings state that women were more effective at completing road projects and hence creating infrastructure for growth. Moreover, women legislators were less likely to be criminal and corrupt, more efficacious, and less vulnerable to political opportunism. They were less likely than men to exploit their offices for personal financial gains (Baskaran et al., 2018).

In general, among the main barriers for women's advancement are unconscious biases that may manifest themselves in the association of leadership and managerial roles with men rather than women. Data from the OECD's GID-DB 2019 report indicates that just over half of the population (52 per cent) in India agreed with the statement 'on the whole, men make better political leaders than women do' (OECD Report, 2019, p. 121).

Prohibitive expenses for elections and women's financial dependence are major hurdles for women aspiring to get elected. Parties hardly offer any financial support to them and they have no money for organizing campaigns, meetings, and rallies. Women work for the family and people around them but they have very few resources of their own to support their political activities. Women's invisible work remains invisible to the public eye and pushes them to economic dependence. Though women's work sustains society, it is taken for granted and regarded as a natural outcome of their nurturing nature. Interestingly, some parties in the last assembly elections took note of women's work and announced some amounts for homemakers in recognition of their work. But rarely do they provide funds for election drives for women. Women's share in the economy is now being discussed; women are noticed in key financial positions.

However, a large number of women are engaged in the informal sector and devoted to their families. Women's unrecognized and unpaid work and feminization of poverty are harsh realities. Gender inequalities in the labour market, lack of opportunities to be self-sufficient and well qualified, and very few openings for enhancing their potential put limitations on women's pursuit of power. The fact remains that women hardly have any independent resources of their own and if they do not get support for child care, health and related issues, they cannot think of entering politics. Institutions and offices for party work are mostly designed for men. There are insufficient facilities for women like child care or maternity leave or suitable working hours. Moreover, there are laws to protect women but often imperfect laws leave many loopholes adding to their insecurity.

Patriarchal socialization, traditional norms, and cultural practices in India hold women in their firm grip. Rising cultural prejudices add to limitations on women's activities. Patriarchy operates at many levels, sometimes overtly and at times subtly. In this context, it is important to refer to the force of the backlash. Reactions from powerful social orthodox elements create a huge obstacle in the women's way and progressive steps in the political arena. According to Susan Faludi (2006, p. 11), 'the anti-feminist backlash has been set off not by women's achievement of full equality but by the increased possibility that they might win it'. The most adverse effect of the backlash is when women internalize it and decide to stay within the structured boundaries and do not think of going to the public domain.

Often women do not have strong networking with organizations that can support their political aspirations. Once again the shaky link between women's movements and candidatures of women is obvious. Moreover, rarely are women able to establish and strengthen their links with other organizations like trade unions and professional bodies. Interestingly, the family is also important in this context. Women do need the support of their families, especially their spouses, in fulfilling their political ambitions. As pointed out by Susan Moller Okin (1989, p. 4), 'Until there is justice within the family, women will not be able to gain equality in politics, at work, or in any other place'.

The role of the media, in this context, is also very important. Instead of what a woman has achieved or how well she is trying to perform her role as a leader, it pays attention to frivolous details like her dressing or behaviour. Very often questions are asked not about women's policies but about their personal lives; discussions with them focus not on political but on trivial issues. A woman's feminine qualities, her looks and clothes are emphasized. Bindi on the foreheads of Sushma Swaraj or Brinda Karat often became a focal point for the media.

When a woman gets a prominent position in politics, she is often given an identity by her familial ties rather than as an independent leader. Jayalalitha was known as Amma (mother), Mamata Banerjee as Didi (elder sister), and Mayawati as Behenji (sister). Dimple Yadav is known as Bhabhi (brother Akhilesh Yadav's wife), Indira was called *goongi gudia* (dumb doll) when she entered the political arena, and Sonia Gandhi was called the 'videshi bahu' (foreigner daughter-in-law). Rabri Devi's image is that of a dutiful wife. Women politicians are casually connected with their mentors as Jayalalitha with M.G. Ramachandran and Mayawati with Kanshi Ram. The media is by and large unsympathetic to women politicians and does not hesitate to use negative connotations. Portrayal of women as weak and dependent on men helps create an impression of a weak woman leader. The trend in media of presenting women in stereotypical roles or as objects is a deterrent to women's entry into politics.

The prevailing political culture inhibits women's political ambitions. With the shadows of crime and violence hovering over politics, women are hesitant to join politics. Violence against women in politics is a huge deterrent to women's entry into politics in India as also in other countries. Violence against women in politics originates 'in structural violence, is carried out through cultural violence, and results in symbolic violence against women' (Krook and Sanin, 2020, p. 741). Women politicians face violence during their election campaigns and even later after getting elected to the legislative bodies, both from the opposition as well as their own parties. A study based on the experiences of 55 women parliamentarians from 39 countries highlights this grim reality. These women parliamentarians said that they suffered not only psychological violence but also sexual, physical, and economic violence. Media, especially social media, was abusive to them by disseminating images or comments that were contemptuous or sexually charged (IPU Report, 2016).

UN Special Rapporteur Dubravka Simonovic's report on violence against women draws attention to violence against women in politics which violates a woman's human right to live free from gender-based violence in political and public life. The aim of such violence is to discourage women from being politically active and to preserve traditional gender roles and stereotypes and maintain structural and gender-based inequalities. It is worrisome that violence against women in politics is often normalized and tolerated. There is an urgent need to design, adopt, and enforce laws and policies that will effectively combat and prevent violence against women inclusive of political violence (Simonovic, 2020).

The situation in India is also dampening. Contemporary studies and reports in the media often draw our attention to this. Women members in the Parliament and assemblies often have to face rude comments, sexist expressions, and are trolled for their dress and appearance. Seasoned politicians like Jayalalitha and Jaya Prada as well as newcomers like Nusrat Jahan and Mimi Chakraborty had to bear the brunt of such behaviour from the media and male politicians. Increasing criminalization of politics is equally worrisome. If women want to enter politics, they have to realize that money power and muscle power are important for winning elections. Crime and corruption are inter-connected.

Women politicians have to survive in such a hostile political environment. They are drawn into this vortex, knowingly or unknowingly once they accept the importance of winning a seat and retaining it. Economic forces, changed standards of politics, and political exigencies rule over other considerations. In this context, Narendra Kumar Arya in his analysis of women and politics in Bihar draws attention to a report by ADR.

The journey to gender-balanced representation is not a smooth sail. Obstacles are like icebergs; one realizes when any of them hits the ship. It is also to be noted that women are not a homogeneous group, but divided on lines such as caste, class, ethnicity, and religion and there are women from differently abled/minority groups. Women's citizenship rights in India are framed within the social structures of caste, class, and ethnicity (Chari, 2009).

There is no magic wand that will bring women to politics. Political parties have to take concrete and positive steps to bring more women into politics. Steps like strategic planning and institutional innovations, measures for strengthening women's capacities, endeavours to promote gender equality in public institutions at all levels, and raising political awareness are needed. Also, support for domestic responsibilities and facilities like affordable crèche services will be beneficial. Conscious and concrete steps by the government are also required.

Equally important are efforts to change the mindset that discriminates against women and this needs to be coupled with institutional changes. Norms of equality and an egalitarian approach have to be instilled in the young generation. In the larger context, a commitment to democratic norms, respect for the rule of law and democratic institutions, and fervour for gender equality are undoubtedly important. India has yet to develop a culture that respects a reproductive role for a woman politician and have a baby-friendly legislature like in New Zealand where the Prime Minister took maternity leave and later took her child with her to a UN General Assembly meeting. Women too have to break the cocoon and come out of their concept of being *becharis* (helpless). The narrative has to change.

Frustrated with the harsh realities and difficulties in entering the seemingly impregnable fortress of power, feminist theorists and political practitioners are forced to relook at the strategies and mechanisms. In this context a debate on the Women's Reservation Bill in India and its fate is called for.

Reservation of seats for women

Gender quotas have enabled many countries like Argentina and Rwanda to increase women's representation in decision-making bodies. It is now increasingly felt that women's negligible presence in decision-making bodies is a serious issue that needs definite strategies. Despite all the criticism against them, quotas have become a part of the contemporary political discourse and practice. They are no longer regarded as archaic and obsolete but are considered a new mechanism for gender equality. With imagination and democratic inputs, these can be converted into a powerful tool for achieving gender equality. It will be useful, at this juncture, to get an overview of their trajectory in India.

The issue of reservation of seats for women in India has had a 'chequered history'. Most of the authors in this volume, because of under-representation of women in their respective state assemblies, argue for reservation of seats for women in the Parliament and state assemblies. Importance of having special provisions for women's representation in the legislative bodies is also being recognized at the international level. It is significant to note, however, that the issue of reservation was raised much earlier in India.

The issue of reservation of seats for women came up formally in the Constituent Assembly of India at the time of drafting of the Constitution and the view that prevailed was that 'working of democracy in the normal course would ensure the representation of all sections of Indian society' (Menon, 2000). Paradoxically, the only 15 women members of the Constituent Assembly too toed that line and in their idealism, categorically rejected the idea of reservation of seats for women. Renuka Ray is on record to say that women were particularly opposed to reservation of seats for women. 'Ever since the start of the women's movement in this country, women have been fundamentally opposed to special privileges and reservations ... Women in this country have striven for their rights, for equality of status, for justice and fair play'. Reservation of seats, emphatically observed

Renuka Ray, 'was an impediment to our growth and an insult to our intelligence and capacity' (Ray, 1947, pp. 668–669).

Even if the women founding mothers of the Constitution rejected any kind of reservations for women, women's organizations had struggled hard and vociferously campaigned for right to franchise and to be elected without any qualifications. It may not be out of place to mention here that women first got entry into state legislatures through nominations, though limited, in the 1920s and the Government of India Act, 1935 formally reserved seats for women along with SCs and minorities in both Houses of the federal legislature and the provincial legislatures.

The faith of women members of the Constituent Assembly was misplaced as women never got a fair chance to represent themselves either in Parliament or state assemblies in the years to come. In the first elections to the Lok Sabha in 1952, only 5 per cent women were elected and state assemblies had even lesser representation of women. It prompted Jawaharlal Nehru, the then Prime Minister of India, to write a letter to the chief ministers (March 18, 1952) expressing his concern and drawing their attention to the few elected women (Parthsarthi, 2018, p. 614).

Even when the Congress had the dominant position, it did nothing with respect to Nehru's suggestion to field at least 15 per cent women candidates. A culture of patriarchal dominance prevailed and the democratic space that the framers of the Constitution, including women members, had envisioned and were quite confident of was denied to women.

The demand for reservation was made by women's groups before the first committee was constituted by the Government of India on the Status of Women in India (CSWI, 1974). The committee, in its report *Towards Equality*, too rejected the demand with a dissenting note from two of its members (Lotika Sarkar and Vina Mazumdar). It listed a number of reasons for rejecting the demand, conceding to which they thought would be a retrograde step (*Towards Equality*, 1974). It, however, did recommend reservations in local bodies. Statutory women's panchayats were recommended at the village level to provide greater opportunities to women to actively participate in the decision-making process and to do away with the existing tokenism. The committee also recommended reservation of seats in municipalities in all the states as a transitional measure, though no percentage of such seats was mentioned (*Towards Equality*, 1974, p. 304). The chair of the committee, Phulrenu Guha with another member Maniben Kara, unequivocally opposed reservations at any level. Echoing the same line of argument as that of the women members of the Constituent Assembly, the chair said in her dissent note: 'Separate seats will weaken the position of women. They must come up on the strength of their own abilities and not through special provisions'. She had the apprehension that reservations will 'only help women of a particular class who are already privileged' (*Towards Equality*, 1974, p. 354).

The committee further recommended that 'political parties should adopt a definite policy regarding the percentage of women candidates to be sponsored by them for elections to Parliament and State Assemblies' (*Towards Equality*, 1974, p. 305) and proposed that parties could start with 15 per cent reservations and gradually increase it. But this recommendation has not found favour with either the parliamentarians or women's organizations.

Two divergent views emerged from the arguments of the members of the committee. Those who opposed reservations, as noted earlier, felt that reservations would help women from the privileged class, whereas the dissenters (Sarkar and Mazumdar) argued that the background of the women legislators was considerably narrower and represented the dominant upper strata of our society. 'When one applies the principle of democracy to a society characterized by tremendous inequalities, such special protections', wrote the two, 'are only spearheads to pierce through the barriers of inequalities' (*Towards Equality*, 1974, p. 357).

No action was initiated on CSWI's recommendations by the Government of India but the states of Karnataka, Andhra Pradesh, and Maharashtra did take the initiative on their own in the early 1980s to introduce reservation for women in panchayats. Later it was the National Perspective Plan for Women, 1998–2000, prepared under the leadership of Margaret Alva, the then union minister of state for women and child development, that made a clear-cut recommendation for '30 per cent seats at Panchayat to Zila Parishad level and local municipality bodies for women' and 'wherever possible, higher representation of Dalits/tribals, women of weaker sections should be ensured' (NPPW, 7.5). It further recommended that '30 per cent executive heads of all bodies from village panchayats to district level' must also be reserved for women (NPPW, 7.5). Reservations for women in Parliament and state assemblies did not find mention in this plan.

A year later, in 1989, the 64th and 65th Constitutional Amendments were introduced in the Lok Sabha reserving 33 per cent seats for women in Panchayati Raj Institutions and municipal bodies with reservations within reservations for SC/ST women. These were passed in the Lok Sabha without any obstruction but fell in the Rajya Sabha for want of presence of the required minimum number of members in the House. These were re-introduced in 1992 and were passed as the 73rd and 74th Constitutional Amendments. One-third positions of chairpersons were also reserved for women. As a result of these amendments, a 'silent revolution' took place in the country.

Since then, more than 20 states have increased the percentage from 33 to 50 per cent both in rural and urban local bodies. Close to 1.4 million women have been elected. Some women get elected unopposed but a majority face a contest, engaging nearly the same number of women in electoral politics at the local level (MoSPI, 2020). Rajasthan has the highest percentage of elected women in panchayats (56.49 per cent) followed by Uttarakhand

(55.66 per cent) (MoSPI, 2020). Men are finding it hard to adjust to this change and slippage of power. Some of the chapters in this volume indicate how there are attempts by men to control and run the panchayats by proxy. But change is taking place and studies are showing the transformative change that these women leaders are bringing in their panchayats. A UN-Women paper (2021) provides evidence of the fact that women-led panchayats delivered 62 per cent higher drinking water projects than those led by men. Many women elected on reserved seats, particularly in municipal bodies, are now daring to contest from the general seats and increasing instances of upward mobility are noticeable.

Incidentally, the Government of India ratified CEDAW, after enacting the 73rd and 74th Constitutional Amendments. At the local level gender parity has been achieved with most states adopting 50 per cent reservations but the state and national scenario is still dismal. In the absence of reservation of seats for women in Parliament and state assemblies, the incremental increase in women's participation has been rather slow. In the seven decades since the first general elections in India, there has not even been a three-fold increase in women's representation in Parliament. In 1952, only 5 per cent women were elected to the Lok Sabha and in 2019, the percentage rose only to 14.4 per cent. Eight states and five Union Territories have zero women's representation in the Lok Sabha (MoSPI, 2020). In the state assemblies, out of 4,235 MLAs, only 476 are female, which is just 11 per cent. The Nagaland and Mizoram assemblies continue to be all male assemblies (MoSPI, 2020).

A democratic deficient quotient thus continues leading to renewed calls for reservation of seats for women in Parliament and state assemblies. Responding to it and to win over an increasing number of women voters, prior to the 11th Lok Sabha elections (1996), the major political parties promised reservation of seats for women in their election manifestos (Dhawan, 2008). How genuine these political parties were became clear soon after, as not once but many a times, the Women's Reservation Bill was introduced but lapsed. The Deve Gowda government introduced the 81st Constitutional Amendment Bill in 1996, reserving 33 per cent seats for women and a quota within this quota for SC/ST women. There was near volte face and the bill could not be passed. The bill was referred to the Joint Select Committee chaired by Geeta Mukherjee. The committee submitted its report with recommendations on December 9, 1996, but the ill-fated bill lapsed as the government lost its majority (Dhawan, 2008).

The bill was re-introduced as the 84th Constitutional Amendment Bill by the NDA government in the 12th Lok Sabha but it again lapsed as the Vajpayee government lost its majority and the Lok Sabha was dissolved. It was re-introduced in the 13th Lok Sabha in 1999 and again in 2002 and 2003 but the government deferred it as a consensus could not be built and it lapsed again (*Deccan Herald*, March 9, 2010). In 2004, the UPA government

INTRODUCTION

included the reservation issue in its Common Minimum Programme and in 2008 tabled the bill in the Rajya Sabha so that it did not lapse. The bill was referred to the Standing Committee on Law and Justice. After the committee presented its report, the bill was tabled in both the Houses amid protests from Samajwadi Party, JD(U), and RJD. The bill was moved in the Rajya Sabha on Women's Day (March 8) in 2010. Interestingly, the law minister at the time of introducing the bill sat between two women MPs (Kumari Selja and Ambika Soni) while other women MPs stood guard to ward off any attack on him (*The Hindu*, March 7, 2015). Voting on the bill was deferred due to unruly scenes and also threats of withdrawal of support to the government by its alliance partners, in particular the SP and RJD. They demanded a quota within the quota for women from backward classes. The next day (March 9, 2010), however, the Constitutional (108th Amendment) Bill was passed in the Rajya Sabha with support of BJP and Left parties. The 33 per cent reservation was on a rotational basis and valid for 15 years. It was neither applicable to Rajya Sabha (Upper House) nor the Vidhan Parishads (legislative councils in the states).

Arun Jaitley, the then leader of opposition, called it a myth that reservations would create a privileged society. Reservations, he said, 'is an affirmative action, which is intended to wash away the reality of inequality and translate it into a vision of equality ... Reservation quotas for women, therefore, become an essential instrument to jump-start the process of equality'. Jaitley also favoured the principle of rotation. He argued that it would ensure that 'in 15 years, the life of this amendment, each constituency in the country sends, at least once a women representative to Parliament. This will increase the horizontal spread of activism' (*The Economic Times*, March 10, 2010).

Lalu Prasad (RJD), however, dubbed the bill as a 'political blunder', meant to suppress the representation of women belonging to OBC, ST/SC, and Muslim communities and it served only 'the interests of the elite classes' (Banerjee, 2010).

CPM leader Brinda Karat speaking in the Rajya Sabha trashed such arguments and cited statistics on female representation from Bihar and UP to show that OBC women were not disadvantaged. In Bihar, in 2010, 70.8 per cent of the 24 women legislators belonged to the OBCs, SCs, and minorities and in the case of Uttar Pradesh the figure was an impressive 65 per cent (*The Economic Times*, March 10, 2010).

The bill was passed in the Rajya Sabha but was fiercely opposed in the Lok Sabha. The House witnessed the worst kind of pandemonium, with the papers being snatched from the Speaker and being torn off. There hangs the fate of the Women's Reservation Bill. It may not be out of place to mention here that reservation for women at the local level through the 73rd and 74th Amendments was smooth and it did not ruffle feathers in political circles as the parliamentarians did not feel the heat of the reservations at that level.

But the WRB did send ripples through the sitting members as in the rotation some may lose their well-nursed and guarded constituencies. Who would be the 181 of the 543 male members of Lok Sabha and 1,370 MLAs out of the 4,109 legislators in state assemblies, who would have to surrender in case their constituency got reserved for women? This insecurity and fear, though not acknowledged openly, is one of many reasons for stalling the passage of the bill.

Quotas within quotas have been used as a divisive tool by parties opposing the Women's Reservation Bill. 'Caste identity politics' is played up to project that it is the elite and upper caste women who will gain at the cost of marginalized and backward class women. Despicable and misogynistic language has been used by the opposing leaders. A senior leader went to the extent of saying 'Do you think these women with short hair (*par kati*) can speak for women, for our women?' (*The Hindu*, March 7, 2015).

Within 'the broad feminist camp, the suggestion of quotas within quotas, has received mixed response' (Menon, 2000). While a feminist case for women's reservation is made in terms of the need for affirmative action to redress women's situation, there are others like Gail Omvedt who consider that reservations will only bring to the fore the 'beevi-beti brigade' and is being pushed by women in the 'creamy layer' (Menon, 2000). The beevi-beti brigade is a reality of Indian politics, reservation or no reservation and is not true of only upper castes. A vehement critic of the bill, Lalu Prasad Yadav, is not free of putting up that variety of brigade. His wife was the Chief Minister of Bihar and daughter is a member of the Rajya Sabha.

Women's organizations have been quite active in seeking reservation of seats for women. After the bill lapsed in 1996, women's groups undertook a 'Train Yatra' (train courtesy of the then railway minister, Nitish Kumar) from Delhi to Kanyakumari to mobilize support in favour of the bill. More than 1 million signatures were collected in favour of reservations, according to Mohini Giri, former chairperson of the National Commission for Women, who led the Train Yatra which was flagged by the late Mridula Sinha (BJP associate) who later became the Governor of Goa. The support signatures were submitted to the government. Thereafter, joint memoranda have been submitted to the political parties, women's groups have met the Prime Minister(s) and Speaker(s) of the Lok Sabha, organized dharnas, and have marched to Parliament a couple of times. They met the Chief Election Commissioner (M.S. Gill) requesting him to withdraw his proposal that the political parties should mandatorily give a certain percentage of tickets to women. The parties, it is argued, would invariably put up women candidates in the constituencies in which they have the least chances of winning.

As the bill is still pending, women's organizations observed the 25th anniversary of their struggle for reservations in September 2021 with a call to pass the bill.

All the chapters in this volume refer to 'winnability' as the main criterion while giving a ticket to a woman, notwithstanding the fact that winnability of women candidates, as established by many studies, is higher than that of men. The proposal for double member constituency has also not found favour with women's groups.

There is backtracking by political parties, either in the name of 'quota within quota' or in the name of 'consensus'. The latter is a convenient tool, when the issue is of sharing power with women. On other issues, the political parties issue whips to see that they win and have their way but women's reservations issue is not high on their priorities and so does not invite invocation of such a strategy. The manifestos of most political parties do reiterate their commitment but it is more lip service and meant to win women's votes rather than actually sharing power with them and giving them their due right. In the 17th Lok Sabha, as in the 16th Lok Sabha, the NDA has absolute majority and now in the Rajya Sabha too it has a clear majority, yet the passage of the reservation bill is elusive. Even in the assembly elections held in 2021 in four states and one Union Territory, and in five state assemblies in March 2022, the number of women candidates fielded by political parties (except by the Congress in Uttar Pradesh) did not show any change in the thinking of the parties.

In the 2021 elections in Assam, where the percentage of women voters is 49.35 per cent, there were only 7.8 per cent women candidates, which included independent candidates (74 women candidates out of the total 946 candidates). Only six women were successful. In Kerala, which has 52 per cent women voters, NDA fielded 13 per cent (22) women candidates, followed by LDF – 11 per cent (15), and UDF at just 8.5 per cent (12) for 140 seats. Out of a total of 103 women contestants, only 11 (7.9 per cent) made it to the assembly, this number is slightly higher than that of women in the 2016 assembly (6 per cent). In West Bengal the position is slightly better. The ruling TMC is headed by a woman leader, Mamata Banerjee, which fielded 16.7 per cent women candidates as against 13 per cent by the BJP and 9.6 per cent by the Left parties. While TMC cornered 15.5 per cent seats, BJP won 9.1 per cent but the Left drew a blank as none of their women contestants won. Overall women's representation in the West Bengal assembly remains the same with 40 women elected as against 41 in the 2016 elections. In Tamil Nadu, however, the number of women legislators drastically declined from 21 in 2016 to 12 in 2021.

In the 2022 elections to the five state assemblies, the scenario was no better. In Punjab, 7.13 per cent were women candidates, Manipur had 6.2 per cent, and Goa 8.6 per cent. In Uttar Pradesh there were 560 women candidates of which only 46 could win (7.3 per cent) with BJP getting the lead (30+3 allies) followed by SP (12). The Congress which gave 40 per cent tickets to women could win only one seat.

INTRODUCTION

It is significant to note that while successive governments at the Centre have so far failed to pass the Women's Reservation Bill, a couple of state assemblies on their own have passed a resolution for 33 per cent seats for women. The Odisha legislative assembly was the first one (2018) followed by West Bengal and Punjab. It is a resolution on paper only. TMC failed to put up 33 per cent women candidates in the recent assembly elections (2021) though women voters strongly supported the party which won with a thumping majority. There is hardly any change in political parties' attitudes while giving tickets to women candidates.

While there appears no urgency in giving priority to the representation issue and passing the WRB, India's rank among 190 odd countries in its representation of women in Parliament is down at 148, with Sri Lanka only below it in South Asia (IPU Report, 2021). Globally in the backdrop of Covid-19, there is a renewed call for gender parity in decision-making bodies. The Agreed Conclusions of the 65th Session of the United Nations Commission on the Status of Women (E/C N.6/2021/L.3) on women's full and effective participation in public life call for:

> Encourage the implementation of measures and mechanisms, including appropriate mechanisms to track progress to achieve, the goal of 50/50 gender balance at all levels of elected positions;

> Take all necessary measures to encourage political parties to nominate equal number of women and men as candidates, promote equal leadership in party structures and mainstream a gender perspective into party programmes.

> (E/C N.6/2021/L.3)

India being a member of the Commission on the Status of Women (2021–25) has an onerous obligation to follow the Agreed Conclusions and take necessary steps. Sumitra Mahajan, the then Speaker of the Lok Sabha, addressing a large national gathering at Amravati urged all the political parties to back women's reservation but maintained that reservations should be given respectfully (*The Hindustan Times*, February 12, 2017). The High Level Committee on the Status of Women too has recommended 50 per cent reservation of seats in Parliament and state assemblies for women (HLCSW Status Report, 2015). Intriguing, however, is the silence and missing support for the Women's Reservation Bill by 1.37 million elected women to the panchayats through reservations.

As seen earlier, there are many barriers that obstruct gender parity in representation and Drude Dahlerup rightly observes that gender quotas are no miracle cure for all the barriers that women face in politics. Political parties are the gatekeepers to elected positions, and their selection and nomination processes should be internally formalized and transparent to avoid recruitment within 'old boy's networks' (2021). Equally valid is the view point of Rainbow Murray (2014) who turns the argument to say that the need is for (max) quota for men, since men's over-representation is the real problem to be addressed. Struggle for gender equality is far from over.

Experts and theorists have deliberated on the various dimensions of women's political participation, including descriptive and substantive equality, and have argued about the imperative of women's participation in public and political life as equal citizens and for good government with near unanimity on the quota system.

International actors, in particular the United Nations and its bodies, have as much been engaged in building a strong jurisprudence in this regard through declarations, resolutions, and conventions in the framework of human rights. With the blurring of boundaries between national and inter-national activism and governments' commitments in the global fora, it is imperative to look at the UN position and where India stands as an active member of the UN and its various organs.

The United Nations and women's political representation

The issue of women's rights has come to the centre stage from the margins in various international fora, catalysing and accelerating the demand for equal spaces without any discrimination, gender parity in decision-making bodies, and gender-responsive institutions. A prismatic view of the global initiatives of the UN and other bodies and gender advocates for women's equal rights is called for. This is meaningful not only for a better under-standing of women in politics but also because India is committed to many decisions/covenants initiated by the UN.

Within the framework of international human rights first set in the Universal Declaration of Human Rights (UDHR, 1948), premised on equality and non-discrimination has evolved the global framework of women's rights, including political rights. Women who were engaged at the international level in drafting UDHR ensured 'equality of men and women' in the Preamble and other articles of the Declaration (Adami, 2018).

One of the earliest references to women's political rights is the United Nations Convention on the Political Rights of Women (1952), which rec-ognized women's right to vote, contest elections to publicly elected bod-ies, and hold public office without discrimination. Hereafter, the normative framework for women's participation in political and public bodies evolved at the international level through the International Covenant on Civil and Political Rights (1966), the Convention on Elimination of All Forms of Discrimination Against Women (CEDAW, 1979), Global Conferences on Women (Copenhagen 1980 and Nairobi 1985), the ECOSOC Resolution 1990, and elaborated at length in the Beijing Declaration and Platform for

INTRODUCTION

Action (BPFA) adopted at the UN Fourth World Conference on Women (1995), the Outcome Document (2000), and Sustainable Development Goal 5 (2015).

Reinforcing the Political Rights Convention, CEDAW, which is called the 'International Charter of Women's Rights', mandates the state to take all appropriate measures to eliminate discrimination against women in political and public life in the country and to represent their government at the international level (Articles 7 and 8).

Following CEDAW's adoption, the two Global Conferences on Women too emphasized women's participation in political and other decision-making bodies. Both the Programme of Action adopted at Copenhagen at the Second World Conference (Copenhagen, 1980, paras 69–75) and the Forward Looking Strategies adopted at Nairobi at the Third World Conference (Nairobi, 1985, paras 86–92) recognized the criticality of women's representation in decision-making bodies for equality, development, and peace.

Notwithstanding the fact that CEDAW sought de jure and substantive equality, the Economic and Social Council noted in its Resolution 1990 that women continued to be grossly under-represented in political decision-making and that decisions on public policies that affect women's equality were still in the hands of men, who may not have the same incentive to pursue them as women (para 6). Moving towards a target-oriented approach, the Resolution recommended that governments, political parties, trade unions, and professional and other representative groups should aim at targets to increase the proportion of women in leadership positions to at least 30 per cent by 1995 and equal representation by 2020 (ECOSOC Resolution, 1990).

The UN Fourth World Conference on Women (1995), another milestone in the journey of women's rights, included Women in Power and Decision Making as one of the 12 Critical Areas of Concern. The BPFA adopted at the conference echoed the ECOSOC Resolution 1990, while noting that 'little progress was made in attaining political power in legislative bodies or in achieving the target endorsed by the Economic and Social Council of having 30 per cent women in positions in decision-making levels by 1995' (UN BPFA, 1995). It points out that discriminatory attitudes and practices, and unequal power relations within the family, have resulted in inequalities in public areas. Achieving the goal of equality in representation was needed not only to deepen and strengthen democracy but also as a necessary condition for women's interests and gender-specific concerns to be taken into account (UN BPFA, 1995, paras 181, 182, and 189).

In its strategic objectives, BPFA lists the measures that governments, political parties, and the UN should take to ensure equal access to and full participation of women in power structures and decisions. It emphasizes on gender balance and equal representation if necessary through positive action in all governmental and public administrative positions at all levels. The expression 'critical mass' of women leaders finds a categorical mention when BPFA talks of the need to take positive steps in that direction (UN BPFA, 1995, para 192(a)).

The Outcome Document that emerged out of the five-year Beijing review and the UNGA Special Session for Further Actions (UNGASS 2000) noted that a gap between de jure and de facto equality persisted and that gross under-representation of women in decision-making bodies in all areas hindered the inclusion of a gender perspective in the critical spheres of influence (Beijing Declaration and Platform for Action with the Beijing +5 Political Declaration and Outcome Document (OD), 2001). The Outcome Document reiterated the need for time-bound targets and quotas to promote progress towards a gender balance and women's equal access and full participation on a basis of equality in all areas and at all levels of public life. The goal of 50/50 gender balance in all posts is envisioned in the document. In addition, there is special mention of opportunities for women of all ages to enter politics, the indigenous and marginalized women and the need to address the barriers they face in accessing and participating in decision-making (UN Outcome Document (OD), 2001, paras 66, 81, and 88).

The CEDAW Committee revisited Articles 7 and 8 of CEDAW in the light of the gap between de jure and de facto equality in public life as pointed out by BPFA and framed a General Recommendation 23 in 1997. In its observations, the General Recommendation (GR) notes,

> The principle of equality of women and men has been affirmed in the constitutions and laws of most countries and international instruments. Nonetheless in the last fifty years, women have not achieved equality and their inequality has been reinforced by their low level of participation in public and political life.

Highlighting the impact of cultural traditions and religious beliefs in confining women to the private sphere and limiting their participation in public life, the GR reiterates that 'concept of democracy will have real and dynamic meaning and lasting effect only when political decision-making is shared by women and men and takes equal account of interests of both' (CEDAW Committee, GR-23, 1997).

Apart from elaborating on Articles 7 and 8, the GR mandates the states to invoke Article 4 of the Convention for taking Temporary Special Measures to give full effect to these articles as an essential pre-requisite to true equality in political life. The reporting framework under Articles 7 and 8 makes it mandatory for the states to provide statistical data disaggregated by sex.

The issue of women's representation in decision-making bodies continues to engage the attention of the UN and other organizations as is discernible from the Agreed Conclusions of the thematic sessions of the 41st and 50th

INTRODUCTION

sessions of the Commission on the Status of Women (Agreed Conclusions, (1997/2), 1997), the 2003 UN General Assembly Resolution (58/142), the 2011 UN General Assembly Resolution on Women's Political Resolution (66/130), and the latest the Sustainable Development Goals (SDGs). In each meeting with reaffirmations of already made commitments, more and diverse measures have been suggested to strengthen participation and making it truly representative.

The Agreed Conclusions, broad based as they are, refer to women's participation in areas inclusive of macroeconomic policy, trade, labour, budgets, defence, foreign affairs, the media, and judiciary. To foster an enabling environment, measures for eradication of poverty, equal access to education and gender-sensitive education, access to decent work and productive employment, and strategies for elimination of stereotypes in all spheres of life are recommended. For monitoring and reviewing the implementation of CEDAW, BPFA, and the Outcome Document, a Parliamentary Standing or ad hoc Committee with cross party representation is recommended (Agreed Conclusions (ECOSOC 2006/9), 2006).

The UN General Assembly too has from time to time seized the issue of women's representation. The GA Resolution 58/142 (2004) on women and political participation stipulates that governments, the UN system, NGOs, and other actors develop a comprehensive set of policies and programmes to increase women's participation in decision-making, including in conflict resolution and peace processes (UN GA, 2004).

The 2011 General Assembly Resolution on Women's Political Participation (66/130) also calls upon the states to take a number of measures including a review of the differential impact of electoral reforms on the political participation of women and reform systems where appropriate; encouraging political parties to remove discriminatory barriers against participation of women; investigating allegations of violence, assault, and harassment of women elected officials and candidates and creating an environment of zero tolerance for sexual offences; and encouraging greater involvement of marginalized women, including indigenous women, women with disabilities, women from rural areas, and women of any ethnic, cultural, or religious minority.

The member states have thus reiterated, be it through the adoption of the Conventions, World Conferences, Agreed Conclusions of the Commission on the Status of Women, ECOSOC, or General Assembly Resolutions, the rights of women to full and effective representation and participation in decision-making at all levels from local to national to international, Special Temporary Measures in the form of quotas/targets, electoral reforms, changes in social norms, zero tolerance for violence and harassment, inclusion of marginalized women, and the role of political parties as the gateway to ensure effective participation of women in national and international affairs.

INTRODUCTION

On the 20th anniversary of the Beijing Conference, Planet 50:50 by 2030 became the refrain. 'In 2030 we want to be able to talk about a world that has achieved gender equality', said the UN Women Executive Director in her inaugural message to the 59th Session of the Commission on the Status of Women (UN Women, 2015).

On the side lines of the Global Summit in September 2015 to adopt Agenda 2030, UN Women, with China as co-host, hosted a Global Leaders Meet on Gender Equality and Women's Empowerment: A Commitment to Action. This historic meet was attended by about 80 heads of state and governments. Commitments from leaders covered a broad range of issues including reaching parity for women at all levels of decision-making, eliminating discriminatory legislations, and addressing social norms that perpetuate discrimination and violence against women (September 27, 2015). Addressing the assembled leaders, the then UN Secretary General Ban ki-Moon said, 'As Heads of State and Government you have the power and responsibility to ensure that gender equality is – and remains – a national priority' (UN Women, 2015). He outlined three areas of action:

> First, I urge you to create and energetically implement coherent gender equality policies. Second, provide significant financing for gender equality so that commitments become reality. And third, monitor progress so that all governments will hold themselves and each other accountable for the pledges made here today.
>
> (UN Women, 2015)

Civil society had given a call for 'Step It Up' (September 24, 2015) and the same was echoed by the UN Women Executive Director Phumzile Mlambo-Ngcuka at the closing session where she asserted that there can be no 'business as usual'.

However, with all these commitments and high expectations, the 2021 Inter-Parliamentary Union (IPU) Report shows no signs of gender parity. Even when many countries have had recourse to what Drude calls a 'fast track mode' to equal representation the overall scenario is not promising. To quote Phumzile Mlambo-Ngcuka, 'we have created a world where women are squeezed into just 25.5 per cent of the space in parliaments and other critical decision-making spaces'. We still need, she said, 'bold decisive action across the world to bring women into the heart of decision-making spaces in large numbers and as full partners. There is no doubt this can and should be done. It should be done now' (Mlambo-Ngcuka, 2020).

Twenty-nine countries have women heads of state/governments and according to the UN Secretary General, it will take 130 years to achieve gender parity. The proportion of women ministers and women speakers, however, is at an all-time high with 21.9 per cent women ministers and 22 per cent speakers. Fourteen countries have 50 per cent women in their cabinets. None of these countries are from Asia, the region which has the slowest growth rate in women's representation in parliaments. It stands at 21.1 per cent. In Asia on the whole, only three states have crossed the 30 per cent mark, Timor-Leste (38.5 per cent), Nepal (32.7 per cent), and Uzbekistan (32.7 per cent). Quotas have been a pushing factor, yet in 2021, only five countries had 50 per cent or more representation in the Lower House of Parliament and just one country among these has over 60 per cent seats (Rwanda, 61.3 per cent) (IPU, 2021).

The pendulum of power continues to swing to the side of the male custodians of power, who have been 'guarding it jealousy' for millennia (UN SG, 2020). The inequalities were further exacerbated in all spheres during Covid-19. Affirming this the UN Secretary General in his Policy brief: The Impact of Covid-19 observes: 'The pandemic is deepening pre-existing inequalities, exposing vulnerabilities in social, political and economic systems which are in turn amplifying the impacts of the pandemic' (UN Secretary General, Policy Brief, 2020). The Policy Brief, laying emphasis on the 'women's role as backbone of recovery in countries', stipulates three cross-cutting priorities and one of these requires 'women's equal participation in all COVID-19 response planning and decision-making' (UN Secretary General Policy Brief, 2020).

Women 'who are considered the drivers of economic recovery and resilience' (W20 and UN Women 2020) are, however, poorly represented in the task forces/advisory bodies to handle the pandemic's impact even when globally it is reported that states headed by women leaders have provided effective leadership with their decisiveness, sensitivity, and grit, in handling Covid-19. A study done on 194 countries, 'Leading the Fight Against Pandemic: Does Gender Really Matter?' by Supriya Garikipati and Uma Kambhampati (2020), validates this. The UN Rights Chief, Michelle Bachelet, too acknowledges that during the pandemic countries led by women leaders adopted sound policies based on scientific expertise for the people's good and 'not soundbites based on noisy drama and the interest of elites' (Bachelet, CSW, 2021). However, the invisibility, and gender gap in decision-making task forces, is clearly borne out by the BMJ Global Health study which shows that 115 expert and decision-making Covid-19 task forces from 87 countries had 85.2 per cent men, 11.4 per cent predominantly women, and a mere 3.5 per cent exhibited gender parity; 81.2 per cent of these task forces were headed by men. This was true of global task forces too. In India, as per this study, there were 12.5 per cent women (2 women, 14 men) in the Covid-19 task forces (BMJ Global Health, 2020).

Be that as it may, the normative framework of women's rights continues to be used by gender equality advocates at all fora, be these regional commissions or regional groupings like G7 and G-20. Women 20 (W-20), an official engagement group of G-20 countries, in its 2020 communiqué issued during the Saudi Arabian presidency, in the eight key measures to support economic recovery, called upon the G-20 leaders to immediately 'ensure equal representation of women at all levels of decision-making in national and global political and economic bodies including in the private and public sectors' (Communique, 2020). The chair of W-20, 2020, Thoraya Obaid, a champion of a gender equal world, has been unequivocally saying that, gender parity, 'if not now, when?' It's time 'to move from the side table to the negotiating table' (W20 German Project Handbook, 2017).

The Political Declaration issued by the UN as part of its 75th year of founding too affirms:

> We will place women and girls at the centre. Conflicts will not be resolved and sustainable development will not occur without the equal and active participation of women at all levels ... We will accelerate action to achieve gender equality, women's participation and empowerment of women and girls in all domains.
>
> (UN GA Declaration, 2020)

The priority theme of the 65th session of CSW (2021) again was 'Women's full and effective participation and decision-making in public life'. The Agreed Conclusions based on a very comprehensive Report of the UN Secretary General (CSW 65, 2021) and the recommendations of the Expert Group constituted by the UN Women (EGM, 2020) call for strengthening the normative, legal, and regulatory framework; criminalization of violence against women in political and public life both online and off-line; and strengthening gender-responsive institutional reforms (CSW 65 Agreed Conclusions, 2021).

It is intriguing to note that while the CSW Agreed Conclusions or for that matter the ECOSOC or General Assembly Resolutions are agreed upon by all the member states, back home, very few states actually act upon them. The power dynamics do not provide elbow space for these conclusions to be implemented and there are no accountability mechanisms for realizing the commitments and resolutions de facto. These remain alive to be recognized and reaffirmed in successive meetings and help to keep the issue alive.

Planet 50:50 by 2030, end of patriarchy by 2030, and that no one shall be left behind are ideal goals to be achieved, given the equalitarian human rights framework. The United Nations and its other bodies keep revisiting and further substantiating the normative framework to realize gender equality, nay parity. But given the socio-cultural and systemic barriers, patriarchal structures, and above all the absence of political will, there does not appear a chance of realizing these goals in this time frame. Masculine politics is a reality. To use the words of Michelle Bachelet, reality cannot be 'air-brushed'. Addressing the 65th Session of CSW (2021), she acknowledged that women's equal representation in political life is advancing slowly and that at current rate, gender parity in legislatures would not be reached before 2063 (Bachelet, 2021). Her assessment is on the positive side in comparison to that of the 2022 World Economic Forum report. According to the Global Gender Gap, it will take 155 years to close the political empowerment gender gap (Global Gender Gap, 2022). Notwithstanding these estimates, the Generation Equality Forum in Paris (2021) with a Global Action Plan to accelerate gender equality by 2026 offers another hope.

Towards new horizons

The scarcity of women in political institutions has been a cause of concern for feminist scholars and practitioners of democracy. Increasingly women realize that they have to constantly negotiate with the state. The state plays a key role in the construction of gender and gender relations and in the construction of the public–private divide. Scholars like J.B. Elshtain (1981), Carole Pateman (1988), and Catharine A. MacKinnon (1989) have provided important feminist perspectives. Under-representation of women and ways to expand opportunities for them in public life have attracted the attention of scholars like Anne Phillips (1995) and Pippa Norris (2004).

Women have to enter the political structures, have to survive there, and have to challenge the oppressive and patriarchal norms and practices from inside and outside. They have to work 'in and against' the state, within and outside the boundaries of the structures collectively and ceaselessly. The objective is to change the prevailing unequal power structures and to ensure a better life for all citizens including the deprived and women. In fact, the very definition of governance needs to be engendered. Women need to be empowered so that they can interrogate their oppression in all spheres, from the family to the state, and can claim their rightful places in gender-responsive governance (Jayal, 2003).

The legislature is an important site for the continuous process of democratization. Women members here learn to walk through the labyrinth of almost impenetrable structures, build alliances, formulate strategies, and shape the policies of the nation. It cannot be confidently predicted that women members will always promote women's issues and display feminist traits. Sometimes even if they wish, gender issues may not get priority. It is important to remember in this context that the identity of a 'woman' is not singular in India as in other countries; the differences of class, caste, religion, region, ethnicity, language, community, and consequent complexities as well as difficulties encountered in handling them cannot be overlooked. Women members have to fight many battles at one time. As elaborated by Sarah Childs and Mona Lena Krook (2008), more nuanced and comprehensive frameworks are required to understand the links between descriptive and substantial representation of women.

The descriptive representation of women is visible to some extent in the states in India but not the substantive. The glass ceiling is yet to be shattered and with few women in positions of power, they continue to be haunted by the threatened spaces syndrome. There is no hand holding. Many in power play masculine politics to continue to stay in power, and thus attract the comment: 'they are no different'. The feminist vision of transformative politics gets on hold. Bella Abzug said once: 'We will not simply be mainstreamed into polluted stream. Women are changing the stream, making it clean and green and safe for all, every gender, race, creed, sexual orientation, age and ability'.

These words seem to be a distant dream given the ground realities of state politics in India, yet despair is not the answer. The answer lies in the energy of the youth and women. India has the advantage of a demographic dividend, with half of that being young women, who must be empowered in the four sets of empowerment well spelt by Pippa Norris (2020): Cultural Empowerment, Civic Empowerment, Decision-Making Empowerment, and Policy Empowerment along with removing the socio-cultural and other barriers and providing a violence-free environment.

The UN Secretary General observed in his opening remarks at the GEF that 'Gender Equality is, essentially about power' and that 'power is very rarely given. You have to take it' (Guterres, 2021). However, power must be nurtured to be humanistic and caring and not divisive and devious. It is imperative to assimilate women's perspectives in politics. Some years back, organizing a 'Women's Parliament' in Delhi was an energizing experience (Pam Rajput was elected the Speaker of this Women's Parliament in 2009). Women from diverse backgrounds representing all states and all parliamentary constituencies (543) in this Parliament reflected not only on their leadership talent as they shared voices of both experience and dissent but also their understanding of issues as the legislative business was enacted. Going beyond gender budgeting, the budget presented in this 'House' had a feminist touch as it was based on Gross National Happiness (GNP) and not Gross Domestic Product (GDP). This experience put at rest any 'ifs' and 'buts' about women's capacity to be feminist leaders in their own right to effectively participate in people-oriented governance.

In India it is close to three decades now that women got reservations in local bodies, but the 1.37 million elected women, not known anywhere in the world, have yet to emerge as a political force and be as much the nurseries for leadership at the state and central level, so that the political dividend of this great political investment can be reaped. They have made their presence felt at the local level, now they have to turn their enormous potential into a robust political force, facilitating women to go from local to the state and central levels. It is time they play a meaningful and predominant role in state politics to end the hegemony of a misogynist culture.

Women in independent India are discovering their innate individual and collective strength, are developing capacity to build democratic institutions from the panchayat to the Parliament, and are claiming their rightful place as citizens in the messy political arena. It is time that gender parity is provided in representation through reservations. This is a unique opportunity to re-work the basic principles of political life and to infuse new energy and new imageries into them as we celebrate 75 years of our independence. Powerlessness of many has the power to change, power to translate the participatory form of democracy into an emancipatory/transformative one. The future – the sustainable future – is with SHEROS and now is the time to change the vocabulary of politics.

Bibliography

Adami, R. (2018). *Women and the Universal Declaration of Human Rights*. London: Routledge.

Bachelet, M. (2021). *Fast-track Women's Participation in Public Life 'for Everyone's Benefit*. Speech at 65th CSW Session. Available at: https://news.un.org/en/story /2021/03/1087532, accessed on May 2, 2022.

Banerjee, S. (2010, March 7). 'A Political Blunder. Lalu', *The Hindu*. Available at: https://www.thehindu.com/news//article60602725.ece, accessed on June 16, 2021.

Baskaran, T., S. Bhalotra, B. Min, Y. Uppal (2018). *Women Legislators and Economic Performance*. WIDER Working Paper 2018/47. UNU-WIDER. Available at: https://www.wider.unu.edu/sites/default/files/Publications/Working -paper/PDF/wp2018-47.pdf, accessed on July 6, 2021.

Basu, A. (2016). 'Women, Dynasties and Democracy in India', in K. Chandra (ed.), *Democratic Dynasties: State, Party and Family in Contemporary Indian Politics* (pp. 136–172). Delhi: Cambridge University Press.

Bhandare Namita (2019). 'Muslim Women Are 6.9 % of Population Have Just 0.7% Representation in LS', *Business Standard*, April 26, Available at: https://www .business-standard.com/article/elections/muslim-women-are-6-9-of-population -have-just-0-7-representation-in-ls-119042600134_1.html, accessed on June 1, 2021.

BMJ Global Health (2020). 'Symptoms of a Broken System: The Gender Gaps in COVID-19 Decision-making', *Science Daily*. Available at: https://gh.bmj.com/ content/5/10/e003549, accessed on April 5, 2021.

Chari, A. (2009). 'Gendered Citizenship and Women's Movement', *Economic and Political Weekly*, 44 (17), 47–57.

Chaturvedi, S. (2015). 'The (Slow) Rise of Women-oriented Political Parties', *Business Standard*, April 3. Available at: https://www.business-standard.com/ article/specials/the-slow-rise-of-women-oriented-political-parties-115033100532 _1.html, accessed on June 15, 2021.

Childs, Sarah and Mona Lena Krook (2008). 'Theorizing Women's Political Representation: Debates and Innovations in Empirical Research', *Femina Politica*, 2, 20–29. Available at: https://www.budrich-journals.de/index.php/ feminapolitica/article/viewFile/1698/1331, accessed on July 1, 2021.

Dahlerup, D. (ed.) (2006). *Women, Quotas and Politics*. London: Routledge.

Dahlerup, D. (2021). *Women in Decision-Making in Public Life: Types, Usage, and Effects of Temporary Special Measures, Including Gender Quotas.* UN Women, Expert Group Meeting, Sixty-fifth session of the Commission on the Status of Women (CSW 65). New York. Available at: https://www.unwomen.org/sites/default/files/Headquarters/Attachments/Sections/CSW/65/EGM/Dahlerup_TSMs_EP3_EGMCSW65.pdf, accessed on June 30, 2022.

Deccan Herald. (2010, March 9). *Women's Reservation Bill: Chronology.* Available at: https://www.deccanherald.com/content/57134/womens-reservation-bill-chronology.html, accessed on May 30, 2021.

Deshpande, R. (2009). 'How Did Women Vote in Lok Sabha Elections 2009?', *Economic and Political Weekly*, 44 (39), 83–87.

Dhawan, R. (2008). 'Reservations for Women: The Way Forward', *National Law School of India Review*, 20 (1), 1–45.

Elshtain, J.B. (1981). *Public Man, Private Woman: Women in Social and Political Thought.* Princeton: Princeton University Press.

Faludi, S. (2006), *Backlash: The Undeclared War Against American Women.* New York: Three Rivers Press.

Garikipati, S. and U. Kambhampati (2021). 'Leading the Fight Against the Pandemic: Does Gender Really Matter?' *Feminist Economics*, 27(1–2), 401–418.

Government of India (1974). *Towards Equality. Report of the Committee on the Status of Women in India.* New Delhi: Ministry of Education and Social Welfare.

———— (1988). *National Perspective Plan for Women 1988–2000 A.D.* New Delhi: Ministry of Human Resources, Department of Women and Child Development.

———— (2015). *Status Report of the Government of India High Level Committee on the Status of Women.* New Delhi: Ministry of Women and Child Development.

Guterres, A. (2021, July 1). [Tweet]. Available at: https://mobile.twitter.com/antonioguterres/status/1410320946058117120, accessed on June 30, 2022.

Inter-Parliamentary Union (2016). *Sexism, Harassment and Violence Against Women Parliamentarians.* Available at: http://archive.ipu.org/pdf/publications/issuesbrief-e.pdf, accessed on June 30, 2021.

———— (2021). *Women in Politics: 2021.* Available at: https://www.ipu.org/women-in-politics-2021, accessed on May 6, 2022.

Jayal, N.G. (2003). 'Locating Gender in the Governance Discourse', in *Essays on Gender and Governance* (pp. 96–143). New Delhi: Human Development Resource Centre, UNDP.

Jensenius, F. R. (2016). 'Competing Inequalities? On the Intersection of Gender and Ethnicity in Candidate Nominations in Indian Elections', *Government and Opposition*, 51 (3), 440–463.

———— (2019). *Women and Minorities in the Lok Sabha: Intersectionality in the Indian Elections.* The Asia Dialogue, April 15, Available at: https://theasiadialogue.com/2019/04/15/women-and-minorities-in-the-lok-sabha-intersectionality-in-the-indian-elections, accessed on June 30, 2021.

Jolliffe, G. (2019). *Where Are the Muslim Women in Indian Politics?* May 6. Available at: https://www.videovolunteers.org/where-are-muslim-women-in-indian-politics/, accessed on November 3, 2020.

Kapoor, M. and S. Ravi (2014). 'Women Voters in Indian Democracy: A Silent Revolution', *Economic and Political Weekly*, 49 (12), 63–67.

Khan, N. (2020). *Role of Women in Politics of Jammu and Kashmir*, unpublished paper.

Krook, M.L. and J.R. Sanin (2020). 'The Cost of Doing Politics? Analyzing Violence and Harassment against Female Politicians', *Perspectives on Politics*, 18 (3), 740–755. Available at: https://www.cambridge.org/core/journals/perspectives-on-politics/article/cost-of-doing-politics-analyzing-violence-and-harassment-against-female-politicians/997569433135FA170B2789, accessed on March 25, 2021.

Kumar, A. (ed.) (2011). *Rethinking State Politics in India, Regions within Regions*. New Delhi: Routledge India.

Kumar, S. (2021a). 'Women Voters to Play Critical Role in Bengal and TN Elections', *Deccan Chronicle*, March 18. Available at: https://www.deccanchronicle.com/opinion/columnists/170321/sanjay-kumar-women-voters-to-play-critical-role-in-bengal-tn-elect.html, accessed on August 10, 2021.

———— (2021b). 'West Bengal Assembly Elections: Women Rally Behind Trinamool', *Deccan Chronicle*, May 6. Available at: https://www.thehindu.com/elections/west-bengal-assembly/women-rally-behind-trinamool-finds-csds-lokniti-survey/article34494083.ece, accessed on August 10, 2021.

MacKinnon, C.A. (1989). *Towards A Feminist Theory of State*. Cambridge, MA: Harvard University Press.

Manorama, R. (2019). 'Dalit Women in Politics: Women with Strong Ideologies Who Enter Politics Face Targeted Violence', *Firstpost*, March 13. Available at: https://www.firstpost.com/india/dalit-women-in-politics-women-with-strong-ideologies-who-enter-politics-face-targeted-violence-says-ruth-manorama-6244661.html, accessed on August 10, 2021.

Menon, N. (2000). 'Elusive 'Woman': Feminism and Women's Reservation Bill', *Economic and Political Weekly*, 35(43/44), 3835–3939 and 3841–3844.

Ministry of Statistics and Program Implementation (MoSPI). (2020). *Women and Men in India 2020*. New Delhi: Ministry of Statistics and Program Implementation.

Mlambo-Ngcuka, P. (2015). 'In 2030 We Want to be able to talk about a world that has achieved gender equality', CSW 59th Session, March 9. Available at: http://beijing20.unwomen.org/en/step-it-up, accessed on August 13, 2021.

———— (2020). In 2020, World "Cannot Afford" so Few Women in Power. Available at: https://www.ipu.org/news/press-releases/2020-03/in-2020-world-cannot-afford-so-few-women-in-power, accessed on August 13, 2021.

Murray, R. (2014). 'Quotas for Men: Reframing Gender Quotas as a Means of Improving Representation for All', *American Political Science Review*, 108 (3), 520–532.

Narain, I. (ed.) (1967). *State Politics in India*. Meerut: Meenakshi Prakashan.

NITI Aayog. (2021). *SDG India, Index and Dashboard 2020–21, Partnerships in the Decade of Action*. New Delhi: NITI Aayog. Available at: https://www.niti.gov.in/writereaddata/files/SDG_3.0_Final_04.03.2021_Web_Spreads.pdf, accessed on February 2, 2022.

Norris, P. (2004). *Electoral Engineering, Voting Rules and Political Behaviour*. Cambridge: Cambridge University Press.

———— (2020). 'The state of women's participation and empowerment: New challenges to gender equality', Background paper, EGM/CSW/2021/BP1. Available at: https://www.unwomen.org/sites/default/files/Headquarters/Attach

ments/Sections/CSW/65/EGM/Norris_State%20of%20Womens%20Participation%20and%20Empowerment_BP1_CSW65EGM.pdf, accessed on September 8, 2021.

OECD Report. (2019). *From Promises to Action: Addressing Discriminatory Social Institutions to Accelerate Gender Equality in G20 Countries*. Paris: OECD. Available at: https://www.oecd.org/dev/development-gender/OECD_DEV_W20 -report_FINAL.pdf, accessed on September 6, 2021.

Okin, M. S. (1989). *Justice, Gender and the Family*. New York: Basic Books, Inc.

Pai, S. (1989). 'Towards a Theoretical Framework for the Study of State Politics in India: Some Observations', *The Indian Journal of Political Science*, 50 (1), 94–109.

Parthasarathi, G. (ed.), (1952) *Jawaharlal Nehru: Letters to Chief Ministers, Vol. 2 (1950–1952)*. New Delhi: Jawaharlal Nehru Memorial Fund.

Pateman, C. (1988). *The Sexual Contract*.Stanford: Stanford University Press.

Phillips, A. (1995). *The Politics of Presence: The Political Representation of Gender, Ethnicity and Race*. Oxford: Oxford University Press.

Poojari, O. (2021). 'The Crisis of Under-representation of Women in Parliament and Assemblies', *The Leaflet*, March 8. Available at: https://www.theleaflet.in /the-crisis-of-under-representation-of-women-in-parliament-and-assemblies/#, accessed on July 30, 2021.

Quraishi, S.Y. (2020). 'Time Women Got 33% Quota for Seats in Houses', *The Tribune*, March 9. Available at: https://www.tribuneindia.com/news/comment /time-women-got-33-quota-for-seats-in-houses-53061, accessed on July 30, 2021.

Ramachandran, R. (2021). 'Kerala: IUML's First Female MLA Nominee in 25 Years Triggers Debate on Women in Politics', *The Wire*, March 16. Available at: https:// thewire.in/politics/kerala-assembly-elections-iuml-noorbina-rashid-women -politics-representation, accessed on June 10, 2022.

Ray, R. (1947). *Constituent Assembly Debates*. Vol. 4. Available at: https://www .constitutionofindia.net/constitution_assembly_debates/volume/4/1947-07-18, accessed on May 20, 2021.

Raychaudhury, P. (2021). 'How Mamata Won Woman Vote', *The Indian Express*, May 7. Available at: https://indianexpress.com/article/opinion/columns/west -bengal-assembly-elections-mamata-banerjee-tmc-women-candidates-7305104, accessed on August 10, 2021.

Roy, P. and D.R. Sopariwala (2019). *The Verdict: Decoding India's Elections*. Gurgaon: Vintage.

Sardesai, S. (2020). 'Stunning Gender Gap: Women Voters Powered AAP's landslide in Delhi', *The Indian Express*, February 15. Available at: https://indianexpress .com/article/cities/delhi/stunning-gender-gap-women-voters-powered-aaps -landslide-in-delhi-6267107/, accessed on May 19, 2021.

Simonovic, D. (2020). 'Violence Against Women in Politics. UN Women', Expert Group Meeting, Sixty-fifth session of the Commission on the Status of Women (CSW 65). New York. Available at: https://www.unwomen.org/sites/default/ files/Headquarters/Attachments/Sections/CSW/65/EGM/SRVAW_VAW%20in %20Politics_EP9_EGMCSW65.pdf, accessed on December 5, 2021.

The Economic Times (2010). 'Brinda Reels Off Statistics to Show OBC Women Not Disadvantaged', March 10. Available at: https://economictimes.indiatimes.com

/news/politics-and-nation/brinda-reels-off-statistics-to-show-obc-women-not -disadvantaged/articleshow/5665412.cms?from=mdr, accessed on April 6, 2021.

The Hindu (2015). Women's Reservation Bill: The story so far, March 7. Available at: https://www.thehindu.com/news/national/Womens-Reservation-Bill-The -story-so-far/article60515381, accessed on April 6, 2021.

The Hindustan Times (2017). Reservation should be given respectfully to women, says Lok Sabha speaker, February 12. Available at: https://www.hindustantimes .com/india-news/reservation-should-be-given-respectfully-to-women-says-lok -sabha-speaker/story-0qKAIKn2gsSHq1yt13NgxL.html, accessed on May 30, 2021.

The Indian Express (2021). Her due opportunity, May 10. Available at: https:// indianexpress.com/article/opinion/editorials/woman-voter-bengal-elections -mamata-banerjee-lok-sabha-elections-schemes-for-women-7308646/, accessed on April 8, 2021.

The Times of India, 14 August 2018, Rajendra Sharma, Madhya Pradesh: Ahead of assembly polls, BJP women's wing seeks 25% share in tickets,. Available at https:// timesofindia.indiatimes.com/city/bhopal/madhya-pradesh-ahead-of-assembly -polls-bjp-women-wing-seeks-25-share-in-tickets/articleshow/65398176.cms accessed on 13 December 2021.

The Tribune, February 14, 2019. Mahila Cong demands 50% tickets for women. Available at https://www.tribuneindia.com/news/archive/haryana/mahila-cong -demands-50-tickets-for-women-728670 accessed on 13 December 2021.

The Tribune, September 8, 2019. Sushil Manav, Haryana Mahila Congress chief Sumitra Chauhan quits party: joins BJP Available at https://www.tribuneindia .com/news/archive/haryana/haryana-mahila-congress-chief-sumitra-chauhan -quits-party-to-join-bjp-today-829303 Accessed on 3 December 2021

The Tribune (2020). JP Nadda announces new team of BJP's national office-bearers, September 26. Available at: https://www.tribuneindia.com/news/nation/jp-nadda -announces-new-team-of-bjps-national-office-bearers-146933, accessed on June 22, 2022.

——— (2021). BJP releases 80-member national Executive list, October 7. Available at: https://www.tribuneindia.com/news/nation/bjp-releases-80-member-national -executive-list-321428, accessed on June 22, 2022.

UN Commission on the Status of Women (1980). *Report of the World Conference on the U.N. Decade for Women: Equality, Development and Peace, Copenhagen.* New York: United Nations. Available at: https://www.un.org/womenwatch/daw /beijing/otherconferences/Copenhagen/Copenhagen%20Full%20Optimized.pdf, accessed on April 22, 2021.

UN Commission on the Status of Women (1985). *Report of the World Conference to Review and Appraisal of the Achievements of the U.N. Decade for Women: Equality, Development and Peace. Nairobi.* New York: United Nations. Available at: https://digitallibrary.un.org/record/113822?ln=en, accessed on April 22, 2021.

UN Commission on the Status of Women (1995). *Beijing Declaration and Platform for Action (A/CONF.177/20 and A/CONF.177/20/Add.1).* New York: United Nations.

UN Commission on the Status of Women (2001). *Beijing Declaration and Platform for Action with the Beijing+5 Political Declaration and Outcome Document.* New York: United Nations.

INTRODUCTION

UN Commission on the Status of Women (2006). 'Follow-Up to the Fourth World Conference on Women and to the Special Session of the General Assembly Entitled 'Women 2000: Gender Equality, Development and Peace for the Twenty-First Century': Review of Gender Mainstreaming in Entities of the United Nations System', *CSW50 Agreed Conclusions* (E/CN.4/2006/59–E/CN.6/2006/9). Available at: https://documents-dds-ny.un.org/doc/UNDOC/GEN/N05/650/23/PDF/N0565023.pdf?OpenElement, accessed on March 10, 2021.

UN Committee on the Elimination of Discrimination Against Women (CEDAW) (1997). *CEDAW General Recommendation No. 23: Political and Public Life.* (A/52/38). Available at: https://www.refworld.org/docid/453882a622.html, accessed on April 19, 2021.

UN CSW (1997). *Women in Power and Decision-making: CSW41 Agreed Conclusions (1997/2)* Available at: https://www.unwomen.org/-/media/headquarters/attachments/sections /csw/41/2_e_ final.pdf?la=en&vs=1647, accessed on April 19, 2021.

UN General Assembly (2004). *Women and Political Participation (A/RES/58/142).* Available at: https://documents-dds-ny.un.org/doc/UNDOC/GEN/N03/503/10/PDF/N0350310.pdf?OpenElement, accessed on March 3, 2021.

UN General Assembly (2011). *Women and Political Participation (A/RES/66/130).* Available at: https://documents-dds-ny.un.org/doc/UNDOC/GEN/N11/466/62/PDF/N1146662.pdf?OpenElement, accessed on March 7, 2021.

———— (2015). *Transforming Our World: The 2030 Agenda for Sustainable Development.* United Nations General Assembly Session 70. New York: United Nations.

———— (2020). *Declaration on the Commemoration of the Seventy-Fifth Anniversary of the United Nations (A/RES/75/1).* United Nations General Assembly Session 75. New York: United Nations.

UN Women (2000). *Five-year Review of the Implementation of the Beijing Declaration and Platform for Action (Beijing + 5).* Available at: https://www.un.org/womenwatch/daw/followup/beijing+5.htm, accessed on March 3, 2021.

United Nations (1948). *Universal Declaration of Human Rights.* Available at: https://www.un.org/en/udhrbook/pdf/udhr_booklet_en_web.pdf, accessed on March 4, 2021.

———— (1952). Convention on the Political Rights of Women. Available at: http://www.un-documents.net/cprw.htm, accessed on March 4, 2021.

———— (1966). *International Covenant on Civil and Political Rights.* Available at: https://treaties.un.org/doc/Treaties/1976/03/19760323%2006-17%20AM/Ch_IV_04.pdf, accessed on March 7, 2021.

———— (1979). Convention on the Elimination of All forms of Discrimination Against Women. Available at: https://www.un.org/en/development/desa/population/migration/generalassembly/docs/globalcompact/A_RES_34_180.pdf, accessed on March 9, 2021.

United Nations Economic and Social Council (1990). *(E/RES/1990/15).* New York: United Nations.

UN Commission on the Status of Women (2021). *Women's Full and Effective Participation and Decision Making in Public Life. CSW65 Agreed Conclusions.* (E/CN.6/2021/L.3). Available at: https://documents-dds-ny.un.org/doc/UNDOC

/GEN/N21/079/07/PDF/N2107907.pdf?OpenElement, accessed on March 10, 2022.

UNWOMEN (2015). *Global Leaders' Meeting on Gender Equality and Women's Empowerment: A Commitment to Action*. New York: United Nations. Available at: https://www.unwomen.org/sites/default/files/Headquarters/Attachments /Sections/Library/Publications/2016/UNW_GLM_layout_final_web2.pdf, accessed on March 19, 2021.

UN Women (2020). *UN Secretary-General's Policy Brief: The Impacts of COVID-19 on Women*. Available at: https://www.unwomen.org/en/digital-library/ publications/2020/04/policy-brief-the-impact-of-covid-19-on-women, accessed on March 23, 2021.

United Nations Secretary-General, António Guterres (2022). The secretary-general's message on International Women's Day. Gender equality today for a sustainable tomorrow, March 8. Available at: https://www.un.org/en/observances/womens -day/messages, accessed on June 24, 2022.

W20 Germany (2017). *W20 Germany Project Handbook*. Available at: http://www .w20-germany.org/fileadmin/user_upload/documents/W20_Projecthandbook -final-web.pdf, accessed on August 10, 2021.

W20 Saudi Arabia (2020). *Women 20 Communique*. Available at: https://drive .google.com/file/d/16WkRnv7r-6oZz5LZL7Z_06sTD2FKKbAT/view, accessed on August 9, 2021.

W20 and UN Women (2020). *UN Women and Women 20 Call on G20 Members to Recognize Women as Drivers of Economic Recovery and Resilience During COVID-19 and Beyond*. Available at: https://www.unwomen.org/en/news/ stories/2020/7/press-release-un-women-and-w20-call-to-recognize-women-as -drivers-of-recovery-and-resilience, accessed on August 7, 2021.

WOMEN'S eNews (2008). *Women in India Form Their Own Political Party*, January 7. Available at: https://womensenews.org/2008/01/women-in-india-form -their-own-political-party/, accessed on August 6, 2021.

World Economic Forum (2022). *The Global Gender Gap Report 2022*. Available at https://www.weforum.org/reports/global-gender-gap-report-2022/digest/, accessed on July 26, 2022.

Weiner, M. (ed.) (1968). *State Politics in India*. Princeton, NJ: Princeton University Press.

Yogendra, Y. and S. Palshikar (2008). 'Ten Theses on State Politics in India', Seminar, 591, 14–22.

INTRODUCTION

Annexure 1

SDG India Index and Dashboard 2021

SDG 5 : Gender Equality Index Score of States/Union Territories

State	Score	Percentage of Elected Women in State Assemblies
1. Chhattisgarh	64	14.44
2. Kerala	63	5.71 (7.85%, 2021#)
3. Himachal Pradesh	62	7.35
4. Tamil Nadu	59	8.51 (5.12, 2021#)
5. Andhra Pradesh	58	8.00
6. Sikkim	58	9.38
7. Karnataka	57	3.14
8. Goa	55	5.00 (7.5, 2022#)
9. Madhya Pradesh	55	9.13
10. Mizoram	54	0
11. Jharkhand	51	12.35
12. Maharashtra	51	8.33
13. Meghalaya	51	5.08
14. Uttar Pradesh	50	10.61 (11.4, 2022#)
15. Gujarat	49	7.56
16. Bihar	48	11.52
17. Nagaland	48	0
18. Odisha	46	8.90
19. Uttarakhand	46	8.45 (11.4, 2022#)
20. Punjab	45	5.13 (11.1, 2022#)
21. Haryana	43	10.00
22. Manipur	41	3.3 (8.3, 2022#)
23. Telangana	41	5.04
24. West Bengal	41	13.61
25. Rajasthan	39	12.00
26. Tripura	39	5.00
27. Arunachal Pradesh	37	5.00
28. Assam	25	6.35 (4.76, 2021#)

Source: NITI Aayog (2021), p. 104.
As per recent election results.

1

WOMEN AND POLITICS IN JAMMU AND KASHMIR

Rekha Chowdhary and Vibhuti Ubbott

Introduction

The question of women in the erstwhile state of Jammu and Kashmir (now a Union Territory) has to be posed from a number of perspectives. To begin with, Jammu and Kashmir's (J&K) peculiarity lies in its diversity and plural character. This is one rare political state in India which is a Muslim majority with a significant minority of Hindus. However, its context of diversity extends much beyond its religious demography and gets reflected in its multiple ethnic, cultural, linguistic, tribal, and caste identities. These diversities are so manifested that they provide a context for the complexity that defies any simplistic understanding of its plurality. Thus, it would be a misconception to state that this erstwhile state has been internally undifferentiated. There are multiple layers of identities which overlap in certain spaces and stand in divergence with each other in other spaces (Chowdhary, 2010).

Further, the former state has been conflict ridden and besides its external context of conflict, it has also faced an internal dimension of the conflict. Not only does it have volatility on its borders both during war and peace times but it has also been facing internal turbulence. For the last three decades this erstwhile state in general, and the Kashmir Valley in particular, has been confronted by militancy and separatism. The context of conflict has various implications for society in general and for politics in particular (Bose, 2003; Chowdhary, 2016; Puri, 1993).

Till very recently, this was the only state in India which was granted special constitutional status and it enjoyed formal constitutional autonomy under Article 370 of the Indian Constitution. However, a major change in its status was brought about by the Nation Democratic Alliance (NDA) government in August 2019. Besides withdrawing its special constitutional status, the erstwhile state was also bifurcated into three union territories.

This chapter discusses women mainly in the context of the Union Territory of Jammu and Kashmir. However, it also refers to the Union Territory of Ladakh.

DOI: 10.4324/9781003374862-2

53

The social set-up and women's position in
Jammu and Kashmir and Ladakh

Being a plural society with multiple social diversities, women's position in the erstwhile state of Jammu and Kashmir is also reflective of multiple patterns. Though women's overall position is characterized by patriarchal norms there are a lot of internal variations. The social set-up of Dogra society dominated by upper castes is quite different from that of the Kashmiri society characterized by the peasantry and artisan classes or the Ladakhi tribal society. There are also different patterns related to the role and status of women among the marginal sections, including the Gujjars, Paharis, and Dalits. Historically, both in Jammu as well as in the Kashmir regions, women from the upper classes have faced severe implications of patriarchal norms. Thus, purdah was much more prevalent among the Dogra Rajput and Kashmiri Muslim elite as compared to the lower castes and classes. Like the rest of northern India, the tradition of female infanticide was very common in the Dogra belt and the Dogra state had to take legal steps to enforce its abolition.

It was the same situation when it came to sati and child marriages (Soodan, 1999). In Kashmir, patriarchal values were strictly enforced among the middle- and upper-class women and they also observed the purdah. On the other hand, women from the lower strata, being part of an agrarian economy, trading or cottage industries, did not adopt the veil and were granted a lot of freedom, especially before the onset of conflict in the region. However, despite contributing to the work and the incomes of their households, women had negligible control over resources and property (Lawrence, 1995).

On the whole, the erstwhile state represents a varied and complex picture vis-à-vis women. Traditions and social norms in all the three regions are different. While the plains of Jammu were impacted by north Indian social practices, the Kashmir Valley was insulated from the influence of north India. Ladakh, on the other hand, was more linked to Tibet and Central Asia and had its own peculiarities. Due to paucity of land, there was fraternal polyandry with two or more brothers marrying the same woman (Mann, 2002).

Notwithstanding these traditional peculiarities, modernity influenced all the three regions equally allowing not only the opening up of opportunities for women including those related to education and employment but also in modernizing patriarchal structures. Thus, while statistics from the post-1947 period reflects a lot of changes in women's status, they also reflect a continuation of discriminatory practices against women and even the extension of these practices to places where they did not exist earlier. Kashmiri society, which was traditionally not known for dowry or for violence against women, has started showing these trends in the recent past (Dabla, 2014).

As far as the overall socioeconomic profile of women in this erstwhile state is concerned, they suffer from many gender-specific disabilities like low sex ratio, low work participation, and lower health status. They have been lagging behind in almost all the indices of growth and well-being. The Census of India (2011) recorded the sex ratio in J&K at 889. The child sex ratio showed a downward trend at 862.

Female literacy rate has consistently been lower than the male literacy rate in J&K. For 78.26 per cent male literates, there were only 58.01 per cent female literates (Census, 2011). Similar is the case with women's employment status. Of the total workers (both main and marginal) in the state, only 26.09 are women (Government of Jammu and Kashmir, 2018). Though with the passage of time and with the forces of globalization and modernization sweeping the world, the state has not been left untouched. Women are also taking advantage of new opportunities offered by these forces and are progressing on many fronts. Their enrolment ratio in educational institutions, especially in higher education, has been very encouraging in the state.

Political consciousness, rights, and political transformation – Women and their position in Jammu and Kashmir

The political transformation that started taking place in the 1930s and 1940s introduced the language of rights and ideals of 'equality'. The political movement in Kashmir against the monarchical and feudal system politicized the peasantry and artisan classes and the political discourse that evolved referred to the emancipation and empowerment of marginal sections of society (Bazaz, 1954). National Conference (NC) emerged as a progressive and pro-people party in 1939 which adopted the New Kashmir Manifesto in 1944 that had separate charters for peasants, artisans, and women. The Women's Charter promised various rights to women with a view that 'men and women must collaborate with each other in shouldering the weighty responsibility of nation building'.

The comprehensive charter lists many socioeconomic, political, and legal rights, including women's right to be elected to institutions, right to employment, right to follow any trade and profession that the women are capable of, social insurance, healthcare and maternity benefits, free education, and right to choose her husband and to get a divorce (New Kashmir Manifesto, 1944). All these rights enunciated in the charter were later incorporated in the state's Constitution.

Women's question that was addressed in a very progressive manner during the 1940s and early 1950s was put on the back burner later. As the state got engulfed in a conflict situation in the post-1950 period, NC's progressive agenda and the state were side-lined. The issue of 'Kashmiri identity' was privileged over other issues confronting the state.

With the removal of the socioeconomic agenda from popular politics in the state, progressive and socially purposive politics, including women's politics that captured the imagination of the nation in the 1970s, virtually bypassed the state. While northern India was impacted by the Dalit movement, the women's movement, and the right to information movement, Jammu and Kashmir remained totally untouched by these. The question of political identity became so important that not only was the politics of Kashmir dominated by it, but Jammu and Ladakh's regional response too was defined by it. While it was Kashmiri nationalism and Kashmiri political identity that was asserted in Kashmir, it was Jammu and Ladakh's regional identities that were asserted in these two regions. Despite a clear distinction in the nature of politics on a regional basis, what remained important was the primacy of a 'political identity' and 'political questions' over socioeconomic questions.

This was clear in Kashmir where there was continued political mobilization in the post-1950 period. Here, Kashmiri identity became the central point underlying politics and all political mobilization took place around this identity. The gender question was not raised and if anything, it was made subservient to the politics of a Kashmiri identity. By implication, women's concerns were neither addressed nor were they considered important. The progressive agenda of the New Kashmir Manifesto no more dominated Kashmiri politics. What was worse, patriarchal trends in Kashmiri identity politics remained totally unquestioned.

The patriarchal approach to Kashmiri identity politics became quite visible around a very important question of a domicile-related law in the state – the rights of permanent residents of the state. As per the law, which was protected by Article 35A, a category of 'Permanent Residents of the State' was defined who enjoyed special privileges related to ownership of land, state government employment, state fellowships, admissions to state-run professional institutions, and the right to vote and contest in state panchayats and the state's legislative assembly. However, as per administrative practices, a distinction was made between male and female permanent residents of the state. Permanent residence certificates (PRCs) for women were generally stamped as 'valid till marriage' and in case a woman married a person from outside the state, she was no longer considered a permanent resident of the state. It was only in 2004 that that this practice was discontinued following a High Court decision. However, the discriminatory content of the law continued as women who married outside the state could not transfer their property to their children. While children of males married outside the state enjoyed full rights to be considered permanent residents of the state, children of females married outside the state were not granted PRCs.

Notwithstanding the discriminatory nature of the law, there remained a consensus in Kashmir Valley in its favour. Any discussion around the

WOMEN AND POLITICS IN JAMMU AND KASHMIR

need to change it was strongly resisted as it was seen to be endangering the 'Kashmiri identity'. The argument was that extending the right to be permanent residents to women married outside the state or their children would amount to changing the demography of the state and endangering the 'Muslim majority character of the state'. This was a clear case of subordinating gender rights and submerging the question of women in the larger question of Kashmir's 'political identity'.

Women in formal politics

Like elsewhere in India, women have failed to become a significant political constituency in Jammu and Kashmir. They are not seen voting en bloc as women and are not seen as a political force significant enough to be wooed by political parties. Unlike caste, religion, and community which form important categories in electoral politics, gender does not have any significant space. Women are not considered important even as voters for changing electoral outcomes. Hence, gender specificity or gender sensitivity in political parties' manifestoes or in their electoral campaigns is not seen. No specific appeal is made to women as voters. No political programmes are specifically targeted at women.

Women in electoral politics are not visible beyond the level of voting. But even at this level, a large gap remains between men and women. Electoral data available since 1972 brings out some clear trends in the context of female voters. The gap between male and female voters was around 15 per cent in 1972 which decreased in successive elections. In 1977, it was around 13 per cent and in 1983 around 5 per cent. It increased slightly in 1987 (around 8 per cent). By this time, around 70 per cent women as compared to around 75 per cent men were participating in elections as voters. There was sufficient progress in women's voter turnout when compared to 1972 when their participation was around 54 per cent (see Table 1.1).

Women's participation as voters in the state was severely affected by armed militancy. Though overall voter participation was also affected by the violence, female voters' participation was affected more severely and female voter participation went down from 70.36 per cent in 1987 to 46.98 per cent in 1996 and 38.27 per cent in 2002. One can clearly see that women were more affected by the conflict as compared to men, since the gap between male and female voters increased to around 15 per cent in 1996. Although the gap reduced in the 2002 elections, the overall percentage of female voters was as low as 38.27 per cent. A large majority – around 60 per cent women voters – kept away from the electoral process. However, this gap showed a reverse trend in 2014 with higher women voters' participation as compared to men (Table 1.2).

Table 1.1 Women voters in the assembly elections (1972–87)

Year of Election	Percentage of Male Voters	Percentage of Female Voters	Gap between Male and Female Voters
1972	69.27	53.92	15.35
1977	73.14	60.39	12.75
1983	75.56	70.48	5.08
1987	78.65	70.36	8.29

Source: Compiled by the authors from various sources.

Table 1.2 Women voters in the assembly elections (1996–2014)

Year of Election	Percentage of Male Voters	Percentage of Female Voters	Gap between Male and Female Voters
1996	60.57	46.08	14.49
2002	48.26	38.27	9.99
2008	63.28	58.86	4.42
2014	64.85	66.27	−1.42

Source: Compiled by the authors from various sources.

Women as contestants in elections

The extent of women's participation in activities beyond voting is quite low. As the recorded electoral data shows, there is a very large gap between the number of male and female contestants. The number of women contestants remains quite insignificant. Similarly, women are not very visible in party politics. This despite the fact that almost every political party has a women's wing. However, this wing is a subordinate political organ and is marginalized in decision-making processes. Rather than rising from the cadres, women in leadership positions are nominated by party leaders and very often they are relatives of male leaders in the parties.

On the whole, the percentage of women contestants has not exceeded 5 per cent. This is a reflection of how the electoral process is still dominated by men. The electoral contest remains the monopoly of men. During the 1972 assembly elections, only 8 of the 342 candidates were women. The number of women contestants was the lowest in 1977 when only four women joined the electoral fray. The percentage of women candidates in this election was less than 1 per cent. The number of women candidates slightly increased in subsequent elections but their percentage remained quite minimal. In 1996 when the number of candidates increased two-fold compared to the 1983 and 1987 elections, the number of female candidates remained quite low. In the 1996 elections, there was less than 2 per cent participation of women as contestants. Since this was the peak of the militancy, not many women could come forward to contest elections.

The number of women candidates increased to 30 in 2002 and this was by far the largest number and percentage of women contestants. As against the 1.46 per cent female contestants in 1996, this number went up to 4.23 per cent in 2002. The number of women contestants reached its peak in 2008 when 67 women contested the assembly elections. At 4.92 per cent this was by far the highest percentage of female contestants in any assembly elections. But the number went down again in 2014 as 28 women contested in these assembly elections (Table 1.3).

The number of women elected as members of the legislature is much more disappointing. While four women were elected in 1972 only one woman was elected in 1977. No woman could win in the 1983 assembly elections. In the 1987 assembly elections, only one woman won. Two female candidates each were elected in 1996 and 2002. The number of elected female legislators in the 2008 elections was three while it was two in the 2014 elections.

A study of the data related to female contestants provides interesting insights. There is a regional difference in female participation. In the 1972 assembly elections, there were eight women contestants. Of these, three contested from the Kashmir region and five from the Jammu region. In 1977, of the four contestants, three were from the Jammu region and only one contested from the Kashmir region. In 1983, all the seven contestants were from the Jammu region; no female contested from the Kashmir region. A similar story was repeated in the 1987 elections. All the 13 women contestants were from the Jammu region and there was no representation of women from Kashmir or Ladakh regions.

The situation was different in 1996 since there were seven female candidates each from the Kashmir and Jammu regions and one female candidate from Ladakh. This was the first time that the number of female contestants

Table 1.3 Women contestants in the assembly elections (1972–2014)

Year of Election	Total Number of Candidates	Number of Female Candidates	Percentage of Female Candidates
1972	342	8	2.33
1977	409	4	0.97
1983	505	7	1.38
1987	528	13	2.46
1996	1,027	15	1.46
2002	709	30	4.23
2008	1,354	67	4.95
2014	831	28	3.37

Source: Compiled by the authors from various sources.

from Kashmir was so high. In 2002, of the 30 female contestants, 16 were from the Jammu region and 14 from the Kashmir region. One can clearly see that since the 1996 elections, women have started contesting elections in the Kashmir region, though in small numbers. This can also be seen in the 2008 assembly elections when 36 female candidates contested from the Kashmir region. There were 31 female candidates at that time from Jammu. No female candidate contested the elections in Ladakh in these elections.

Women political leaders in formal politics

Begum Abdullah has been one of the most visible faces of women politicians from the state. As Sheikh Abdullah's wife, she played a prominent role in the politics of the state, especially as a Member of Parliament. Though she entered the political arena through the family route and remained under the shadow of her husband for a long time, she grew in politics after his death and played an important role as the patron of the National Conference.

More recently, there have been a few women politicians whose rise in politics has also been because of the families that they belong to. Mehbooba Mufti, as the leader and one of the co-architects of the People's Democratic Party (PDP), has been an important political leader of Kashmir in her own right. Though she came into politics because of her family (her father Mufti Sayeed was a veteran politician of Kashmir), she evolved into a powerful political leader. One of the reasons that the PDP was successful in establishing itself as another regional party in Kashmir along with the National Conference was the role played by Mehbooba. Soon after PDP's launch in 1999, she was involved in political mobilization. As part of PDP's 'Healing Touch' policy, she moved from village to village in Kashmir to develop personal contact with the people and offered them succour during the conflict. She, in fact, became a face of new politics in the mainstream sphere and because of her significant presence, the PDP could popularize itself and could win enough seats in the 2002 assembly elections to form the government. Though she did not join the government at that time, she was known as the most influential leader of the party besides her father. She contested the parliamentary elections a number of times and represented South Kashmir in Parliament. She eventually became the first woman Chief Minister of the erstwhile state of Jammu and Kashmir after her father's death.

As a woman president of PDP, Mehbooba Mufti's role vis-à-vis women in J&K was full of paradoxes. Though she was the first woman leader of Kashmir who played an effective role in Kashmir's politics, she did not always take gender-sensitive positions. One of the situations in which she actually took a negative stand was on discrimination against women in the state subject law. After the J&K High Court set aside the discriminatory nature of this law, as the president of the ruling PDP, she pushed a bill in the state legislature which sought to undo the relief provided by the High Court. The

Women Disqualification Bill sought to disqualify women marrying outside the state from the privilege of being considered as permanent residents of the state.

After becoming the Chief Minister, she sought to pursue a few gender-sensitive policies in the state. Some of these policies were related to providing special women's buses, abolishing stamp duty for women registering their property, and establishing all-women police stations. But besides this, not much attention was paid by her government to empowering women.

Among the other women who have been active in formal politics is Sakina Ittoo of the National Conference. Her entry into politics was abrupt and was not her choice. After her father, a senior NC leader's assassination, she had to sacrifice her medical career for filling up the 'family vacancy'. For her, joining politics was a compulsion as the elections were approaching and she was fielded as a candidate in the 1996 assembly elections. After winning the elections, she also became a minister.

Another woman who joined politics in Kashmir because of her family is Shabnam Lone, daughter of separatist A.G. Lone. A legal professional, she claimed to be representing the legacy of her father's politics, though two of her brothers, Sajjad Lone of People's Conference and Bilal Lone, a Hurriyat member, were already active in Kashmir's politics. She contested the assembly elections at a time when there was a boycott call from the separatists which reflected her autonomy not only in her family but also in the separatist politics of Kashmir.

On the whole, one can say that there are not too many women political leaders in mainstream politics in the state. Family connections were very important for women like Mehbooba Mufti and Sakina Ittoo to rise to become ministers. However, that is not to argue that women joining politics through family connections lack political competence. As the case of Mehbooba Mufti clearly shows, though she entered politics because of her family she was able to make a mark for herself and play an effective role in her party.

Protest politics and women

While the women of Jammu and Kashmir have been marginalized in formal politics, they have been visible in agitational/protest politics. This is truer of the Kashmir region. Women became visible during the Amarnath agitation in protest politics in the Jammu region in 2008. In Kashmir, they have been the face of protest politics and have been at the forefront of all agitations.

Women's role in the Amarnath agitation in the Jammu region

The women of Jammu region have been subject to strong patriarchal norms with all the conservative and patrilineal standards and caste restrictions. Moreover, the region lacks overall gender awareness due to a paucity of gender-based movements or gender politics in the region. What prompted women's participation in the Amarnath agitation was something inherent in the agitation. The Amarnath shrine is one of the most revered religious sites for Hindus and it is popular even outside Jammu and Kashmir.

The agitation took place both in Kashmir and Jammu regions. In the first phase, the Kashmir region was affected by the agitation as the state government's decision to transfer 40 hectares of land to the Shri Amarnath Shrine Board was opposed by the political class in Kashmir. The agitation that took a separatist turn was so massive in Kashmir that the government was forced to withdraw the land order. This resulted in an agitational response in the Jammu region. Known as the Amarnath agitation, this was a prolonged agitation which lasted for over two months. Though the question of 'hurt religious sentiments' underlay the agitation, the agitation was also known for Jammu's regional and nationalist assertion.

The mass agitation had a huge participation of women. Women belonging to the Hindu majority districts of Jammu region formed the largest number of people demanding restoration of the land to the shrine. One of the reasons for women's participation in this agitation was the nature of the agitation. To begin with, the issue was linked to religious sentiments and in the process of mass mobilization, the religious factor was clearly overplayed. Not only was the religious issue central but even the tools of the agitation were religious in nature. There were bhajan *kirtans*, *prabhat pheris*, and religious slogans. Women were central in this religious manifestation of the agitation (Ubbott, 2010). Keeping in view the mobilization of a large number of women, the Shri Amarnath Yatra Sangharsh Samiti, formed especially for this purpose, fixed Tuesdays as all women's protest days during the Jail Bharo Andolan. Thousands of women from various parts of Jammu got arrested and made their way to police stations.

In a traditional society, where women are subject to strong social norms and are confined mostly to the homes, temples, and ashrams, religious places provide a legitimate public space to interact and carry out various activities without disturbing the boundaries ascribed by gender. In the Amarnath agitation too, the role played by women's religious groups (bhajan *mandalis*), religious heads of various sects (gurus) adopted by women, and the heads of various temples (pundits) in mobilizing women was remarkable. Emotive and provocative speeches by some of these leaders played a major role in arousing religious sentiments among the people (Ubbott, 2010).

However, there was also a class factor in women's participation in this agitation. While women from the rural areas and those belonging to lower-middle classes and lower castes participated in the agitation through religious processes, urban and upper class/upper caste women participated in various other ways like in rallies and organizing peace marches and signature campaigns.

One reason for women's participation in the agitation in large numbers was that the protest became familial and their male relatives were already participating in it. The agitation was seen as a legitimate activity by the larger society and there was no contradiction between males and females when it came to participation in the agitation. Further, participation in a religion-oriented agitation seemed an extension of their ascribed religious duties.

Though women's participation in this agitation was unprecedented it did not lead to furthering their gender interests. The agitation did not get linked to issues related to women. Despite the fact that women came out in the public space and played a major political role, there was no linkage between the agitation and their concerns. Moreover, women's participation in the agitation seemed to be exceptional. It did not train them politically to occupy the political space later. As soon as the agitation was over, they went back to their traditional roles and did not use this experience for entering politics in either a big or small way. The only exception was Shilpi Verma who entered electoral politics in the 2008 assembly elections which took place immediately after the Amarnath agitation. However, her entry into electoral politics did not reflect her gender agency much. She was seen to be a fit candidate for the simple reason that her husband had committed suicide during the elections and as the 'widow' of a 'martyr' who had died for 'religious' and 'regional' reasons, her entry was a reflection of the emotions of the people of Jammu. She lost the elections and her political career came to an end.

Women's role in protest politics in the Kashmir region

In contrast to the Jammu region, women have always been at the forefront of protest politics in the Kashmir region. Much before the separatist and militant manifestation of politics, women were part of the massive demonstrations that took place in the region. They were a part of the huge rallies that were organized by the Plebiscite Front in the post-1950s period. They were also visible in the processions organized by the National Conference. However, they became the face of protest politics during the period of separatism and militancy. In 1989–90, they were an important part of the demonstrations. Like men, they came out in large numbers and participated in the demonstrations (Chowdhary, 2010). There were mass protests and huge protest demonstrations almost every day and women were a part of these. Women across the class divide were visible in the public space during the early period of militancy. Of course, there were some class differences since women from the very elite class did not participate in the processions. In fact, many rich people who could afford to send their families outside the Kashmir Valley sent them to places like Delhi and Jammu.

Besides participating in mass politics, women also played an important role in legitimizing armed militancy. This process of legitimization involved a number of things ranging from eulogizing the militants, giving them the status of public heroes to encouraging young boys including their own children to join militancy. Militants who died were given the status of martyrs and women venerated at their funerals like during wedding festivities. One can get a glimpse of the way the women responded to armed militancy in the way they used *wunwoon* (traditional marriage folk songs) during the funerals for legitimizing militancy.

One consequence of the intense political upsurge was that women became highly politicized. However, due to the stringent security environment by the end of 1990, women's visibility in the public space was almost nil. This was a phase of aggressive militancy on the one hand and the repressive role of state forces on the other. The kind of mass protests that were visible earlier were not possible in this environment.

As the conflict became more complex, its implications for women also started becoming more intricate. Women were caught in the conflict in different roles – as informers, couriers, and sources. Women started becoming visible once again in the post-militancy period. By 2004, armed militancy had started declining and in the new environment, protest politics again started assuming importance. By 2006–7, Kashmir had started witnessing protest politics and there were numerous public demonstrations in 2007 highlighting various issues; in a few cases the issues were governmental, but in most cases the issues were related to violations of human rights. There was a mass upsurge in 2008 that echoed the separatist politics of the 1990s. Women were mobilized in large numbers and they participated in the demonstrations almost on a daily basis. Women were quite active during the prolonged separatist protests in Kashmir in 2009, 2010, and 2016 (Chowdhary, 2016).

However, despite their participation in mass separatist politics, women could not develop an independent space for themselves even though they did become more politicized and more politically conscious. Women may have been active supporters of separatist politics but not many of them were visible in leadership positions. Seen from this perspective, the separatist leadership is totally male dominated. There are exceptional cases of women leaders like Aasia Andrabi and Zamruda who have some presence in separatist politics but generally there are no women in either higher leadership positions or in the lower or middle levels of the separatist cadres. There appears to be a dividing line between men and women when it comes to leadership (Chowdhary and Ubbott, 2016).

Aasia Andrabi's case is very complex. She is the sole woman leader who entered the male bastion of separatist politics and her organization, Dukhtaran-e-Millat (DeM), formed much before the onset of armed militancy, is the only all-women's organization which has some visibility in Kashmir. What remains important about this organization is that it is not only led by a woman but it also has women in its cadres. Rather than operating like other women's organizations in ancillary roles vis-à-vis separatist politics, DeM has been a mainstream separatist organization. Though DeM's members have not been directly involved in armed militancy as combatants, they have been very closely associated with militants and separatists. Security agencies believe that during the peak of the militancy, DeM's cadres made strategic use of the veil when working for militants for carrying arms and providing other support to them.

However, there is a paradox about the DeM and Aasia Andrabi's politics. Her organization is the only women's organization that has succeeded in penetrating the male-controlled separatist politics of Kashmir. However, her gender politics is confined to the limits of religion. She has been identifying with the radical Islamist movement at the global level and supporting the idea of a global jihad. She has chosen to wear the veil and all members of her organization wear the veil. The veil is recommended for the women of Kashmir as well. Besides the veil, DeM has been recommending a strict dress and moral code for women and its members have been conducting raids and picketing beauty parlours, restaurants, and cyber cafes. Aasia is opposed to the idea of women paying attention to their bodies or the free mixing of sexes; by extension, she is also opposed to the idea of women being visible in public spaces.

Politics and women's voice in Jammu and Kashmir

A traditional patriarchal culture with a demarcation of roles for men and women keeps women away from politics. Women, despite being educated and pursuing careers, are essentially seen as homemakers. Political roles that fall in the realm of public roles are therefore not easily accessible to them unless there is familial support. With the exception of certain 'political families' which provide such support to women, generally women are not encouraged to be visible in the public space. Under extraordinary circumstances like a conflict situation, when women attain visibility, this is mainly in relation to the roles which can be seen as an extension of their familial roles. That is why it is 'motherhood' which gets celebrated. Alternatively, women are visible as widows or half-widows which is again a reflection of their status not as individuals but in relation to the men in their families.

The domestic space arguably is a 'private' space where women are supposedly protected and secure and therefore even when they enter the 'public space' it is for the specific purpose of getting educated or for working or pursuing their careers. Beyond this purpose, the public space is not considered 'proper' for women and in general social understanding it carries all the possibilities not only of endangering women's 'security and safety' but also upsetting the social and ethical order.

Though there has been much political discourse within conflict politics in the name of women there is no way of knowing what women want. Since there are not many women's organizations representing the women's side in the conflict situation, women's gender concerns have not been articulated as a mainstream discourse in the conflict situation. Issues related to women and their concerns remain at the periphery of the 'main' political discourse.

Like in mainstream politics, even in separatist politics the lack of women's collective voice pushes them and their concerns to the margins. Even here they do not seem to form a political constituency. This is the reason why women's participation is taken for granted, and their support is seen as unquestioned.

That women's voices are not represented in separatist politics gets clear from the numerous cases of victimized women who are living lives of destitution. The victimization of these women (whether they are raped, or widowed, or living as 'half-widows') is raised loudly in separatist discourse. But the way the victimization has impacted the lives of these women and the way they are coping with this victimization does not become the central point of this discourse (Chowdhary and Ubbott, 2016).

Women, community, and politics

In both Jammu and Kashmir regions the discourse on issues related to women has been articulated within the limits of community identity. Women have not been able to carve out gender politics or a gender identity for themselves. They are seen as a part of the political, religious, or ethnic community. All gender issues are debated within the realm of this community identity. Thus, women's politics remains a part of 'regional' politics, 'ethnic' politics, or 'religious' politics and women are seen as 'Muslim women', 'Gujjar women', 'Pahari women', 'Kashmiri women', or 'Dogra women'. Fragmented in as many identities as the competing political identities that there are in Jammu and Kashmir, their gender identity gets underplayed and submerged in some other 'larger' identity. This is the reason that we see them being mobilized for the purpose of these identities but not for gender-related issues. This is true as much of the women of Kashmir who have been part of conflict politics as is of the women of the Jammu region. The kind of political mobilization witnessed in Kashmir is not visible in the Jammu region. However, as and when there is any significant protest or agitation which is regional in nature, women are mobilized. As we saw in the Amarnath agitation, which was a rather sustained and region-wide agitation, women were quite actively mobilized. However, they have never been mobilized for gender-related issues. This point gets clearer in the case of Kashmir where there has been continuous mass mobilization of women for the last three decades.

Rarely is there a debate on issues related to women and gender. Women's identity is already pre-defined either as religious beings or as part of the

Kashmiri community. It is in this process that the contradictions between gender and community/religious identity are obviated. Nyla Ali Khan in her study of women in the Kashmir conflict (*Islam, Women, and Violence in Kashmir: Between India and Pakistan*) notes, 'In effect, the Kashmiri woman is constructed as a parchment on which the discourses of religious nationalism, secular nationalism and ethno-nationalism are inscribed'. She further notes,

> The equation of the native woman to the motherland in nationalist rhetoric has, in recent times, become more forceful. In effect, the native woman is constructed as a trough within which male aspirations are nurtured, and the most barbaric acts are justified as means to restore the lost dignity of women. ... If a woman's body belongs not to herself but to her community, then the violation of that body purportedly signifies an attack upon the honour (izzat) of the whole community.
>
> (Khan, 2010, pp. 109–110)

That the widely available trend of attaching a community identity to women's bodies during the Partition as reflected in Kashmir during the armed militancy has been noted by many. Women here have been under pressure to adopt cultural, religious, and moral codes in the name of 'honour' of the community.

Women's agency

However, despite the fact that community identity overtakes gender identity, the protracted conflict situation has reflected women's agency in a variety of ways. One of the ways in which this can be analysed in the context of Kashmir is in relation to women's participation in protest politics. To quote Misri, 'Agency-oriented roles are highly visible in the political participation and mobilization of women. Outnumbering men at times, they have made their presence felt in a big way in protest rallies and dangerous political missions' (Misri cited in Khan, 2010, p. 119). Besides participating in mass demonstrations, women have also been quite active in their own localities and neighbourhoods. They clearly reflect their approval of armed militants. In fact, armed militancy and Kashmiri youth taking to violence attained a sense of legitimacy in Kashmir due to the women. Women considered militants their heroes, called them 'our boys', sung songs in their praise, and were ready to provide whatever support they could to them. They gave them shelter when required and felt a sense of pride in having contributed to the 'cause'.

Women's agency vis-à-vis Kashmir's conflict politics is clearly explained with reference to their role both in legitimizing and de-legitimizing militancy. Militancy got social approval in the early period largely due to the role played by the women in approving and glorifying it. Later as the women started disapproving of it, it lost its legitimacy. As they were themselves subject to the multiple consequences of violence, women's attitude towards violence as a means of political resistance also changed. Their changed response to militancy resulted in a wider political debate on the relevance of militancy and the need to shift to more political ways of resistance.

Women have been using their agency in many more ways. It has been noted by many that women have been negotiating for their husbands and sons after they are picked up by the security forces. According to Mushtaq Ul Haq,

> Illiterate women, whose sons, spouses, brothers or fathers were serving jail sentences in different parts of Kashmir and India, began to follow their legal suits, contact lawyers, learn about the draconian laws under which their near and dear ones were imprisoned. They began to visit the various jails, and detention centres and travelled to far-off places. Thus their personal tragedies empowered them.
> (Mushtaq Ul Haq, 2012, p. 23)

In asserting their agency, women have not necessarily been vocal. There are many examples of women silently but forcefully taking a position both individually as well as collectively. They silently fought against the fundamentalist forces at a time when violence dominated and there was no civil society or political opposition in Kashmir and there were no women's political groups.

Throughout the period of armed militancy, women were not able to organize themselves on a common platform to speak for themselves or to confront the issues from a gender perspective in the form of collective resistance. The political movement was so overarching in Kashmir that it did not leave much space for a women's movement and gender politics. In other words, every other movement or struggle had to be subsumed in the larger struggle and would have had a place, if any, only after the political struggle was fruitful.

In this lack of space for gender politics, women responded in the only way they could be most effective – silently rejecting the pressure of fundamentalist politics. This becomes clear from women's response to wearing the burqa. Whenever a diktat was issued that women needed to cover their faces and bodies, they followed it but did not make it a part of their routine lives. There are a lot of stories in Kashmir of how women subverted the very use of the veil and used it for their benefit, using the anonymity that the burqa provided for availing their freedom of mobility and even visiting forbidden places like restaurants with their male friends.

Not only the veil, women have also silently resisted various other pressures. In the early 1990s, attempts were made to introduce the idea of sex segregation in public places, for instance, in buses which they resisted.

Conclusion

Despite all kinds of pressures, women have continued the cultural traditions of Kashmir. However, though affected by the prolonged abnormal situation, women's education has remained a priority for Kashmiri society. Two decades after militancy started, one can see that women have continued with their own cultural traditions. For most of the women wearing a veil is a 'non-Kashmiri' phenomenon. They proudly inform you that Kashmiri women were never traditionally veiled and had the freedom of mobility. In rural areas, women were involved along with their men in agricultural activities and could not have veiled themselves. Even in urban areas, there was no tradition of women wearing the veil. As far as education is concerned, though there has always been a gap between male and female educational levels, the number of educated women has increased since 1947. What is more important is that society values women's education and does not place any restrictions on their mobility and their being educated in co-educational institutions.

In general, one can agree with Dasgupta (2001) that

> even amidst this atmosphere of violence and terror the women of Kashmir have shown resistance and a sense of discrimination. They have refused to give up their traditional value system and cherished heritage. Had they not resisted the pressures to succumb to social customs that were alien to the Kashmiri way of life, perhaps Kashmir would have gone the way of Afghanistan.

Bibliography

Bazaz, Prem Nath (1954). *The History of Struggle for Freedom: Cultural and Political*. Srinagar: Kashmir Publishing Company.

Bose, Sumantra (2003). *Kashmir: Roots of Conflict, Paths to Peace*. Delhi: Vistaar.

Butalia, Urvashi (1999). *Gender, Religion and Ethnicity in the Context of Armed Conflict and Political Violence in India*. Washington, DC: The World Bank.

Chenoy, Anuradha M. (2005). 'Women and the Breakdown of the Public Space', in Rajeev Bhargava, Helmut Reifeld, Konrad-Adenauer-Stiftung (eds), *Civil Society, Public Sphere, and Citizenship: Dialogues and Perceptions*. Berlin: Sage.

Chowdhary, Rekha (ed.) (2010). *Identity Politics in Jammu and Kashmir*. Delhi: Vitasta.

——— (2016). *Jammu and Kashmir: Politics of Identity and Separatism*. Delhi: Routledge.

Chowdhary, Rekha and Vibhuti Ubbott (2016). 'Conflict and the Peace Process in Jammu and Kashmir: Locating the Agency of Women', in Asha Hans and Swarna Rajagopalan (eds), *UNSCR 1325, Women and Security in India*. Delhi: Sage.

Dabla, Bashir A. (2014). *Violence Against Violence in Kashmir Valley*. Jammu: Jay Kay Books.

DasGupta, Sumona (2001). *Breaking the Silence: Women and Kashmir*. New Delhi: WISCOMP.

Government of Jammu and Kashmir (2018). *Digest of Statistics, Jammu and Kashmir*. Srinagar: Directorate of Economics and Statistics.

Hans, Asha (2004). 'Women Across Borders in Kashmir: The Continuum of Violence', in Ranbir Samadar (ed.), *Peace Studies: An Introduction to the Concept, Scope and Themes*. New Delhi: Sage.

Khan, Nyla Ali (2010). *Islam, Women, and Violence in Kashmir: Between India and Pakistan*. Delhi: Palgrave Macmillan.

Lawrence, Walter (1995). *The Valley of Kashmir*. Delhi: Asian Educational Services.

Mann, Rann Singh (2002). *Ladakh Then and Now: Cultural, Ecological and Political*. Delhi: Mittal Publications.

Menon, Ritu and Kamla Bhasin (1998). *Borders and Boundaries: Women in India's Partition*. Delhi: Rutgers University Press.

Mushtaq Ul Haq, Ahmad Sikander, 2012, 'Women in Conflict: Surviving and Struggling in Kashmir', *Economic and Political Weekly*, 47 (9), 21–24.

Puri, Balraj (1993). *Kashmir Towards Insurgency*. Delhi: Orient Longman.

Soodan, Surjit Singh (1999). *Jammu under the Reign of Maharaja Hard Singh: A Study of Socio-Economic Conditions*. Jammu: Vinod Publications.

Ubbott, Vibhuti (2010). 'Gender Identity and Participation of Women in Amarnath Agitation', in Rekha Chowdhary (ed.), *Identity Politics in Jammu and Kashmir*. Delhi: Vitasta.

2

WOMEN IN HARYANA'S POLITICS
Myth of empowerment

Ranbir Singh and Kushal Pal

Introduction

Haryana is a small state located next to the national capital Delhi in north-western India. The state developed a peculiar model of politics after its formation as a result of the linguistic reorganization of the bilingual state of Punjab on the recommendations of the Parliamentary Committee on Punjabi Suba headed by Sardar Hukam Singh on November 1, 1966.

This state is a classic paradox of economic development and social decay. On the one hand, Haryana, which was a backward region of Punjab before it got statehood, has become one of the most developed states in the Indian Union due to the success of the green, white, and blue revolutions; rapid industrialization; development of communication; and its emergence as an information and technology hub. However, Haryana has also acquired notoriety because of a large number of incidents of female foeticide, atrocities against Dalits, and crimes against women. Despite women's significant contributions to the success of the three revolutions and industrial development, the sex ratio in Haryana remains the most adverse in the country, the literacy rate among women is also 20 per cent lower than that among men, anaemia among women is higher than in men, and life expectancy is lower among women.

This relatively disadvantaged position of women in Haryana may be attributed to the persistence of a patriarchal society mainly having a traditional and neo-feudal culture on the one hand and the failure of successive political dispensations to focus on social development and gender justice on the other hand. The absence of social reform movements and the persistence of a weak civil society have also been instrumental in the prevalence of this dismal state of affairs. But despite this, whenever they have got a chance, women have excelled in education and sports and brought laurels to the state (Chaudhary D.R., 2007; Chaudhary Prem, 2010).

DOI: 10.4324/9781003374862-3

Caste dynamics in state politics

Caste dynamics plays an important role in the politics of the state. Brahmins, Banias, and Punjabis (30 per cent) belong to high castes. The dominant agricultural caste is the Jats (27 per cent). Ahirs, Rajputs, Rors, Sainis, Gujjars, Meos, and Bishnois belong to minor agriculturist castes. Ravidasias, Balmikis, Dhanaks, Khatiks, and Jatias are the Scheduled Castes. There are also some Backward Castes – Kambojs, Khatis, and Jhimars.

Representation of women in state politics and the government

Women from Haryana have had a nominal representation in the Lok Sabha and Rajya Sabha. Only Chandrawati, Kumari Selja, and Sunita Duggal from the state have been able to win elections to the Lok Sabha. Chandrawati, a self-made Jat widow with an Arya Samaj background and a legal practitioner having links to the legendary peasant leader Devi Lal, was able to win from Bhiwani in the 1977 parliamentary elections as a candidate of the Janata Party. She defeated Bansi Lal, a former Chief Minister and Defence Minister of India, at that time by riding on the Janata wave against the Congress' excesses during the Emergency (1975–77) in general and in the implementation of the family planning programme in particular. Her image as a brave woman who dared to challenge Bansi Lal's might at the time of the Riwasa episode, in which a woman was allegedly humiliated in her brother's presence, enabled her to get a Janata Party ticket for contesting the elections.

Kumari Selja (Ravidasia), daughter of former union minister Dalbir Singh, won the elections to the Lok Sabha in 1984, 1991, and 1996 from Sirsa (reserved constituency) and from Ambala (reserved constituency) in 2004 and 2009 as a candidate of the Congress Party. She also served as a union minister from 2009 to 2013. Her success can be ascribed to her family background, good education, and Congress leader Sonia Gandhi's political patronage. But sitting Rajya Sabha MP Kumari Selja was elbowed out to allow Deepender Singh Hooda to enter the Rajya Sabha in 2020.

Sunita Duggal (Dhanak), a former Indian Revenue Service (IRS) officer and wife of an Indian Police Service (IPS) officer, was able to make it to the Lok Sabha from Sirsa (reserved constituency) as a Bharatiya Janata Party (BJP) candidate due to the powerful impact of the Modi factor in the 2019 parliamentary elections.

Only three women, Sushma Swaraj, whose husband Swaraj Kaushal was close to George Fernandes; Sumitra Mahajan, Punjabi widow of former Punjab MLA O.P. Mahajan from Hisar having links with the former Chief Minister of the state O.P. Chautala; and Kumari Selja, have been able to make it to the Rajya Sabha from Haryana. Sushma Swaraj, an outstanding orator belonging to the Brahmin community who became a member of the legislative assembly (MLA) in 1977 as a candidate of the Janata Party and also served as a minister in the Bhajan Lal-led Janata government (1979–80), was elected to the Rajya Sabha as a BJP candidate in 1989.

Sumitra Mahajan made it to the Rajya Sabha as a candidate of the Indian National Lok Dal (INLD) in 2002. Kumari Selja was a nominee of the Congress in 2013 as she was not inclined to contest from Ambala (reserved) Lok Sabha constituency in the 2014 parliamentary elections due to her differences with Bhupinder Singh Hooda who headed the Congress government in the state at that time. She was also inducted as a cabinet minister in the union government on account of her closeness to Congress leader Sonia Gandhi.

Sunita Duggal of the BJP was elected from Sirsa (SC) parliamentary constituency in the 2019 elections because of the split in the INLD and a division of its votes between INLD candidates and those of the Jannayak Janata Party (JJP) floated by Dushyant Chautala, a grandson of INLD supremo O.P. Chautala. The number of Lok Sabha and Rajya Sabha seats from Haryana is ten and five, respectively.

Only five women MLAs from the Haryana region – Om Prabha (Jain), Chandrawati (Jat), Rajkumari Sumitra Devi (Ahir), Parsanni Devi (Jat), and Shanno Devi (Punjabi) – were elected from Kaithal, Loharu, Rewari, Rajound, and Yamuna Nagar constituencies, respectively, as candidates of the Congress in the 1962 elections to the Punjab assembly. They became members of the first 54-member Haryana state assembly in 1966. Women MLAs only had a 9.25 per cent share in this assembly. All of them, except Chandrawati and Shanno Devi, belonged to leading political families. Om Prabha Jain is related to the former Chief Minister of Madhya Bharat (a Part B state, which existed before the formation of Madhya Pradesh), Takhat Mal Jain; Sumitra Devi is the great granddaughter of Rao Tula Ram, a hero of the Revolt of 1857; and Parsanni Devi is the niece of former Congress MLA, Samar Singh. All of them, except Rajkumari Sumitra Devi, took an active part in the deliberations in the Haryana assembly. Shanno Devi also became the first Speaker of the assembly. Chandrawati and Om Prabha Jain were included in the cabinet and both of them played important roles in the decision-making processes in their ministries.

In 1967, the representation of women in the Haryana assembly reduced to 6.27 per cent as only five women (Raj Kumari Sumitra Devi, Sneh Lata (Bania), Parsanni Devi, Om Prabha Jain, and Lekhwati Jain) were elected as Congress candidates from Hisar, Rewari, Indri, Kaithal, and Naggal constituencies, respectively, in a House of 81 members. Chandrawati was defeated in Badhra by an independent candidate, Major Amir Singh; Shanno Devi was declined a ticket by her party because Chief Minister Bhagwat Dayal Sharma decided to shift to the safe constituency of Yamuna Nagar from Jhajjar where he anticipated defeat.

None of these elected women could take an active part in the deliberations in the assembly as it rarely met during its short span of eight months during the tenure of the Rao Birender Singh-led Samyukta Vidhayak Dal (SVD) government which was dismissed by the then Governor B.N. Chakraverti to bring an end to the *Aaya Ram, Gaya Ram* politics (Aaya Ram Gaya Ram were the names given to the politics of defection and counter-defection in Haryana after the 1967 elections). Om Prabha Jain also served as a minister in the short-lived Congress government headed by Bhagwat Dayal which was toppled within two weeks because of defections by over a dozen Congress MLAs from the party. The SVD government did not have a woman minister.

The representation of women, however, increased to 8.68 per cent in the 1968 mid-term elections as their numbers increased from five to seven in a House of 81. Sharda Rani, Parsanni Devi, Lekhwati Jain, Chandrawati, and Om Prabha Jain were elected on Congress tickets from Ballabgarh, Indri, Ambala city, Badhra, and Kaithal, respectively, whereas Raj Kumari Sumitra Devi and Shakuntla (Jatia) were elected as candidates of the Vishal Haryana Party floated by Rao Birender Singh from Rewari and Salhawas (reserved) constituencies, respectively. All of them, except Shakuntla, were from leading political families. Shakuntla got a party ticket because she belonged to party head Rao Birender Singh's village Ram Pura (Rewari). All of them, except Rajkumari Sumitra Devi and Sakuntala, took an active part in the deliberations in the assembly. Om Prabha Jain and Parsanni Devi became ministers; Lekhwati Jain was elected as the deputy Speaker. However, Om Prabha Jain was side-lined by Chief Minister Bansi Lal as she had been aspiring to become the Chief Minister of Haryana. Prasanni Devi remained powerful because of her proximity to Bansi Lal. Lekhwati Jain, who had been elected deputy Speaker, played an effective role only when she got a chance to preside over the deliberations in the assembly in the absence of the Speaker Banarsi Das Gupta.

Despite the fact that Haryana made remarkable progress from 1968 to 1972 due to developmental activities undertaken by the Bansi Lal government, the number of women MLAs in the state assembly declined from seven to five (6.17 per cent) in the 1972 elections. Only Chandrawati (Loharu), Lajjawati (Jat) (Badhra), Sharda Rani (Rajput) (Ballabgarh), Lekhwati Jain (Ambala City), and Parsanni Devi (Indri) could be elected as candidates of the Congress Party. All of them, except Chandrawati and Lekhwati Jain, belonged to political families. Lajjawati is the widow of former minister Major Amir Singh and Sharda Rani is wife of a former MLA and a former president of the zila parishad, Gurgaon, Gurdit Singh. Om Prabha Jain was defeated by an independent candidate Charan Das Shorewala backed by Chief Minister Bansi Lal who had started seeing her as a serious rival. Raj Kumari Sumitra Devi also lost from Jatusana as a candidate of the Vishal Haryana Party because of her decision to change her constituency from Rewari; Shakuntla was denied a party ticket.

Sharda Rani, Parsanni Devi, and Chandrawati were inducted in the cabinet but they could only play an insignificant role in the decision-making process because all the powers were centralized in the office of Chief Minister Bansi Lal during 1972–75. Chandrawati was dismissed in 1974 for daring to question the activities of Bansi Lal's son Surinder Singh. Sharda Rani remained powerful during Banarsi Das Gupta's tenure as Chief Minister during 1976–77 because of her proximity to him.

Elections in the post-Emergency period were held in 1977 during the Janata wave against the excesses committed during the Emergency and the Congress was routed in the 1977 parliamentary elections and a Janata government was formed at the Centre and the Banarsi Das Gupta-led Congress government was dismissed in Haryana. But these changes failed to bring any change in the representation of women in the Haryana assembly. Although the strength of the House increased from 81 to 90 following the delimitation of the constituencies, only four women were elected to the assembly. Hence, their share declined to 4.44 per cent.

All the winners were new faces and all of them were elected as nominees of the Janata Party. All those who contested as Congress candidates or as independents were defeated. The new women MLAs were Shakuntala Bhagwaria (Ravidasia) (Bawal), Shanti Rathi (Jat) (Kailana), Sushma Swaraj (Brahmin) (Ambala Cantt), and Kamla Verma (Kamboj) (Yamuna Nagar). All of them, except Kamla Verma, got a chance to serve as ministers. They handled the responsibilities of their ministries fairly competently. Their socio-political background was different from earlier women MLAs. None of them belonged to political families. Shanti Rathi had served a jail term in the agitation by government teachers against the Bansi Lal government. Kamla Verma was in jail during the Emergency and Sushma Swaraj earned her ticket on the strength of her oratorical skills during the 1977 parliamentary elections. Bhagwaria made it to the Haryana assembly because of her links with Chand Ram, a prominent Dalit leader at that time.

The representation of women marginally increased in the 1982 elections in which they won seven seats (7.15 per cent) in a House of 90 members. They included Shanti Rathi of Congress from Kailana, Sharda Rani of Congress (Jagjivan Ram) from Ballabgarh, Parsanni Devi of Congress (I) from Indri, Shakuntala Bhagwaria of Congress (I) from Bawal, and Vidya Beniwal (Jat) of the Lok Dal from Darba Kalan. The latter had been given the Janata Party ticket after her husband Jagdish Kumar's murder soon after the 1977 elections. In addition, Shanti Lather (Jat) was elected from Karnal on a Congress (I) ticket. She was a well-known social worker. Besides, Basanti Devi, granddaughter of the legendry Jat leader Sir Chhotu Ram, was elected on a Lok Dal ticket from Hassangarh. Shanti Devi, Shakuntala Bhagwaria, and Sharda Rani had also served as ministers in the Bhajan Lal-led Congress government and Parsanni Devi in the Bansi Lal government in 1986. It goes to the credit of all of them that they handled their ministries fairly competently. However, the key factor in their dominant positions was the support they enjoyed from chief ministers Bhajan Lal and Bansi Lal.

The percentage of women's representation declined in the 1987 Haryana assembly elections as only five (5.05 per cent) women were elected: Sushma Swaraj (Ambala Cantt) and Kamla Verma (Yamuna Nagar) from the BJP; and wife of a former Chief Minister of Haryana and then a union minister (Aadampur) Jasma Devi (Bishnoi) from the Congress. She was a substitute for Bhajan Lal who had been sent to the Centre as a union minister; Medhavi Kirti (Ravidasia), granddaughter of the well-known Scheduled Caste leader Babu Jagjivan Ram (Jhajjar); and Vidya Beniwal (Darba Kalan) of the Lok Dal. However, none of them got a chance to become ministers in governments headed by Devi Lal, O.P. Chautala, Banarsi Das Gupta, and Hukam Singh during 1987–91.

There was a marginal increase in women's representation in the 1991 Haryana assembly elections in which 6.65 per cent women were elected: Kartari Devi (Ravidasia) (Kalanaur reserved), Shanti Rathi (Rohat), Janki Devi (Jat) (Indri), Shakuntala Bhagwaria (Bawal reserved), and Vidya Beniwal (Darbakalan). The first two were elected on Congress tickets, the third was a candidate of the Haryana Vikas Party, the fourth was as an independent, and the fifth was a candidate of Samata Party (Lok Dal). Among them, Kartari Devi was the only new face. She had joined Congress after unsuccessfully contesting as a candidate of the Samyukta Socialist Party in the 1967 and 1968 assembly elections. Janki Devi, who belonged to a leading political family of Karnal district, was also a first timer. Kartari Devi, Shanti Rathi, and Shakuntala Bhagwaria became powerful ministers due to their proximity to Chief Minister Bhajan Lal.

Women's representation in the Haryana assembly declined significantly in the 1996 elections as only four (4.44 per cent) women were elected in these elections. This was because those contesting on Congress tickets were defeated because of the Bhajan Lal-led regime's (1991–96) image as a corrupt government. The women who made it to the assembly were Kamla Verma of the BJP (Yamuna Nagar), Vidya Beniwal of the Lok Dal (Darba Kalan), Sarita Narian (Ravidasia) of the BJP (Kalanaur), and Krishna Gahlawat (Jat) of HVP (Rohat). Among them Gahlawat was a first timer. She was close to party leader Bansi Lal and Sarita Narian is the daughter of a former BJP MLA, Jai Narian.

Only Kamla Verma was included in the Haryana Vikas Party–BJP alliance-led government headed by Bansi Lal and she handled her ministry effectively (the Haryana Vikas Party was formed by Bansi Lal). The other elected women, by and large, remained passive members of the House. Even Kamla Verma did not have a free hand as the reins of power were in the hands of the dominant political leader of the party. HVP lost power in 1999 after the BJP withdrew its support following the defeat of the BJP–HVP alliance in the 1998 parliamentary elections on the issue of prohibition.

WOMEN IN HARYANA'S POLITICS

Women's representation in the Haryana assembly remained unchanged in the 2000 assembly elections as once again only four (4.44 per cent) women could make it to the House because all the Congress women candidates, except Anita Yadav (Ahir), were defeated. Others who made it to the Haryana Vidhan Sabha were Sarita Narian (SC) (Kalanaur reserved) and Veena Chhibber (Punjabi) (Ambala city) of the BJP and Vidya Beniwal (Darba Kalan) of the INLD. Anita Yadav and Veena Chhibber did not belong to political families. It is also pertinent to mention here that Kamla Verma of the BJP, who had served as a minister in the Bansi Lal-led HVP–BJP government, was defeated from Yamuna Nagar as the elections were allegedly sabotaged by the party's alliance partner, the Indian National Lok Dal. It is also worth mentioning here that no woman legislator was included in the council of ministers headed by O.P. Chautala from 2000 to 2005. Among the women legislators, only Vidya Beniwal had political clout because she was a close relative of the Chief Minister.

There was, however, a quantum jump in women's representation in the 2005 elections when 11 women (12.20 per cent) made it to the Vidhan Sabha. Among them, Anita Yadav (Ateli), Parsanni Devi (Naultha), Kartari Devi (Kalanaur), and Shakuntala Bhagwaria (Bawal) had earlier been members of the Haryana assembly. But Raj Rani Poonam (Ravidasia) (Aasandh), Meena Mandal (Balmiki) (Jundla), Krishna Pandit (Brahmin) (Yamuna Nagar), Geeta Bhukkal (Ravidasia) (Kalayat), Sharda Rathore (Rajput) (Ballabgarh), and Sumita Singh (Jat) (Karnal) were elected for the first time to the assembly on Congress tickets. Krishna Pandit is the widow of a former MLA, J.P. Sharma, from Yamuna Nagar and Sumita Singh had been president of the Haryana Mahila Congress. Kavita Jain is the wife of BJP leader Rajiv Jain and was elected as a candidate of that party from Sonepat. Rekha Rana, a Rajput and wife of former MLA Ramesh Rana, won from Gharaunda as an INLD candidate. Two women were elected in the by-elections, Savitri Jindal (Bania), widow of Haryana minister O.P. Jindal and Kiran Chaudhary (Jat), widow of another Haryana minister Surinder Singh. Kiran Chaudhary had earlier been the deputy Speaker of Delhi assembly.

This enhanced the number of women in the Haryana assembly to 13 (14.44 per cent). Anita Yadav, Shakuntala Bhagwaria, Kartari Devi, Geeta Bhukkal, Meena Mandal, Raj Rani Poonam, Sharda Rathore, and Sumita Singh did not belong to political families. However, all of them had links with Congress leaders Bhajan Lal or Bhupinder Singh Hooda. Kiran Chaudhary, Savitri Jindal, Kartari Devi, and Meena Mandal were made ministers and Krishna Pandit and Sharda Rathore were appointed as parliamentary secretaries in the Haryana government. Kiran Chaudhary was more influential because of her links with the Congress high command but none of them could be considered powerful.

Women's representation in the Haryana assembly reduced in 2009 to nine (10 per cent) because Meena Mandal and Poonam Rani's constituencies were abolished in the delimitation. While Poonam Rani did not contest, Meena Mandal shifted to a new constituency and, being an outsider, was defeated from Nilokheri. Sumita Singh (Jat), Savitri Jindal, Kiran Chaudhary, Shakuntla Devi (Khatik), Anita Yadav, and Sharda Rathore of the Congress were able to get re-elected from their old constituencies. Geeta Bhukkal of the Congress won from a new constituency, Jhajjar (reserved), after her old constituency, Kalayat, was de-reserved. Kavita Jain of the BJP was also able to retain her seat. Saroj Mor (Jat) of the INLD (Narnaund constituency) was elected for the first time. Savitri Jindal, Kiran Chaudhary, and Geeta Bhukkal were made ministers once again by Bhupinder Singh Hooda and Anita Yadav and Sharda Rathore were made chief parliamentary secretaries.

Despite the fact that all the powers continued to be concentrated in the hands of Chief Minister Hooda, all the women ministers and chief parliamentary secretaries handled their departments fairly effectively. Geeta Bhukkal was more powerful than the others because she enjoyed the confidence of the Chief Minister. Kiran Chaudhary also continued to retain her clout due to her proximity to the Congress High Command (Chaudhary D.R., 2007; Chaudhary Prem, 2010)

The 2014 elections to the Haryana assembly, held after the Modi wave had catapulted the Narendra Modi-led BJP-dominated NDA government to power at the Centre, brought about a significant change in the Haryana assembly by giving a clear majority to the BJP. However, this did not change the representation of women in the assembly as women were able to win only 13 of the 90 (14.44 per cent) seats in the House. Most of them were new faces. Those who won on BJP tickets included Latika Sharma (Brahmin) (Kalka); Santosh Sarwan (Balmiki) (Mulana); Rohita Rewri (Punjabi) (Panipat Urban); Kavita Jain (Sonepat); Prem Lata, wife of then union minister, Birender Singh (Jat) (Uchana Kalan); Santosh Yadav (Ahir) (Ateli); Bimla Chaudhry (Ravidasia) (Pataudi); Seema Trikha (Punjabi) (Badhkal); and Naina Devi (Jat) (Dabwali). All of them, except Kavita Jain, were elected for the first time. Santosh Sarwan, Kavita Jain, and Prem Lata belonged to political families while Kiran Chaudhary (Tosham), Shakuntla (Kalanaur), and Geeta Bhukkal (Jhajjar) were elected on Congress tickets. All of them had won in the 2009 assembly elections as well. Naina Devi is the wife of INLD leader Ajay Chautala and daughter-in-law of O.P. Chautala. She was elected from Dabwali.

Renuka Bishnoi (Bishnoi) of HJC who won from Hansi was a second timer as she had earlier been elected in a by-election from Aadampur in 2011 after her husband Kuldeep Bishnoi had been elected to the Lok Sabha in a by-election held in 2010 (Singh, 1999; Chahar, 2004; Prasad, 2010).

Women's representation declined to nine in the 2019 assembly elections from 12 in 2014. Among the sitting MLAs Geeta Bhukkal, Shakuntala Khatak, and Kiran Chaudhary of the Congress were re-elected. While

Bhukkal and Khatak's victories were due to the support extended by the former Chief Minister of Haryana Bhupinder Singh Hooda, that of Kiran Chaudhary was on account of the Bansi Lal family's influence in her constituency. Renuka Bishnoi (Hansi) decided to stay away from the electoral fray this time after her son Bhavya Bishnoi was defeated from her constituency in the 2019 parliamentary elections.

Naina Singh Chautala, who had been elected as an INLD candidate from Dabwali in 2014, was returned from Badhra as a Jannayak Janata Party candidate because of her husband Ajay Chautala's (grandson of Devi Lal and a former MP) hold over the constituency. Shally Chaudhary, granddaughter-in-law of Gujjar leader Ram Kishan Chaudhary, was elected for the first time as a Congress candidate because of support from the Jats. Renu Bala, a former chairperson of the Yamuna Nagar zila parishad, was elected for the first time from Sadhaura (SC) because of a combination of SC, Jat, and Muslim votes in her favour.

Among the second-term women MLAs of the BJP only Seema Trikha from Badkhal (Gurugram) could win in the 2019 elections because of her personal popularity in the constituency. Latika Sharma (Kalka), Kavita Jain (Sonepat), and Prem Lata (Uchana Kalan) were defeated. Santosh Yadav (Ateli), Bimal Chaudhary (Pataudi-SC), and Rohita Rewri (Panipat city) were denied party tickets. Nirmal Chaudhary (Jat) was elected from Gannaur (Sonepat) because her caste dominated in her constituency. Similarly, Kamlesh Dhanda, wife of former minister Nar Singh Dhanda, was elected from Kalayat because of voters' dissatisfaction with the performance of the Congress candidate Jai Parkash who had been elected as an independent in the 2014 elections but who joined the Congress on the eve of the 2019 assembly elections.

None of the BJP and JJP women MLAs were included in the Manohar Lal Khattar-led BJP–JJP coalition government which assumed office after the 2019 assembly elections.

It is observed that among the minor agriculturist castes, only Rajput, Ahir, and Bishnoi women have been able to get elected to the state assembly. Only one woman from the Backward Kamboj caste, which is a landowning caste, was able to reach the Haryana assembly. Among the Scheduled Castes, it is mainly Ravidasia women who have been elected to the state assembly as it is numerically, socially, educationally, economically, and politically stronger than the other Scheduled Castes. Some Scheduled Caste women also got some representation due to reservations for them. But they made it to the Haryana assembly for the same reasons that helped women from the dominant agriculturist castes, the minor agriculturist castes, and the upper castes – a political background or linkages with powerful political leaders like Bhagwat Dayal Sharma, Rao Birender Singh, Bansi Lal, and Devi Lal. No Muslim or Sikh woman has become a member of the assembly.

Women in political parties and election campaigns

The presence of women in political parties in Haryana is limited. Earlier Om Prabha Jain, who was the first woman finance minister of Haryana in Bansi Lal's government during 1968–72, and Kumari Selja who was a union minister were prominent in the Congress Party. Although Kumari Selja had been president, Haryana Pradesh Congress Committee, her position was weakened after she lost by a huge margin from Ambala reserved constituency in the 2019 parliamentary elections. No woman leader has been important in the BJP in the state after Sushma Swaraj moved to national politics and contested the elections to the Lok Sabha from Madhya Pradesh in the 2004 parliamentary elections and thereafter.

It may also be added here that there was a quantum jump in the number of women leaders who participated in campaigning in the 2019 parliamentary elections in the state. All the women candidates, Shruti Chaudhary (Bhiwani-Mahendergarh) and Kumari Selja (Ambala) of the Congress, Sunita Duggal (Sirsa) of the BJP, Raj Bala Saini (Sonepat) and Shashi Saini (Kurukshetra) of the Loktantra Suraksha Party, and Swati Yadav of the Jannayak Janata Party, actively campaigned in their respective constituencies. Besides, all the women MLAs in the state also actively campaigned in these elections. But the most interesting feature of these elections was canvassing by mothers for their sons and daughters. Naina Chautala campaigned for her sons Dushyant Chautala (Hisar) and Digvijay Chautala (Sonepat). Kiran Chaudhary campaigned for her daughter Shruti Chaudhary in Bhiwani-Mahendergarh, Prem Lata campaigned for her son Brijinder Singh in Hisar, and Renuka Bishnoi campaigned for her son Bhavya Bishnoi. On account of her appointment as the president of the Haryana Pradesh Committee on the eve of the 2019 Haryana assembly elections, Kumari Selja campaigned vigorously for Congress candidates in all the constituencies.

Women's share in Panchayati Raj Institutions (PRIs)

Before the 73rd Constitutional Amendment, women had a token share in gram panchayats, panchayat samitis, and zila parishads through a system of co-option. But the one-third reservation of membership and offices for women under the act enabled them to get more than 33.33 per cent representation in the 1994–95, 2000, 2005, and 2010 elections to PRIs. Apprehensions that the required minimum educational qualifications of middle pass for general, Backward, and OBC women and of Class 5 pass for SC female candidates contesting elections to PRIs and other requirements would restrict their entry have been belied.

Women's strength in zila parishads increased from 37.7 per cent in 2010 to 43.5 per cent and from 35.4 to 41.6 per cent in panchayat samitis. For the office of sarpanches of gram panchayats, women's strength increased from

37.6 per cent in 2010 to 41.3 per cent in 2016. For *panchs*, it increased from 35.7 per cent in 2010 to 42.2 per cent in 2016 (Malik, 2016). However, women's improved share at all the three levels of PRIs did not lead to their empowerment at any of the three levels. Their roles are often played by their male relatives. A study on women sarpanches elected in the 2016 Haryana panchayat elections shows that in place of *sarpanch pati* (husband of a sarpanch), now we have *sarpanch bhai* (brother of a sarpanch) and *sarpanch pita* (father of a sarpanch) in those gram panchayats where unmarried daughters had to be fielded as candidates because the wives did not have the minimum educational qualifications for contesting elections (Sangwan, 2016). Even women's educational background has not helped in their empowerment due to cultural constraints.

Conclusion

Haryana's failure in empowering its women has largely been attributed to the persistence of a traditional conservative culture in rural areas and also to a considerable degree in urban areas due to the virtual absence of social reform movements in the state on the one hand and the failure of successive political dispensations to address the problem of social development on the other.

The Haryana government has established the Haryana State Commission for Women and has initiated some policies and programmes for women and girl children like Ladli, Incentive Awards for improving the sex ratio, education loan schemes for girls, and awards for rural adolescent girls.

Though the women's movement is not well entrenched in Haryana, some changes can be noticed as women took an active part in an anti-liquor movement in Haryana during 1995–96 that enabled the Bansi Lal-led HVP–BJP coalition government to come to power in 1996 (this was a major issue in the 1996 assembly elections which helped the party to come to power).

During recent years, Dalits, including women, have attempted to assert their self-respect and dignified identity on various issues related to livelihood (like food security, MNREGA, and land) on the one hand and against caste discrimination or sexual violence on the other.

Some women's organizations and NGOs like Himmat and some Dalit outfits like the Gyan Vigyan Samiti and the All India Democratic Women's Association (AIDWA) have been instrumental in attracting Dalit women to grassroots activities. It is not easy for women to make a dent in the traditional set-up and open up political avenues for themselves. However, it is an encouraging sign that some efforts are being made in this direction.

Bibliography

Chahar, S. S. (2004). *Dynamics of Politics in Haryana, Vol. II*. New Delhi: Sanjay Prakashan, 375–392.

Chaudhary, D. R. (2007). *Haryana at Crossroads: Problems and Prospectus*. Delhi: National Book Trust.

Chaudhary, Prem (ed.) (2010). *Understanding Politics and Society (1910–1997). Hardwari Lal*. New Delhi: Manak Publications.

Malik, Varinder Singh (2016). 'Panchayat Chanuv me Sharto se Jamini Star pe Kamjor Hua Loktantra', *Panchayat Raj Update, (ISS)*, 5, 6–7.

Prasad, Gopal (2010). 'Representation of Women in Haryana Legislative Assembly', *Women's Link*, 16 (2), 44–50.

Sangwan, S. S. (2016). 'Haryana Panchayats More Inclusive Now', *The Tribune (Chandigarh)*, February 9, p.9.

Singh, Ranbir (1999). 'Women, Politics and Developing Nations-A Case Study of Indian State, Haryana', *Journal of Haryana Studies*, XXI (1&2), 1–11.

—— (2016). 'Haryana Mein Sarpanchon ka Kshamata Vardhan Karyakram', *Panchayati Raj Update*, July, 1, 5.

3

WOMEN IN PUNJAB POLITICS
Missing, voiceless, inactive

Simrit Kahlon and Seema Thakur

Introduction

The venue: Jantar Mantar, New Delhi; date: July 26, 2021; event: Kisan Mahila Sansad. Two hundred women associated with agriculture, mostly from Punjab, came together to enact a parody of the Indian Parliament, which at that time was in the midst of a stormy monsoon session. While the actual parliamentary proceedings were marred by disruptions and adjournments, the Mahila Kisan Sansad at Jantar Mantar passed two significant resolutions in a single day: one, to promote opportunities for women to play a proactive and visible role in the farmers' agitation and two, to provide 33 per cent reservation for women in the central and state legislatures. Both resolutions underscored the need to increase women's role and visibility in decision-making in the political arena.

In fact, over a period of eight months the farmers' agitation in Punjab provided a space and visibility to women like never before (*The Tribune*, 2021). From Swaran Kaur, a septuagenarian driving a tractor on her way to an agitation site along with a group of women eloquently speaking of the damage that poorly thought-out policies had wrought on agriculture in Punjab and how they planned to make a success of the agitation, to Amrit Kaur a young post-graduate student speaking on issues relevant to the country, particularly the youth which remain unaddressed, the agitation brought to the fore a variety of female voices and opinions. What appeared most remarkable was the confidence expressed by these women in their own ability to find a solution to their problems. No one can say that these women had been brought along as mere poster girls of the agitation or their speeches had been tutored. If anything, the farmer's agitation helped them stand next to men as equals.

Observers of the feminist movement (or the lack of it) in Punjab see this as a turning point in the women's struggle to carve out a space and identity within the largely male-dominated political system of Punjab.

DOI: 10.4324/9781003374862-4

No role for women in the political process

This positive outlook regarding the likely empowerment of Punjabi women and their enthusiastic participation in the mass movement notwithstanding, the fact remains that women's presence and involvement in decision-making in general and decision-making in the political process in particular has remained negligible at most. In fact, the ironic tale of the role of Punjabi women in the political arena was most aptly summed up by Savitri Devi, wife of the seventh Chief Minister of Punjab when she spoke on the pre- and post-independence scenarios in Punjab:

> *jaloosan wich nahre lagaan layi sadi lor si. Jadon rajnitik takat wandan da waqt aya ta sanu kiha giya, tusi ta ghar dian ranian ho, iss kichar wich hath gande karan di ki lor hai?*
>
> (Mohan, 2006)

> (We were considered useful for raising slogans as volunteers in nationalist agitations. But when the time came for sharing political power, our husbands, who were active in politics, told us 'you are the queens of the domestic realm, why do you soil your hands in dirty politics?').

It is in fact such a paradoxical situation with regard to women in the arena of Punjab politics. This chapter does an analysis of past trends in political participation viewed in the context of Punjab's socio-cultural and political climate. It is rooted in an understanding that women's participation in the political process is germane to their overall well-being, particularly their empowerment. This understanding both at the global and national level is by no means a recent phenomenon.

In 1993, India implemented the 73rd and 74th Amendments to the Constitution, thereby ensuring that not less than one-third of all elected seats at each level of the three-tier local governance structure would be reserved for women out of which one-third would further be reserved for women belonging to Scheduled Castes and Scheduled Tribes. Doubtless this measure was expected to stimulate women's political participation in the higher echelons as well. Available data, however, has a different tale to tell.

Despite all efforts on the part of the Indian state to promote women's participation in politics, women are not yet visible in sizeable number in decision-making bodies. Considering that India had its first woman Prime Minister in 1966, its first woman Cabinet Minister in 1947, its first woman Governor in a state in 1947, its first woman Chief Minister in 1963, and the first woman President of a major political party as far back as 1925, this is a perplexing situation.

The story of Punjab is no less puzzling. A state which is considered one of the developed states, and has had a woman in the union cabinet (Rajkumari

Amrit Kaur), a woman Chief Minister (Rajinder Kaur Bhattal), and women cabinet ministers, is low on the score of Sustainable Development Goal (SDG) 5 (46) which places it among the 'Aspirant States'. It has a long way to go in terms of women's participation in politics (NITI Aayog, 2021).

Punjab: Region, state, and culture

Punjab as we see it today is a result of a complex set of dynamics which played out over its historical past stretching back to the early Vedic times. This region was the stage where the epic battle of *Mahabharata* was enacted and the initial narratives and role models of Indian femininity as well as masculinity were developed.

As a territorial entity, the region has remained a borderland though not with immutable boundaries. Inhabited by mobile martial tribes and exposed to repeated foreign incursions, violence, particularly violence perpetrated on women, has become a part of its cultural ethos. It is no surprise then that patriarchy is deeply rooted in its culture: higher value is placed on men and masculinity while women are seen as the repositories of tribal, clannish, and familial honour and as begetters of male heirs to carry forth the bloodline.

As an administrative entity, Punjab has seen several divisions and sub-divisions ever since it first became a tangible administrative unit under the British in 1904. The bloodiest of these accompanied the Independence of India which saw Punjab being ripped in two along its north–south axis. East Punjab was the name given to the portion of the state left to India which was inhabited by Hindus and Sikhs (Government of Punjab, n.d.). This was followed by the reorganization of Punjab along linguistic lines in 1966, dividing it into two successor states: Punjab and Haryana and transferring its hilly areas to Himachal Pradesh (Government of Punjab, n.d.). Consequent to this reorganization, Punjab also became a Sikh majority state. Ever since, the state has never seen a non-Sikh Chief Minister. Very recently the suggestion of a woman as the Chief Minister was brushed aside on account of her being a non-Sikh.

The Partition of 1947, the most cataclysmic event of the recent past, only served to strengthen the cultural legacy of violence, gendered violence, and patriarchy in the state. India's Independence dawned but at a huge cost for the women of Punjab. Excesses were committed on them as their bodies were transformed into sites of violence and annihilation which left deep scars on the collective consciousness of the entire Punjabi community. Doubtless this troubled consciousness manifested itself in the form of a reassertion of patriarchal patterns of behaviour.

The British regime in Punjab also transformed its physical and economic landscape. The carving out of Canal Colonies converted a primarily tribal scrubland into a settled agricultural landscape where power was drawn through the ownership and control of land. From being perceived as war booty, women started being seen as instruments of land acquisition. This colonial legacy persisted in independent Punjab despite the consolidation and redistribution of landholdings. While the dominant caste group has remained that of the land-owning Jats, who also remain a decisive political force, the feudal dispensation necessitated the presence and participation of a considerable proportion of lower as well as menial castes. Punjab being the state with the largest proportion of Scheduled Castes in its population, Dalits and their issues remained an important factor in its political theatre. Punjab most recently got its first Dalit Chief Minister (*The Indian Express*, 2021).

The assertion of the Dalit identity has manifested in their moving out from the fold of the Sikh religion. This shift was facilitated by the emergence of a number of informal socio-religious sects known as *deras* in Punjab. Having a considerable following, particularly among women, often it is these *deras* and their god-men who decide the outcome in state elections.

The foundations of a more socially just and egalitarian society in Punjab, which allowed the Dalit movement to prosper, were no doubt laid in the Sikh religion which accorded equal respect to people from all castes and faiths while compiling the *Guru Granth Sahib*. However, even here one finds no female voice. It is another matter that the first Guru did accord women an equal status to that of men by heralding them as all men's friends, companions, and mothers.

Various communities in Punjab were identified as *kurhi-maars* (killers of daughters) and even today female foeticide remains a shameful reality of Punjabi society. At 895 females per 1,000 males, Punjab has one of the most adverse sex ratios in the country. The sex ratio in the 0–6 years age group is worse at 846 girls per 1,000 boys (Census, 2011). The fact that the sex ratio for this age group is even lower in the rural areas as compared to the urban areas is all the more worrisome and telling. Even more shameful is the fact that Sikhs as a community have the most adverse sex ratio in the 0–6 years age group at 828 girls per 1,000 boys (Census, 2011).

When it comes to the mean age of females at marriage, Punjab features among the top two states in the country. The state's female life expectancy at birth (74.8 years) in 2014–18 was among the top four states in the country, while the maternal mortality rate in the state in 2016–18 at 129 far exceeded the national average and was three times that of Kerala (43) which was the best performing state (Census, 2011).

Female literacy levels (78.5 per cent) have shown a tremendous improvement over the last two decades but still remain far below that of Kerala (95.2 per cent) (Census, 2011). Making matters worse, the Annual Status of Education Report (ASER) (2019) shows that close to one-fifth of all mothers of school-going children in rural Punjab were illiterate. Data also shows that households invested more on the education of male children than female children. Whereas girls were more likely to be educated in government-run schools, boys were often admitted to the more prestigious and expensive private schools. In terms of social development, Punjab has had a mixed performance (Table 3.1).

Table 3.1 Punjab: Socioeconomic profile

Population	Total Population			SC Population		
	2001			2011		
	Total	Male	Female	Total	Male	Female
	24,358,999	1,298,5045	11,373,954	7,028,723 (28.85)	3,714,350 (28.60)	3,314,373 (29.14)
	27,743,338	1,463,9465	1,310,3873	8,860,179 (31.94)	4,639,875 (31.69)	4,220,304 (32.21)
Sex ratio in the 0–6 age group (females per 1,000 males)	2011			2018		
	Rural	Urban	Total	Rural	Urban	Total
			893			
Life expectancy in Punjab (2014–18)	Male			Female		
	71			74.8		
Maternal mortality ratio (1,00,000 live births)			2016–18 129		2007–9 172	
Population below national poverty line (%)			2018 8.26			2019 8.26
Under-5 mortality rate (1,000 live births)				33		

(*Continued*)

Table 3.1 Continued

Literacy		Total			Rural			Urban		
		M	*F*	*T*	*M*	*F*	*T*	*M*	*F*	*T*
	2001	75.2	63.4	69.7	71.05	57.75	64.72	83.05	74.49	79.10
	2018	88.5	78.5	83.7	85.5	74.0	80.0	93.8	86.7	90.5
Workers		*Total Population*			*Total Workers (in % to Total Population)*			*Non-workers (in % to Total Population)*		
		M	F	T	M	F	T	M	F	T
		52.77	47.23	100.0	55.15	13.91	35.67	44.85	86.09	64.33

Source: Census of India, Punjab (2001 and 2011); Various Government of Punjab, Statistical Abstracts of Punjab; and *Ministry* of Statistics and Programme Implementation (MoSPI) (2020). *Women and Men in India*. Government of India.

Women's participation in economic activities in Punjab has remained consistently low since 1971 when only 1.2 per cent of all women in Punjab identified themselves as workers. This figure increased to 6.2 per cent in 1981, fell again to 4.4 per cent in 1991, increased to 19.1 per cent in 2001, and fell again to 13.9 per cent in 2011 (Census, 2011). The high degree of commercialization and mechanization, which was necessitated by the model of intensive agricultural development adopted by Punjab, systematically excluded women from economic production, thus placing a relatively low economic value on them with the result that 2011 saw Punjab with the lowest female work participation rate in the country. Further, the female workforce in Punjab is found mostly in low-paid jobs such as agricultural labour or in the urban informal sector. Such jobs are seasonal or part-time and generally lack security of tenure. This has led to the feminization of poverty in the state.

Punjab's socio-cultural and economic realities have a strong bearing on its political climate. The region is a classic example of how deep-rooted patriarchy born of a long historical experience of violence (primarily perpetrated on women's form and psyche) coupled with the concentration of power in the hands of the land-owning castes led to the social backwardness of women (in terms of numbers, health, and education) and their marginalization in the economic sphere. Political decision-making is influenced by religious and caste considerations and political bargaining is done using money and muscle power. This results in women's marginalization in the political arena.

Women in mass movements

Punjabi women have a strong tradition of participating in mass movements having socio-political overtones. Be it the Gurdwara Reform movement, the Ghadar movement, the Babbar Akali movement, the Naujawan Bharat Sabha, the Kirti Kisan movement, or the Indian National movement, women from Punjab have actively participated in a variety of protests and reform movements (Kaur, 1968; Mohan, 2006). These women took training in manufacturing bombs, established liaison among the freedom fighters, helped them escape from the authorities, and provided them with food and shelter. They also organized and participated in protest marches and congregations to express resentment against British rule. However, it should be noted that the women involved in these revolutionary activities were always related to the male revolutionaries.

Punjabi women also took part in other aggressive programmes of the Indian National movement like picketing of foreign cloth and wine shops. During the Civil Disobedience movement launched in 1930, Rajkumari Amrit Kaur played a pivotal role. Several girl students also participated in the Quit India movement primarily in processions and distributing anti-government literature; 22 girls were arrested in Lahore for their participation (Kaur, 1968). During the entire national movement, 21 women were arrested in the Revolutionary movement, 78 were arrested during the Civil Disobedience movement, 42 during the Satyagraha movement, and 41 in the Quit India movement (Pal, 2012). Mass movements in Punjab did not come to an end with India's Independence and its Partition. Punjab being a border state was always vulnerable to influences from across the border whether full-scale wars like the ones in 1965 and 1971 or subversive infiltrations in the form of drugs, weapons, and discourse. The 1960s saw Punjab under the influence of the Naxal movement while two decades later Punjab had to wrestle with the Sikh radical movement and its demand for Khalistan. Both these movements were active all over the state though they had deeper roots in rural areas and in border districts.

Literature and historiography have sadly maintained a heavy silence regarding women's role in these movements. One does find a suggestion that these movements were largely masculine in nature and the few women who did become a part of them did so as wives or female dependents of the male recruits.

The more recent farmers' agitation also did seem to have a strong presence of women among the protestors. Farmers' unions recruited several women farmers as their members at the village level who worked to mobilize villagers for the protest and even kept the spirit of the protest from flagging. Most important is the fact that women protestors and particularly 'old' women became icons of the agitation. What was lacking, however, was a female face among the leaders of the farmers' unions. The lone female who was part of the delegation of farmers' union leaders was not a farmer herself. Nevertheless, the movement served to highlight the potential and possible contribution of women during the mass protest movement.

Women in formal politics

Women's participation in formal politics may be evaluated along four fronts: first, women's voter turnout; second, the proportion of women in the legislative bodies at the central and state levels; third, the proportion and role of women at the grassroots level of governance; and fourth, women's proportion and roles in political parties' organizational structures. However, it is prudent to first understand the situation in Punjab vis-à-vis the rest of the country.

India and Punjab

Among the states having a reasonable representation in the Lok Sabha, those with a relatively higher proportion of women include Odisha (33 per cent), West Bengal (26 per cent), and Chhattisgarh and Gujarat (23 per cent each) (MoSPI, 2020). Punjab with women comprising 15 per cent of its contingent was a laggard state performing only marginally better than the national average of 14 per cent. Women's voter turn-out in Punjab for the general elections held in 2019 was 65.62 per cent, much lower than the all-India average of 67.18 per cent and far behind states such as West Bengal (81.79 per cent), Andhra Pradesh, Himachal Pradesh, and Kerala (MoSPI, 2020). At the level of the state legislature, with 11.11 per cent women among the legislators, though higher than the national average of 9 per cent, Punjab is far behind in the representation of women in the assemblies of states like Chhattisgarh, Jharkhand, and West Bengal.

The proportion of women representatives in the Panchayati Raj Institutions in Punjab rests at 41.79 per cent. This is below the national average of 46 per cent and the figure for the best performing state Jharkhand (59 per cent). Even the neighbouring states of Haryana (37 per cent) and Himachal Pradesh (50 per cent) have put up a much better show.

Women voters

Rajkumari Amrit Kaur from Punjab was a prime mover in the Women's Suffrage movement at the national level. One of the most strident voices of the British Women's Suffragette movement, Sophia Duleep Singh was the daughter of Punjab's last ruler Maharaja Duleep Singh. While women the world over took a century and more to get the right to vote, India adopted universal adult suffrage from the moment of its independence. Even so, the proportion of women voters has traditionally remained low. Less than half (46.6 per cent) of the total registered women voters turned up to vote in the third general elections. From the following general elections, this percentage increased to more than half and consistently remained above 50 per cent till the 16th general elections when it shot up to 65.6 per cent and further increased to 67.2 per cent in the 17th general elections. It was during the last general elections that for the first time in India, women's voter turnout was more than that of men (67 per cent).

Punjab exhibits a relatively healthier turnout of women voters in state elections (Table 3.2). Despite the fact that women voter turnout in the lat-est Lok Sabha elections at a mere 65.62 per cent was lower than even the national average, the figure in the state elections in 2017 stood at 77.9 per cent. This compares well with the figures for male voter turnout. The voter turnout in successive state elections has varied between a low of 21.59 per cent in 1992 and a high of 77.90 per cent in 2017. Close to two-thirds of the women have consistently been turning up to vote and elect a government of their choice. It is evident that women in Punjab identify more with political issues and elections at the regional level than at the national level. Higher

Table 3.2 Punjab: Women voter turnout during successive assembly elections

Year of Elections	Total Electors	Registered Women Electors	No. of Women Voters	Women Votes Polled (in per cent)
1952	6522434	NA	NA	NA
1957	4,462,127	NA	NA	NA
1962	10,745,652	4,871,615	2,888,094	59.09
1967	6,311,063	2,904,999	1,989,796	68.50
1969	6,692,111	3,087,194	2,148,855	69.61
1972	7,244,663	3,354,118	2,235,027	66.64
1977	8,764,980	4,015,734	2,555,815	63.65
1980	9,857,228	4,527,749	2,843,445	62.80
1985	10,728,825	4,849,800	3,235,557	66.72
1992	13,171,851	6,056,447	1,307,817	21.59
1996	15,225,395	7,183,287	4,873,478	67.80
2000	15,816,169	7,469,417	4,800,619	64.27
2007	16,775,702	8,083,650	6,100,419	75.40
2012	17,764,755	8,383,335	6,614,316	78.90
2017	20,029,646	9,407,337	7,328,107	77.90
2022	21,609,482	10,203,440	7,335,923	71.89

Source: Various reports of the Election Commission of India.

voter turnouts are accompanied by a constant increase in the number of women contestants in the fray.

Women in the central legislature

Women from Punjab have generally exhibited an above average presence within the contingent of MPs from the state in the Lok Sabha. Despite the fact that few women contestants from Punjab tasted success in the first six general elections (three out of eight), ever since the seventh general elections in 1980, the contingent of MPs from Punjab has always included women. Their percentage has ranged from a low of less than 8 per cent to a high of more than 30 per cent. In absolute terms, since the 1980s, women MPs from Punjab have ranged from one to four in the Lok Sabha. The heartening news is that over the years the number of women contesting the polls has been increasing but the sad news is that the success ratio of the women candidates is falling (Table 3.3).

Seven women from Punjab have been members of the Rajya Sabha over the last seven decades. Five of them were from the Congress, and one each from the BJP and the Shiromani Akali Dal (SAD). This speaks volumes about the lack of gender equality in these parties. On an average, one woman from Punjab has reached the Rajya Sabha every ten years (Table 3.4). Of these, Rajkumari Amrit Kaur was the Health Minister at the Centre.

Table 3.3 Representation of women from Punjab in the Lok Sabha (1952–2019)

Year	Total No. of Lok Sabha Seats from Punjab	Total No. of Contestants	No. of Women Contestants	No. of Seats Won by Women	Percentage of Elected Women
First (1952–57)	14	101	2	Nil	–
Second (1957–62)	17	78	1	1	5.88
Third (1962–67)	22	112	Nil	Nil	–
Fourth (1967–70)	13	75	3	2	15.38
Fifth (1971–77)	13	83	1	Nil	–
Sixth (1977–79)	13	79	1	Nil	–
Seventh (1980–84)	13	146	3	2	15.38
Eighth (1984–89)	13	74	5	1	7.69
Ninth (1989–91	13	227	8	3	23.07
Tenth (1991–96)	13	81	4	2	15.38
Eleventh (1996–97)	13	259	17	2	15.38
Twelfth (1998)	13	102	9	1	7.69
Thirteenth (1999–2004)	13	120	14	2	15.38
Fourteenth (2004–9)	13	142	10	2	15.38
Fifteenth (2009–14)	13	218	13	4	30.76
Sixteenth (2014–19)	13	233	20	1	8.0
Seventeenth (2019–	13	278	25	2	15.38

Source: Election Commission of India and Who's Who of Punjab Vidhan Sabha (1952–2012 and 2017).

Table 3.4 Women members of the Rajya Sabha (1952–2003)

Name of the Member	Period	Party
Amrit Kaur, Rajkumari	1957–58 and 1958–64	CONG
Amarjit Kaur	1976–82 and 1982–88	INC
Sita Devi	1972–74	CONG
Rajinder Kaur	1978–84	SAD
Gurcharan Kaur	2001–4	BJP
Sukhbans Kaur Bhinder	2004–06	INC
Ambika Soni	1976, 2000– till now	INC

Source: Election Commission of India and Who's Who of the Punjab Vidhan Sabha (1952–2012 and 2017).

Women in the state assembly

Punjab has had a unicameral state legislature since 1970. The proportion of women in the Punjab state assembly varied from nil in 1969 to less than 12 per cent in 2022 (Table 3.5). Only twice in all the years of independence has

Table 3.5 Representation of women in Punjab's assembly (1952–2017)

Year of Elections in the State	Total No. of Seats	Total No. of Contestants			No. of Women Contestants			Seats Won by Women	Percentage of Women MLAs
		Total	General	SC	Total	General	SC		
1952	154	843	NA	NA	13	NA	NA	5	3.24
1957	12	661	NA	NA	19	NA	NA	9	7.43
1962	154	756	595	161	14	NA	NA	8	4.54
1967	104	602	462	140	8	NA	NA	2	1.92
1969	104	471	389	92	8	NA	NA	Nil	–
1972	104	468	380	88	14	12	2	6	6.73
1977	117	682	509	173	18	13	5	3	2.56
1980	117	722	556	166	19	13	6	6	5.12
1985	117	857	655	202	33	26	7	4	3.43
1992	117	579	NA	NA	22	NA	NA	6	5.12
1997	117	693	541	151	52	41	11	7	5.98
2002	117	923	699	224	71	43	28	8	6.83
2007	117	1,055	818	237	56	42	14	7	5.98
2012	117	1,078	792	286	93	64	29	14	11.97
2017	117	1,145	834	311	81	55	26	6	5.13
2022	117	1,304			93			13	11.11

Source: Election Commission of India and Who's Who of Punjab Vidhan Sabha (1952–2012 and 2017).

the share of women among the legislators touched double digits. What also needs to be noted is the success rate enjoyed by women contestants in the state assembly. While the success rate for total candidates has varied from a high of 22 per cent to a low of 10 per cent, the range in case of women candidates extends from 0 to 57 per cent. However, in the last few elections this success rate is showing a declining trend. Here two issues come to light: (1) the relatively small proportion of women contestants albeit one which is showing a slow but consistent rise over successive elections and (2) the falling success rate of women contestants.

Women in political parties

The two major political parties in Punjab are the Indian National Congress (INC) and the Shiromani Akali Dal (SAD). Both parties have well established women's wings: the Punjab Pradesh Mahila Congress and the Istri Akali Dal, respectively. These wings have only women members but the presence of women in the organizational structures of the parties is extremely poor. Bibi Jagir Kaur and Upinderjit Kaur are the only two female faces visible among the SAD's organizational structure. The INC despite having propped up the only female Chief Minister of the state does not give adequate representation to women in its organizational structure.

Women's wings are used for mobilizing ground sentiment and motivating people to attend political rallies; these almost never function as pressure groups during the distribution of tickets as one needs male support to obtain a ticket. A cursory glance at the list of women MLAs from Punjab reveals that a majority of the elected women hail from political families apart from being exceedingly rich. They, however, have little or no experience of politics or governance at the grassroots level.

A perusal of the performance of women candidates in successive Punjab assembly polls shows that the number of women candidates being fielded by different parties is on the rise and yet the number of successful women candidates remains more or less static (Table 3.6). Ironically while the number of independent candidates contesting elections has risen sharply, most of them end up forfeiting their security deposits. The importance of being affiliated to political parties thus cannot be over-emphasized. However, not all political parties fare equally well in Punjab. While the BJP's performance has remained static over the years, the Bahujan Samaj Party (BSP) turned out to be the least successful party as far as its women candidates are concerned. Over the years it has not secured a single seat and 36 out of the 38 candidates fielded by it forfeited their deposits. The Aam Aadmi Party (AAP) on the other hand has performed rather well, having contributed half the successful women candidates in 2017. In 2022, this proportion rose to 84.6 per cent. Another heartening development

Table 3.6 Performance of women candidates in successive assembly polls in Punjab (1967–2022)

Political Party	Con/Won/FD	1967	1969	1972	1977	1980	1985	1992	1997	2002	2007	2012	2017	2022	Total 1967–2022
INC	CON	3	3	6	4	6	15	6	9	12	10	11	11	11	107
	Won	2	0	5	0	4	3	4	1	5	4	6	3	1	38
	FD	0	0	0	1	0	1	0	4	0	1	0	0		7
SAD	CON	0	0	1	3	3	2	3	6	5	5	10	5	4	47
	Won	0	0	1	3	2	1	0	4	3	2	6	0	1	23
	FD	0	0	0	0	0	0	3	0	0	0	0	0		3
IND	CON	3	4	5	11	8	12	8	20	19	22	45	32	29	218
	Won	0	0	0	0	0	0	0	0	0	0	0	0	0	0
	FD	3	4	5	10	8	10	8	20	18	22	44	31	0	183
BSP	CON							2	5	16	6	6	3	1	39
	Won							0	0	0	0	0	0	0	0
	FD							1	5	16	6	6	2	0	36
BJS#/ BJP	CON	2					3	2	2	1	1	3	2	8	24
	Won	0					0	1	2	0	1	2	0	0	6
	FD	2					2	0	0	0	0	1	0	0	5
AAP	CON												9	12	21
	Won												3	11	11
	FD												0	0	0
OTH	CON	0	1	0	0	2	1	1	10	18	12	18	19	28	110
	Won	0	0	0	0	0	0	1	0	0	0	0	0	0	1
	FD	0	1	0	0	0	0	0	10	18	12	18	19	0	78
Total	CON	8	8	12	18	19	33	22	52	71	56	93	81	93	485
	Won	2	0	6	3	6	4	6	7	8	7	14	6	13	76
	FD	5	5	5	11	8	13	12	39	52	41	69	52		260

Source: Election Commission of India and Who's Who of Punjab Vidhan Sabha (1952–2017 and 2022).

in the latest assembly elections was the success of relatively ordinary and unknown entities, a fact that holds true for women as well but only those who belong to AAP.

An indifference towards the conscious inclusion of women by the political parties leads to a neglect of issues relevant to women and their lives. Seldom do election manifestoes highlight or prioritize issues that are germane to women's development and empowerment. The Congress Party's 2017 election manifesto, for instance, only proposed free education for girls from the weaker sections till the level of PhD and SAD promised an enhancement in the Shagun scheme to reach Rs 51,000 in the name of gender sensitivity. In the most recent elections AAP offered various sops to the electorate including that of giving Rs 1,000 to every female above the age of 18 years. Issues such as providing economic opportunities to women, mitigating violence against them, or correcting the imbalance in the sex ratio does not find a mention in the manifestoes. A document enunciating the State Policy on Women in Punjab framed in the last decade of the last millennium continues to gather dust while the status of women in Punjab moves from bad to worse. Table 3.6 gives the performance of women candidates in assembly polls in Punjab from 1967 to 2022.

The situation in the state conforms with the national picture where women in political parties tend to be restricted to the grassroots level or in performing supporting roles without access to established networks of influence.

Women and political agency: Factors and impediments

Leaving aside numbers, women's participation in state politics can also be gauged from their performance in the House as manifested in their presence in the House, their interventions, their presence in various committees, and their identification with Punjab; very few women legislators make regular interventions on women's issues.

Studies (Kaur, 1968; Sultana, 2015) show that very few women legislators from Punjab make regular interventions through the legislative procedure of asking questions by participating in the question hour. This is particularly sad when one considers the fact that unlike their male counterparts, a majority of the women legislators hold graduate degrees and some are also professionally qualified. A perusal of the questions that have been raised by women shows that these covered a broad spectrum of issues related to the state and constituency problems. Further, most of the women legislators did not identify themselves solely as representatives of women and their issues though they did raise questions dealing with women's issues. The findings also show that the most questions were raised by Vimla Dang and Laxmi Kanta Chawla.

The presence of women in various in-house committees of the state assembly is negligible but that may be attributed to their generally negligible presence in the House. Very few women legislators have built their legislative careers through working in local representative bodies like zila parishads, panchayat samitis, gram panchayats, municipalities, and municipal corporations. This could be the reason for their remaining mute spectators during the functioning of the House. Data also shows that most of the women legislators were elected only once. Thus, it is clear that in the legislative leadership in Punjab there is quite a high turnout of new entrants.

The reasons for a lack of a sustained career in politics for women are not hard to find. Most women enter the political arena only once they are in their 50s and hence have short active political lives before them. Many times, women candidates may be fielded as proxy candidates in case of a male relative's death or elevation to the central legislature or higher political positions. Gurbinder Kaur Brar, Karan Kaur Brar, Rajinder Kaur Bulara, Bimal Khalsa, and Charanjit Kaur Bajwa are examples of this. Some women candidates from political families like Aruna Choudhry have had a sustained innings.

Fieldwork shows the characteristic features of Punjab politics, including dynastic politics, use of money, muscle power, and violence to achieve and retain power which leads to the marginalization of women in politics. In the course of an informal conversation, a lady holding a ministerial position in the Punjab government revealed that it was difficult for women to network for positions at odd places and awkward times, particularly over cocktail parties.

Another elected woman representative at the grassroots level echoed similar thoughts when she said that the night prior to the polling day was referred to as the night of *qatl-e-aam* or massacre since mass transfer of votes from one candidate to the other took place at this time.

However, most inhibiting for women is the patriarchal mindset where a woman political leader or a representative is seldom treated with the same respect and seriousness as her male counterparts.

Things have particularly worsened since the political power centre of Punjab shifted from Majha to Malwa. Till the Green Revolution bore fruit it was the Majha region that was the cultural, political, and economic hub of the state. Here the size of landholdings was small and there were ample opportunities for the not-so-rich to participate in politics. Women like Vimla Dang, Laxmi Kanta Chawla, and Sukhbans Kaur Bhinder tasted political success in Punjab due to this. The sub-region of Malwa is marked by large landholdings retained through the use of muscle power and political influence. Just as the control of land rests in a few hands, so does political power. Further, there have been matrimonial alliances between families which have cemented their position further in the corridors of power. No matter the political party that one belongs to, a position of power and pelf is always ensured for a privileged few. To quote just two examples, the wife of SAD's president addresses the erstwhile Congress Chief Minister as uncle owing to their family relations and the Kairon and Badal families are bound by matrimonial alliances.

Conclusion

All is not lost yet. The 2017 state assembly polls which saw women's participation in Punjab at a very low level also witnessed the entry of three women candidates who were marginalized in terms of caste and economic status. They defied the stereotype of the Punjabi woman politician both in terms of age and family lineage. They seemed to be performing their duties with a rare sense of vigour, conviction, and commitment. The most recent state assembly polls (2022) which returned the Aam Aadmi Party to power with an overwhelming majority also saw the entry of women from the grassroots into the corridors of power, that too after defeating stalwarts like erstwhile ministers and party presidents. It is thus equally the duty of the electorate to elect the right kind of people.

Bibliography

Anand, J. C. (1976). 'Punjab: Politics of Retreating Communalism', in I. Narain (ed.), *State Politics in India* (pp. 262–98). New Delhi: Meenakshi Prakashan.

Census of India. (1991, 2001 and 2011). *Census of Punjab (1991, 2001, and 2011)*. Chandigarh: Directorate of Census Operations, Punjab.

Election Commission of India (various years). *Statistical Report, Punjab Legislative Assembly Elections (various years)*. New Delhi: Election Commission of India. Available at: www.ecl.nic.in, accessed on March 19, 2022.

Government of Punjab (n.d.). *History*. Available at: https://punjab.gov.in/know -punjab/history/, accessed on March 16, 2022.

Government of Punjab (various years). *Statistical Abstracts of Punjab*. Chandigarh: Government of Punjab.

Kaur, M. (1968). *Role of Women in India's Freedom Struggle (1857–1947)*. New Delhi: Sterling Publishers.

Kumari, B. (2008). 'Women's Movement and Indian Politics', in J.K. Soni (ed.), *Women Empowerment the Substantial Challenges* (pp. 104–112). New Delhi: Authors Press.

Ministry of Statistics and Programme Implementation (MoSPI) (2021a). *Women and Men in India 2020*. New Delhi: Ministry of Statistics and Programme Implementation (GoI).

——— (2021b). *Sustainable Development Goals National Indicator Framework: Progress Report 2021*. New Delhi: Ministry of Statistics and Programme Implementation, Government of India.

Mohan, K. (2006). *Towards Gender History*. New Delhi: Akbar Books.

NITI Aayog (2021). *SDG India, Index and Dashboard 2020–21, Partnerships in the Decade of Action, United Nations and NITI Aayog*. Available at: https://www

.niti.gov.in/writereaddata/files/SDG_3.0_Final_04.03.2021_Web_Spreads.pdf, accessed on June 5, 2022.

Pal, Savinder (2012). Role of Punjabi women in Indian struggle for independence 1885 to 1947. Ph.D. Thesis, Panjab University. Available at http://shodhganga .inflibnet.ac.in:8080/jspui/handle/10603/79854 accessed on December 10, 2021

Parvin, R. M. (2005). *Empowerment of Women: Strategies and Systems for Gender Justice*. New Delhi: Dominant Publishers.

Punjab Vidhan Sabha *Compendium of Who's Who of members (1937-2017). (Updated till 25-10-2019)*, Chandigarh: Punjab Vidhan Sabha Secretariat.

Singh, B. (2010). *Punjab Politics: Retrospect and Prospect*. New Delhi: Readworthy Publications.

Sultana, A. (2015). *Gender and Politics: Role Perception and Performance of Women Legislators*. New Delhi: Regal Publications.

The Indian Express (September 21, 2021). 'Explained: Why Dalits and a Dalit CM matter in Punjab's Politics'. Available at: https://indianexpress.com/ article/explained/punjab-dalit-chief-minister-charanjit-singh-channi-congress -7523739/, accessed on December 23, 2021.

The Tribune (July 26, 2021). 'Women Farmers Hold 'Kisan Sansad'; Pass Resolution Demanding 33 Percent Representation in Parliament'. Available at: https:// www.tribuneindia.com/news/nation/women-farmers-hold-kisan-sansad-pass -resolution-demanding-33-per-cent-representation-in-parliament-288538, accessed on September 26, 2021.

4

POLITICAL PARTICIPATION OF WOMEN IN POLITICS OF UTTAR PRADESH

Manuka Khanna

Introduction

The Indian Constitution grants equal legal and political status to both men and women. As far as their administrative skills, organizational capacities, and political insights are considered, women are not behind men (Kuldeep, 2014). They have proved that they can effectively run a party and a government which is still by and large considered a male bastion. Yet there are only a few women in decision-making bodies. There is a strong patriarchal ideological construct that firmly believes in giving second citizenship to women. In this backdrop this chapter discusses the role that women play in the politics of Uttar Pradesh (UP).

UP's political significance

Uttar Pradesh has special political significance on the basis of its population, demographics, cultural heritage, and contributions to the freedom movement. It is the heart of political institutions in the country. Located in northern India, lying in the Gangetic plains, it is the most populous state in the Indian Union with an area of 2,40,928 square kilometres which is equal to 7.3 per cent land area of the country. The state shares its borders with states like Bihar, Madhya Pradesh, Rajasthan, Delhi, Himachal Pradesh, Haryana, and Uttarakhand as well as with Nepal. For administrative facilitation, it has 18 divisions, 75 districts, and 822 development blocks.

UP was created as the United Province of Agra and Oudh during the British rule in 1937 and renamed Uttar Pradesh in 1950. A new state of Uttarakhand was carved out of its Himalayan hill region on November 9, 2000. It has one of the most fertile lands for agriculture and is the largest producer of food grains. The state has an agriculture-based economy and there are variations in production in different regions due to large variations

DOI: 10.4324/9781003374862-5

101

in geophysical conditions like land, soil, rainfall, and climate. Consequently, there are regional disparities and inequalities in the state.

UP is ranked the lowest in almost all social indicators with only Bihar and Odisha lagging behind it. The status of women in traditional set-ups puts many limitations on their political participation, though efforts are being made to change this situation. UP has a sex ratio of 912 girls for every 1,000 boys. Its maternal mortality rate is 216 and workers' population is 9.6 per cent females against 47.1 per cent males in rural areas and 7.3 per cent against 48.5 per cent in urban areas (NSO, 2020).

Unfortunately, the number of crimes against women in UP is alarming. As per the National Crime Records Bureau (NCRB) data, Uttar Pradesh and Madhya Pradesh fare the worst when it comes to women's security. According to NCRB, 3.78 lakh cases of crime against women were reported in 2018, with Uttar Pradesh registering 59,445 cases – the most (Crimes Against Women, 2020).

Women's political participation

The issue of women's participation in state politics is entangled with the larger issues of caste and religion. The political scene in Uttar Pradesh is often explained as one that has been greatly influenced by the caste system since independence. The Indian National Congress dominated the politics of the state for many years after 1950 and had support from the upper castes along with a large share of votes of the lower castes. Thereafter politics has made space for three main parties –the Bharatiya Janata Party (BJP), Bahujan Samaj Party (BSP), and Samajwadi Party (SP) – which have played the caste card for polarizing votes. Though castes have retained their importance, the last Vidhan Sabha elections in 2017 gave different signals.

The Mandal Report (1983, implemented in 1990) served as a powerful force for creating new caste-based alliances. In 1993, the leader of the Samajwadi Party Mulayam Singh Yadav united the Other Backward Castes (OBCs) under the Yadav leadership along with support from Muslim voters. Muslims had traditionally voted for the Congress. To further restrict the Congress' influence, Mulayam Singh Yadav built the BSP–SP alliance. The success of this alliance was able to project an upsurge of the lower castes (Chandra, 1998); this coalition was short-lived due to the opportunistic strategies followed by both the partners. Though the alliance was created for securing power for the lower castes and BSP leader Mayawati had projected herself as the sole custodian of the downtrodden when the alliance was created, she changed her stand to retain power. She entered into an alliance with BJP, which is considered an upper caste party to form a new government. Her 'social engineering' was based on the 'destruction of the social order from below' (Pai, 2001). This brought her success.

Mulayam Singh Yadav attempted a similar move by using another caste card (Dheeraj, 2019) but Mayawati proved to be a better political strategist who brought together the Dalits and upper castes. Over the years, the two leaders have used their caste cards alternately and state politics has moved on the caste track with little or no influence of gender. As a consequence, Mayawati was able to get elected four times to the state government.

Uttar Pradesh is also the home of many religions. As per the Census of India (2011), Hindus constitute 79.73 per cent of the population of the state while Muslims constitute 19.26 per cent of its population. The population of all other religious groups is less than 1 per cent. This makes Muslim votes important.

A new trend in state politics

The state assembly elections in 2017 reflected a new trend in UP politics. A state which had voted on caste lines over the last few decades appeared to have given caste a miss this time. The Samajwadi Party with its core voter base of 9 per cent Yadavs and BSP with its core voter base of 12 per cent Jatavs had planned their campaigns on caste lines. A *maha gathbandhan* was formed to get together the combined strength of their core voters to defeat the BJP. However, BJP was able to cut across caste lines and secure a strong majority raising the question: 'Has the caste factor been replaced?' The BJP won 312 seats, BSP 18, SP 47, and INC 7 in the 2017 state assembly elections.

In these elections in a state where one of every five people is a Muslim, the BJP did not give a single ticket to Muslim candidates (Rukmini, 2018). Of 24 Muslim members of the legislative assembly (MLAs) who won in 2017, more than half (14) won from the same constituencies. A sixth of the Muslim MLAs have represented their constituencies for the last 15 years at least. None of the Muslim members are women (Saldanha, 2017).

UP's caste and religion matrices are such that roughly 20 per cent of the state's population is upper caste, 20 per cent is Dalits, 20 per cent is Muslims, and 40 per cent is OBCs. This political arithmetic is a good starting point for a political analysis (Varshney, 2019). In the last elections the issue of national security, especially the Balakot air strikes in the aftermath of the Pulwama terror attack and the success of flagship schemes Ujjwala and Swachh Bharat, overshadowed caste factors (*The Times of India*, 2019). Gender therefore did not play a significant role in voting patterns. However, schemes like Ujjwala and building toilets helped the BJP in wooing female voters.

Women from UP in national-level politics

Women do not share political power equally with men. However, it is important to remember that women's contribution during the national movement was significant. Laxmibai of Jhansi and her shadow Jhalkari Bai's valour and grit gave Uttar Pradesh a place of pride in India's history. Women from UP participated actively in the national movement under Gandhi's leadership and some of them became prominent leaders in independent India. Women from the state like Sucheta Kriplani, Kamla Chaudhary, Purnima Banerjee, and Begum Qudsia Aizaz Rasul played an important role in framing the Constitution.

Sucheta Kriplani, a committed freedom fighter, an effective parliamentarian, and a competent administrator, played an important role in UP's politics. She was the first woman Chief Minister in India (from 1963 to 1967). She set high standards of efficiency and honesty in the political arena. It is important to note that she was a member of the Lok Sabha thrice (the first, second, and fourth Lok Sabhas) but effortlessly went to state politics when the situation demanded it. Mayawati, the second woman Chief Minister of the state, also kept channels of both state and national politics open by being elected to both the Lok Sabha and the state assembly. The state also had another first, the first woman Governor, Sarojini Naidu. She was a close associate of Gandhi, a freedom fighter, poet, and was often called the 'Nightingale of India'.

Vijay Laxmi Pandit (Jawaharlal Nehru's sister), who was the first woman and the first Asian to be elected president of the United Nations General Assembly, was elected to the first, third, and fourth Lok Sabhas. She started her political career with her election to the Allahabad Municipal Corporation and thereafter was a member and a minister in the assembly of the United Provinces in 1937.

Begum Qudsia Aizaz Rasul, a progressive politician, was the only Muslim woman (a member of the Muslim League) in the Constituent Assembly. She made notable contributions to UP's politics after being elected in 1937 and post-independence as a member of the Uttar Pradesh legislative assembly for a long time and as a member of the Rajya Sabha (her autobiography *From Purdah to Parliament: Memoirs of a Muslim Woman in Indian Politics* traces the journey of a Muslim woman in the political and constitutional space).

After independence, women politicians in UP came from different social and cultural backgrounds as well as professions. Some had high educational qualifications while some had the richness of experience.

Some women who participated in the struggle for independence were active in politics in independent India like Sushila Nayar, a close associate of Gandhi and Kasturba, who was elected to the second, fourth, and sixth Lok Sabhas and was an able health minister in independent India. A few women entered politics mainly due to their family ties and thereafter carved their own political paths. Often the seat of power was vacated by the patriarch either due to death or circumstances. Jawaharlal Nehru's daughter, Indira Gandhi, initially branded a 'dumb doll' (*goongi gudiya*) emerged as one of the most powerful leaders and a strong Prime Minister; she was also the first woman Prime Minister of India (in 1966–77 and again in 1980–84; she was assassinated in 1984). Initially a member of the Rajya Sabha, she was elected to the fourth, fifth, sixth, and seventh Lok Sabhas. She handled many portfolios and provided a strong leadership at critical junctures like at the time of the creation of Bangladesh. The Emergency proclaimed by her in 1975 evoked fierce criticism and protests that led to elections in 1977 in which Congress (her party) lost the majority.

Sonia Gandhi was propelled to prominence after her husband Rajiv Gandhi was assassinated in 1991 and she became the president of the Indian National Congress. She wielded power though she never accepted any position in the government. She remains the unquestioned leader of the party. She was elected to the 13th, 14th, 15th, 16th, and 17th Lok Sabhas. Indira Gandhi's younger son Sanjay's wife Maneka Gandhi was undeterred by the family fights and emerged as a strong politician with eight terms as a member of the Lok Sabha; she was also a union minister.

Meira Kumar, the first woman Speaker of the Lok Sabha and the daughter of freedom fighter and important political leader Jagjivan Ram, fought one election from Uttar Pradesh and was elected to the eighth Lok Sabha from a SC constituency. Rita Bahuguna Joshi, daughter of H.N. Bahuguna, a former Chief Minister of UP and Kamala Bahuguna, was a member of the sixth Lok Sabha. She covered her political journey from the local to the central decision-making bodies. She was the mayor of the Municipal Corporation of Allahabad, and thereafter a member of the Uttar Pradesh state assembly and a minister. After almost 24 years in the Congress, she joined the BJP in 2016. She defeated Mulayam Singh Yadav's daughter-in-law Aparna Yadav in the 2017 UP assembly elections and became a minister in the state assembly. In 2019, she was elected to the 17th Lok Sabha from Allahabad.

Tazeen Fatma (SP) won a seat in the Uttar Pradesh state assembly from the Rampur assembly constituency which was vacated by her husband Azam Khan, who was elected to the 17th Lok Sabha. Dimple Yadav (SP) has been a two-term member of the Lok Sabha.

Some women politicians in the state got support from their families while some others undertook the journeys on their own. Mayawati (BSP) is an intriguing example of political participation of women from the lower classes. Her political graph moved from being a protégée of Kanshi Ram to the Chief Minister (the first Scheduled Caste woman Chief Minister). Mayawati was elected to the 9th, 12th, 13th, and 14th Lok Sabhas from SC constituencies. She remained a powerful member of the Uttar Pradesh state assembly and was elected as the Chief Minister in 1995, 1997, 2002 (short tenures), and 2007–12. She was a member of the Rajya Sabha in 1994, 2004, and 2012.

Some women like Ganga Devi and Sheela Gautam got elected to the Lok Sabha more than once. While some women entered the political arena directly in the Lok Sabha, some preferred to start at the state and local levels and then move forward based on this experience. It is interesting to explore the trajectories of these women. Sheila Kaul (Congress) was elected to the fifth, seventh, eighth, ninth, and tenth Lok Sabhas and headed important ministries. Earlier she had been a member of the Lucknow Municipal Corporation and the Uttar Pradesh legislative council. She was later appointed the Governor of Himachal Pradesh. Rajendra Kumari Bajpai also started her political career as a member of the Allahabad corporation and then moved to the UP state assembly where she held ministerial portfolios to finally being elected to the seventh, eighth, and ninth Lok Sabhas. Later she was appointed Lieutenant Governor of Puducherry. After getting elected to the Uttar Pradesh state assembly, Krishna Raj (BJP) was elected to the 16th Lok Sabha and became a union minister.

Mohsina Kidwai (INC), one of the few Muslim women politicians in UP, was elected to the sixth, seventh, and eighth Lok Sabhas and was a union minister of state. Before entering national politics, she was a member of the Uttar Pradesh legislative council and the state assembly, where she was also a minister. Among other Muslim women politicians from the state are Begum Abida Ahmed (Cong-I) (wife of the former President of India, Fakhruddin Ali Ahmed), Noor Bano Begum (INC), and Begum Tabassum Hasan (BSP). Hamida Habibullah was an elected member of the Uttar Pradesh state assembly and a minister in the early 1970s. Thereafter she became a member of the Rajya Sabha.

The state has a wide spectrum of women politicians with different backgrounds and cultures. There have been members from elite families. On the other hand, there is Phoolan Devi, whose exploits as a bandit were covered widely by the media including the film *Bandit Queen* based on her life. She entered politics after getting support from the Samajwadi Party. She was elected to the 11th and 13th Lok Sabhas and was shot dead during her second term as a Member of Parliament. Women like Hema Malini (BJP) and P. Jaya Prada Nahata (SP) brought glamour from the film world to the state.

In the council of ministers constituted during the Modi government's second term at the Centre, UP is represented by ten members including two women – Smriti Irani as a cabinet minister and Sadhvi Niranjan Jyoti as a minister of state. Smriti Irani has emerged as a powerful leader who dared to defeat the scion of the Gandhi family in the 17th Lok Sabha elections from a constituency that was considered to be a family fiefdom. Current members of the Rajya Sabha from the state include Jaya Bachchan (SP) and Kanta Kardam (BJP) (Table 4.1). Table 4.1 shows that the number of women elected to the Lok Sabha from UP is low.

POLITICAL PARTICIPATION OF WOMEN IN POLITICS OF UTTAR PRADESH

Table 4.1 UP women's representation in the Lok Sabha (1952–2019)

Lok Sabha	Year	Total Seats in the State	Number of Women Contestants	Number of Women Elected
First	1952	93	–	6
Second	1957	92	6	3
Third	1962	92	14	7
Fourth	1967	92	13	8
Fifth	1973	87	16	6
Sixth	1977	87	13	4
Seventh	1980	92	35	8
Eighth	1984	88	44	10
Ninth	1989	86	41	6
Tenth	1991	86	50	3
Eleventh	1996	85	107	9
Twelfth	1998	85	56	9
Thirteenth	1999	83	61	9
Fourteenth	2004	88	61	7
Fifteenth	2009	81	100	13
Sixteenth	2014	83	126	14
Seventeenth	2019	81	104	11

Source: loksabhaph.nic.in, accessed on June 15, 2022.

Women in the state assembly

After independence, the first elections to the state assembly were held in 1952 in which 25 women contested of whom only 11 won (3.17 per cent). There were fluctuations in the percentage of successful women members in the first 13 elections to the state assembly but during the 1990s the number of elected women representatives increased (Table 4.2). Though the numbers indicate that more women were successful in winning elections, political parties were not able to fulfil their declarations of giving 15–20 per cent tickets to women. Data shows that parties are still male centric and women account for only 5–10 per cent of the candidates. No serious attempt has been made by political parties to involve women in political pressure groups and women members need to put in greater efforts for establishing their positions within the parties. The Indian National Congress had the highest representation of women in the state assembly till the tenth assembly. At this point we need to remember that the Congress was in power at the national level also. The other parties had very few women members.

However, male members outnumbered women members at any point of time. After the downfall of the Congress, the period after 1977 saw more women being fielded by other political parties. Yet the number of male candidates exceeded the number of female candidates. Even the BSP led by Mayawati and INC led by Sonia Gandhi were no different. Thus, it can be

107

Table 4.2 Women's representation in the UP state assembly (1952–2022)

Year	Assembly	Total Seats	Number of Women Contestants	Number of Women Elected
1952	First	447	25	11
1957	Second	440	39	26
1962	Third	436	61	20
1967	Fourth	428	39	7
1969	Fifth	438	55	19
1974	Sixth	426	92	21
1977	Seventh	435	63	12
1980	Eighth	439	85	23
1985	Ninth	432	168	31
1989	Tenth	426	207	19
1991	Eleventh	419	226	10
1993	Twelfth	430	253	16
1997	Thirteenth	451	190	19
2002	Fourteenth	436	344	33
2007	Fifteenth	430	370	30
2012	Sixteenth	403	582	36
2017	Seventeenth	396	445	42+2 in by-elections
2022	Eighteen	403	560	44

Source: http://uplegisassembly.gov.in, accessed on June 15, 2022.

said that women are still kept away from power and there is more 'symbolism' than substance in giving them representation.

A profile of the elected women members of the 17th state assembly shows that they have higher educational qualifications as compared to the previous incumbents. Still the larger issue of women's political participation demands attention.

It is significant to see young women entering the legislative assembly. Anupama Jaiswal (BJP) and Archana Pandey (daughter of BJP leader late Ram Prakash Tripathi) were elected to the Uttar Pradesh assembly and were also ministers of state. Swati Singh, Gulabo Devi, Neelima Katiyar, and Kamala Rani Varun (a cabinet minister who succumbed to Covid-19 in August 2020) were ministers during Yogi Adityanath's first term as Chief Minister. In his second term, five women were inducted in the council of ministers on March 25, 2022. Baby Rani Maurya and Gulabo Devi have been given berths in the cabinet while Pratibha Shukla, Rajni Tiwari, and Vijaylakshmi Gautam have been sworn in as ministers of state.

Over the years the number of women not only increased on the electoral rolls but also in terms of their casting of votes in the state – 62.8 per cent of women electorate cast its votes as compared to 59.56 per cent men. District-wise voter turnout figures indicate that out of 75 districts in the state, the voter turnout among women was higher than that of men in 43 districts in 2022.

The number of female contestants in the fray for the 18th Vidhan Sabha was also commendable. As compared to 445 in 2017, 560 women contested the elections in 2022. Forty-six women candidates were elected, including 30 from the BJP, 12 from the Samajwadi Party, three from Apna Dal (S), and one from the Indian National Congress.

Before the elections major political parties presented programmes to win women's support. The Indian National Congress put forth the Pink Manifesto promising 40 per cent tickets to females and brought the issue of reservation for women to the fore but was able to get only one win (Aradhana Mishra from Pratapgarh). The BJP and SP also promised women voters free rations and incentives for the education of the girl child. Women voters were definitely seen as the major factor behind the success of BJP in these elections. Their 'silent vote' appears to be behind the success of the BJP. The perception of better law and order, the Ujjwala yojana, and free rations wooed the women voters towards the BJP. In the Muslim major- ity polling stations including Mantola, Dhonkhar, Sadarbhatti, Kotwali, Azampada, Nai ki Mandi, Wazirpura, and Tajgunj, the number of votes for BJP increased four times. The triple talaq law is being seen as a major mobilizer of women's votes in these constituencies.

It is important to note that at present Anandiben Patel is the Governor of UP. She was the first woman Chief Minister of Gujarat and has also been the Governor of Chhattisgarh and Madhya Pradesh.

Women in Panchayati Raj Institutions

Uttar Pradesh is a pioneering state as it recognized Panchayati Raj Institutions (PRIs) as being important and it passed the United Provinces Panchayat Raj Act, 1947. Consequent to the 73rd Constitutional Amendment, the United Provinces Panchayat Raj Act, 1947 and the Uttar Pradesh Kshetra Panchayat and Zila Panchayat Adhiniyam, 1961 were amended and Panchayati Raj was revitalized through the Uttar Pradesh Panchayat Laws (Amendment) Act, 1994. The state has 75 zila panchayats (district panchayats), 826 kshetra panchayats (intermediary panchayats), and 58,189 gram panchayats (village panchayats) (Panchayati Raj Department, Uttar Pradesh). The total number of elected women in PRIs is 272,733 (Ministry of Panchayati Raj, 2019). In accordance with the provisions of the 74th Constitutional Amendment, the state passed the Uttar Pradesh Urban Local Self-government (Amendment) Act, 1994 which replaced the five categories of urban local bodies by three categories of nagar nigams (municipal corporations), nagar palika parishads (municipal boards), and nagar panchayats (town panchayats). There are 17 nagar nigams, 200 nagar palika parishads, and 517 nagar panchayats in the state (Urban Development, Government of Uttar Pradesh).

Reservation of seats for women has been a progressive step for their development. Now women are visible in local bodies. In the municipal corporation elections held in 2017, BJP won 14 of the 16 mayoral posts. The municipal corporations of Lucknow, Kanpur, Ghaziabad, Varanasi, Meerut, Firozabad, and Allahabad got women mayors (all BJP). Sanyukta Bhatia became the first woman mayor of the Lucknow Municipal Corporation in a century. This seat was reserved for women this time.

However, it is not easy for women to make their presence felt in decision-making bodies. In a study conducted by Garima Mishra (2016) in Lucknow district, 92 per cent of the rural and 80 per cent of the urban respondents agreed that reservations were responsible for increased participation of women in politics. However, 96 per cent rural and 92 per cent urban respondents believed that without her husband's support, a woman's entry into politics was not possible. The remaining 4 per cent and 8 per cent rural and urban respondents, respectively, held the view that the son or some other male member had to support a woman's entry into politics. The study showed certain obstacles which came in the way of women's participation in politics, including inadequate education, reproductive role, lack of financial independence, and cultural and religious beliefs. It also pointed out that women faced different types of problems at different levels – firstly at the entry level and secondly being accepted in the political atmosphere. At the same time, women were less likely to obstruct corruption or question alleged persons. The study concluded that women showed that they were dependent on their male family members. Even the contact numbers given by elected women representatives were of some male members of their families and often there was insistence that communication should be with them and not with the women.

Though there is growing acceptance of women in local governance decision-making is still not in their domain.

Issues of concern

Traditional patriarchal and feudal attitudes condition social attitudes. Patriarchy is influenced by other factors like caste, class, region, language, and religion. At the same time, preoccupation with household chores and children does not leave women enough time for active participation in politics (Khanna, 2001). Politics continues to be visualized as a 'male domain' and a 'dirty game' best left to the men folk.

It is often felt that most of the women who are actively engaged in politics come from economically well-off families and have at least one close relative involved in active politics. Even the women leaders from Scheduled Castes and Scheduled Tribes belong to the higher educational category and are economically well-off. In such cases where a woman candidate has strong family linkages, resistance to her participation in politics is almost non-existent. For example, Priyanka Gandhi Vadra does not have to face the hurdles and struggles in politics, as the space has been created and nurtured for decades by her family and the organizational position in the party also came to her without any hurdles. Thus, it is observed that gender alone is not a determinant of political participation and success. In UP it is seen that widow succession is pervasive. After a man dies his wife is given a ticket to contest elections in the belief that she will be able to draw votes on sympathetic grounds and reap the fruits of her husband's toil (Singh and Pundir, 2002).

Participation in formal politics also requires availability of excessive resources, both monetary resources and social capital. Women lack access to resources as well as ownership of productive resources (Khanna, 2009). This limits the scope of their political work.

Women also lack social capital since they are often not heads of their communities, tribes, or families, which leads to the absence of a constituency base. It is normally the father, brother, husband, or father-in-law who has control over a constituency and the women are only there to take on the 'responsibility' of contesting elections in circumstances when they are not able to contest. This situation was seen when Akhilesh Yadav surrendered his seat in the Lok Sabha to enter state politics and his wife Dimple Yadav bore the 'responsibility' of keeping the constituency safe for the family. Similarly, when seats are reserved for the women in the Panchayati Raj Institutions, often the woman who is entrusted the responsibility by the male member holds the seat for that term only. This compulsory sharing of political space does not immediately give the women political skills, education, training, access to information, or economic resources. The positions they acquire are seen as transient and not taken seriously by them as well as by their male counterparts.

Seventy years after independence there is a huge increase in the number of women voters in Uttar Pradesh. However, it is likely that women may not be making independent choices when they vote. Apathy towards politics and lack of time and awareness may be leading to decisions being forced on them. In a traditional society in which a female is socialized to look up to the patriarch to decide her fate, it is natural that the decision to cast a vote is generally taken on a family level. A family, community, or village votes together. A survey conducted in Uttar Pradesh points out that women are much less likely to report being part of other electoral activities such as participation in campaigns, listening to candidates' speeches, or becoming members of political parties (Iyer and Mani, 2019).

There has been an increase in the number of women contestants over the years. At the national level, the total number of candidates fielded in the 2019 Lok Sabha elections was 8,049 with over 700 female contestants. Uttar Pradesh fielded the highest number of female candidates, 104, followed by Maharashtra, Tamil Nadu, Bihar, and West Bengal (Dantewadia, 2019).

However, the cultural, social, and economic structures form barriers for all contestants as they are the basis of the political structure. Politics can be seen as an 'articulation, or working out of relationships within an already given power structure' (Randall, 1987, p. 46). This task is more difficult for new entrants and women coming from non-political backgrounds. The culture of formal political structures hinders women's genuine participation.

Women candidates are generally evaluated on the basis of their dressing and outward appearance and often they also attempt to present 'the traditional look' to win over the public. When film stars like Hema Malini come to their constituencies they dress in a saree with their heads covered just like the other women there. Priyanka Gandhi leaves her western outfits back home when in Amethi. Another weapon used by society to clip women's wings is character assassination, threats, and violence. In the 2019 Lok Sabha elections, Jaya Prada Nahata, a popular cinema actress, was humiliated by the opposition and unparliamentary language was used against her on several instances during the campaign.

The 'hereditary factor' counters this bias in certain instances as in the case of Indira Gandhi or Priyanka Gandhi Vadra. Women politicians without a male political mentor very often do not even reach local-level organizational positions. If we see Mayawati at the helm of the party the credit goes to Kanshi Ram or in the case of Jayalalitha to M.G. Ramachandran. Power is not shared, it is often transferred to a successor like Jawaharlal Nehru was succeeded by Indira Gandhi and Rajiv Gandhi was succeeded by Sonia Gandhi. This trend was shaken when Smriti Irani won from Amethi constituency in the last Lok Sabha elections. Women occupying top positions are an exception and not the rule.

When policies are to be made or decisions to be taken, male leaders have their own perspectives that tend to ignore that of women; women's perspectives are supposed to be too soft or subjective. Women, who enter the political arena within this 'patriarchal context of modern democracies', are not willing and/or are not able to bring about radical changes. They prefer to largely play their political roles on the terms of the male members (Bari, 2005).

If we analyse the policies and decisions taken during Mayawati's tenure as Chief Minister, do we notice any striking differences with those taken during the tenures of other male chief ministers? When in power Mayawati pursued the policies of her predecessors. Her conduct and language were not different from the earlier male leaders. Female leaders attempt to 'masculine' themselves so as to survive in the political arena. Consequently, the expected 'feminization of politics' is a distant dream.

Women are usually regarded as delicate, vulnerable, and requiring guidance and protection. Male members' attitude does not credit them with the capacity to lead or take decisions. Thus, they are not chosen as decision-makers in political parties. The Left parties and Janata Dal have no women member in their political affairs committees. BJP and the Indian National Congress claim active participation of women legislators in their parties. However, in most of the cases, women leaders toe the party line on general issues. Only when there are incidences of violence and atrocities committed against women do they unite cutting across party lines. At times, they also raise issues which are not specifically related to women but the frequency of such instances is entirely dependent on their experience in terms of time and exposure to political activities at the grassroots level. Only women who have 'participated' in active mainstream politics are in a position to take an independent stand.

The 73rd and 74th Constitutional Amendments are path-breaking initiatives that ensure the presence of women in local governance. However, reservation is a first step. It requires many more steps and a multipronged approach to reach the goal. Effective representation cannot be achieved by reservations alone till the structural constraints of women's exclusion are addressed (Khanna, 2001). Socioeconomic redistributive justice is needed to make an effective change in society.

It should also be realized that women are not a homogeneous group. They are divided along lines of class, caste, language, region, and religion. In most places, women from the elite groups dominate an organization and women from sections considered lower in terms of class are suppressed. Social hierarchy prevents a large section of women from playing an effective role in politics. Reservations for women along with reservations on caste lines in local governments have been converted more to 'tokenism' or 'symbolism' rather than real power wielding (Kaushik, 2000, p. xix).

Conclusion

Despite all the obstacles, women have been forging ahead. Women's participation in the Chipko movement in Uttarakhand (earlier UP) made the headlines in the mid-1970s. It was a movement against degradation of forests and the environment. Women came to the forefront of this movement and transformed the struggle into their own movement. Chipko means clinging or hugging. Women expressed their love for trees by hugging them and not allowing forest officers and contractors to fell the trees for profit. The movement subsequently included protests against alcoholism and wife-beating. During the movement, the women said, 'The forest is our mother's home. We shall protect it with all our might'.

Growing awareness about their status and rights as Dalits has encouraged Dalit women to think about their course of action. While they have been with the men of their communities, they are also conscious of the way ahead. According to Radhika Govinda, Dalit women are now using their caste identity alongside their identity as village-level activists or members of women's self-help groups. They are doing this to make their interests go beyond women's activism to local electoral politics (Govinda, 2006).

In UP the status of women in the political sphere is conditioned by class, caste, and religion as well as their own inability to recognize their capabilities. Over the years their socialization makes them accept a lower position within the family as well as society. Many a times they doubt their capabilities and do not challenge the belief that the power structure is a protected zone. Women need to strive for their rights and exert themselves instead of feeling ashamed or scared of the heights.

With its advantage of a larger number of seats in the Lok Sabha and Rajya Sabha, Uttar Pradesh has the potential of leading a change in the country. It has given the country women leaders in the past and may continue to do so in the future to alter the gender imbalance in the political scenario.

Bibliography

Baldwa, Shreya and Sonakshi Awashi (2019). 'Lucknow's Muslim Women Tip Toe Around Triple Talaq, but Issue Might Have Given BJP a Toehold', *The Indian Express*, May 5.

Bari, Farzana (2005). 'Women's Political Participation: Issues and Challenges', United Nations Expert Group Meeting, Bangkok, Thailand. Available at: https://www.un.org/womenwatch/daw/egm/enabling-environment2005/docs/EGM-WPD-EE-2005-EP.12%20%20draft%20F.pdf, accessed on January 19, 2020.

Chandra, Kanchan (2000).'Post Congress Politics in Uttar Pradesh: The Ethnification of the Party System and its Consequences', in Ramashray Roy and Paul Wallace (eds.), *Indian Politics and the1998 Elections: Regionalism, Hindutva and State Politics* (pp.55–104). New Delhi: Sage Publications.

Dantewadia, Pooja (2019). *Lok Sabha Election Results: How Women Candidates Fared*, May 24. Available at: https://www.cnbctv18.com/politics/lok-sabha-results-2019-how-women-candidates-fared-in-the-election-3453211.htm, accessed on February 20, 2021.

Dheeraj (2019). *Caste and State Politics in India*. Available at: https://www.yourarticlelibrary.com/caste/caste-and-state-politics-in-india/49343, accessed on February 18, 2021.

Fadia, Kuldeep (2014).'Women's Empowerment through Political Participation in India', *Indian Journal of Public Administration*, 60 (3), 537–548.

Government of India (2019). Ministry of Panchayati Raj, Basic Statistics of Panchayati Raj Institutions, Available at: https://www.panchayat.gov.in/documents/20126/0/Statistical+handbook_MoPR+02082019.pdf/4988ca1b-4971-1f3b-54e7-980228eb47f9?t=1564729098415, accessed on February 20, 2021.

Govinda, Radhika (2006). 'The Politics of the Marginalised: Dalits and Women's Activism in India', *Gender and Development*, 14 (2), 181–190.

Gupta, Manika (2017). 'Uttar Pradesh Assembly Election Results 2017: Did Muslim Women Vote for BJP in Triple Talaq Issue?' *The Financial Express*, March11.

Iyer, L. and A. Mani (2019). 'The Road Not Taken: Gender Gaps Along Paths to Political Power', *World Development*, 119, 68–80.

Kaushik, Susheela (2000). 'Women's Political Participation in Politics', in Niroj Sinha (ed.), *Women in Indian Politics*. Delhi: Gyan Publishing House.

Khanna, Manuka (2001). 'Reservation for Women and Political Equality: A Note', *Punjab Journal of Politics*, 25 (1), 117–126.

———— (2009).'Political Participation of Women in India', *The Indian Journal of Political Science*, 70 (1), 55–64.

Mishra, Garima (2016). 'Women's Participation in Decentralized Governance: A Study of Selective Districts of Uttar Pradesh', PhD thesis, University of Lucknow. Available at: https://shodhganga.inflibnet.ac.in/handle/10603/123847, accessed on January 8, 2020.

National Statistical Office (2020). *Women & Men in India 2019*. New Delhi: Social Statistics Division, National Statistical Office, Ministry of Statistics and Programme Implementation, Government of India.

Pai, Sudha (2001). 'From Harijans to Dalits: Identity Formation, Political Consciousness and Electoral Mobilisation of the Scheduled Castes in Uttar Pradesh', in Ghanshyam Shah (ed.), *Dalit Identity and Politics* (pp. 258–287). New Delhi: Sage Publications.

Panchayati Raj Department, Uttar Pradesh. Available at: panchayatiraj.up.nic.in, accessed on June 24, 2022.

Panda A.N. (2010). 'Political Participation of Tribal Leaders', in B.R. Raju (ed.), *Development Issues in Contemporary India*. New Delhi: Concept Publishing Co. Pvt. Ltd.

Rai, Siddhartha (2017). 'Triple Talaq: 1 Million Muslim Women Sign RSS-backed Petition against the Practice', *India Today*, March17.

Randall, Vicky (1987). *Women and Politics: An International Perspective*, 2nd Edition. England: Macmillan Education Ltd.

Rukmini, S. (2018). 'How India Votes: What Does It Take for Muslims to Get a Ticket from the BJP?', *Scroll.in*, November 28. Available at: https://scroll.in/article/903613/how-india-votes-what-does-it-take-for-muslims-to-get-a-ticket-from-the-bjp, accessed on January 6, 2021.

Saldanha, Alison (2017). 'Muslim Representation in UP Assembly Plummets with 2017 Elections', *The Wire*, March 14. Available at: https://thewire.in/culture/muslim-representation-up-plummets, accessed on January 10, 2020.

Scroll.in (2020). *Crimes against Women*, January, 10, NCRB Report. Available at: https://scroll.in/tag/NCRB, https://scroll.in/latest/949408/crimes-against-women-uttar-pradesh-again-tops-list-madhya-pradesh-reported-most-rapes-in-2018, accessed on January 9, 2021.

Singh, Pitam and J.K. Pundir (2002). 'Women Legislators in UP: Background, Emergence and Rule', *Economic and Political Weekly*, 37 (10), March 9–15, pp. 923–928.

The Times of India (2019). 'Editorial, How Modi Magic Trumped Caste in UP', May 24.

Urban Development, Government of Uttar Pradesh. Available at: urbandevelopment .up.nic in, accessed on June 24, 2022.

Varshney, Ashutosh (2019). 'Caste and Religion Still the Bedrock of People's Political Understandings in U P', *The Indian Express*, May16.

5

WOMEN IN POLITICS IN HIMACHAL PRADESH

Bhawana Jharta

Introduction

Women exercise their franchise in large numbers, but when it comes to enjoying power positions or occupying prestigious political offices, they lag far behind men. This situation is found in almost all the states in India and Himachal Pradesh is no exception in this disappointing state of affairs with regard to women's participation in politics.

Himachal Pradesh is a small hill state located in North India. After the Anglo-Gorkha War (1814–16), the British colonial government came to power and the land now comprising Himachal Pradesh became a part of the Punjab Province of British India. Himachal Pradesh came into being as a centrally administered territory on April 15, 1948, after the integration of 30 erstwhile princely states of Punjab and Shimla Hills. At that time, the state had four districts – Chamba, Mahasu, Mandi, and Sirmour. In 1951, it was made a Part 'C' state under a Governor with a 36-member legislative assembly and a three-member cabinet. In 1956, it was made a Union Territory under an administrator designated the Lieutenant Governor and its assembly was abolished.

In 1963, the assembly was revived and a popular ministry was formed. On January 25, 1971, Himachal got full statehood and became the 18th state of the Indian Union (Government of Himachal Pradesh, 2015).

According to the Census of India (2011), Himachal Pradesh with a population of 68,64,602 persons (50.73 per cent males and 49.27 per cent females) constitutes 0.57 per cent of India's total population; 89.96 per cent of the population of the state lives in rural areas. The sex ratio is 972 females per 1,000 males.

Himachal Pradesh is one of the most literate states in the country. According to the 2011 Census, the literacy rate in the state was 82.80 per cent (89.53 per cent for males and 75.93 per cent for females) which was higher than the national average of 69.62 per cent. Himachal Pradesh is a beautiful land inhabited by people of various castes, creed, and religious

DOI: 10.4324/9781003374862-6

groups. The state's cultural heritage is very diverse, colourful, and rich. Hinduism (95.17 per cent) is the main religion in Himachal Pradesh.

About 90 per cent of the people living in the villages earn their livelihood directly or indirectly from agriculture and horticulture. The state's economy is undergoing big changes. It has shed off some elements of backwardness and acquired some characteristics of developed economies.

The momentum of growth and development picked up after the state attained statehood in 1971. An *India Today* report (2019), 'State of the States', ranked Himachal Pradesh as the best performing big state in education and healthcare. Himachal was also the first state to achieve universalization of primary education and 100 per cent literacy faster than Kerala. Himachal Pradesh has been ranked the second-best state after Kerala for achieving the targets under the Sustainable Development Goals (SDGs) Index of NITI Aayog for 2019–20. 'The state has performed well in providing clean water and sanitation, power, industry and other social services sector such as health, education, nutrition and gender equality' (*The Statesman*, 2019).

Women in Himachal Pradesh

Due to its prevailing topographical and geographical conditions, women are involved in physical activities outside their homes like working in the fields and orchards and rearing animals and are also engaged in small cottage industries. A large number of women are also holding jobs in the public and private sectors. In Himachal Pradesh, women enjoy a greater degree of freedom than those elsewhere in the country. They are very hardworking and the backbone of the rural economy. One of the distinctive features of the state is a high level of female labour-force participation. As per the 2011 Census, the workforce participation rate for females in the state was the highest (44.82 per cent) in the country.

The Government of Himachal Pradesh is giving priority to the empowerment of women. The state has been honoured with the prestigious 'Diamond State Award' for the work that it has done for the upliftment of women. It has launched various schemes and programmes for the welfare and upliftment of women in the state. Special incentives are given for promoting the girl child ratio and female education in the state. Apart from this, the State Women's Commission has been set up for redressal of women's grievances and to make them aware of their legal rights. The commission is providing counselling services and legal aid to women. The commission also looks into complaints of violence and atrocities against women.

Thus, there has been a significant participation of women in various fields like education, occupation, and employment during the last few decades in Himachal Pradesh. They have held important positions in various capacities in the state but they are still marginal in politics. They are not getting adequate representation in Parliament, the state legislature, and other decision-making bodies. A strong women's political activism is still not visible among Himachali women. State politics is dominated by men. Like elsewhere in India, gender bias has always been there in state politics.

Women in the freedom movement

Although not many in number, women remained an integral part of the freedom movement in the state. Evidence shows that there were some prominent women activists who played an active role in the national freedom movement and various Praja Mandal movements in the state. The main objective behind the formation of praja mandals in the *reyasats* was fighting against the tyranny and exploitation by local rulers and establishing responsible governments in these *reyasats*. Some notable women activists who took part in these movements are Durga Bai Arya; Lalita Kumari, popularly known as Rani Kheragarhi; Raj Kumari Amrit Kaur; Naura Richard; Sarla Sharma; Susheela; Ram Rakhi; Meera Ben; Dev Vati; Sunhari Devi; Almo Devi; and Sakno Devi (Government of Himachal Pradesh, 1992, pp. 68–165; Government of Himachal Pradesh, 1993, pp. 50–53).

However, it needs to be pointed out that the women who took part in these movements were either from royal families or were wives or daughters of some revolutionaries. General womenfolk remained indifferent towards the freedom struggle in Himachal Pradesh.

Women in politics in the post-independence era

With independence and the framing of the Constitution of India, women were guaranteed political equality with men. In consonance with the right to universal adult franchise and all other political rights conferred by the Constitution, women's participation in political activities increased and improved. However, this impact is more visible in voting than in other political activities. In Himachal Pradesh, though the number of women voters has been nearly equal to men voters and at times it has been even higher, their representation in the state legislature, Parliament, and decision-making bodies has been very disappointing.

In Himachal Pradesh, there is a unicameral legislature consisting of 68 members. Out of these 68 legislative assembly constituencies, 16 are reserved for Scheduled Castes and 3 for Scheduled Tribes. The state is represented by seven members in the Indian Parliament (three members in the Rajya Sabha and four members in the Lok Sabha).

Women as voters

In a country like India, most of the citizens participate in governmental affairs only through voting. Voting is the most common mode of political participation among women too (Jharta, 1996). In Himachal Pradesh, elections to the state legislative assembly were first held in 1952 when Himachal Pradesh became a Part 'C' state of the Indian Union. After the dissolution of the assembly on October 31, 1956, the next elections for the territorial council (which replaced the assembly) were held in 1957 and 1962. After the revival of the assembly on July 1, 1963, elections have been held at regular intervals in 1967, 1972, 1977, 1982, 1985, 1990, 1993, 1998, 2003, 2007, 2012, and 2017. Till today, 13 elections have been held for the Himachal Pradesh legislative assembly. Table 5.1 shows the participation of women in voting during the different assembly elections in the state.

Table 5.1 shows that there was not much difference in the number of male and female voters in different assembly elections in the state. In 1982 and 1985, women voters were more than male voters. The data also shows that women's voting percentage has substantially increased in the last few elections. In the last five assembly elections in 1998, 2003, 2007, 2012, and 2015, trends show that more women exercised their franchise than men. This indicates that with the spread of education among the women, they have realized the value of their votes. They are conscious of their voting rights. The increase in women's voting percentage shows that their interest in politics is increasing and this increasing participation of women in voting may be considered a sign of the strengthening of political democracy in the hill state.

Further, the increase in women's voting percentage in elections, especially after the implementation of 73rd and 74th Constitutional Amendment Acts in the state (1995), may also be attributed to the fact that women representatives of Panchayati Raj Institutions (PRIs) and municipalities and other women political activists are mobilizing women voters to take on an active role in voting in the elections.

Women's representation in the state assembly

There is no doubt that as voters women are playing a very significant and decisive role in the formation of the government in the state, but their representation in the state assembly has been very disappointing. Women's representation in the state assembly/territorial council remained appallingly low before 1972. Women who were members of the state assembly and territorial council before 1972 include Umavati, Satyavati Dang, Devindra Kumari, Subhadra Amin Chand, and Sarla Sharma. Umavati was elected to the assembly after the integration of the Part 'C' state of Bilaspur with Himachal Pradesh in 1954. Satyavati Dang was nominated to the territorial

Table 5.1 Women voters in different legislative assembly elections (1972–2017)

Year	Voters (in lakh)			Voting Percentages			Difference in Male and Female Voting Percentages
	Total	Men	Women	Total	Men	Women	
1972	18.05	–	–	49.95	–	–	–
1977	19.97	10.27	9.70	58.57	62.16	54.76	–7.40
1982*	22.12	11.02	11.10	71.06	73.29	68.85	–4.44
1985*	23.52	11.73	11.84	70.36	71.91	68.83	–3.08
1990	30.58	15.47	15.11	67.73	69.48	65.97	–3.51
1993	32.67	16.43	16.24	71.72	72.21	71.21	–1.00
1998**	36.28	18.27	18.01	71.23	70.24	72.23	+ 1.99
2003**	41.01	20.81	20.20	74.51	73.14	75.92	+ 2.78
2007**	46.04	23.36	22.68	71.61	69.67	74.55	+ 4.88
2012**	46.08	23.73	22.35	72.69	69.39	76.20	+ 6.81
2017**	50.26	25.69	24.57	74.17	70.58	77.92	+ 7.34

Note: Data before 1972 is not available. The voting percentages for men and women do not include postal votes.
*More women voters than men.
**More percentage of women voters as compared to men.
Source: Reports on General Elections to Himachal Pradesh state legislative assembly from 1972 to 2017 (Chief Electoral Officer and Financial Commissioner, Government of Himachal Pradesh, Shimla).

council (1957–62), Devindra Kumari was elected to the territorial council/ legislative assembly (1962–67), and Subhadra Amin Chand was a nominated member of the territorial council/legislative assembly (1962–67). Sarla Sharma became a member of the state assembly after the reorganization of the state of Punjab in 1966. There was no woman member in the state legislature from 1967 to 1971 (*Himachal Pradesh Vidhan Sabha Ki Karyawahi*, 1952–56 and 1963–66; and *Who's Who*, Himachal Pradesh Legislative assembly, 1952–71).

Table 5.2 shows the representation of women in the Himachal Pradesh assembly from 1972 to 2017.

Table 5.2 shows that the representation of women in the state assembly has been very small as compared to men. Their number has never exceeded seven (10.29 per cent) and that was in 1998. In 1972, soon after Himachal Pradesh attained statehood, five (7.35 per cent) women entered the legislative assembly. In 1977, there was only one woman representative in the state assembly. After that, except in 1998 their representation in the state assembly revolved around three (4.41 per cent) to five (7.35 per cent). In 1972, four women from the Indian National Congress – Sarla Sharma, Chandresh Kumari, Lata Thakur, and Padma – contested the assembly elections and interestingly, all of them won. After the death of Congress MLA Lal Chand Stokes, his wife Vidya Stokes was elected to the Vidhan Sabha in a by-election in 1974.

In 1977, nine women contested the elections but only one from the Janata Party (Shyama Sharma) got elected. There were three women each in 1982 (Vidya Stokes and Chandresh Kumari from INC and Shyama Sharma from JP) and 1985 (Vidya Stokes, Viplove Thakur, and Asha Kumari from INC) elected to the state assembly. In the 1990 state assembly elections, four women (Shyama Sharma of JP, Vidya Stokes of INC, and Leela Sharma and Sushma Sharma of BJP) were elected to the state assembly whereas in the next elections in 1993, their number reduced to three (Viplove Thakur, Asha Kumari, and Krishna Mohini). In a by-election in 1994, one more woman, Anita Verma, was elected on a Congress ticket from the Hamirpur assembly constituency.

Women's performance was the best ever in the 1998 assembly elections, when seven women were elected, four on Congress tickets (Vidya Stokes, Viplove Thakur, Asha Kumari, and Krishna Mohini) and three on BJP tickets (Urmil Thakur, Sarveen Chaudhary, and Nirmla Devi) but one of the members, Krishna Mohini, was unseated by a Supreme Court judgement in 1999. In the 2003 assembly elections, again four women from the Congress Party were successful (Vidya Stokes, Asha Kumari, Anita Verma, and Chandresh Kumari). In 2007, five women (Vidya Stokes from the Congress Party and Sarveen Chaudhary, Urmil Thakur, Renu Chaddha, and Vinod Kumari Chandel from the BJP) were elected to the state assembly. In 2012, only three women (Asha Kumari and Vidya Stokes from INC and Sarveen

Table 5.2 Representation of women in the HP assembly (1972–2007)

Year	Total Seats	Total Contestants	Women Contestants (%age to the Total Contestants)	Seats won by Women (% age to the Total Seats)	Party-wise Distribution of Winning Women Contestants				Winning Rate of Women Contestants (% age)
					INC	JP	BJP	JD	
1972	68	–	5	5 (7.35)*	5	–	–	–	–
1977	68	330	9 (2.72)	1 (1.47)	–	1	–	–	11.11
1982	68	441	9 (2.04)	3 (4.41)	2	1	–	–	33.33
1985	68	294	8(2.72)	3(4.41)	3	–	–	–	37.50
1990	68	454	17 (3.74)	4(5.88)	1	–	2	1	23.53
1993	68	416	16 (3.85)	4(5.88)*	4	–	2	–	25.00
1998	68	369	25 (6.78)	7(10.29)	4	–	3	–	28.00
2003	68	408	31 (7.60)	4(5.88)	4	–	–	–	12.90
2007	68	336	25 (7.44)	5(7.35)	1	–	4	–	20.00
2012	68	459	34 (7.41)	3 (4.41)	2	–	1	–	08.82
2017	68	337	19 (5.64)	5 (7.35)*	1	–	4	–	26.31

* One woman member was elected in a by-election.
Source: *Reports on General Elections to Himachal Pradesh state legislative assembly from 1972 to 2017* (Chief Electoral Officer and Financial Commissioner, Government of HP, Shimla).

Chaudhary from the BJP) were elected to the state assembly whereas in 2017, four women (Asha Kumari from INC and Reeta Devi, Sarveen Chaudhary, and Kamlesh Kumari from the BJP) got elected. Reena Kashyap of the BJP was elected to the Vidhan Sabha in a by-election in 2019. Thus, there are five women in the present state assembly.

These figures present a very disappointing picture of women's representation in the Himachal Pradesh assembly. In 1972–2017, women were elected only on 44 seats. Some women representatives have been elected more than once. Vidya Stokes was elected eight times; Asha Kumari six; Sarveen Chaudhary four times; Viplove Thakur, Shyama Sharma, and Chandresh Kumari three times each; Anita Verma, Krishna Mohini, and Urmil Thakur two times each; and Nirmla Devi, Leela Sharma, Sarla Sharma, Sushma Sharma, Padma, Lata Thakur, Renu Chaddha, Vinod Kumari Chandel, Reeta Devi, Kamlesh Kumari, and Reena Kashyap once. The reason why most of the women members of the assembly in Himachal get re-elected is because they are professional and successful politicians and are popular in their constituencies. They also tend to have an elite profile and a political family background.

There is a perception that parties tend to give more tickets to women for reserved seats than for general seats. However, this is not the case in Himachal Pradesh where 40 of its 44 women MLAs so far have won from general seats. In 1972, Lata Thakur of the Congress Party won from a Scheduled Tribe seat in Lahaul–Spiti and in 2017, for the first time two Scheduled Caste women, Reeta Devi in Indora and Kamlesh Kumari in Bhoranj (both from the BJP), were elected on seats reserved for Scheduled Caste candidates. In 2019, Reena Kashyap of the BJP was also elected from a Scheduled Caste constituency (*Reports on General Elections to Himachal Pradesh legislative assembly*, 1972–2017).

One of the reasons for the low representation of women in the state assembly is that there has always been a very small number of women contestants (between 2.04 and 7.60 per cent), though their winning rate has remained quite satisfactory. Table 5.2 shows that till 1985, there were between five and nine women contestants. In 1990, their number increased to 17 (3.74 per cent) which further increased to 25 (6.78 per cent) and then 31 (7.60 per cent) in the 1998 and 2003 elections, respectively. However, the number of women contestants decreased to 25 (7.44 per cent) in the 2007 assembly elections. In 2012, it increased to 34 (7.41 per cent) but decreased to 19 (5.64 per cent) in the next elections in 2017 despite loud demands made by the women's frontal organizations in the two main political parties in the state – BJP and Congress – for fielding women candidates on at least 33 per cent of the total seats. It is a rather disappointing and discouraging number of women contestants in comparison to their voting strength. Political parties seem very reluctant to field women candidates. Though some women have contested elections as independents but they have never won a seat. Thus, contesting elections still remains a male prerogative.

Women in party hierarchies

It is seen that women also constitute a very small proportion of the total membership of various political parties in Himachal Pradesh. Table 5.3 shows the share of women in the hierarchies of the two main political parties, Congress and BJP, in Himachal Pradesh.

The Congress seems a little more liberal in giving party positions to women as compared to the BJP. It has even appointed women to the highest position in the party. Sarla Sharma and Vidya Stokes were presidents of the Himachal Pradesh Congress Committee. It is also observed that women's position in other political parties' hierarchies in the state is almost negligible. This indicates that all the political parties in the state are biased against women when it comes to nominating them to different positions in the party hierarchies. On the issue of giving tickets to women to contest elections, it may be stated with some justification that this hesitation arises from the perception that women have less chances of winning. Thus, a small percentage of women is put up by different political parties to occupy important positions in the party hierarchies or as candidates in the elections.

Women in the council of ministers

Like the assembly, women's representation in the council of ministers has also remained very low in the state. There was no woman in the council of ministers from 1952 to 1971 and there were very few women ministers from 1972 to 2017. Sarla Sharma and Shyama Sharma were ministers of state in 1972 and 1977, respectively. Chandresh Kumari was made deputy minister in 1977 and minister of state in 1984. In 1985, Vidya Stokes was appointed as the first woman Speaker of the state assembly and she was also the leader of opposition from 1990 to 1992 and 2007 to 2012. Leela Sharma was made parliamentary secretary in 1990. In 1995, after the expansion of the council of ministers, Asha Kumari and Viplove Thakur were inducted as ministers of state and Anita Verma was made parliamentary secretary. In 1998, two women, Urmil Thakur and Sarveen Chaudhary, were made parliamentary secretaries. In 2003, in the Virbhadra government three women were appointed as cabinet ministers – Vidya Stokes, Asha Kumari, and Chandresh Kumari – for the first time. But Asha Kumari had to resign due to a judicial case in the High Court and Chandresh Kumari had to lose the ministry due to the downsizing of the council of ministers to 15 per cent of the total number of members in the state assembly according to the 91st Constitutional Amendment Act of 2003.

124

WOMEN IN POLITICS IN HIMACHAL PRADESH

Table 5.3 Women in party hierarchies

Party	General House/State Executive Committee			Executive Body/Office Bearers			Members AICC/Members National Executive Committee		
	Male	Female	Total	Male	Female	Total	Male	Female	Total
Congress	160 (82.05)	35 (17.95)	195 (100.00)	83 (81.37)	19 (18.63)	102 (100.00)	14 (73.68)	5 (26.32)	19 (100.00)
BJP	181 (89.60)	21 (10.40)	202 (100.00)	29 (82.86)	6 (17.14)	35 (100.00)	–	–	–

Source: Offices of the Congress (I) and the BJP (2021).

In 2005, Anita Verma was made parliamentary secretary but was dropped after four months. In this way, the representation of women was again reduced to one in the11-member council of ministers. In 2007, 2012, and 2017 also only one woman each – Sarveen Chaudhary in 2007 and 2017 and Vidya Stokes in 2012 – was included in the council of ministers as cabinet ministers (*Who's Who*, Himachal Pradesh legislative assembly, 1952–2017).

Women's representation in Parliament

Like the state assembly, women's representation in Parliament has also remained appallingly low from Himachal Pradesh. From 1952 till date, only three women have been elected to the Lok Sabha from the state. In the first general elections to the Lok Sabha in 1952, Raj Kumari Amrit Kaur was elected from the Mandi-Mahasu parliamentary constituency on a Congress ticket. She was also included in the central council of ministers as health minister with a cabinet rank. She was the only woman member of the Lok Sabha till then from the state who became a minister at the Centre. After that till 1980, five elections were held to the Lok Sabha, but no woman could reach the Lower House of Parliament from the state. Chandresh Kumari was elected from Kangra parliamentary constituency in 1984 and Pratibha Singh, wife of the then Chief Minister Virbhadra Singh, was elected to the Lok Sabha from the Mandi parliamentary constituency in 2004. All three women elected to the Lok Sabha were from the Congress Party (*Who's Who*, first to the fourteenth Lok Sabhas).

Women's representation in the Rajya Sabha from Himachal Pradesh is comparatively better than in the Lok Sabha. Leela Devi Mahajan (1956–62) of Mandi from the Congress Party was the first woman to represent the state in the Rajya Sabha. After that, Satyawati Dang (1968–74), a prominent politician of the state; Mohinder Kaur (1978–84); Usha Malhotra (1980–86); Chandresh Kumari (1996–2002); Viplove Thakur (2006–12 and 2014–20); Vimla Kashyap (2010–16); and Indu Goswami (2020–26) were members of the Rajya Sabha from Himachal Pradesh. Of these, except Mohinder Kaur (Janata Party), Vimla Kashyap (BJP), and Indu Goswami (BJP), the rest were from the Congress Party (*Who's Who*, Rajya Sabha, 1968 onwards).

Sarla Sharma, Chandresh Kumari, Vidya Stokes, and Asha Kumari are important women leaders in Himachal Pradesh politics. They all belong to the Congress Party. Sarla Sharma was a freedom fighter and a Gandhian. She actively participated in the national freedom struggle and was jailed during the Quit India movement. She was a member of the Punjab assembly from Hamirpur in 1957 and 1962 and became a member of the Himachal Pradesh assembly in 1972. She was also a minister of state and president of the Himachal Pradesh Congress Committee (*The News Himachal*, 2013).

Chandresh Kumari belongs to the Kangra and Jodhpur royal families. She joined politics by contesting her first assembly elections in 1972. After that she remained quite active in national and state politics and held many positions. She was a member of the Himachal Pradesh assembly thrice (1972, 1985, and 2003) and was a member of the state council of ministers as deputy minister (1977), minister of state (1984), and cabinet minister (2003). She is the only woman in Himachal Pradesh who got an opportunity to be a member of both the Houses of Parliament as well as the state assembly. She was elected to the Lok Sabha in 1984 from Kangra parliamentary constituency and was nominated to the Rajya Sabha in 1996 *(Royal Kangra*, 2021).

Vidya Stokes, the daughter-in-law of American missionary Satyanand Stokes, became active in state politics in 1974 after the death of her husband, Lal Chand Stokes. She was elected to the Himachal Pradesh assembly eight times in 1974, 1982, 1985, 1990, 1998, 2003, 2007, and 2012. She was the irrigation and public health minister (2012–17) and minister for power (2003–7). She was also the president of the Himachal Pradesh Congress Committee, leader of opposition in the assembly, and Speaker of the state assembly. She remained active in state politics for more than four decades (*The Hindustan Times*, 2014).

Asha Kumari also belongs to an erstwhile royal family. She was a member of the Himachal Pradesh assembly six times from Banikhet (1985, 1993, 1998, and 2003) and Dalhousie (2012 and 2017). She was minister of state for primary education (October 1995–March 1998) and education minister with a cabinet rank (March 2003–February 2005) (*eVidhan-Himachal Pradesh*, 2021).

Women in PRIs and municipalities

The 73rd and 74th Constitutional Amendment Acts (1993) are a revolutionary landmark in the history of women's participation in politics in India. These acts provided 33 per cent reservation of seats for women in PRIs and municipalities. These acts laid a strong foundation for women's participation in decision-making at the grassroots level. The Himachal Pradesh government passed the Panchayati Raj and Municipalities Act in 1994 and the first elections to PRIs and municipalities according to the new act were held in December 1995. Till date, six elections have been held to PRIs and urban local bodies in the state in 1995, 2000, 2005, 2010, 2015, and 2021.

To ensure equal participation and representation of women in PRIs and municipalities, the Himachal Pradesh state assembly passed the Himachal Pradesh Panchayati Raj (Amendment) Bill (2008), raising the reservation for women in PRIs from 33 to 50 per cent. It also passed the Himachal Pradesh Municipal Corporation (Amendment) Bill (2008) and the Himachal Pradesh Municipal (Amendment) Bill (2008) to provide 50 per cent reservation to women in place of the 33 per cent in municipal corporations, other municipalities, and urban local bodies.

Before 1995, women's representation in PRIs and municipalities was up to two women in all the bodies. After 1995, it increased to a minimum of 33 per cent and has been 50 per cent since the 2010 elections to PRIs and urban local bodies. The representation of women in these bodies has shown an increasing trend. In the last five elections to PRIs and urban local bodies in the state, women have been elected even from unreserved seats and their representation has been more than the fixed quota allotted to them. They are gradually learning to assert themselves, using their power for the good of the community and are succeeding.

Women in protests and agitational politics

If we go beyond formal politics, we find that Himachali women have always remained the mainstay of various movements and protests. They have always raised their voice for their rights and other issues which affect their home and hearth like dowry, rape, domestic violence, price rise, alcoholism, and deforestation. For example, Rattan Manjari, a tribal woman from Kinnaur district, is working to secure property rights for tribal women. Despite having the Hindu Succession Act (1956) that grants daughters an equal share in ancestral property, to this day women cannot stake a claim to family property in the districts of Kinnaur, Lahaul–Spiti, and some tribal belts of Chamba district in the state. This is due to the legacy of about a century-old customary law called 'Wajib Ul Urj' (1926) which allows only men to inherit ancestral property if not bequeathed. It even side-lines widows. This patriarchal customary law stems from the belief that giving inheritance rights to women will give an opportunity to outsiders to become owners of agricultural land (which is in scarcity in tribal areas) if the women marry outside the community. But owing to this discriminatory law, women, especially widows and divorced and unmarried women, are treated badly by their male family members. They are treated as a burden and are sometimes abandoned by their families.

Rattan Manjari founded the Mahila Kalyan Parishad (MKP) in 1989, a rights group based in Kinnaur district that campaigns for educating women about their right to ancestral property. With the help of hundreds of activists in over 300 women's groups in the district, Manjari has been organizing panchayat meetings and signature campaigns to get the law overturned. In June 2015, a Himachal High Court ruling gave land inheritance rights to tribal women. But in February 2016, this judgement was challenged in the Supreme Court which stayed the High Court's order and the case is still pending. In 2017, Manjari and MKP filed a PIL under Article 32 in the Supreme Court, demanding property rights for tribal women in Himachal Pradesh but it was withdrawn after one hearing in 2018. A year later, in

April 2019, under Article 226, MKP again filed a petition in the High Court. Manjari is determined to see the PIL through and is also willing to approach the Supreme Court if the High Court pronounces an unfavourable verdict. She is hopeful that the day is not far when tribal womenfolk will get their due right to property and get justice like other women in the state (*Deccan Herald*, 2010; *The Wire*, 2019).

Kinkri Devi, an uneducated poor woman from a small village in Sirmaur district, waged a war on illegal mining and quarrying in her district. In 1985, she started a fight for environmental protection through a voluntary organization, People's Action for People in Need, and continued it till her last breath. Through hunger strikes and memoranda of protests, she not only made people aware of environmental protection but also fought against the mining mafia. In December 1991, the Himachal Pradesh High Court gave a ruling in favour of a PIL filed in 1987 and banned mining and quarrying (*The Better India*, 2016).

The visible women's faces in the politics of Himachal Pradesh either belong to royal families or they are wives, widows, daughters, or daughters-in-law of prominent politicians. In other words, we may say that the 'Bibi-Beti-Bahu' syndrome is in operation and the general womenfolk are kept away from power politics in the state.

Reasons for low participation of women in politics

There are many factors responsible for the low participation of women in state politics. Various socio-cultural, economic, and political factors obstruct women from taking part in politics. As we know, political roles are shaped by the socio-cultural milieu in which the people live. Himachali women have to face many obstacles because of traditions, prejudices, and social conditions of the hill society. Social traditions look at women as a part of the household and not as a part of public life. The male-dominated society is generally reluctant to accept women as decision-makers. Men like to retain their monopoly over power and do not want to share power with women. Womenfolk themselves are also reluctant to engage in political activities due to lack of political ambition, lack of economic resources, fear of dislocation of domestic life, lack of awareness and experience, lack of political exposure, criminalization of politics, lack of safety and security, and the rough and tumble of political life.

Women's engagement in household chores, child care, family responsibilities, and agricultural activities burden them and hamper their active participation in political activities. Further, too many restrictions on their mobility and lack of familial and community support also prevent them from participating in political activities.

Political parties are also reluctant to field women candidates in the elections because of their perceptions that women have less prospects of winning. Political parties do not want to give tickets to women despite the loud promises that they make with regard to allotting party tickets to women from time to time. Political parties use the winnability criteria while allotting tickets to women. It is interesting to note that while all the political parties in principle support the Constitutional Amendments for 33 per cent reservation for women in the Parliament and state legislatures, no party has so far come forward to give this percentage of seats to women for contesting elections to the Lok Sabha and state assemblies. Women are welcomed by them as voters but not as representatives.

Conclusion

Education, political awareness, competencies, willingness, self-confidence, motivation, encouragement, and support from family, society, and political parties will help in bringing women to the mainstream of the political arena. Women themselves have to become more conscious and assertive about their political rights and duties. They have to come out of their home-bound commitments and find time to take part in political activities. Women who have calibre and leadership qualities should join politics. Spreading education among women can play a very important role in bringing about desirable behavioural changes among women and make them well equipped in terms of knowledge, awareness, skills, self-confidence, and capacity to deal with different problems.

Women's participation in politics is influenced by their families to a large extent. Hence, family support and cooperation are necessary for enhancing women's participation in politics.

Further, political parties must encourage women to take part in political activities by providing them important offices in party hierarchies, allotting party tickets to them to contest elections, and if elected they must be encouraged by giving them important portfolios in the government and various other decision-making bodies. There is a need for political parties to promote the candidature of more women. The reservation of seats for women in Parliament and state legislatures as is the case in PRIs and municipalities should be adopted and implemented as a transitory measure. However, mere reservations will not solve the problem unless and until women are given commensurate powers to function effectively.

It is also essential to discard criminalization of politics by taking stern action against the culprits. In our male-dominated patriarchal society, sometimes it has been seen that women political activists and even elected women representatives become victims of sexual abuse, exploitation, violence, and harassment. Women should feel secure and safe in all spheres including politics. Unless the fear of dirty politics is removed from the minds of the women, they will always be reluctant to be active in politics.

Women still have to climb many steps to be able to contribute equally in the political sphere with men. Now it is being globally and nationally recognized that women's equal participation in politics as voters, candidates, representatives, and decision-makers is essential not only for the success of a democratic political system but it is also a fundamental pre-requisite for gender equality, gender justice, and the reconstruction of society.

Bibliography

Deccan Herald (2010).'Rattan Manjari: A Crusader for Women's Property Rights', March 7. Available at: https://www.deccanherald.com/content/56745/rattan -manjari-crusader-womens-property.html, accessed on August 7, 2021.

eVidhan- Himachal Pradesh (2021). 'Hon'ble Member Legislative Assembly-Asha Kumari', Available at: https://hpvidhansabha.nic.in/Member/Details/4, accessed on August 7, 2021.

Government of Himachal Pradesh (1992). *Himachal Pradesh Mein Swatantrata Sangram Ka Sankshipt Itihas*. Shimla: Language and Culture Department.

——— (1993). *Swadhinta Ki Aur*. Shimla: Language and Culture Department.

——— (2015). *Brief Facts: Himachal Pradesh*. Shimla: Department of Economics and Statistics.

Himachal Pradesh Vidhan Sabha Ki Karyawahi (1952–1956 and 1963–1966). Shimla: HP Vidhan Sabha Secretariat.

India Today (2019). 'State of the States 2019', 22 November. Available at: https:// www.indiatoday.in/india/story/state-of-states-2019-full-winners-list-1621684 -2019-11-22, accessed on August 6, 2021.

Jharta, Bhawana (1996). *Women and Politics in India*. New Delhi: Deep and Deep Publications.

Reports on General Elections to Himachal Pradesh Legislative Assembly (1972–2017). Shimla: Chief Electoral Officer and Financial Commissioner, Himachal Pradesh.

Royal Kangra (2014). 'The Fight for Freedom', Available at: http://www.royalkangra .com/fightforfreedom.html, accessed on August 5, 2021.

The Better India (2016). 'How Kinkri Devi Fought against Quarrying in Himachal Pradesh', 25 January. Available at: https://www.thebetterindia.com/40364/kinkri -devi-himachal-pradesh/#:~:text=She%20initiated%20her%20fight%20by ,ground%20of%20irresponsible%20limestone%20quarrying, accessed on August 1, 2021.

The Hindustan Times (2014), 'I Work Harder than Many Half My Age: Vidya Stokes at 86', July 17. Available at: https://www.hindustantimes.com/chandigarh /i-work-harder-than-many-half-my-age-vidya-stokes-at-86/story-GUYTgNYqi8I WEUUHEOwb8H.html, accessed on August 2, 2021.

The News Himachal (2013). 'Veteran Congress Leader and Freedom Fighter Sarla Sharma Passes Away', May 3. Available at: https://thenewshimachal.com/2013 /05/veteran-congress-leader-and-freedom-fighter-sarla-sharma-passes-away/, accessed on August 2, 2021.

The Statesman (2019). *Himachal Ranks 2nd in Niti Ayog's SDG Index*, 31 December. Available at: https://www.thestatesman.com/cities/shimla/himachal-ranks-2nd -niti-ayogs-sdg-index-1502839760.html, accessed on August 2, 2021.

The Wire (2019).'Why Rattan Manjari Fights for Tribal Women's Land Rights in Himachal Pradesh', 11 December. Available at: https://thewire.in/rights/why-rattan-manjari-fights-for-tribal-womens-land-rights-in-himachal-pradesh, accessed on August 2, 2021.

Lok Sabha members since 1952. available on https://loksabha.nic.in/members/lokprelist.aspx?lsno=1 accessed on March 1, 2022

Government of *Himachal Pradesh*. *Himachal Pradesh Legislative assembly, Who's Who* (1952–71). Shimla: HP Legislative Assembly Secretariat.

Rajya Sabha members Biographical sketches 1952–2019. Available at https://cms.rajyasabha.nic.in/UploadedFiles/ElectronicPublications/Member_Biographical_Book.pdf accessed on March 2, 2022

6

WOMEN AND STATE POLITICS IN HARYANA

Reicha Tanwar

Introduction

Politics, the sphere of 'public life' that deals with establishing, interpreting, and enforcing the rules of personal and community relations, has not been a field that has welcomed women. Yet, it is important that women find their voice in the public sphere, because it is only then that they will be able to take control of their lives and realize their potential. Various studies have established that improved levels of education and household incomes do not necessarily translate into women's increased participation in decision-making, both private and public. At times, it has also been noticed that relatively wealthy, educated women may be restricted more within their households as compared to poor, illiterate women who by necessity are forced to play a more independent role.

Although there are various legal provisions for women in India, the laws have their own limitations and legal obligations alone cannot lead to any drastic changes in the society's mindset.

From the local to the global level, women's political participation and leadership are restricted. Women are under-represented as voters as well as elected representatives. According to UN Women, only 24 per cent of all national parliamentarians were women in November 2018, a slow increase from 11.3 per cent in 1995. As of January 2019, 11 women were serving as heads of state and 10 were serving as heads of government. Evelin Hust (2004) lists four successive stages that are linked to the inclusion of women in political decision-making bodies which need to be analysed. The first stage is who are the women who have moved into positions of power? Second, whether women who have moved into political positions are actually exercising their power. Third, are they autonomous and do they participate in decision-making? Fourth, whether women who are serving in political institutions have gained status and visibility at home and in public life and whether they have gained a new consciousness and confidence? And

DOI: 10.4324/9781003374862-7

133

lastly, whether reservation for women in political bodies has been able to change the political narrative.

Women in Haryana's politics

Participation of women in governance is an integral part of the democratic process and in strengthening the quality of civic life. Very often social structures and social norms are barriers and stem from social conditioning which inhibit women from participating in public life. So far very few women in Haryana have been successful in reaching the highest level of political life. But after the 73rd and 74th Amendments to the Constitution, women in large numbers have been able to occupy positions in local bodies of governance, be it panchayats or municipal councils. But despite an increase in their numbers how many women are actually decision-makers or are actively contributing to these bodies is an area of concern.

Institutional factors related to society's organizations, their norms and values are the greatest hindrance to women moving up the political ladder. Women are also hampered by their family and care-taking tasks as well as society and family's attitudes.

Representation of women in India's politics has always been low. If we look at the all-India figures for the general elections in 1967, there were only 33 women candidates who could make a successful entry into the Lok Sabha. The percentage of elected women candidates among all the candidates was a mere 5.9 per cent. In the 2014 general elections, the number of women members in the Lok Sabha increased to 68 and their percentage almost doubled but it was still quite low as compared to male representation in the Lok Sabha. In the 2019 Lok Sabha elections, 81 women were elected out of the 542 seats (14.39 per cent), which is the highest number ever.

A gender analysis of women's political participation in Haryana shows the absence of women at the decision-making level in political life. At the time of its creation, Haryana had nine parliamentary constituencies, while now there are ten constituencies. Table 6.1 shows that in the 1967 Lok

Table 6.1 Number of elected members in the Lok Sabha from Haryana

Year	Total Seats	Male	Female
*1967	9	9	0
**2014	10	10	0
** 2019	10	9	1

Source: *www.election.in/parliamentary-Constituencies/1967-election-result.html, accessed on November 30, 2020.
**www.elections.in/haryana/assemble-constituecies/2014-election-result.html, accessed on November 30, 2020.

Sabha elections all the nine seats were held by men and in the recent 2014 elections also no woman from Haryana could win any parliamentary seat. Only four women have entered the Lok Sabha from Haryana – Chandrawati (sixth Lok Sabha), Kumari Selja (10th, 11th, 14th, and 15th Lok Sabhas), Kailasho Devi (12th and 13th Lok Sabhas), and Sunita Duggal (17th Lok Sabha). In the 2019 Lok Sabha elections, only Sunita Duggal managed to enter the Lok Sabha defeating state Congress chief Ashok Tanwar from the Sirsa (reserved) constituency.

Other women candidates like Kumari Selja (Ambala), Shruti Chaudhary (Bhiwani), and Raj Bala Saini (Sonepat) of the Loktantra Suraksha Party could not win the elections. Chandrawati, a former Janata Party leader, became the first ever woman MP from the state in 1977. Significantly, at no time has Haryana had more than one woman representative in the Lok Sabha.

A similar situation prevails with respect to women's representation in the Upper House (Table 6.2). Only four women have represented Haryana in the Rajya Sabha – Vidya Beniwal (1991–96), Sushma Swaraj (1990–96), Sumitra Mahajan (2002–8). Currently, the fourth woman representing Haryana in the Rajya Sabha is Kumari Selja who was elected as a member of the Rajya Sabha in April 2014.

Table 6.3 shows an equally gloomy picture of women's representation in the state legislative assembly. Of the total 81 seats in the assembly in 1967 there were only four women elected candidates. Now the number of seats has increased to 90, but women's representation has increased only marginally. Out of these 90 seats there are 77 men and only 13 women.

If we look at women contestants in various Haryana legislative assembly elections, in the 1967 elections there were only eight women contestants, out of which four won their seats. In the 2014 elections, the number of women contestants increased to 116 but the number of winning candidates did not increase in the same proportion.

In the 2019 Vidhan Sabha elections, out of a total of 105 women candidates in the fray, only nine succeeded in making it to the assembly as against 13 in 2014. The BJP fielded 12 women candidates, Congress 10, JJP 8, and INLD 15 in the 2014 elections. In 2014, the total number of women candidates was

Table 6.2 Number of Rajya Sabha members from Haryana

Year	Total Seats	Male	Female
1984	5	5	0
2016	5	4	1
2019	5	5	0

Source: www.newincet.com/haryana/list-of-rajya-Sabha-maps-of-haryana-html, accessed on November 30, 2020.

Table 6.3 Women's representation in the legislative assembly (1967–2019)

Year	Total Number of Seats	Number of Women Contestants	Number of Seats Won by Women	Percentage of Women MLAs
1967	81	8	4	4.9
1968	81	12	7	8.6
1972	81	12	4	4.9
1987	90	35	5	5.5
1991	90	41	6	6.7
1996	90	93	4	4.4
2000	90	49	4	4.4
2005	90	60	11	12.2
2009	90	69	9	10
2014	90	116	13	14.4
2019	90	105	9	10

Source: Election Commission of India.

116 of whom 13 were elected, which was the maximum since 1966. INLD had given tickets to 15 women candidates but none of them won. Out of nine women candidates who got elected, four were first-time MLAs.

As far as the voting percentage of women electors in the Haryana assembly elections held in 2019 is concerned, their participation was the lowest in the last 23 years. The overall turnout in 2019 was 68.31 per cent. A little over 69 per cent of the voters were males and 67.12 per cent were females. In the 2014 Vidhan Sabha elections, of the 76.13 per cent voter turnout, 76.59 per cent were males and 75.59 per cent were female electors. In 2009, 71.11 per cent women exercised their franchise. Even though it is difficult to define the reasons for this decline in numbers, what can be said is that masculine norms which preserve the right to decision-making are by and large vested in men. Women do not have an independent voice, whether as voters or as contestants.

Among the prominent women legislators, Shakuntala Bhagwaria was elected for the first time in 1968 and subsequently in1977, 1982, and 1991. Another senior member Parsanni Devi was elected to the Vidhan Sabha in 1967, 1972, 1982, and 2005; Sushma Swaraj, a prominent BJP leader, got elected from Ambala in 1977 and 1987. Probably the youngest women legislator to be made a cabinet minister at the age of 25 years, Swaraj played an active role in the national political arena right up to her demise in 2019.

With regard to the number of contestants in the Lok Sabha elections from Haryana it can be observed from Table 6.4 that in the 1971 elections no woman contested the Lok Sabha elections on Haryana's parliamentary seats. However, in the 2014 Lok Sabha elections, out of the 230 contestants there were 11 women candidates though none of them won. The number of women contestants in the 2019 Lok Sabha elections remained the same at 11.

Table 6.4 Contestants in Lok Sabha elections from Haryana (1971, 2014, and 2019)

Contestants	1971*	2014**	2019**
Total	63	230	223
Men	63	219	212
Women	0	11	11

Source: *http://eci.nic.in/eci_main/statisticalReport/LS_1971/Vol_I_LS71.pdf, accessed on November 30, 2020.
**http://ceoharyana.nic.in/docs/pdf/GLANCE.pdf, accessed on November 30, 2020.

Imbalance in the sex ratio among the electorate

The percentage of women and men voters shows an imbalance in successive elections to the Lok Sabha. Women constituted 46.96 per cent of the total electorate in 1971 and in 2016 this percentage went down to 46.25 per cent. The number of women electors in the 2019 Lok Sabha elections increased from 77,82,301 to 83,40,173.

However, women's participation in decision-making at the grassroots level has increased at all the levels but this does not necessarily prove women's increased political participation at the grassroots level. Following the 73rd and 74th Amendments to the Constitution women have entered panchayats and municipal councils as 33 per cent seats are reserved for them.

In 1994–95 when the first panchayat and municipal council elections were held in Haryana after the 73rd and 74th Amendments to the Constitution, there were just 33.46 per cent women sarpanches in Haryana and 20 years after the amendments, in the 2016 panchayat elections this figure had increased to 41.44 per cent.

Similarly, the percentage of women elected as *panchs* in gram panchayats increased from 33.10 per cent in 1994–95 to 42.18 per cent in 2016. The maximum increase in the number of sarpanches can be observed in Karnal district as in 1994–95 there were just 33.33 per cent women sarpanches in this district while this percentage increased to 45.78 per cent in the 2016 elections. The maximum increase in the number of *panchs* is noticed in Kurukshetra district which had 32.95 per cent women *panchs* in 1994–95 while 47.02 per cent women *panchs* were elected in the 2016 panchayat elections.

With regard to block samiti members there were 34.54 per cent women block samiti members in 1994–95 which increased to 41.97 per cent in 2016 and the percentage of women zila parishad members which was 33.33 in 1994–95 increased to 43.50 per cent in 2016. The highest percentage of block samiti women members was in Mahendergarh district (47.77 per cent) and the highest percentage of women zila parishad members was in Kaithal district (57.14 per cent) in the 2016 elections.

Similarly, in 1994–95, 33.46 per cent women were elected as sarpanches in Haryana which increased to 41.44 per cent in 2016. Women's increased participation in local governance is a healthy trend in Haryana. The Government of Haryana laid down Class 8 as the minimum educational level for women contestants to panchayats and urban local bodies in the 2016 elections. It is very heartening to note that in 2016 out of a total of 2,565 female candidates who were elected as sarpanches, 833 women were Class 8 pass, 1,145 women were Class 10 pass, 318 women were Class 12 pass, and 245 were graduates or above.

Role of *khap* panchayats in local politics in the state

It is pertinent to mention the role and influence of *khap* panchayats in local politics in Haryana. *Khap* panchayats are essentially community groups which comprise of elderly men from the Jat community. These all-male bodies seek to enforce age-old taboos such as prohibition of Sagothra marriages and have also been instigating honour killings in inter-caste or inter-faith marriages. Their role has been questionable and under the scanner of the judiciary. In 2011, the Supreme Court called *khap* panchayats 'Kangaroo courts' and declared them illegal. In 2018 again, the Supreme Court directed police officers to persuade the *khaps* to desist from making illegal decisions. The *khaps* nonetheless continue to remain active in the social and political life in the rural areas where their diktats have to be followed.

Lack of women's organizations

Haryana is not known to have many women's organizations and as such there is no women's movement in the state. All India Democratic Women's Association (AIDWA) is one organization which has a strong base in the state. It started working in Haryana in 1985 and now has over 48,000 members operating in 11 districts in the state. AIDWA works on social issues, particularly on violence against women and honour killings; it is also active in creating political awareness at the grassroots level. Its area of concern has been honour killings in Haryana which has been supported to quite a large extent by *khap* panchayats. It supported the filing of a public interest litigation in the Supreme Court by the women who could not contest panchayat elections because of the minimum educational qualifications laid down by a law enacted by the state. The Supreme Court, however, upheld the 2015 legislation. AIDWA's leader Jagmati Sangwan, was in the fray for the mayoral election in Rohtak as a CPI(M) candidate in 2018, the first woman candidate from the party in Haryana. She lost the elections and later resigned from CPI(M).

Conclusion

Although there has been a substantive increase in the number of women representatives in panchayats and local bodies, their active participation in politics has been limited to family connections rather than their own convictions and commitments. Consequently, they have been left at the periphery of political life. The most crucial obstacle in their journey in political participation is the nomination of their candidatures. Most of the women fill the seats because of pressure from male members or due to the pressure of political parties. Many are surrogates for husbands and fathers who cannot contest because of reservation limits. Some have been put in place by the wealthy and powerful for their malleability – puppets to serve their vested interests while appearing to be elected representatives.

Even today the political field is considered a male domain. Elections in India, as in all other modern democracies, have become very complicated, violent, dirty, and expensive inviting many legitimate and many not so legitimate ways of funding and managing them. Women cannot obviously fit into this matrix of elections. Participation costs are very high and violence has come to dominate elections in many areas. As a consequence, women lack the required skills and confidence to contest elections on their own might. Lack of knowledge and awareness about elections and the electoral process among women is also a major barrier to their political participation. Haryana being a rural agrarian state where patriarchal norms are more pronounced, decision-making powers and positions are considered a male domain. At all political levels, one observes that elected women play a subordinate role. In the final analysis, one can conclude that very few women have achieved visibility, confidence, and the ability to make a difference in their own lives as well as in the lives of other women in the state.

Bibliography

Arun, R. (1996). 'Role of Women in Panchayat Raj', *The Administrator*, April and June, 115–126.

Asthana, P. (1988). *Party System in India: Development or Decay*. New Delhi: Criterion Publications.

Bajpai, A. and M.S. Verma (1995 and 1997). *Panchayati Raj in India: A New Thrust*. Vols. 1 & 2. Delhi: Sahitya Prakashan.

Bhattacharya, M. (1997). 'Democracy and Reservation', *Seminar*, 457, 23–24.

Dreze, J. and A. Sen (1999). *India: Economic Development and Social Opportunity (1995)*. New Delhi: Oxford University Press.

Everett, J.M. (1979). *Women and Social Change in India*. New Delhi: Heritage.

Ghadially, R. (ed.) (1988). *Women in Indian Society: A Reader*. New Delhi/Newbury Park/London: Sage.

Hust, Evelin (2004). *Women's Political Representation and Empowerment in India: A Million Indiras Now?* New Delhi: Manohar Publisher and Distributors.

Indira, R. and P.K. Behra (eds) (1999). *Gender and Society in India*. Vol. 2. New Delhi: Manak.

Kaushik, S. (1993). *Women and Panchayati Raj*. New Delhi: Har-Anand.

——— (1995). *Panchayati Raj in Action: Challenges to Women's Role*. New Delhi: Friedrich-Ebert-Stiftung.

——— (1997). *Women Panches in Position: A Study of Panchayati Raj in Haryana*. New Delhi: Centre for Development Studies and Action.

——— (1999). Political Empowerment and Gender Justice', in M.C. Bhandare (ed.), *The World of Gender Justice* (pp. 183–191). New Delhi: Har-Anand.

Menon, N. (2001). 'Introduction', in N. Menon (ed.), *Gender and Politics in India*. New Delhi: Oxford University Press.

Panda, Snehlata (1990). *Determinants of Political Participation: Women and Public Activity*. New Delhi: Ajanta Publications.

Panda, Snehlata (1992). *Women and Social Change in India*. New Delhi: Ashish Publishing House.

Panda, Snehlata (1995). *Gender Environment and Participation in Politics*. New Delhi: M.D. Publications.

Rajput, P. (1993). 'Women Leadership at the Grassroot Level in Punjab', in S. Kaushik (ed.), *Women's Participation in Politics* (pp. 31–44). New Delhi: Vikas Publishing House.

Sharma, K. (1991–92). 'Grassroots Organizations and Women's Empowerment: Some Issues in the Contemporary Debate', in *Samya Shakti*, 5. New Delhi: CWDS.

7

KERALA

Beyond the politicking of gender politics

Meena T. Pillai

Introduction

This chapter examines the paradoxical nature of Kerala's polity by looking at how mass politics has shaped and responded to gender politics in the state. It also discusses the manner in which political parties tap into discourses on gender and morality for claiming public consensus and for maintaining a regime of power. The communalization of politics in Kerala has seen an increasing masculinization of its public sphere. This chapter focuses on how majoritarian and minoritarian identity politics hitch on to the fault lines of gender and come together to enshrine repressive and socially reactionary political forces in the state.

According to the official data released by the Election Commission of India, women in Kerala voted more as compared to men in the 2016 Kerala state elections. While 74 per cent of the women voted, only 73.95 per cent of the men exercised their franchise in the 2014 general elections. As shown in Table 7.1, in the 2019 general elections this margin further increased when the women voter turnout was a significant 78.78 per cent against the 76.48 per cent male voter turnout as 10,611,000 women out of the total 13,469,000 women voters in Kerala exercised their franchise. This data seems to buttress the obvious belief that one of the most literate states in the country should also necessarily have women with very high levels of political consciousness.

The Kerala model of development

The much-hyped 'Kerala model of development', despite its spectacular social development indicators which helped transport Kerala's image to enviable heights, has not augured well for the women of the state in terms of a liberatorial potential that would translate into their everyday lives. The commendable indices like high levels of female literacy, employment, sex ratio, and health achievements together with 50 per cent reservation of seats

DOI: 10.4324/9781003374862-8

141

Table 7.1 State-wise women voter turnout for general elections (2019)

(Figures for electors and voters in thousands)

State/UTs	Women Electors	Women Voters	% Women Turnout	Total Electors	Total Voters	% Total Turnout
(1)	(2)	(3)	(4)	(5)	(6)	(7)
Andaman and Nicobar Islands	149	98	65.47%	318	207	65.12%
Andhra Pradesh	19,881	15,818	79.56%	39,406	31,675	80.38%
Arunachal Pradesh	404	326	80.78%	804	660	82.11%
Assam	10,757	8,748	81.33%	22,050	17,993	81.60%
Bihar	33,533	19,980	59.58%	71,216	40,830	57.33%
Chandigarh	305	216	70.79%	647	457	70.61%
Chhattisgarh	9,482	6,689	70.55%	19,016	13,623	71.64%
Dadra and Nagar Haveli	118	95	81.17%	250	199	79.58%
Daman and Diu	61	46	75.47%	122	87	71.85%
Delhi	6,444	3,876	60.14%	14,328	8,682	60.60%
Goa	580	442	76.16%	1,136	854	75.14%
Gujarat	21,697	13,214	60.90%	45,152	29,128	64.51%
Haryana	8,340	5,800	69.55%	18,057	12,701	70.34%
Himachal Pradesh	2,606	1,936	74.31%	5,330	3,860	72.42%
Jammu and Kashmir	3,777	1,650	43.67%	7,923	3,563	44.97%
Jharkhand	10,667	7,281	68.26%	22,405	14,967	66.80%
Karnataka	25,249	17,080	67.65%	51,095	35,159	68.81%
Kerala	13,469	10,611	78.78%	26,205	20,397	77.84%
Lakshadweep	27	24	86.78%	55	47	85.21%
Madhya Pradesh	24,837	17,055	68.67%	51,867	36,928	71.20%
Maharashtra	42,249	24,853	58.82%	88,677	54,111	61.02%

(*Continued*)

KERALA

Table 7.1 Continued

(Figures for electors and voters in thousands)

State/UTs	Women Electors	Women Voters	% Women Turnout	Total Electors	Total Voters	% Total Turnout
(1)	(2)	(3)	(4)	(5)	(6)	(7)
Manipur	996	838	84.13%	1,960	1,620	82.69%
Meghalaya	965	714	73.93%	1,915	1,368	71.43%
Mizoram	404	252	62.40%	792	500	63.14%
Nagaland	599	495	82.69%	1,214	1,007	83.00%
Odisha	15,835	11,750	74.20%	32,498	23,817	73.29%
Puducherry	514	419	81.52%	973	791	81.25%
Punjab	9,832	6,452	65.62%	20,893	13,777	65.94%
Rajasthan	23,395	15,335	65.55%	48,956	32,476	66.34%
Sikkim	212	167	78.60%	434	353	81.41%
Tamil Nadu	29,542	21,362	72.31%	58,503	42,392	72.46%
Telangana	14,776	9,245	62.57%	29,709	18,647	62.77%
Tripura	1,286	1,054	81.97%	2,615	2,155	82.40%
Uttar Pradesh	67,056	39,941	59.56%	146,135	86,532	59.21%
Uttarakhand	3,713	2,391	64.39%	7,856	4,861	61.88%
West Bengal	34,049	27,850	81.79%	70,001	57,230	81.76%
All India	437,807	294,103	67.18%	910,512	613,656	67.40%

Source: *Election Commission of India – General Elections, 2019 (17th Lok Sabha).*

MEENA T. PILLAI

Table 7.2 State-wise women's participation in the 17th Lok Sabha elections

Name of the State/UTs	Women MPs	Total Seats	% Women	First Time Elected		
				Women	Total	% Women
(1)	(2)	(3)	(4)	(5)	(6)	(7)
Andaman and Nicobar Islands	0	1	0%	0	0	
Andhra Pradesh	4	25	16%	4	18	22%
Arunachal Pradesh	0	1	0%	0	0	
Assam	1	14	7%	1	9	11%
Bihar	3	40	8%	2	17	12%
Chandigarh	1	1	100%	0	0	
Chhattisgarh	3	11	27%	3	10	30%
Dadar and Nagar Haveli	0	1	0%	0	0	
Daman and Diu	0	1	0%	0	0	
Delhi	1	7	14%	0	2	0%
Goa	0	2	0%	0	0	
Gujarat	6	26	23%	2	10	20%
Haryana	1	10	10%	1	4	25%
Himachal Pradesh	0	4	0%	0	2	0%
Jammu and Kashmir	0	6	0%	0	3	0%
Jharkhand	2	14	14%	2	5	40%
Karnataka	2	28	7%	1	11	9%
Kerala	1	20	5%	1	10	10%
Lakshadweep	0	1	0%	0	0	
Madhya Pradesh	4	29	14%	2	16	13%
Maharashtra	8	48	17%	2	19	11%
Manipur	0	2	0%	0	2	0%
Meghalaya	1	2	50%	0	0	
Mizoram	0	1	0%	0	1	0%
Nagaland	0	1	0%	0	0	
Odisha	7	21	33%	6	16	38%
Puducherry	0	1	0%	0	1	0%
Punjab	2	13	15%	0	5	0%
Rajasthan	3	25	12%	2	8	25%
Sikkim	0	1	0%	0	1	0%
Tamil Nadu	3	39	8%	3	27	11%
Telangana	1	17	6%	1	12	8%
Tripura	1	2	50%	1	2	50%
Uttar Pradesh	11	80	14%	5	31	16%
Uttarakhand	1	5	20%	0	2	0%
West Bengal	11	42	26%	6	22	27%
All India	78	542	14%	45	266	17%

Source: *Lok Sabha Secretariat as on January 3, 2020.*

in local governance bodies for women are often believed to indicate that Kerala's women have achieved a fair degree of social and political empowerment in the public domain. It has also contributed to the creation of 'the myth of the empowered Malayali woman' and its mystique. However, none of these indices seem to find a positive echo when it comes to Malayali women in the public domain of politics.

Table 7.2 gives the state-wise percentage of elected women representatives in the 17th Lok Sabha elections. It can be deduced that the prioritization of male candidates in Kerala continues unabated despite the high number of women turning out to vote.

Women in the state assembly

The situation is the same when it comes to women's participation in elections to the state assembly.

Table 7.3 gives women's participation in state assemblies. It is evident from the table that in the 2016 Kerala state elections, only 6 per cent of the seats were occupied by women in contrast to the 132 men who were elected. This stands in contrast to states like Haryana and Bihar which exhibit a more favourable percentage of women's performance (14 per cent) in state assembly elections.

It is interesting to note in Table 7.4 (which gives the state-wise percentage of women representatives in Panchayati Raj Institutions), that as opposed to the number of women elected to the Kerala state assembly and the Lok Sabha, Malayali women's representation in panchayat elections is as high as 52 per cent, which is one of the highest in the country (Women and Men, 2017, p. 108). According to the Ministry of Statistics and Programme Implementation's report *Women and Men in India – 2017* (p. 102), the percentage of women voters' turnout in the general elections in 2014 in Kerala was as high as 74 per cent. However, the positive image projected by the number of women voters in Kerala becomes bleak once we look deeper into the statistics on Malayali women's participation in mainstream politics and the way women politicians work in the public sphere and respond to questions concerning women and gender.

In 2009, under the Left Democratic Front government, Kerala became the sixth state to implement 50 per cent reservation for women in local bodies after Bihar, Uttarakhand, Himachal Pradesh, Madhya Pradesh, and Chhattisgarh. Thus, 52 per cent of the members in PRIs in Kerala are women representatives (Table 7.4). However, when it comes to Kerala's state legislature, women members make up only 6 per cent of the total strength of the current assembly. This nominal representation is an extension of a past in which women's representation in Kerala's elected bodies remained marginal.

Table 7.3 Participation of women in the state assembly

	Assembly					Council			
State	Year of Constitution of the State/Assembly	Year of Assembly Election	Male	Female	% Women	Male	Female	% Women	Total
Andhra Pradesh	1955	2014	156	20	11%	53	5	9%	58
Arunachal Pradesh	1978	2014	58	2	3%				
Assam	1937/1951	2016	118	8	6%				
Bihar	1937/1951	2015	209	34	14%		68		75
Chhattisgarh	2000/2003	2013	80	10	11%				
Delhi	1992/1993	2015	64	6	9%				
Goa	1987/1967	2017	38	2	5%				
Gujarat	1960/1962	2017	160	13	8%				
Haryana	1966/1967	2014	77	13	14%				
Himachal Pradesh	1971/1951	2017	65	4	6%				
Jammu and Kashmir ^	1934/1962	2014	85	2	2%	32	2	6%	36
Jharkhand	2000/2005	2014	69	8	10%				
Karnataka	1956/1957	2013	218	6	3%	71	3	4%	75
Kerala	1957	2016	132	8	6%				
Madhya Pradesh	1957	2013	200	30	13%				
Maharashtra	1960/1962	2014	268	20	7%	74	4	5%	78
Manipur	1972/1967	2017	58	2	3%				
Meghalaya	1972	2013	56	4	7%				
Mizoram	1987/1972	2013	40	0	0%				
Nagaland	1963/1964	2013	60	0	0%				

(Continued)

KERALA

Table 7.3 Continued

State	Year of Constitution of the State/Assembly	Assembly				Council			
		Year of Assembly Election	Male	Female	% Women	Male	Female	% Women	Total
Odisha	1937	2014	136	11	7%				
Punjab	1937	2017	111	6	5%				
Puducherry	1963	2016	30	0	0%				
Rajasthan	1956	2013	172	28	14%				
Sikkim	1975	2014	29	3	9%				
Tamil Nadu	1937	2016	218	16	7%				
Telangana	2014	2014	111	9	8%	35	1	3%	40
Tripura	1972	2013	55	5	8%				
Uttar Pradesh	1937	2017	361	42	10%	94	4	4%	100
Uttarakhand	2000	2017	66	4	6%				
West Bengal	1937	2016	255	39	13%				
Total			3759	359	9%	427	23	5%	462

^ 6-Year Term.

Women and Men in India – 2017 (2018), Ministry of Statistics & Programme Implementation, Government of India, New Delhi, p. 104.

Table 7.4 Women's representatives in Panchayati Raj Institutions

States/UTs	No. of Panchayats*				Elected Representatives #	
	District Level	Intermediate Level	Village Level	Total	Total Women	Women (%)
Andaman and Nicobar Islands	3	9	70	NA	NA	–
Andhra Pradesh	13	660	12,920	156,049	78,025	50
Arunachal Pradesh	20	177	1,835	9,356	3,094	33
Assam	21	191	2,199	26,844	13,422	50
Bihar	38	534	8,378	136,325	70,400	52
Chandigarh	1	1	12	NA	NA	–
Chhattisgarh	27	146	10,996	158,776	87,549	55
Dadar and Nagar Haveli	1	NA	20	136	47	35
Daman and Diu	2	NA	15	97	28	29
Goa	2	NA	192	1,559	514	33
Gujarat	33	248	14,263	132,726	43,670	33
Haryana	21	126	6,204	68,152	24,876	37
Himachal Pradesh	12	78	3,226	27,832	13,947	50
Jammu and Kashmir	22	319	4,204	33,282	11,169	34
Jharkhand	24	263	4,398	51,327	30,373	59
Karnataka	30	176	6,024	95,307	50,892	53
Kerala	14	152	941	19,089	9,897	52
Lakshadweep	1	NA	10	NA	NA	–
Madhya Pradesh	51	313	22,825	396,819	198,409	50
Maharashtra	34	351	27,887	203,203	101,466	50
Manipur	4	NA	161	1,784	868	49
Odisha	30	314	6,806	100,791	49,697	49
Puducherry	NA	10	98	NA	NA	–
Punjab	22	147	13,016	97,180	33,609	35

(*Continued*)

Table 7.4 Continued

States/UTs	No. of Panchayats*			Elected Representatives #		
	District Level	Intermediate Level	Village Level	Total	Total Women	Women (%)
Rajasthan	33	295	9,891	121,008	70,531	58
Sikkim	4	NA	185	1,099	549	50
Tamil Nadu	31	385	12,524	119,399	39,975	33
Telangana	9	438	8,685	103,468	46,702	45
Tripura	8	35	591	10,939	3,930	36
Uttar Pradesh	75	821	59,019	718,667	297,235	41
Uttarakhand	13	95	7,955	61,451	35,537	58
West Bengal	22	342	3,341	59,296	29,579	50
Total	621	6626	248,891	291,1961	1,345,990	46

* As on December 2017.
# November 2016.
Women and Men in India – 2017 (2018), Ministry of Statistics & Programme Implementation, Government of India, New Delhi, p. 108.

For a state that elects 141 legislative assembly members once every five years, Kerala has elected only 87 women MLAs since 1957 (Deshabhimani, *Randu Stree Mantrimar*, 2016). On the national level, the total number of elected women in the 16th Lok Sabha stood at 62 out of a total of 543 members. While this was a record high for India in terms of women's membership to the Lower House, these figures are not praiseworthy when compared with the gendered indices of other nations. *The Economic Times* (2016) emphasized that

> India has slipped from a rank of 117 among 188 countries in 2014 to 144 among 191 countries as on February 1, 2016, in terms of the proportion of women in Parliament. Barely 12 per cent of MPs in the Lok Sabha are women and the figure stands at 12.8 per cent in Rajya Sabha. This is well below the global average of around 22 per cent in both Houses.

This disheartening trend continues as we look at Kerala women's participation in the Lok Sabha and Rajya Sabha elections especially considering that the much-lauded participation of 27 Malayali women candidates constitutes only a small percentage of the 269 candidates contesting from various Lok Sabha constituencies in Kerala (*The Economic Times*, 2014). In spite of sending 20 MPs to the Lok Sabha every term, Kerala elected only eight women Lok Sabha MPs between 1951 and 2014 (*Kaumudi Online*, 2019). In the case of the Rajya Sabha, Kerala has sent only four women MPs including Bharati Udayabhanu who was elected in 1958 and T.N. Seema who was elected in 2010 (Thottappuzha, 2019).

In the 2019 Lok Sabha elections, among the six women candidates, Ramya Haridas was the only woman who got elected. There are no women in the current nine Rajya Sabha MPs from Kerala (Rajyasabha.nic.in, 2019). Though larger electoral participation could be a result of awareness among women about the need to exercise their electoral rights and the role played by self-help groups (SHGs) and the Panchayati Raj system, all of which have helped in raising political consciousness, the data reflects interesting points regarding the gender paradoxes of Kerala's polity.

Firstly, after 14 assembly elections since the formation of the state in 1956 and the first election in 1957, fewer women seem to actually win seats to the upper echelons of political power. For instance, although Kerala has elected 87 women MLAs belonging to different political parties in the last six decades, so far only six of them have become ministers and no one has become the Chief Minister (Deshabhimani, 2016). The LDF government of 2016 was the first in the state's history to have two women ministers in the cabinet.

What is even more significant is that even as the number of women candidates contesting the elections to the legislative assembly has increased by leaps and bounds in the last two decades, the women actually elected showed poorer numbers. 'The percentage of female members of the legislative assembly (MLAs) fell from 10.23 per cent in 1996 to 6.06 per cent in 2016, even as the number of women candidates doubled over these five elections' (Sreedevi, 2016).

Hence, there are more women willing to stake a claim to their right to be part of electoral politics but less women, and men for that matter, are willing to permit them to do so. Even in those instances where women's representation in the governing bodies is legally ensured through reservations, as in the case of PRIs, it becomes important to ask how far such measures have translated into real agency for women in terms of the power to engage in the decision-making process and to make informed choices regarding one's personal and political life (Devika and Thampi, 2012).

Even those women who successfully make it to the higher echelons of power in legislatures and other elected bodies often end up playing complex and sometimes, paradoxical roles within Kerala's public sphere. Many of the elected women representatives in Kerala have responded to issues regarding women's health, education, and employment and have often taken a progressive stance in relation to women's empowerment and welfare. Some have even recognized and expressed concerns about the marginal presence of women in mainstream politics. For instance, T.N. Seema, the sole woman member from Kerala in the Rajya Sabha in 2010–16, acknowledged the larger societal prejudices that work against women candidates and responded in favour of legal reservation for women in legislative bodies, stating that '[u]ntil we have a system for legal reservation, chances are remote that change happens in representation of women in parliament and assembly' (quoted in Kumar, 2019).

However, in the context of the emergence of vociferous feminist, subaltern, Dalit, and most recently queer counter publics and pressure groups within Kerala since the last decades of the twentieth century, women in mainstream politics often find themselves performing paradoxical roles, sometimes adopting politically progressive stances that unsettle the structures of patriarchy that govern the political groups which they formally identify with, while at other times taking a stance that is at odds with the opinions held by counter-hegemonic pressure groups. This is particularly so as debates related to sexuality, desire, mobility, morality, and tradition increasingly get articulated in contemporary Kerala.

The paradoxes

Some of the reasons for these curious ironies could be located in the central paradoxes of Kerala's tryst with modernity and the resolution of 'the woman question' under its aegis. One of the most literate states in India, Kerala still remains a polity governed by groupings and political parties with historical ties to religious, caste, and community associations. The paradoxical nature of Kerala's civil order is best reflected in the recent rise of right-wing politics that brings under its ambit religious, political, cultural, social services, and militant associations that have media and muscle power, and whose interventions in Kerala's public sphere of late have exposed the links between politicking of gender politics and the maintenance of regimes of power.

What is even more interesting is the manner in which minoritarian politics in Kerala often invokes majoritarian religious and ideological commitments enshrining repressive and socially reactionary political forces. Thus, gender becomes one of the fault lines across which minoritarian and majoritarian politics build their bridges and forge consensus. The containment of gender politics thus becomes an agenda whereby an entire set of social relations and practices, which by themselves do not form a political coalition, pave the way for the historical emergence of a bloc, cutting across different political parties with differential ideological leanings, whose articulations of dominance and consent through political and civil society apparatuses seek to maintain the myth of the empowered Malayali woman.

Mobilizations involving women

I take three instances of progressive mobilizations around women's rights and the politics of gender to talk about this issue and how political parties and women in politics have addressed them. The first is the agitations led by a group of youngsters who organized a symbolic 'Kiss of Love' (KOL) protest in Kochi in 2014 against the rising instances of moral policing in the state, the second is the more recent furore over women's entry into the Sabarimala temple, and the third is *Pembilai Orumai*, the non-party-affiliated spontaneous agitation in 2015 of over 5,000 women workers in the Munnar tea estates for increased wages.

The KOL campaign was launched on social media after the vandalizing of a coffee shop in Kozhikode, prompted by the alleged public display of affection by couples who frequented the place. Those who opposed the KOL march mostly included right-wing parties and their youth outfits. Many of them came out in protest against KOL strikers, sloganeering against the loss of moral values and the contamination of Indian culture. Many of the people who came to express solidarity with the youth were attacked by these protestors. The 50-odd young men and women who constituted the kiss crusaders were bundled off by the police. The 'pro-culture' group came out with a poster which congratulated the solidarity displayed by all religious factions of Kerala in vindicating 'Indian culture' and defeating the 'obscenity' of the KOL campaign, pointing out that this was 'true secularism'.

One can see here a falling in line of majoritarian and minoritarian communalism. The concerted efforts to forge associations based on caste and communal identities and faith communities, which began under the sign of colonial modernity in the late nineteenth and early twentieth centuries, have, over the years, sought to erase the markers of social, economic, educational, and cultural differences that underlie each community group in Kerala. The elites of such groups, including the Sree Narayana Dharma Paripalana (SNDP) Yogam, the Nair Service Society (NSS), and Muslim and Christian associations, sought to project themselves as single units to reap the benefits of social and developmental policies. This process, negating democratic ideals within communal politics, contributed significantly to the re-feudalization of the public sphere in Kerala, establishing the hegemony of community elites.

This resurfaced in more clear formats during the Sabarimala controversy, when a patriarchal Brahmanical ritualistic base and 'royal' decrees of the once royal family of Pandalam sat in judgement over a Supreme Court verdict allowing women of all ages entry into the Sabarimala temple. Moreover, this re-invocation of traditional and exclusive structures of domination is repeatedly legitimized by many, including women political leaders in Kerala's public domain.

The complicity between the social and economic elites in a community and its religious leadership has often led to a totalization of politics in the state. Communities of minority faith become synonymous with a political community. This, along with majority fundamentalism, has seriously undermined the process of women's empowerment and the crusade for their rights in Kerala that was initiated in the first half of the twentieth century through its famed social reforms movements. Political-communal solidarity has often led to a reduction of citizenship rights at the cost of communitarian politics. Citizens organized under liberal and secular interests have become suspect. This minoritarian politics echoes a significant ideological shift away from caste politics that characterized Kerala's project of modernity at the beginning of the twentieth century, which was a move for equal social rights and justice.

It should also be added here that the myth of Kerala as a haven of social democratization and communal harmony founded on secular and egalitarian principles has acted as a smokescreen for the increasing communalization of the public sphere. It is significant that those who protested against the KOL march and were in the forefront to hold women's constitutional rights as hostage in the Sabarimala protests brought in notions of pollution and contamination aplenty in their sloganeering, significantly re-writing upper-caste rituals and practices revolving around pollution and cleansing. Women political leaders of many non-Left parties repeatedly invoked the language of both patriarchy and hegemonic masculinity to reiterate women's roles in the inner spiritual domains of the family as upholders of age-old 'traditions'. *Acharasamrakshanam* (conservation of tradition/rituals) was the recurring rhetoric of most of these leaders. It is interesting to note that in some of the speeches of women leaders there is an aspiration to toughness and ruthlessness, playing up to the stereotype that it requires male aggressiveness and macho-ness to be successful in politics.

However, the difficulty of accessing power and maintaining conventional femininity is affected through sartorial choices that mark them as 'hyper feminine', adhering to traditional Kerala women's attire while imitating the leadership styles and keeping to the political priorities of their respective parties, no matter how misogynist they might be.

One of the prime manifestations of the communalization of politics in Kerala has been the masculinization of the public sphere. A great deal of recent scholarship has bust the myth and mystique of the 'Kerala woman', exposing the fact that Kerala's high rate of female literacy does not translate into either women's freedom or agency (Mukhopadhyay, 2007). Moreover, it is largely within the undemocratic precincts of a chauvinistic and conservative family space that large sections of Malayali women seem to find themselves groomed and grounded. Most of them are sabotaged by intimate and affective economies, and it is on such manufactured consent that women's citizenship rights, especially the right to mobility and choice, are curtailed and monitored. It has been drilled into Kerala's collective unconscious that women belonging to 'good families' will not be seen outside their homes after sunset, until and unless properly chaperoned by male members of the family. Women's bodies which were co-opted by different movements and agendas in the history of Kerala, including conjugal, caste, and agrarian reforms, are now co-opted by counter-democratic communal forces to forge an emotional and ideological unity among themselves, at whatsoever minimal a level.

Even women-led resistance movements like *Pembilai Orumai*, with its assertions that oppose and reveal the dominant capitalist–communal nexus of mainstream politics, when mobilized into systems of legislative power are often seen as being co-opted under the logic of dominant political structures of a masculinized political sphere (Paul, 2016).

Ethno-caste political entities are seen to establish their links with the body politic through the act of sacralizing and policing women's bodies. Regional minoritarian and majoritarian communal politics arrive at their consensus on the tropes of the Indian women and Indian culture. This politics exudes solidarity of a different kind when it comes into conflict with situations, events, or practices where men and women refuse to write themselves into conventional social scripts, be it the controversy over sex education in Kerala, or the 'secularization' of school textbooks, or the recent attempt to forge a creative protest towards imagining the body as a site of resistance to state and community surveillance.

The mobilization of communal politics to counter both Sabarimala and the KOL rally and the ensuing controversy it kicked up, with large sections of the Malayali public expressing their unwillingness to support *acharalanghanam* in the former case and a blatant show of 'obscenity' in the latter, is a pointer to the widespread perception of traditions and conventions as constitutive features of the public sphere instead of rational-critical debates.

The Temple Entry Proclamation, the first of its kind in India, which allowed non-caste Hindus to enter temples was a milestone in the social and political history of Kerala and it happened way back in 1936. It is ironic that neither the people who gained entry into temples by that edict, nor the 'benevolent' elites who condescendingly consented to it, have since bothered to examine why pre-menopausal women continue to be 'culturally' banned from entering the famous Sabarimala temple, even after the legal ban was lifted by a Supreme Court verdict. Women being mobilized by women leaders, consenting to be active participants in constructing their bodies as polluted, thus become illustrative of the ways in which consent can be manufactured to maintain hegemonic religious and cultural structures. Both Congress and BJP women leaders were active organizers of women's collectives that chanted bhajans and proclaimed that they did not want to exercise their constitutional rights to enter Sabarimala. However, it is worth mentioning here that Bindu Krishna, who is the president of the Kollam District Congress Committee (the second woman DCC president in the state's history), took a controversial stance that opposed her party's attitudes against women's entry into Sabarimala (Kairali TV, 2018).

In contrast to the dominant opposition by the Congress and the BJP, the Left parties had women leaders who under the patronage of the Chief Minister organized a 640-km women's wall, pledging to protect Kerala's renaissance values. On New Year's day in 2019, 5 million women lined up, offering a rekindled hope that this would spark off a new movement that would seek to unshackle Kerala's women from the tyranny of patriarchy. The BJP organized a counter campaign called *Ayyappa Jyothi* which had women lining up on the streets to light lamps and chant prayers.

The fact that religion and culture are increasingly being used as forces of mobilization for preserving hegemonic masculinity in both private and public spaces reveals a continued resistance to a feminized and democratized public sphere despite the presence of large numbers of women as public actors. Moreover, in a media-saturated society like Kerala, the 'public' is more an imagined subject, constituted primarily through male authoritative voices, misogynist talk shows, and the much-hyped television channel discussions with their regular stereotypes and clichés, as also one constituted under the sign of the 'benevolent patriarchy' of print media (Mukhopadhyay, 2007, p. 26). This makes it possible for upper-class male public subjects to offer legitimacy and endorsement to lesser players like women and members of other marginal communities, on condition that they confirm dominant hegemonic rules.

Many of the right-wing women political leaders were seen to endorse and mimic a patriarchal logic and language. Some of their leaders became notorious in the way they retaliated to opponents on TV shows with no semblance of democratic ideals or political decorum. They claimed to represent the true feelings of the common woman, the 'real' bhakt, as opposed to the socially engineered policies of gender equality that the Marxists were seeking to endorse.

However, as prominent political parties and caste and community associations have started owning TV channels and newspapers, voice and visibility constitute the chief feature of the modern public sphere in Kerala. The politics manifested in the concerted efforts to remove the intimate from public gaze and the constant policing of private subjectivities reveal the technologies of power, the politics of its inclusions and exclusions, and the manufacturing of consent through populism. Thus, constant invocations of 'Indian culture' become the singular marker of the secularist presumptions of such a public sphere.

The KOL and Sabarimala debates have, in a sense, destabilized the notion of a secular, liberal public sphere in Kerala. The patriarchal and communal regimes of 'discipline and punish', to borrow Foucault's words, are also revealed in the redrawing of the boundaries between the public and the private, morality and transgression, culture and anarchy, tradition and modernity. The unpardonable sin was that young Malayali women who expressed a wish to go to Sabarimala or supported KOL indulged in performative acts that signalled their break from tradition and evinced a refusal to be governed by gender laws and regulations imposed by religion and culture regarding the licit and illicit. Though both men and women kissed in public, the media visuals were almost entirely of women, and most of the social media discussions focused on the necessity to discipline recalcitrant feminine subjects. Though the women who went to Sabarimala said they were believers, there were recurring debates on the necessity to test their faith and prove their spiritual and religious 'purity' like Sita's *agnipareeksha*.

The allegation was that many of these women were activists, as though activism for women is a pollutant that drains away their moral right to be devotees. The figure of the *kulasthree* (high-born woman) began to haunt Kerala's social imaginary and it is interesting that many of the women politically lay claim to that label through sartorial choices that wrote them into its registers.

The need to sanitize Kerala's public spaces from the threat of 'unruly' and 'activist' women, the fear instilled by fundamentalists about 'our culture' being polluted, and the blatantly repressive grooming in academic and educational institutions have all contributed to a warped state of events. Many of the girls who come from the upper echelons of Kerala society today choose to migrate to other cities for higher education and work. One needs to talk about the new demographics of gender migration from Kerala. Even while girls who are victims of the ideological bandwagon that constitutes Kerala's civil and political culture remain mired in the bog of their oppression, most of them are so steeped in the patriarchal ethos as to be blissfully ignorant of their rights.

Women in Kerala continue to function as sexual and ideological reproducers, irrespective of their education and work. Gendered bodies and sexualities – and, specifically, women's mobility and dress – continue to be brought under caste, class, and community scrutiny. The attempt to communalize the masses has gender as its key focus, the rock bed on which the populist discourses around tradition and modernity, the private and public, religious and secular can be unleashed for political purposes.

As large numbers of Malayali women enter the public arena and girls outnumber boys in educational institutions as also in workplaces, women seem to be placed under a constant threat of policing and mandatory community control. Caste and religious fundamentalism are bound to escalate in a context where the global media and markets infiltrate traditional societies, triggering a crisis in masculinity. An increasing feeling of emasculation, a palpable fear of the erosion of masculine control, and the need to invoke caste and religion to circumscribe the secular and liberal are symptoms of this disease. Women's presence in politics has hardly made a dent in this situation or moved beyond 'symbolic representation' to 'substantive representation' as elaborated by Mackay where at one level, women act on behalf of women 'and ensure women's interests, needs and concerns are more fully represented in the policy process with consequent policy outcomes', while on the other hand they also act 'like women' 'with consequent outcomes in changes to masculinist political behavior and institutional norms' (Macay, 2005, p. 101). Thus, patriarchy and androcentrism continue to co-opt women leaders.

In this larger context of what women's presence in mainstream politics failed to accomplish for the women of Kerala, the 2015 struggle by over 5,000 women workers of the Munnar tea estates for increased wages becomes a relevant third instance that merits discussion. The Munnar plantation strike was a distinct moment in the history of women's resistance in Kerala as it saw women from some of the most marginalized, impoverished, and underprivileged sections of society coming together to protest for something as fundamental as minimum wages and human rights. Although the concerns raised by the collective were primarily economic in nature, in the wake of the movement, the strikers succeeded in bringing attention to the gender-specific concerns faced by women labourers that had hitherto remained unaddressed within both the mainstream women's movement and the workers' movement. In retrospect, what remains the most striking about the movement is the fact that it was carried out under the aegis of *Pembilai Orumai*, an all-women's collective that remained unaffiliated to existing political parties or interest groups. Even as it lost its momentum after the initial success due to internal differences of opinion and interests, it largely succeeded in refusing to be co-opted by specific political or communitarian interests.

On the one hand, the movement and the women who took part in it brought attention to how mainstream politics and women politicians have desperately failed in addressing some pertinent issues faced by underprivileged women in Kerala. On the other hand, the fact that their resisting, transgressive presence in the public sphere did not capture the interests of communitarian forces in Kerala also shows how these women, whose subalternity is written in their caste, social location, and profession, are always imagined as not belonging to the ideal of the Malayali woman, who is conceived to be the reproducer of traditions and femininity in communitarian discourses.

However, in any history that seeks to trace women's engagement with politics in Kerala, the *Pembilai Orumai* strike remains a moment worth remembering as it managed to devise alternative and innovative modes and strategies of gendered women's politics in the state.

Postscript

Since this chapter was written in 2018, it does not focus on some of the contemporary trends that marked the 2020 local body elections in Kerala in which more than 36,000 women contested. The local body elections in Kerala in 2020 had historic moments, like the election of the youngest female mayor in the country. Moreover, the Kudumbashree women, who represent an exemplary model of Kerala's self-help groups, bagged more than one-third of the local body seats, a trend that continued from 2015, holding the promise of a potential shift in gender dynamics. This could be taken as a crucial indicator of the changing dynamics of women's social and political mobility, signifying possible positive trends in the forthcoming 2021 state elections, though this falls outside the scope of this chapter.

Bibliography

Deshabhimani (2016). 'Randu Stree Mantrimar Charitram' ('Two Women Ministers Make History'), May 23. Available at: https://www.deshabhimani.com/special/news-special-23-05-2016/562909, accessed on May 14, 2022.

Devika, J. and Binitha V. Thampi (2012). *New Lamps for Old? Gender Paradoxes of Political Decentralization in Kerala*. New Delhi: Zubaan.

Government of India (2018). *Women and Men in India 2017: A Statistical Profile*. New Delhi: Central Statistics Office.

——— (2020). *Women and Men in India: A Statistical Compilation of Gender Related Indicators in India- 2019*. New Delhi: National Statistical Office.

Kairali TV (2018). 'Sabarimalayil Streekale Maatinirthunnathinodu Vyakthiparamayi Yogikkunnillennu Bindu Krishna', *YouTube*, October 5. Available at: https://www.youtube.com/watch?v=yVDt5Y1XuiI, accessed on May 14, 2022.

Kaumudi Online (2019). 'Kerala Elected only 8 Women MPs in 70 Years', Available at: https://keralakaumudi.com/en/news/news.php?id=63225&u=kerala-had-only-eight-women-mps-in-70-years-63225, accessed on May 14, 2022.

Kumar, Aswin J. (2019). 'Kerala with the Highest Per Centage of Females in Total Population Sent Just 12 Women MPs to Lok Sabha in Six Decades', *The Times of India*, March 14. Available at: https://timesofindia.indiatimes.com/city/thiruvananthapuram/kerala-with-the-highest-per centage-of-females-in-total-population-sent-just-12-women-mps-to-lok-sabha-in-six-decades/articleshow/68405704.cms, accessed on May 14, 2022.

Mackay, Fiona (2005). 'Sharing Power? Gender and Multi-level Democracy in the UK', in Yvonne Galligan and Manon Tremblay (eds), *Sharing Power: Women, Parliament and Democracy*, (pp. 107–122). Aldershot: Ashgate.

Mukherji, Anahita (2016). 'Women in House: India's Rank Slips from 117 in 2014 to 144 This Year', *The Economic Times*, March 8. Available at: https://economictimes.indiatimes.com/news/politics-and-nation/women-in-house-indias-rank-slips-from-117-in-2014-to-144-this-year/articleshow/51303875.cms?from=mdr, accessed on May 14, 2022.

Mukhopadhyay, Swapna (2007). 'Understanding the Enigma of Women's Status in Kerala: Does High Literacy Necessarily Translate into High Status', in Swapna Mukhopadhyay (ed.), *The Enigma of the Kerala Woman* (pp. 3–31). New Delhi: Social Science Press.

Paul, Cithara (2016). 'The Powerpuff Girls', December 25. Available at: www.theweek.in/theweek/cover/pembilai-orumai-kerala.html?fb_comment_id=1027683407353524_1035789163209615, accessed on May 14, 2022.

Sreedevi, R. S. (2016). 'In Kerala, More Women are Contesting Elections, but Fewer are Winning', *Scroll.in*, August 2. Available at: https://scroll.in/article/812963/in-kerala-more-women-are-contesting-elections-but-fewer-are-winning, accessed on June 23, 2021.

The Economic Times (2014). 'Lok Sabha Polls 2014: 27 Women Candidates in Fray for LS Polls in Kerala', March 27. Available at: economictimes.indiatimes.com/news/politics-and-nation/lok-sabha-polls-2014-27-women-candidates-in-fray-for-ls-polls-in-kerala/articleshow/32783444.cms?utm_source=contentofinterest&utm_medium=text&utm_campaign=cppst, accessed August 16, 2021.

Thottappuzha, Varghese John (2019). 'Indian Parliamentile Malankara Sabha Angangal', (Members of the Malankara Church in the Indian Parliament), *Malankara*, March 13. Available at: https://ia800900.us.archive.org/3/items/indian-parliament-malankara-church-members/indian-parliament-malankara-church-members.pdf, accessed on June 16, 2022.

8

WOMEN IN TELANGANA STATE POLITICS AND THEIR STRUGGLES

Rekha Pande

Introduction

Telangana is one of the youngest states, the 28th state in the Indian Union which was formed on June 2, 2014, having separated from Andhra Pradesh. Hence, the history of Telangana cannot be separated from that of Andhra Pradesh. Women in Telangana have been very actively involved in various socio-political movements. They have multiple identities and hence they have participated in their own movements or have been part of mixed-gender social political movements. Unfortunately, though women participated very actively in all the agitations and movements for the formation of the separate state, they got a very raw deal at the hands of the male politicians and we have very few women representatives in the assembly and not much is written about their participation in these movements. History by and large focuses more on men and we only have information about men's role in these struggles and not much documentation and information about women.

A conservative, rural, and tradition bound society like that of Andhra and Telangana, attempting to step into the twenty-first century, is fraught with many problems. Society is a combination of tribal, semi-feudal, capitalistic, and monopolistic segments imposed over by a caste and regional structure. This has created tensions in all spheres of life. Over the years, rural unemployment, migration to cities, exploitation by the crime underworld, prostitution, and exploitation of children have increased poverty and widened class differences resulting in crimes. Because of their powerlessness, women have been worst hit and often gender gets subsumed within the larger political scenario. Cultural and religious practices have combined with the assumption of patriarchy to maintain the power of the producer (male) over the reproducer (female). This was made amply clear by the path-breaking report, Towards Equality (1974), which highlighted women's abysmally low status in modern India and focused attention on the fact that women's status had not improved much despite many progressive

160 DOI: 10.4324/9781003374862-9

social laws and constitutional guarantees (Towards Equality, 1974). In its debate on women's status, this study did not include violence as an important issue. However, by 1995, the Indian government had recognized violence against women as one of the 11 critical areas of concern (Country Report, 1995).

Social reform movements

In Andhra Pradesh, the coastal districts were the site of a strong social reform movement during the nineteenth century, whose central emphasis was the improvement of women's status. This was in line with the wider social patterns in the rest of the country. Child marriages, *kanyasulkam* (the tradition of marrying very small girls often to old men in lieu of cash payments), widow remarriages, the abolition of the *dasi* system (women from lower castes made bonded slaves in the houses of upper caste rich landlords), devadasis (temple dancing girls), particularly the education of women became the main focus, with women also taking an active part in these debates. Though education for girls was emphasized, the understanding was that this training was to encourage women to play their traditional roles of mothers and wives more effectively. However, most of these debates and problems were limited to Andhra society's upper castes and not the great mass of women who were engaged in agriculture and the lower castes.

A literary and social revival during the first half of the twentieth century was also experienced in Telangana region (which was part of the princely state of Hyderabad till 1948, when it entered the Indian Union).

Telangana's struggle for a separate state

In Telangana we can divide the politics and struggle for a separate state into six phases based on a chronological history of their development:

1. The first phase, pre-independence, Nizam's period (1946–47)
2. The second phase, the post-independence period (1948–51)
3. The third phase, the underground movement (1960–72)
4. The fourth phase, the anti-arrack movement (1990–95)
5. The fifth phase, the modern-day Telangana struggle and formation of the new state (1969–2014)
6. The sixth phase, post-2014 onwards

The first phase: The pre-independence, Nizam's period (1946–47)

Though not much is known about women's role in the struggle in the pre-independence period, it is a known fact that there was a lot of exploitation of women. The system of ruling by the Nizam was based on a well-knit network at the village level of Police Patels (law and order), Mali Patels (Revenue), and Patwaris (land record and collection) which were hereditary posts. In a Hindu Social Reform Conference in 1922, when a speaker tried to give his address in Telugu, he was hooted out and this led to the establishment of the Andhra Jan Sangham (Andhra People's Association) with the goal of highlighting Telugu language and culture (Pavier, 1981, p. 66). In 1921, the Andhra Mahasabha (AMS) was formally founded with the name Andhra Jan Sangham (Andhra People's Association), and it became concerned with administrative reforms, demands for more schools, land concessions, and civil liberties (Sundarayya, 1972).

The Andhra Mahasabha was an offshoot of the social reform movement initiated by Veeresalingam in the 1890s in Andhra Pradesh. Women members were primarily from the upper and middle classes connected directly or indirectly to the leaders of the social reform movement. In many of the speeches that they delivered in its annual conferences in 1913 and 1914, they gave a lot of emphasis to women's education but this education was to teach women to fulfil their traditional roles as daughters, wives, and mothers in their families. The roles within the family were reinforced and extended to be in tune with the requirements of a family in a changing society (Pande et al., 1987).

The Telangana struggle was one of the post-war insurrectionary struggles of peasants in India (Desai, 1969, pp. 390–397). While the land was with various jagirdars (landlords) under the Sarf-e-khas scheme, Rs 2 crore annually was provided to the Nizam and his family. In addition, the Nizam obtained Rs 70 lakh per year from the state treasury. In those days, these earnings were considered the highest in India (Briggs, 1861). The *paigahs* played a key role in the jagir areas. The Nizam granted *paigahs* to feudal Muslims, in particular to members of his own family and nearest relatives. The Nizam and his feudal officials, his armed *razakars*, tried to mobilize the Muslim masses to support them against the 'Hindus' during the first phase of the Telangana struggle (1946–47) (Hyder, Mohammed, 2012).

The second phase: The post-independence period (1948–51)

The plight of the peasants worsened when the Second World War started as they were subject to rising exploitative taxes and levies by the Nizam. The Telangana movement gave the peasantry tremendous benefits. Women fought against the police and developed resistance against the landlord–police combine and provided shelter and care to the underground revolutionaries. The *vetti* and *vettichakiri* (bonded labour) systems in Telangana were an all-pervasive social phenomena affecting all classes of people in varying degrees (Khusro, 1958). The big success of the Telangana movement led to the end of *vetti* and the end of the shocking system of *adi papa* and the forced making of concubines. The Communists organized men, women, and children from various disgruntled villages into armed guerrilla squads to combat exploitative landlords and the Nizam's armed battalions, called *razakars*, were gradually deployed to suppress the revolution. The *razakars* were a private militia organized by Qasim Razvi which went on a rampage slaughtering more than 100 villagers (Mehender, 2017).

In this period, when their men were killed or had to seek shelter elsewhere, women fought on the frontline, bearing guns and ammunition. Women took up issues such as bonded labour, violence, and sexual harassment in the public space (Sinha, 1989). Parallel governments were created in about 3,000 villages in the area. While the women of the upper and middle classes, both Hindu and Muslim, were able to avoid the oppression faced by the peasant women, the purdah system still governed them. Intentional efforts were made to unite the women and, in doing so, the problems that were particularly important to them were discussed such as unemployment, wife-beating, child care, hygiene, the right to breast-feed infants at work, food, and lavatories. The very fact that these concerns were posed was enough to win women's loyalty and support.

The women in Telangana actively engaged in the land movement, in agricultural labour wage struggles, in seizing landlords' grains, and fighting against the 'Briggs' scheme of evacuating the people of Koya, Chenchu, and Lambadi from their hamlets in the forest areas or from their scattered hamlets in the plains (Sundarayya, 2006). They battled the *razakars* and the Nizam's police with their husbands and brothers and later fought against the Congress and the central government. When armed police stormed the villages, women were at the side of their men, handing them stones for their strings. They faced brutal lathi charges and shootings along with their men folk. Women insisted that they would follow the men. They joined the military and political squads and endured all the difficulties and joys of life. They served as couriers, as political agitators, and as leaders of social movements and mass organizations in new centres (Lalita et al., 1989). On September 17, 1948, the Nizam surrendered his army to the Indian State and Hyderabad was annexed to the Indian Union.

The demand for a separate state of Andhra was getting stronger in independent India. The States Reorganization Commission (SRC) was constituted by the central government. One of the important ideas was that the states should be reorganized on the basis of the languages of India. On February 20, 1956, an agreement was reached between the leaders of Telangana (Telugu-speaking areas) and the leaders of Andhra to merge Telangana and Andhra with promises to preserve the interests of Telangana, this was called the Agreement of the Gentlemen. On November 1, 1956, the central government formed a unified Andhra Pradesh following the Gentlemen's Agreement. The first general elections in 1952 brought to power elected leaders of the people (Kodandaram, 2009). There were 11 elected women members in the House. However, a strong sense of marginalization experienced by the people of Andhra vis-à-vis the Tamils continued.

The people of Telangana faced two main problems after the liberation of Hyderabad and its integration into the Indian Union. Firstly, although the Nizam was overthrown, the Government of India made him Raj Pramukh of Hyderabad. This had a political impact on the governing elite's decision-making. Secondly, because of the prolonged resistance and armed struggle, tens of thousands of leaders were either in prison or in poverty because they still had cases pending against them.

The third phase: The underground movement (1960–72)

The period 1960–70 is crucial as many women joined the Naxal movement. Some women became active participants, wielding guns as members of the banned People's War Group (PWG). They became very vocal and the Left party leaders and groups brought the issues of gender and gender equality within the official discourse of the party. This gave women in Andhra Pradesh an opportunity to fight patriarchy and violence against them. Driven by a revolutionary ideology, thousands of young men and women took up arms to put an end to what they termed an exploitative socioeconomic order and to overthrow the current state power. With great care and comfort, the women offered food to the guerrillas and party leaders and fought battles against the enemy. Many women were tortured and oppressed. They were molested, raped, and beaten and their children were also tortured and killed. In their presence, their husbands and brothers were hunted, imprisoned, and killed (Xavier, 2012). Sundarayya (1972, p. 14) recounts some of his own experiences in his book, expressing his gratitude to women, 'Who can forget those glorious incidents, those inspiring stories of women's courage and suffering?'

The Telangana–Naxalite struggle, although a descendant of the Naxalbari movement and the Srikakulam struggle, acquired a character and identity of its own. The Andhra Pradesh Coordination Committee of Communist Revolutionaries (APCCCR) played an important role in leading the war in Telangana.

Many women were active participants in cultural groups such as Jana Natya Mandali and the Praja Natya Mandali and other groups such as Arunodaya Samskrutika Samakhya. Women from all classes engaged with passion and determination in the campaign, where both the urban middle class and the peasants were slowly but steadily drawing their support into the campaign. The Communist Party took up social reforms for women such as widow remarriages, the prohibition of child marriages, women's education and opportunities, and also started recognizing women with the potential to improve the movement. Dubala Salamma, Ch. Kamalamma, Achamma Regulla, Ailamma Chityala, Satbamma Pesaru, Swarajyam

Mallu, Kausalya Dayani, Tail Pramila, Lalithamma Chakilam, Bullemma, Narasamma, Vajramma, Saidamma, and Suganamma were some of the women who took active part in these campaigns.

Woman Naxalite, Venkatalaxmi alias Nirmala, left her hometown in Andhra Pradesh in 1989, when she was 22, to join the People's War Group. Before moving to Chhattisgarh in 1994, she was closely aligned with top leaders of the Maoist movement. Her political journey led to her studying Tamil, Kannada, Marathi, Hindi, Gondi, and Halbi. She moved to Dandakaranya in 1994 to learn about forest texture and forest group cultures and their organic relationships. She endeared herself to tribal groups as a fast learner in their ways of living. In her political and cultural education, Bastar became her turf. She became an area commander in 1998. She was a prominent female leader of the militant movement for five years. The Government of Chhattisgarh slapped 159 cases on Nirmala (Karnam, 2019).

In what is currently the fiercest guerrilla region, the rebels have long formed a front organization for women, the Dandakaranya Adivasi Mahila Sangh. All women recruited by the Maoists are forced to undergo tubectomy so that they cannot become pregnant, for having children is considered a burden on the *dalam* (a term used for a unit of Naxalites). The operation is performed by in-house physicians. It is appropriate for women to marry, but only within the *dalam*. If there are two suitors, the woman does not have a say. Her fate is determined by either the *dalam* leader or the men themselves. Women do not leave the scene during gunfights with security forces till all the male members of the *dalam* have fled.

Many girls and women, being at an impressionable age, got carried away by the exhortations of visiting Maoist squads through the speeches and the revolutionary songs provided by the cultural troupes. Some women were persuaded by family members to join the movement. For example, Komarayya's wife, Anasuya, a member of the North Telangana Special Zone Committee (NTSZC), which the rebels once depicted as their flagship guerrilla zone, followed in the footsteps of her husband leaving her toddler son behind in the care of her in-laws; the child later passed away.

Nelakonda Rajitha was a student leader of an undergraduate firebrand in Karimnagar district. She came into contact with Sande Rajamouli, who later became a member of the apex and all-powerful Central Committee and Central Military Council, and married her. Rajitha was killed in a July 2002 encounter and Rajamouli was killed in June 2007. There is no single clear explanation as to why women entered the Maoist ranks. Due to desperation, many joined the underground movement. Another explanation is corruption at the hands of the high and mighty in the village. A 14-year-old girl, Narsingojula Padma, ran away from home into the Maoist fold in January 2004 in Karimnagar district, in an effort to escape marriage against her wishes. She became a soldier's girl. The Maoists were pressured by protests from parents and villagers and they finally let her go. In Dandakaranya, the deliberate efforts of the Maoist organization to put an end to different aspects of patriarchy also helped women join either underground or mass organizations. The Maoists had largely succeeded in putting an end to forced marriages, cousin marriages, and the tradition of *gotul* (*gotul* is central to social and religious life in Gond society and girls and boys interact here before marriage to meet their prospective spouses).

While doing a project on the education of tribal youths for the Government of Andhra Pradesh (2005–10), we visited three camps set up for the tribal children. Here we met four girls who had joined the Naxal movement and had returned to join the mainstream. They thought having a gun in their hands was very empowering. But when faced with the hardships, they decided to come back to their families. They had to walk in the jungles for months together, hiding themselves, amidst the fear of being shot by the police. They could not bathe for weeks and there was no routine in their daily life with no proper time for food or rest. They also told us that it was the men who were very important in all aspects of the movement and the girls had to just follow their orders (Pande, 2017).

The novelty of the Telangana movement lies in the fact that it witnessed an armed struggle against feudal powers six decades ago guided by its own economic and social agenda which was joined by a large number of women. Six decades back, mainly leftist movements were fighting for Telangana's peasants to introduce agrarian and tenancy reforms. The student movement raised a banner for a separate Telangana state five decades ago. It was the epicentre of the nation's most vibrant civil liberties movement four decades ago and was home to the Marxist–Leninist *rythu coolie udyamam*, programmes against landlordism.

The fourth phase: The anti-arrack movement (1990–95)

The 1990s saw another very powerful movement of rural poor women, who were facing a lot of violence in their daily lives because their men were drinking arrack (liquor). Rural women in Andhra Pradesh, who for centuries had been marginalized from every sphere of life, were totally illiterate, exploited by the landlords, and targets of domestic and social violence. They suddenly rose in revolt and were able to change the existing government (Pande, 2000). They had pinpointed the root cause of domestic violence and hence had a simple demand, 'No selling and drinking of liquor in our village'. This demand led to an agitation, which soon became a movement involving thousands of women which spread to the urban areas also. This agitation brought in hitherto remote areas and both topographically and politically marginalized areas to the centre of political discussions and soon its waves could be felt in other states also. It focused on an issue hitherto considered private and brought domestic violence to a public platform.

In Andhra Pradesh, the Naxalites and the Left-wing militants made anti-liquor agitation a part of their land movement. The connection of politicians with the arrack business was also formed (Balagopal, 1992). Due to the Varun Vahini (flooding of liquor) programme, liquor and arrack were brought in plastic sachets to the very doorstep of the households. Men spent nearly 75 per cent of their incomes on drinking. Liquor emerged as a major source of revenue without displeasing the rich (Reddy, 1993).

The space provided by adult literacy classes was the reason why women could voice their concerns. The National Literacy Mission (NLM) programme was officially launched in Nellore district on January 2, 1990, after intensive planning for four months and was adopted in January 1991. To spread literacy, it adopted a campaign approach and instead of only teaching alphabets, a three-pronged approach was implemented which included writing of primers based on women's day-to-day experiences, getting the women to a common platform by building sheds for meetings, and using cultural fora to spread the message of literacy. After several debates and discussions by the women sitting in these sheds, the primers were written first.

There were three primers used by the women. One of these was *Seeta Katha* that had the story of Seeta, who committed suicide after not being able to stop her husband from drinking. In the discussion that followed, many women realized that they were also dealing with the same issue at home and had often thought of suicide, and the only reason they had not taken this step was because of their children. Soon all the women resolved to fight the evil of drinking and ensure that there were no drunks left in the village. These women had a very simple solution: the men would not get liquor and thus would not drink if the arrack shops were closed. The next day, these women marched together and were able to shut down the arrack shop in their village and the men were unable to get a drink.

This incident was followed by another lesson, *Adavallu Ekamaite* (if women unite), on how women closed arrack shops in their villages. The lessons in these primers had an electrifying effect on women. In several other villages, women thought that if women had succeeded in Dubagunta, so could they. Women's committees were created in many villages. They first attempted to stop their husbands and other male relatives from drinking, but found that this was a difficult task till the liquor shops in the villages continued to exist. Their struggle entered a new phase beyond the villages and it involved the contractors, the excise department, and the state itself. The women wanted to know why there was no drinking water, children's schools, or decent wages in their villages, but plenty of arrack shops? Why did they get drinking water once in two days but arrack was supplied twice a day? Why was the state so intent on providing arrack? When answers to these questions were sought, the anti-arrack agitation quickly became a movement and it spread like fire across the state because everywhere women were familiar with domestic violence due to liquor. Three districts – Nellore,

Chittoor, and Kurnool – took the lead, spreading into the Hyderabad and Secunderabad urban areas.

The contractors did not take the movement seriously in the beginning. They strongly felt that this was a temporary phase and soon the movement would die a natural death and they would be able to open the arrack shops. However, when the struggle spread to many villages the contractors were alarmed and started attacking the women and filed police cases against them. They gave a memorandum to the government to reduce the costs which they had to pay to the government. They also filed a writ petition in the High Court against their loss of livelihood. The excise commissioner ordered the district administration to re-open the arrack shops. Throughout the agitation the government held the stand that it was not possible to close arrack shops because the revenue from these was utilized for welfare schemes. Women of Nellore district were not convinced with the argument that the government could not run welfare schemes like rice for Rs 2 per kg till it received money from arrack sales.

The police and other government machinery were surprised at the joint front led by the women and the courage they were showing. A voluntary organization, the Progressive Organization of Women (Stree Vimukthi), stepped in and initiated a programme of closing arrack shops in the villages. They campaigned throughout the district by conducting meetings, processions, and dharnas. The women realized that their misery would not be over just by interfering in the auctions of arrack but they had to see that no arrack reached the villages and this was possible only with the closure of arrack shops. They explained to the people that once arrack was not available the men would not drink.

The women had become very revolutionary and vocal in stopping the sale of liquor. The liquor barons in the district were shocked at seeing the anti-arrack movement gain momentum. They feared that this was questioning their authority and it would break their traditional hold over their fiefdom. They tried to deal with the agitators. They sent their henchmen to attack the women agitators. They even threatened the husbands asking them to control their wives and restrict their activities. Sometimes, they showed a stick and sometimes a carrot to woo the women. Women came out openly and spoke against the faction leaders and criticized them. They stated that they would not sit back and rest until all the *sara* shops were closed in their villages. By now, the women had realized that their strength was in their collective, and with this newly discovered strength they were ready to take on the local goons, the arrack contractors, the police, the government officials, and the state (Pande, 2000).

Finally, the government had to bow down to the pressure and it took the bold decision of banning arrack from October 1, 1993, even bearing a revenue loss of more than Rs 600 crores. The women's groups were happy but soon they saw their struggle come to naught. As a result of the ban on arrack, in the following year there was a substantial increase in the consumption of toddy, which was not banned. To give enough kick it was soon adulterated with drugs like diazepam or chemicals like chloral hydrate. All these had lethal side effects. Since Indian-Made Foreign Liquor (being marketed by the government) was not banned, the number of wine shops selling these increased. Thus, the banning of arrack made no difference in reality. The women felt that their struggle had in reality not achieved much.

Soon many women's groups felt that unless there was total prohibition, nothing much could be achieved. All the women now agreed to take up this issue under a common platform irrespective of any particular ideology. A joint action forum was formed with the demand for total prohibition. The movement started again.

On October 2, 1994, women activists of Hyderabad decided that they would go and picket. Elections to the state were held in December and the Telugu Desam Party (TDP) was elected with a thumping majority with 214 seats in an assembly of 294. On December 12, 1994, at the swearing in ceremony, N.T. Rama Rao reiterated his commitment to total prohibition and declared that from January 1, 1995, the state would follow total prohibition. The women had achieved their victory. Private violence, which had started as a small agitation in a village, soon became a movement and spread to other districts (Pande, 2002).

Meanwhile through a coup within the party, Chief Minister N.T. Rama Rao's son-in-law N. Chandrababu Naidu who was also a member of the cabinet wrested power from his father-in-law blaming him to be very arrogant and dictatorial. The new government of N. Chandrababu Naidu again found itself in a Catch 22 situation. It could not give up on prohibition and annoy the women who had supported it wholeheartedly, nor could it deal with the worsening financial situation after the loss of revenue on liquor. The period following this saw an increase in water cess, electricity charges, and other taxes and every one blamed the women and the prohibition for these developments.

Opinions on the prohibition policy were divided. Women's groups felt that this policy had brought in a lot of changes in the rural areas and violence against women in the domestic sphere had reduced. There was an increase in savings and the living standard of the people had improved. Another equally strong lobby felt that the government had no right to impose its rules and regulations on individual social habits. Questions were raised on the freedom of the people to decide for themselves. They did not like the heavy financial burden of the state being passed on to individuals through heavy taxation. Soon the government policy on liquor began to sag and prohibition was lifted in a phased manner from November 1995 and today there is no prohibition in the state, though the prices of liquor are very high when compared to some other states. What is interesting is that the lessons, which sparked the agitation, are no longer a part of the texts used for literacy.

Just because the state went back on prohibition did not mean that women did not achieve much. Once total prohibition was achieved, women's collectives dispersed. Women could not continue the same kind of momentum forever when the prohibition policy was lifted in a staged manner. Women found that they lacked support from other quarters once a political party appropriated the movement. Many of the Left-wing groups and other political parties distanced themselves from this movement because it was no longer a women's achievement but of a political party. The state may have withdrawn the ban but it was done in a very defensive manner. The greatest achievement of the movement was in creating the necessary awareness, raising consciousness among the women in the countryside to take control of their lives, and creating a line of grassroots leadership (Pande, 2019).

The fifth phase: The modern-day Telangana struggle and formation of a new state (1969–2014)

The Telangana movement is not recent. In 1969, both boys and girl students from Osmania University, Kakatiya University, and other colleges participated under the Jai Telangana movement, making it one of the bloodiest students 'movements for more than 360 people died in police firing. Many women actively participated in this. Sadhalaxmi, Shanthabhai, Sumitradevi were the members and Sangam Laxmibhai, Parliament leader was also the member' (Gandhi, 2010, p. 83). On April 12, 1969, after several days of talks with representatives from both the regions, the Prime Minister established an Eight Point Strategy. M. Chenna Reddy formed the political party Telangana Praja Samithi (TPS) in 1969 to spearhead the statehood movement. The Adivasis of the Telangana region have a history of resistance against all forms of hegemony and they provided vital support for the movement.

In 1999, K. Prathibha Bharathi was unanimously elected as the House Speaker by the 11th Andhra Pradesh state and was the first woman to be chosen to this position. On International Women's Day, the Andhra Pradesh state took up many new measures such as providing all women legislators with a Zero Hour opportunity. By congratulating eight women from various walks of life as 'Agents of Change' in appreciation of their exemplary service to society with devotion and zeal, the 13th Andhra Pradesh state paid them some lip service and gave them recognition. By and large women were now no longer on the forefront. The demands for a separate Telangana state, however, persisted and many parties supported this demand. Before the general elections in 2009, the Bharatiya Janata Party (BJP) declared that if it won the elections, it would create two more states, Telangana and Gorkhaland.

Though women participated in all these movements they were pushed to the background as these movements were patriarchal. Women won few victories in the beginning but these were subsumed under the larger movement and only men emerged in leadership roles. Under the broader concept of class struggle, however, the question of gender equality has always taken a backseat.

The sixth phase: Post-2014 onwards

The new state of Telangana was formed on June 2, 2014, but women were by and large absent in the government. Various political parties' slogans about empowering Indian women in politics seem to have remained just lip service. A case in point is low representation of women in the Lok Sabha and the hurdles in the way of passing the Women's Reservation Bill. While almost all political parties immediately declared that they were supportive of the Constitution (108th Amendment) Bill, first introduced by the United Front government of H.D. Deve Gowda in Parliament in 1996, widely referred to as the Women's Reservation Bill, in reality nothing much has been done.

K. Kavitha was the first woman parliamentarian from Telangana in the 16th Lok Sabha and she was a Member of Parliament from the Nizamabad Lok Sabha constituency from 2014 to 2019. She was given a ticket as she was the daughter of the Chief Minister. However, in the 17th Lok Sabha, which began in 2019, only one of the six women candidates from the three major political parties in Telangana was elected. Maloth Kavitha, the TRS candidate from Mahabubabad, won a Lok Sabha seat, and she did so by nearly 1,45,740 votes over her Congress opponent. Andhra Pradesh sent four women members to the Parliament from Andhra Pradesh to the 17th Lok Sabha.

The 2009 state elections saw a higher allocation of seats for women. There were more than 200 female candidates in the fray, with almost every political party offering tickets to women. It is noteworthy that in most constituencies, not many women had to compete against each other as men were their main opponents. Thirty-six women won, and six women were inducted into the cabinet when the government was formed. The home ministry was given to a woman for the first time. Other significant portfolios, including mining, were also given to women. Again, this was the first time women were entrusted with portfolios other than those connected with customary welfare: welfare of women, welfare of girls, social welfare, and so on. Of the 36 women elected in the 2009 elections, 16 were from the region of Telangana; the home minister was from the same region as well.

However, women have by and large got a raw deal after that. Telangana is being ruled by T. Kalvakuntla Chandrashekar Rao's government. He was elected the first Chief Minister of Telangana, following the elections in which the Telangana Rashtra Samithi (TRS) Party got a majority and he was elected for the second term too.

In the 2014 polls, the Congress gave only 11 tickets to women (11 per cent) while the ruling TRS offered just four seats to women (4 per cent). While three women candidates from Congress and six women candidates from TRS made it to the Telangana assembly in these elections, every political party conveniently forgot its pledge of reservations for and promotion of women in politics by the time the 2018 state elections came around. Only five women got elected – two from Congress and three from TRS. While Congress fielded 11 women candidates, its alliance partners TDP, TJS, and CPI fielded one woman candidate each. Overall, the Congress-led alliance People's Front fielded 14 women candidates while the BJP fielded 14 women candidates and the Bahujan Left Front 11 candidates, including a transwoman candidate Chandramukhi from Goshamahal. A considerable number of women, however, contested as independent candidates, put off by the political parties' attitudes. Thus, 135 women stood for elections, making up less than 10 per cent of the 1,821 candidates in the fray.

Women representing the Congress-led front put up a tough battle and lost to their rivals by very narrow margins. BJP candidates, both males and females, did not do well. No seats were held by any of the women who stood as independent candidates. In the 119-member Telangana assembly, women's representation fell to 5 per cent from 7.5 per cent, as only six women made it to the assembly in 2018. All six of them are from TRS and the Congress, the two main political parties. In the previous assembly, which was dissolved by Chief Minister K. Chandrasekhar Rao, there were nine women and none of them made it to Telangana's first cabinet. In comparison to 85 in 2014, 136 women contested the 2018 polls (*The News Minute*, 2018). The recent elections to the state in Telangana, reduced women's representation in the legislature to less than 5 per cent, with only 6 of the 135 women winning the elections. This is just half the national level for women's representation in legislative bodies. Eleven women candidates were chosen by Congress, three of whom won. Telangana had two women ministers for the first time when KCR expanded the cabinet in September 2019.

In many constituencies in Telangana, women voters outnumbered men, but very few women obtained election tickets. It is a fact that during its first legislative assembly elections, women were poorly represented in India's youngest state, and the situation only deteriorated in 2018. The granddaughter of Telugu Desam Party's founder N.T. Rama Rao, Nandamuri Suhasini, who contested from Kukatpally, was defeated despite there being more women voters in some of the state's vital constituencies. If we look at the electoral rolls published by the Election Commission, in many constituencies female voters outnumbered male voters such as in Sircilla (from which KCR's son and former minister K.T. Rama Rao contested), Siddipet

Conclusion

It is fascinating to see how, parallelly but on different roads, the campaign for independent statehood and advocacy for women in politics have travelled and each has contributed to the other. It is a very sad state of affairs but only those women have made it into the echelons of power who are connected to some male politicians, being their daughters, sisters, or mothers.

A few women have consistently raised the issue of whether the new state would guarantee women a safer Telangana. The question was not answered then, but after the establishment of the state, some small attempts were made to counter gender-based violence. A women's safety committee, headed by an IAS officer, Poonam Malakondayya, made some recommendations, but most of them were never followed up. Another proposal was to raise the government's cash gift to girls from Rs 50,000 to Rs 1 lakh at the time of marriage. Significantly, however, no special programme to support women's education was launched. Meanwhile, in every other survey/statistical study published by the government and non-governmental organizations, Telangana continues to show up as one of the top places in the country that is unsafe for women in terms of both gender violence and discrimination based on gender.

To conclude, there were no deliberate attempts to reinforce female leadership after the state of Telangana emerged as an independent state. The Telangana movement was overwhelmingly patriarchal. Women have always been considered secondary and have been overlooked. That is why, unlike among males, we do not see any prominent female faces. Only a few women, related to male politicians, have been noticed, but no one has been given a significant position in politics. In many movements under the broader concept of class struggle, the question of gender equality has always taken a backseat and Telangana is no exception.

Hundreds of women supporters of Telangana were a part of the marches, dharnas, and road and rail blockades during the struggle. There were no direct gains which the women got out of these struggles but they did gain indirectly. Women have become aware of their abilities and capacity to change society. The agendas of the women's groups were not covered by any detailed preparation. Depending on the case, women took action on the spot and devised their own strategies to deal with issues.

Women contributed significantly to the struggle for the creation of the state of Telangana but they were marginalized in state politics when the state emerged as an independent state and power continued to be in the hands of the men.

Bibliography

Balagopal, K. (1992). 'Slaying of a Spirituous Demon', *Economic and Political Weekly*, 27 (46), November 14, pp. 2457–2461.

Briggs, Henry George (1861a). *The Nizam Vol. 1*. London: Bernard Quaritch. Available at: https://archive.org/details/nizamhishistoryr01brig/page/n7/mode/2up?view=theater, accessed on June 13, 2022.

——— (1861b). *The Nizam Vol. II*. London: Bernard Quaritch. Available at: https://archive.org/details/dli.bengal.10689.7583/page/n7/mode/2up, accessed on June 13, 2022.

Country Report (1995). *Fourth World Conference on Women and Child Development*. New Delhi: Ministry of Human Resources Development.

Desai, A. R. (1969). *Rural Sociology in India*. Bombay: Popular Prakashan.

Gandhi, Shoba (2010). *Prathyeka Telangana UdyamaCharithra*, (Telegu), as quoted by KommineniVeeranna in the PhD thesis, 'The role of Dalit bahujans in the political movements of separate state of Telangana 1969–2011', Kakatiya University.

Hyder, Mohammed (2012). *October Coup, A Memoir of the Struggle for Hyderabad*.New Delhi: Roli Books.

Karnam, Murali (2019). 'Battered but Not Broken: The Story of a Woman Naxal', *The Wire*, April 10. Available at: https://thewire.in/rights/battered-but-not-broken-the-story-of-a-woman-naxal, accessed on June 13, 2022.

Khusro, A. M. (1958). *Economic and Social Effects of Jagirdari Abolition and Land Reform in Hyderabad*. Bombay: Orient Longman.

Kodandaram, M. (2009). 'Telangana Marginalised,' *The New Indian Express*, December 8. Available at: https://www.newindianexpress.com/states/andhra-pradesh/2009/dec/08/telangana-marginalised-110966.html, accessed on June 13, 2022.

Lalita. K., Vasantha Kannabiran, Rama Melkote, Uma Maheshwari, Susie Tharu, and Veena Shatrugna, (1989). *We Were Making History: Life Stories of Women in the Telangana People's Struggle*. London: Zed Books.

Mehender, Adepu (2017). 'Bairanpalle Stands Witness to a Gory Past', *The Hans India*. August 28. Available at: https://www.thehansindia.com/posts/index/Commoner/2017-08-28/Bairanpalle-stands-witness-to-gory-past/322100, accessed on June 13, 2022.

The News Minute (2018). Available at: https://www.thenewsminute.com/article/representation-women-telangana-assembly-reduces-5-percent-93252, accessed October 17, 2020.

Pande, Rekha (2000). 'From Anti Arrack to Total Prohibition: The Women's Movement in Andhra Pradesh, India', in *Gender Technology and Development*, 4 (1), 131–141.

——— (2002). 'The Public Face of a Private Domestic Violence', *International Feminist Journal of Politics*, 4(3), 342–367.

——— (2005). 'Solidarity, Patriarchy and Empowerment- Women's Struggle Against Arrack in India', in Luciana Ricciutelli, Angela Miles, and Margaret

M. Mcfadden (eds), *Feminist Politics, Activism and Vision,- Local and Global Challenges* (pp. 212–226). New York: Zed Publications.

——— (2017). 'Mainstreaming Tribal Youth in Andhra Pradesh Through Education: A Case Study', *Journal of Tribal, Folk and Subaltern Studies*, IV (1), 1–30.

——— (2019). 'Emergence of Grass Root Leadership Among Women in the Fight Against Arrack (Liquor)', in Araceli Alonso and Teresa Langle de Paz (eds), *The Time is Now: Feminist Leadership for a New Era* (pp. 86–93). Wisconsin-Madison: University of Wisconsin-Madison.

Pande, Rekha and J. Kameshwari (1987), '*Women's Discourse on Education: A Preliminary Readings of the Speeches Delivered at the Annual Conference of Andhra Mahila Sabha (1913 and 1914)*', in Proceedings of Indian History Congress, Goa, pp. 390–396.

Pande, Rekha, K. C. Bindu, and Viqar Atiya (2007). 'Remade Womanhoods, Refashioned Modernities: The Construction of Good Woman Hood in Annisa an Early 20th Century Women's Magazine in Urdu', in Shafquat Towheed (ed.), *New Readings in the Literature of British India- C. 1780–1947* (pp. 147–172). Columbia University Press.

Pavier, B. (1981). *The Telangana Movement: 1944–51*. New Delhi: Vikas Publishing House.

Reddy, Narasimha D. and Arun Patnaik (1993). 'Anti Arrack Agitation of Women in A.P.', *Economic and Political Weekly*, 28 (21), 1059–1066.

Sinha, Shanta (1989). *Maoists in Andhra Pradesh*. New Delhi: Gyan Publishing House.

Sundarayya, Putchalapalli (1972). *Telangana People's Struggle and Its Lessons*. Calcutta: Communist Party of India (Marxist).

Sundarayya, Putchalapalli (2006). 'Women in the Telangana Movement', in *Telangana Peoples Struggle and Its Lessons* (pp. 246–265). New Delhi Foundation Books.

Towards Equality (1974). *Report on the Committee on the Status of Women*. New Delhi: Ministry of Education and Social Welfare, Government of India.

Xavier, Sreedevi M. (2012), 'Women In Telangana Peasant Movement: An Exploration In Sociology of Literature', *International Journal of Scientific Research*, 1 (4), pp.132–134.

9

WOMEN IN GOA'S POLITICS

The need for fast tracking to achieve gender equality

Alaknanda Shringare

Introduction

The Constitution declares India as a 'Union of States' and each state has shown considerable variations in its politics since independence. The party system and leadership have been changing but what remains unchanged across all states is women's entry into formal politics.

Goa was under Portuguese rule for over 450 years. It was liberated on December 19, 1961, and remained a Union Territory till statehood was achieved in May 1987. Goa witnessed a large number of women participating in the liberation movement but their entry into formal politics remained marginal in the post-liberation period. Goa has good socioeconomic parameters for women with a low infant mortality rate, a high literacy rate, and a better sex ratio as compared to the all-India level. However, when it comes to women's participation in formal politics it is no different from the other states. Patriarchy and gender stereotypes make entry of women in formal politics difficult.

Post-liberation Goa

After liberation, Goa faced many challenges. On the political front, it faced the issue of merger with Maharashtra. The two regional parties Maharashtrawadi Gomantak Party (MGP) and the United Goans Party (UGP) which played an important role in state politics were formed during this period. MGP was formed with the objective of merging Goa with Maharashtra while UGP was formed to retain Goa as a separate state. In a historic 'opinion poll' on January 16, 1967, the merger issue was resolved when the people of Goa voted against the merger. While the Congress formed the first government in most of the states in India, in Goa the first government was formed by a regional party.

MGP formed the first government under the leadership of Dayanand Bandodkar which remained in power for almost two decades. UGP was the

176

DOI: 10.4324/9781003374862-10

main opposition party. MGP also gave Goa its first woman Chief Minister, Shashikala Kakodkar, who came to power after her father, Dayanand Bandodkar's death.

The challenges before the state were different on the economic front. There were no major industries in Goa at the time of its liberation and agricultural productivity was also low. Though MGP gave Goa its first woman Chief Minister, the state's efforts in the initial years were mainly directed towards economic development while gender equality took a backseat. The state gave impetus to setting up new industries and it also explored development of mining and tourism as options which could contribute to its economy. Economic development continued to remain a major concern of subsequent governments. With the emergence of coalition politics in the post-statehood period, political competition increased manifold. Party hopping became a common feature of Goan politics with every government, political party, and leader struggling to maintain itself in power. In such a scenario, no serious efforts were made either by the government or by the political parties to ensure women's entry into politics.

Goa's gender profile

Goa has high socioeconomic parameters for women. Its sex ratio is 973 which is higher than the national average of 940 as per Census 2011. In 2001, Goa's sex ratio was 961 (Census, 2011) and female literacy was 85 per cent. Goa was also reported to have a low infant mortality rate of eight deaths per 1,000 live births in 2016 (NITI Aayog, 2019).

As per the Periodic Labour Force Survey (PLFS, 2019) of the 50 per cent labour force participation rate (15 years and above) in Goa, 70 per cent were male and 30.9 per cent were female (Ministry of Statistics, 2019). More women in rural areas are working as casual labourers while a sizeable number of women in urban areas are regular wage or salaried employees.

However, these indicators alone are no guarantee that women's condition is better in Goa compared to the rest of India. The question instead is how far this gets translated into their increased representation in the legislative assembly and Parliament? Past experience shows a negligible presence of women in Goan politics.

Women's role in the liberation movement

The 450 years of Portuguese rule gave Goa a unique identity. A system of indirect elections was introduced by the Portuguese in Goa in 1822–51. In 1860, the first direct elections took place in the state. However, franchise was limited to the educated and tax-paying elite men. According to Pais (2017) till the nineteenth century, women's participation in politics was a non-issue in Portugal. It was only in 1933 that the Portuguese government passed a law which allowed educated women a right to vote in Portugal but this was not extended to Goa. Goan women enjoyed their voting rights only after 1961 when Goa was liberated from Portuguese rule.

Women were active participants in Goa's freedom struggle. The beginning was made by Sarubai Vaidya who brought out a Marathi-Portuguese monthly for women called *Haldikumkum* in 1910 (Salgaonkar, 2000, p. 38). Other prominent women in the struggle were Premilabai Zambaulikar, Berta Braganca, Sasikala Hardorkar, Asha Phade, and Vilasini Prabhu. Kakodkar (1986) categorizes the nature and extent of women's participation at three levels. Firstly, a small group of women participated in all aspects of the national freedom struggle. Berta Menezes Braganca is a prominent name among this group of women. Secondly, a group of women who got involved with only one particular aspect of the national struggle and a third group of women who participated in political meetings, *prabhat pheris*, and also became satyagrahis. The first confrontation that the Goan women had with the Portuguese police was on June 18, 1946, the day Ram Manohar Lohia addressed a public meeting in Margao (Sardesai, 1986).

Women's political participation in the post-liberation period

The Union Parliament passed the Constitution (12th Amendment) Act, 1962 on June 20, 1962, and conferred the status of a Union Territory to Goa with a 30-member assembly. The first assembly elections were held in 1963 and were historic with seven women contesting and Urminda Lima Leitao Mascarenhas achieving the distinction of becoming the first woman MLA in the assembly (*The Times of India*, 2017a). Later in the 1967 assembly elections not a single woman contested. Many women were active in social life during this period but their political participation was mainly restricted to voting. Women who had actively participated in the freedom struggle and worked equally with men were not equally represented in Goa's legislative assembly in the post-liberation period. The number of women contesting elections increased only after 1984. In 1984, for the first time, ten women contested the elections but unfortunately not a single one got elected. One of the reasons for this could be that out of the ten women who contested, seven contested as independent candidates. One each contested on BJP, CPM, and Janata Party tickets.

Over a period of time, there has been an increase in the number of women contesting assembly elections (Table 9.1). From 7 in 1963 to 26 in the assembly elections in 2022 there has been a gradual increase in the number of women contesting elections. However, the same is not witnessed in more women getting elected to the state assembly. Since the first assembly elections (1963) not more than two women candidates have been elected to the Goa assembly, except for the 1994 assembly elections, when out of the ten women candidates who contested the elections, four were elected. In the

WOMEN IN GOA'S POLITICS

Table 9.1 Gender-wise data of candidates contesting the Goa assembly elections

Year	Contested (Men)	Won (Men)	Contested (Women)	Won (Women)
1963	–	30	7*	1*
1967	226	29	0	1
1972	132	30	6	0
1977	141	29	4	1
1980	174	30	3	0
1984	232	30	10	0
1989	243	38	8	2
1994	301	36	10	4
1999	200	38	10	2
2002	201	39	11	1
2007	188	39	14	1
2012	196	38	10	2
2017	224	38	19	2
2022**	275	37	26	3

Source: Compiled from www.eci.ac.in, accessed on January 12, 2019.
* https://timesofindia.indiatimes.com/city/goa/53-years-on-women-yet-to find-footing-in-goa-assembly/articleshow/57525646.cms, accessed on January 12, 2019.
** 2022 election data retrieved from www.eci.in, accessed on March 14, 2022.

2022 assembly elections, three women candidates were elected which is an increase over the last five elections. Deviya Rane won with the highest vote share among all the candidates who contested in 2022.

The 2017 assembly elections saw more women contesting (Table 9.1). The highest number of women candidates (five) was fielded by the Aam Aadmi Party (AAP) which contested the assembly elections in Goa for the first time. Congress gave tickets to three women candidates of whom one was victorious. Alina Saldanha was the sole woman candidate contesting on a BJP ticket from the Cortalim constituency. During the election campaign for the 2017 assembly elections, she had told the press that as the only elected woman candidate from her party 'it does get little lonely sometimes' (*The Times of India*, 2017b). The same newspaper reported a statement made by the then Chief Minister Laxmikant Parsekar who believed it was easy to give party tickets to women candidates but getting them elected was a challenge because people in Goa wanted their MLAs at their doorstep to fix their problems from electricity to water and help when someone in the family was not well, which was difficult for women to do (*The Times of India*, 2017b).

He further added that it would take another ten years for women to make a mark in politics. The Congress Party's response to the issue was that it was up to the women to come forward and take part in politics and it was ready to give tickets to women candidates if they were found to be viable. There is reluctance on the part of political parties to give tickets to

179

women. The winnability of women candidates is always questioned by the political parties.

The story is no different when it comes to parliamentary elections. Sanyogita Rane of MGP was the first woman to become a Member of Parliament from Goa in 1980. In the 1980 Lok Sabha elections, Shashikala Kakodkar played an active role in ensuring the victory of MGP candidate Sanyogita Rane Sardesai from the North Goa constituency. Sanyogita Rane was the only woman elected to Parliament from Goa.

The two national parties which played an important role in the politics of the state after MGP's downfall have not given party tickets to women candidates to contest in the Lok Sabha elections from any of the two Lok Sabha seats in the state. Though women candidates contested almost all Lok Sabha elections but they did not get elected, as the chances of any candidate contesting from a party other than the BJP or Congress are almost nil.

Since 1987 the state is sending one representative to the Rajya Sabha but till today not a single woman from Goa has become a member of the Rajya Sabha. It is also important to note that most of the women candidates who were able to make it in Goa's politics had their families either rooted in politics or actively involved in social life.

Any discussion on women in Goa's politics is incomplete without a mention of Shashikala Kakodkar, the first woman Chief Minister of Goa and Mridula Sinha, the first woman Governor of Goa. Both of them left their mark on Goa's politics.

Shashikala Kakodkar was sworn in as the Chief Minister of Goa in 1973. Initially seen as Bandodkar's daughter she soon carved out her own image in state politics. Her experience of participating in Goa's liberation movement, social work, and political affairs benefitted her. She contested the assembly elections in 1967 on a MGP ticket and won by a huge margin. During her tenure, she focused on health, education, and provision of drinking water facilities in the state, apart from which her tenure is also known for the enactment of the Goa, Daman and Diu Mundkars (Protection from Eviction) Act and amendments to the Tenancy Act (Biography, n.d.).

Shashikala Kakodkar faced criticism from within and outside her party. After MGP's defeat in the 1980 assembly elections, she joined the Congress but soon resigned and formed her own party, the Bhausaheb Bandodkar Gomantak Party (BBGP). Later she joined MGP by merging BBGP with it. She contested all assembly elections till 2002 and was successfully elected to the assembly till the 1994 assembly elections. After her defeat in the 2002 assembly elections she did not contest any more elections.

Mridula Sinha's entry into Goa's politics as the first woman Governor was a welcome development. She served as the Governor from August 2014 to October 2019. She was also the first Governor to open the gates of the Governor's residence to the public. She had vast experience in political and administrative fields. She was also a renowned Hindi writer. Being an ambassador of the Swachh Bharat Mission appointed by Prime Minister Narendra Modi, she held the view that cleanliness should be part of our culture and declared 2016 as the year of cleanliness in Goa.

Mridula Sinha emphasized the need for creating a single identity for women as Indian women and maintained that a common civil code will strengthen this singular identity (*The Statesman*, 2017). She also initiated a unique project 'The Constitution Week', a week-long celebration every year in January, to popularize constitutional values and ideals among common people of Goa. She also stressed the need of making the Constitution available in the mother tongue. She faced criticism for inviting the BJP to form the government while it was not the single largest party in the House after the 2017 assembly elections.

Women as voters

While women's political representation in the legislative assembly has been limited to 5–10 per cent, there has been a tremendous increase in their participation by way of voting as compared to men. Since 2007 more women have voted compared to men (Table 9.2). Out of the 80 per cent voter turnout witnessed in the 2022 assembly elections, 51 per cent were women voters. However, this increase in the number of women voters is not getting translated into more women candidates getting elected. Despite the fact that more women are voting compared to men, women are not emerging as a political constituency in the state. Women candidates mobilize voters as party members by following their party's ideology and policies.

Table 9.2 Voting percentage in the Goa assembly elections

Year	Male	Female	Total
1963	–	–	–
1967	69.12	67.42	68.25
1972	69.01	69.30	69.16
1977	64.69	61.75	63.22
1980	70.12	68.89	69.51
1984	71.68	72.03	71.86
1989	73.50	71.42	72.47
1994	71.73	70.65	71.20
1999	66.78	63.15	65.00
2002	69.87	67.61	68.75
2007	69.70	70.30	70.51
2012	78.86	84.57	81.73
2017	78.40	83.94	81.21
2022*	78.15	80.96	79.59

Source: Compiled from www.eci.ac.in, accessed on January 20, 2019.
*2022 data retrieved from www.eci.ac.in, accessed on June 14, 2022.

No political party can neglect women voters who can make a difference to election results. Both the Congress and BJP governments have started various schemes for women. Some of the well-known schemes are Mamata, Griha Aadhar, and Ladli Laxmi schemes. The Mamata scheme provides Rs 25,000 to mothers who deliver a female child and who have been living in Goa for at least three years irrespective of their social/economic status (*The Indian Express*, 2018). Griha Aadhar provides financial assistance of Rs 1,000 per month to women whose gross family income is less than Rs 3 lakh (*The Economic Times*, 2012). The amount was increased to Rs 1,500 per month in 2016. One lakh rupees is given to a girl child under the Ladli Laxmi scheme once she turns 18. Initially the money was provided to meet marriage expenses due to which it came under criticism from feminist groups in Goa. Later the scheme was modified to provide financial benefits to meet girls' educational and other expenses.

Political parties acting as gatekeepers

An important factor in an analysis of electoral quotas for women is the fact that 'political parties are the gatekeepers when it comes to nominations and elections to political posts' (Dahlerup, 2006, p. 10). It is the party that decides the candidates and their constituencies for contesting elections (Table 9.3). It has been observed that political parties are reluctant to give tickets to women candidates. Though Shashikala Kakodkar supported Sanyogita Rane to win the Lok Sabha seat she did not encourage or promote more women in politics in the state. This is also true for most of the women who got elected to the Goa assembly. They may have worked for women's welfare but a conscious effort at mobilizing and organizing more women to bring them into politics was missing.

An examination of the distribution of party tickets to women candidates of the two important political parties in Goa shows that compared to the BJP, Congress has given more preference to women candidates (Table 9.3). Only in the 2022 assembly elections did the BJP give party tickets to three women candidates. It was also the first time that most of the women contested on party tickets. Out of 26 women who contested the elections only six were independents (Table 9.4).

It is important to note the factors that hinder or determine women's entry into politics. Some aspects which make women's entry into politics difficult/ easy deserve attention. Firstly, most of the women who contest as party candidates have a family background rooted in politics which makes it easier for them to get party tickets. Thus, women representatives who get elected to the state assembly mainly belong to political families. In the 2022 assembly elections, all the three women candidates elected belonged to political families. Secondly, each party has a women's wing which tirelessly works for the party but when it comes to getting party tickets its members are often

WOMEN IN GOA'S POLITICS

Table 9.3 Party tickets given to women candidates

Year	Political Party	Number of Women Candidates Given Tickets
1989	INC	4
	BJP	0
	Independent	4
1999	INC	3
	BJP	1
	Independent	1
2002	INC	2
	BJP	1
	Independent	4
2007	INC	1
	BJP	2
	Independent	7
2012	INC	2
	BJP	0
	Independent	2
2017	INC	3
	BJP	1
	Independent	5

Source: Compiled from www.eci.gov.in, accessed on February 5, 2019.

Table 9.4 Women candidates in the 2022 assembly elections

Party	Women Candidates
INC	2
BJP	3
AAP	3
TMC	4
Shiv Sena	2
RGP	2
SBP	2
GSP	1
MGP	1
Independents	6

Source: ECI website: https://affidavit.eci.gov.in/CandidateCustomFilter, accessed on March 14, 2022.

neglected. Women's wings are used as agents for mobilizing people. They are at the forefront of party activities like rallies, dharnas, and campaigns. A discussion with the women representatives of political parties as well as party workers reveals that mahila wings are merely used for working for the parties but are hardly given any opportunities to contest elections.

Thirdly, as political parties are reluctant to give tickets to women candidates, many women in Goa have contested as independent candidates. This also indicates that there are many women candidates who aspire to contest elections. This is a positive development as far as women's political participation is concerned but it is found that women candidates representing a political party have higher chances of winning.

The role of money power too cannot be neglected at the time of elections. Compared to independent candidates, party candidates are in a better position to fund their elections as the party also takes up the responsibility of campaign expenditure. In the absence of reservation for women in assemblies and Parliament, women candidates have to compete with men to win elections. Most of the women candidates believe that it is very difficult to fight against the money power used by men.

It has been observed that in Goa candidates have a stronghold over some constituencies. It does not matter if the candidate changes party loyalties. Men's or families' stronghold over constituencies makes women's entry impossible unless they are from the same family as happened in Taleigao constituency where Atanasio Monserrate made his wife contest the elections and Poriem which was represented by Pratapsingh Rane is now represented by Deviya Rane.

PRIs and women's political participation

With the passing of the Goa Panchayati Raj Act (GPRA) 1994, 33 per cent seats are reserved for women in PRIs in Goa. Panchayat elections were the first democratic elections to be held in Goa in 1962. Earlier one seat was reserved for women in panchayats by the Panchayat Regulations (1962).

In the 1997 panchayat elections, 445 women members were elected from the reserved wards while 33 women won from the general category (Salgaonkar, 2000, p. 104). This trend, however, did not continue for long in Goa. As per the Ministry of Panchayat Raj's (MoPR, 2008) study on elected women representatives in Panchayati Raj Institutions (PRIs), Goa was the only state which had less than 33 per cent women representatives elected to PRIs, while in all the other states this figure was more than 33 per cent. Goa which has good socioeconomic parameters for women as well as the best GDP and HDI parameters compared to other states is not able to perform well in political gender parameters.

It is interesting to note that at the panchayat level women voters outnumber men voters, in Goa. Some assertive women panchayats are also found. When women sarpanches were contacted for this study, they said they had control over gram sabha and panchayat meetings. A woman sarpanch from Gaodongrem, Canacona, revealed that she contested the elections for the first time from an open seat and got elected. This competent and married member with young children got the full support of her family members. It is also noticed that most of the women who were assertive and confident had family members as panchayat members.

However, having assertive women representatives in panchayats does not mean that there are no proxy women members in panchayats. As the wards are reserved, in many cases men who represent those wards make their wives, daughters, or daughter-in-law contest from these wards. When women get elected from these wards as first timers, they lack knowledge about the functioning of the panchayat and are termed proxy members if they take help from their family members. Women who get family support in contesting elections from reserved seats may not get the same support and encouragement when the seat is not reserved for women. This is also the reason why the women who have gained some training and knowledge about the functioning of the panchayats are usually not able to contest for a second time. However, there are a few cases when women get elected for the second time from an unreserved seat and emerge as more confident leaders.

It is easier for women whose families have been in politics to get into politics. Albertina Almeida, Goa-based advocate and social activist, believes that things will improve only when a culture of participation for women is developed at all decision-making levels. It is not possible to achieve women's equal participation at all levels unless we address the issue of the gender division of work.

Women's lived experiences

While talking to some of the women representatives it was found that there are occasions when they feel very lonely and do not know whom to look at for support. Many times men do not even recognize their presence in meetings and other gatherings. However, when asked for help, they never say no. This indicates the mindset of most of the men in politics that they think they are superior and women always need to be protected and supported. When women become assertive and demanding they do not get the same support. Women politicians, party workers, and women activists believe that women's representation in politics is a struggle. Gender stereotypes and patriarchal notions are so strongly rooted that women cannot get an equal say in politics. Politics is still very strongly male dominated where women's entry is blocked in different ways.

Women's movements

Goa is the only state which has the Uniform Civil Code and the credit for this goes to Portuguese rule. During Portuguese rule, several legislations were passed that safeguarded women's rights, especially property rights for Christian women. In 1869, the Portuguese Civil Code of 1867 was extended to the colonies which further helped in improving women's status (Gracias,

1996, p. 90). These rights were not extended to Hindu women in the early period. As a result, legislations passed by the Portuguese helped in improving the status of Christian women in particular. The Portuguese never interfered in the religious and customary traditions of Hindus due to which the laws never protected the interests of Hindu women. However, a few years later, an *Alvarado* issued in 1739 decreed that *gentios* of Old Conquest should be governed by Portuguese laws while their counterparts in New Conquest would be governed by their *Usose Costume* (Gracias, 1996, p. 95). This created further confusion as non-Christians from the Old Conquest were governed by different laws and New Conquest areas were governed by different laws.

The Civil Code ensured certain rights to women but it made wives obey their husbands in many contexts. A husband's consent was required for things like preparing a will, moving the court, and publishing her work. During this time, the Portuguese thought of extending the Civil Code to New Conquest areas also. At the request of Hindus, some of the customary practices relating to Hindu marriages and others were retained. Thus, the revised Code hardly improved the condition of Hindu women. The Civil Code (known as the Uniform Civil Code) continued after Goa's liberation. However, the Civil Code is discriminatory towards women and does not hold women as being equal to men.

Women in Goa not only played a significant role during the liberation movement but also worked towards the development of their community during the Portuguese period. Parobo (2015, p. 45) writes that women from the Gomantak Maratha Samaj played a vital role in promoting the interests of their community in Goa at the beginning of the twentieth century. He further writes that many women of the Gomantak Maratha Samaj participated and played lead roles in organizing conferences. All schools set up by the Gomantak Maratha Samaj were financed by the women from this community (Parobo, 2015, p. 45).

In the post-liberation period, movements for gender equality continued. Goa did not witness massive women's movements as such but women's groups in Goa have time and again raised various women's issues of national and state interest. Women's groups were a part of the national movement demanding equality for women in the Uniform Civil Code after the Shah Bano case. All the women's groups got together for the implementation of the Dowry Prohibition Act which was not extended to Goa. They actively supported the act banning prenatal sex determination and during the Nirbhaya case, women's groups actively participated in support of implementing various acts. There was a continuous struggle by women's groups to put a system in place for implementing the Domestic Violence Act. Most of these women's groups came together and formed Bailancho Ekvott (Women Together). Women's groups are also actively involved in demanding the women's reservation bill and raising questions related to livelihood issues.

Sabina Martins, convener of the Goa Bachao Abhiyan (GBA) and a founder member of 'Bailancho Saad', a women's organization, mentions that women were at the forefront in mobilizing people to fight against the scrapping of the Regional Plan, 2011 and also SEZs in Goa, but when it comes to representation in decision-making bodies, they have been neglected. Very few women who were a part of women's movements joined politics.

Martins observes that priorities change when one becomes part of formal politics. The demands of electoral politics are different. Politics has different rules which clash with the activities of the movements. She states that when the GBA was fighting for various causes many political groups became part of the movement but once the question of decision-making arose all these groups took different stands according to their party ideologies or preferences. Alternative groups have also been formed within GBA which has weakened the group. If women from these groups wish to join politics, they have to join one or the other political party. However, getting party tickets is very difficult for women candidates because of existing gender stereotypes and a stronghold of the patriarchal mindset. Women's winnability is always questioned by the political parties unless they have a family member (men) already in politics who can bargain for them. If women activists wish to contest as independent candidates they lack the resources and tactics to win elections.

Albertina Almeida, a women's rights activist and lawyer, believes that the women's groups in Goa have decided not to get involved in active politics. She mentions that the initial women's movements were through the All India Women's Conference (Goa Branch), an NGO functioning in Goa since 1978. There was no women's rights organization at that time in Goa. The first women's rights movement was noticed in the 1980s when the Muslim Women's Association led by Rashida Muzawar resisted extending the Shariat Act to Goa and fought to continue the Uniform Civil Code in the state. This was the first known women's rights group in Goa. Later many women's groups were formed but most of them were loose organizations mainly working in getting people together to fight for women's causes.

In July 1986, a few women, most of whom had been associated with the progressive students union or with the civil liberties movement, got together to form an informal discussion group. Many of these women were disillusioned by the patriarchal nature of the organizations that they had earlier been associated with and viewed the forming of a women's collective without a formal hierarchical organizational structure a refreshing change from those that they had had experience with (Desouza, 2009, p. 135).

Women working at different positions in different organizations realized that they had common needs and interests, so on October 12, 1986, they formed an independent organization called *Bailancho Saad* (Women's Voice). It was the outcome of continuous discussions carried out by most of the women activists who were initially part of various other movements in Goa. *Bailancho Saad* is also an outcome of the realization that women's issues are not addressed adequately by any groups, organizations, or movements in Goa.

Bailancho Saad's founding members decided that they will not participate in active politics but will fight for women's rights and raise women's issues. One of the important developments at this time was the formation of *Bailancho Ekvott* by Auda Viegas, who felt that women's active participation in politics was crucial for raising women's issues. One more important group which was formed but failed to continue its activities was *Bailancho Munch* (Women's Platform). This was mainly formed for mobilizing women to fight for their causes. Mahila mandals which are present-day self-help groups also contributed in raising women's issues.

One of the social activists pointed out that women's groups did not get support from other organizations in Goa as most of them remained patriarchal. Members of these organizations and also some political leaders believe that Goa does not need women's groups/organizations as it is the only state which has a Uniform Civil Code and women are treated equally with men. They do not see Goan women having any problems. Most of the times even those women who hold important offices do not grasp the issues raised by women's groups. One such incident mentioned by Almeida was in the mid-1980s when Goa's assembly did not have any women MLAs and the government appointed three women to represent women's interests. When one of them was approached by Almeida and her group to object to the manner in which women's images were being used for promoting tourism in Goa, they found it difficult to convince not only the MLAs but also the women who were appointed to represent the women. Almeida opined that women's groups' struggle is on but having women in the state legislative assembly is very much needed and this will happen only by reserving seats for women.

There is very little dialogue between women's movements and the women representatives and if at all it is happening it is not fruitful. This is also pointed out by Basu (2010), when she says that the women's movement has fewer links with women who command political power. Women representatives' power is limited by their party ideology and most of these women representatives have family lineage in politics which keeps them away from actively engaging with women activists and women's movements. As a result, women as a political constituency are not emerging forcefully. There is no question that the farmers' movement and caste-based, ethnic, and religious nationalist movements have all had a much bigger impact as compared to the women's movement on electoral politics (Basu, 2010, p. 179).

Conclusion

There is a need for women's groups and women representatives to actively engage in women's issues and work together to bring more women into politics. There are many aspiring women candidates in the women's wings of different political parties and also those who are part of women's movements who should be supported and encouraged to contest elections.

When women are given an opportunity, they make a difference in politics which is noticeable in the women representatives in panchayats in Goa. However, when it comes to state politics, women do not have a voice. It is not that they are not contesting but it is becoming difficult for women to contest elections in a male-dominated political scenario with a patriarchal mindset. Despite having high socioeconomic indicators, women's representation in Goa's legislative assembly is low. This incremental representation is not going to solve the problem of women's meagre representation in politics. Implementing electoral quotas for women is a way of ensuring more women in the decision-making forums of the state legislative assembly and Parliament.

Bibliography

Basu, A. (2010). 'Gender and Politics', in N. G. Jayal and P. B. Mehta (eds), *Politics in India* (pp. 168–180). New Delhi: Oxford University Press.

Biography. (n.d.). *Shashikala Kakodkar*. Available at: https://peoplepill.com/people/ shashikala-kakodkar/, accessed on April 15, 2020.

Census. (2011). Available at: http://www.census2011.co.in/census/state/goa.html, accessed on January 15, 2019.

Dahlerup, D. (2006). *Women, Quotas and Politics*. New York: Routledge.

Desouza, S. (2009). *Organizing Women for Empowerment: A Study of an Experiment in Goa*. Available at: http://shodhganga.inflibnet.ac.in/bitstream/10603/2722/15 /15_chapter%206.pdf, accessed on April 11, 2019.

Freedman, J. (2002). *Feminism*. New Delhi: Viva Books Pvt. Ltd.

Gracias, F.D. (1996). *Kaleidoscope of Women in Goa 1510–1961*. New Delhi: Concept Publishing Company.

Harmony. (2014). *Her Excellency*. Available at: https://www.harmonyindia.org/ people_posts/her-excellency/, accessed on April 20, 2019.

Kakodkar, A. (1986). 'Role of Women in Goan Freedom Struggle', in B. S. Ali (ed.), *Goa Wins Freedom: Reflections and Reminiscences*. Panaji: Goa Printing Press.

Ministry of Statistics (2019). *Annual Report: Periodic Labour Force Survey(PLFS)*. Available at: mospi.nic.in/sites/default/files/publication_reports/Annual%20Rep ort%2C%20PLFS%202017-18_31052019.pdf?download=1, accessed on April 20, 2019.

MoPR (2008). *A Study on Elected Women Representatives in Panchayati Raj Institutions*. Available at: https://www.panchayat.gov.in/documents/10198/0/ ReportOnEWR.pdf, accessed on January 22, 2019.

MoSPI (2013). *Participation in Economy*. Available at: http://www.mospi.gov.in/ sites/default/files/reports_and_publication/statistical_publication/social_statistics /Chapter_4.pdf, accessed on January 22, 2019.

NITI Aayog (2019.). *Infant Mortality Rate (IMR) (Per 1000 Live Births)*. Available at: http://niti.gov.in/content/infant-mortality-rate-imr-1000-live-births, accessed on February 12, 2019.

Pais, C. S. (2017). *History and Politics of Elections in Goa (1821–1963): A Study.* Available at: irgu.unigoa.ac.in, accessed on February 12, 2019.

Parobo, P. (2015). *India's First Democratic Revolution.* New Delhi: Orient BlackSwan.

Salgaonkar, S. (2000). *Women, Political Power and the State in Goa.* Available at: http://shodhganga.inflibnet.ac.in/bitstream/10603/34458/10/10_chepter%204 .pdf, accessed on February 5, 2019.

Sardesai, M. (1986). 'The Role of Women in the Liberation Movement', in B. S. Ali (ed.), *Goa Wins Freedom: Reflections and Reminiscences.* Panaji: Goa Printing Press.

Stokes, W. (2005). *Women in Contemporary Politics.* Cambridge: Polity Press.

The Economic Times (2012). *Goa Government Launches 'Griha Adhar' Scheme for Women.* October 2. Available at: https://economictimes.indiatimes.com/ news/economy/policy/goa-government-launches-grih-adhar-scheme-for-women/ articleshow/16643136.cms, accessed on January 14, 2019.

The Indian Express (2018). *Incentives Under Mamta Scheme for Mothers Hikes to Rs. 10,000.* December 7. Available at: https://timesofindia.indiatimes.com/city /goa/incentive-under-mamta-scheme-for-mothers-hiked-to-rs-10k/articleshow /66978222.cms, accessed on December 12, 2020.

The Statesman (2017). *Goa Common Civil Code Forbids Oral Divorce, Polygamy Among Muslims: Governor*, May 12. Available at: https://www.thestatesman .com/cities/goa-common-civil-code-forbids-oral-divorce-polygamy-among -muslims-governor-1494616629.html, accessed on April 19, 2020.

The Times of India (2017a). *53 Year on, Women Yet to Find Footing in Goa Assembly.* March 8. Available at: https://timesofindia.indiatimes.com/city/goa /53-years-on-women-yet-to-find-footing-in-goa-assembly/articleshow/57525646 .cms, accessed on January 29, 2019.

The Times of India (2017b). *Goa Election 2017: Over 50 % Voters Women, but Candidates? Just 7 %.* January 26. Available at: https://timesofindia.indiatimes .com/city/goa/over-50-voters-women-but-candidates-just-7/articleshow /56787247.cms, accessed on January 9, 2019.

10

MAHARASHTRA

Engendering the dilemmas of democratic politics

Chaitra Redkar

Introduction

Women in Maharashtra have been in public life for long. There is a vibrant tradition of non-party democratic activism in the state. However, this has not been reflected in women's participation in electoral politics. Why has women's vibrant non-party democratic activism not been absorbed in the corridors of power? Why has this political activism not produced a political culture conducive for effective political representation of women in legislative bodies? Why does state politics continue to remain a male-dominated arena? This chapter contextualizes women's role in Maharashtra's state politics in this historical paradox. Translating the historical lineage of widespread gender sensitivity into improving the quality of women's political participation has been a grave challenge.

Women's wings in political parties

Almost all the political parties in the state have their women's wings and women spokespersons. The Indian National Congress (INC) established a women's wing at the national level in 1984. The state-level Congress replicated the structure. The Bharatiya Janata Party's (BJP) Mahila Morcha established in 1980 has its branches at state, district, and local levels. The Shiv Sena also has a women's wing. In INC and NCP the women's wings are four-layered structures: state level, district level, block level, and village level. Each level comprises of a president, vice president, secretary, general secretary, deputy secretary, and a public relations officer. All the positions need to be occupied by women. The state-level women's organization comprises of four types of women's cells – peasant and agricultural women's cell, housewives' cell, employed women's cell, and a cell for other women workers (Dere, 2016, pp. 138–139). Other parties also have similar structures. Most of the women's wings were established in the mid-1980s. Almost all these parties had some prominent women party workers even before the

DOI: 10.4324/9781003374862-11

191

formation of the women's wings. One cannot say that the women's wings have strengthened women's voices in the parties.

In 2002, the state Mahila Congress secretary complained that she had been sexually harassed by party leaders. But later she withdrew the complaint saying it was a mistake on her part and she had put up false allegations because she was denied candidature by the party (*The Times of India*, 2002). In 2014, Shubha Raul of the Shiv Sena, the former Mayor of Mumbai, complained of mental harassment because of a male party worker who was then a corporator in the Mumbai Municipal Corporation, while his father, also a party worker, was the party's candidate in the assembly elections (*The Economic Times*, 2014). When the party did not take any action against the party worker and continued with the father's party candidature, Raul left the Shiv Sena and joined MNS. She contested against this Shiv Sena candidate (the father of the said party worker) but lost the election. In some time, she returned to the Shiv Sena and ultimately succeeded in convincing the party chief to take action against the party worker (*Zee 24 Taas*, 2017). The party worker was expelled from the party but in his place his sister was nominated as a party candidate and the father continued to be the party leader.

In 2019, Priyanka Chaturvedi of the Mumbai INC complained against the reinstatement of some party workers from Uttar Pradesh who had allegedly harassed her during the anti-Rafael campaign by the party. She left the party over this issue to join the Shiv Sena. Chaturvedi is now a Rajya Sabha member from the Shiv Sena. Chitra Wagh of NCP left the party around the 2019 general elections to join the BJP, stating that she was not being heard by the party. The NCP chief, however, stated that she had joined the BJP to stop the Enforcement Directorate's investigation into corruption charges against her husband (*Sakal*, 2019). Such incidents are found across political parties.

Women's role in the legislature

At any given point of time except for the current period, the number of women members representing Maharashtra in the Rajya Sabha has never been more than three (Table 10.1).

In the Lok Sabha, the percentage of women representatives from Maharashtra has revolved around 5 per cent except for the past two tenures when it went up to 15 per cent (Table 10.2).

State legislature

The state has a bicameral legislature. The Upper House – Vidhan Parishad – has 78 members that include 66 elected and 12 nominated members. The second house – Vidhan Sabha – is composed of 288 members. Vidhan

Table 10.1 Women members in the Rajya Sabha from Maharashtra

Name	Party	Tenure
Lilavati Munshi	Congress	1952–58
Violate Alva	Congress	1960–62
		1966–72
Tara Sathe	Congress	1962–68
Vimal Punjabrao Deshmukh	Congress	1967–74
Sarojini Babar	Congress	1968–74
Saroj Khaparde	Congress	1972–74
		1976–82
		1982–88
		1988–94
		1994–2000
Premalatai D Chavan	Congress	1980–86
Sudha Vijay Joshi	Congress I	1984–90
Pratibha Devising Patil	Congress	1985–90
Suryakanta Patil	INC	1986–92
Chandrika A. Jain	Cong I	1990–96
Supriya Sule	NCP	2006–12
Rajani Patil	INC	2013–18
Vandana Chavan	NCP	2012–18
		2018–on going
Fauzia Khan	NCP	2020–ongoing
Priyanka Chaturvedi	Shiv Sena	2020–on going

Source: Using data compiled from the webpages at: https://rajyasabha.nic.in/rsnew/member _site/women.aspx (see Prasanna Kumar et al., 2019), accessed 16 January 2020.

Sabha was constituted for the first time in 1962. Table 10.3 shows women's marginal representation in the Vidhan Sabha. The percentage of women in the Maharashtra Vidhan Sabha was, at times, less than the percentage of women in the Lok Sabha.

The number of women contesting elections is steadily increasing. Though political parties nominate very few women candidates, the number of independent women candidates is very large and is steadily increasing. It is also true that voters have generally preferred party candidates over independent women candidates.

A large number of women candidates have lost their security deposits (Table 10.3). This means that they could not secure even one-sixth of the total votes cast. There is a steady increase in the number of women contesting elections and there is a proportionate rise in the number of women candidates forfeiting their deposits. At times political parties project this gap as grounds for not nominating women candidates in elections. Political parties believe that women lack the 'winnability' factor (Spray, 2014; also see Rai, 2011) and their candidature incurs major political losses for a party. This, however, ignores the fact that the number of persons (of all the sexes) contesting elections is going up and correspondingly the figures of candidates

CHAITRA REDKAR

Table 10.2 Women in the Lok Sabha from Maharashtra

	Party	*Constituency*	*Name*
First Lok Sabha	Congress	Bombay Suburban	Jayashree Naishadh Raiji
	Congress	Kaira South	Maniben Vallabhbhai Patel
	Congress	Poona South	Indira Anant Maydeo
	Congress	Ahmedabad South	Sushila Ganesh Mavalankar
Second Lok Sabha	Congress	Nagpur	Anusuyabai Purushottam Kale
	Congress	Anand	Maniben Vallabhbhai Patel
	Congress	Girnar	Jayaben Shah
Third Lok Sabha	Congress	Amravati	Vimal Deshmukh
	Congress	Chanda	G.M. Tai Kannamwar
	Congress	Ratnagiri	Sharda Mukherjee
Fourth Lok Sabha	Congress	Hatkanangale	Maharani Vijaymala Rajaram Bhosale Chhatrapati
	Congress	Ratnagiri	Sharda Mukherjee
	Congress	Bombay North East	Tara Govind Sapre
Fifth Lok Sabha	Congress	Karad	Premalabai Dajisaheb Chavan
	CPI	Bombay Central	Roza Deshpande
Sixth Lok Sabha	Congress	Karad	Premalabai Dajisaheb Chavan
	Janata Party	Bombay North	Mrinal Gore
	CPI(M)	Bombay North Central	Ahilya Rangnekar
Seventh Lok Sabha	Congress (I)	Amaravati	Usha Prakash Choudhari
	Janata Party	Bombay North Central	Pramila Dandavate
	Congress (I)	Bheer (Beed)	Kesharbai Kshirsagar
	Congress (I)	Sangali	Shalinitai Patil
Eighth Lok Sabha	Congress	Karad	Premalabai Dajisaheb Chavan
	Congress (I)	Amaravati	Usha Prakash Choudhari
	Congress (I)	Bheer (Beed)	Kesharbai Kshirsagar
Ninth Lok Sabha	Congress	Karad	Premalabai Dajisaheb Chavan
	BJP	Mumbai North East	Jayawantiben Mehta
Tenth Lok Sabha	Congress (I)	Beed	Kesharbai Kshirsagar
	Congress (I)	Amaravati	Pratibha Devisingh Patil
	Congress (I)	Nanded	Suryakanta Patil
Eleventh Lok Sabha	BJP	Mumbai South	Jayawantiben Mehta
	BJP	Beed	Rajani Ashokrao Patil
Twelfth Lok Sabha	Congress (I)	Hingoli	Suryakanta Patil

(Continued)

MAHARASHTRA

Table 10.2 Continued

	Party	Constituency	Name
Thirteenth Sabha	Shiv Sena	Washim	Bhavana Gawali
	NCP	Ichalkaranji	Nivedita Mane
	BJP	Mumbai South	Jayawantiben Mehta
	INC	Wardha	Prabha Rau
Fourteenth Lok Sabha	Shiv Sena	Washim	Bhavana Gawali
	INC	Mumbai North West	Priya Dutt
	NCP	Ichalkaranji	Nivedita Mane
	NCP	Hingoli	Suryakanta Patil
Fifteenth Lok Sabha	Shiv Sena	Yavatmal–Washim	Bhavana Gawali
	INC	Mumbai North West	Priya Dutt
	NCP	Baramati	Supriya Sule
Sixteenth Lok Sabha	Shiv Sena	Yavatmal–Washim	Bhavana Gawali
	BJP	Raver	Raksha Khadse
	BJP	Nandurbar	Heena Gavit
	BJP	Beed	Pritam Munde
	NCP	Baramati	Supriya Sule
	BJP	Mumbai North Central	Poonam Mahajan
Seventeenth Lok Sabha	IND	Amaravati	Navneet Rana
	NCP	Baramati	Supriya Sule
	BJP	Beed	Pritam Munde
	BJP	Dindori	Bharati Pawar
	BJP	Mumbai North Central	Poonam Mahajan
	BJP	Nandurbar	Heena Gavit
	Shiv Sena	Yavatmal–Washim	Bhavana Gawali
	BJP	Raver	Raksha Khadse

Source: The Lok Sabha Secretariat (2020).

Table 10.3 Women candidates in the legislative assembly elections

	Contestants	Elected	Fortified Deposits
1962	36	13	NA
1967	19	9	NA
1972	56	28*	22
1978	51	8	30
1980	47	19	22
1985	83	16	NA
1990	147	6	120
1995	247	11	212
1999	86	12	63
2004	157	12	127
2009	211	11	173
2014	277	20	237
2019	239	24	189

Source: ECI (2020).
Note: * The member profiles published by the Maharashtra legislature show that there were at least two by-elections due to the death of the sitting MLAs. In both the cases their wives were elected. This increased the number of women to 22 in this legislative assembly. However, the Maharashtra Human Development Report (2022) gives a figure of 28 which is cited in the table.

losing their deposits are also going up for both the sexes. For instance, in 1972 when 22 women lost their security deposits, 648 men also lost their security deposits. In 2014, women candidates losing their security deposits went up to 237 and the number of men losing their security deposits went up to 3,185 (ECI, 2020). These figures refer to a trend in the Indian political system where a large number of people without party affiliations are participating in the electoral process even when there are rare chances of their winning. But this is often presented as a case against women. This leads to further marginalization of women in electoral politics. Even when party organizations have strong and able women candidates, they prefer to make them work as loyal party workers or at the most they are made party spokespersons.

Ultimately, the women who manage to get a party's candidature normally come from families with political lineage. This is visible across political parties. Sharad Pawar–Supriya Sule, Sunil Dutt–Priya Dutt, Gopinath Munde–Pankaja Munde-Palwe and Pritam Munde, Sushil Kumar Shinde–Praniti Shinde, Eknath Gaikwad–Varsha Gaikwad, Nana Chudasama– Shaina N C, Pramod Mahajan–Poonam Mahajan, and Sunil Tatkare–Aditi Tatkare are powerful father–daughter duos in Maharashtra politics.

Across party affiliations women members of the Maharashtra state assembly have had a strong political lineage whether it was Shalinitai Patil (wife of late Chief Minister Vasantdada Patil) or Premalatai Chavan (wife of Dajisaheb Chavan). Women representatives, even when not from the immediate family of a politician, normally come from the same political clan or lineage. The other side of this reality is reflected in the way the Upper House of the Maharashtra legislature – the Vidhan Parishad – is composed.

The Vidhan Parishad has 78 members. From this the 22 elected members are supposed to represent local self-government bodies. In view of the provision of 50 per cent reservations for women in the local bodies, elections to these 22 seats become crucial. The Vidhan Parishad's track record shows that women representatives in urban and rural local bodies have not got their due share in this House ever since the provision for reservations (initially 33 per cent) was made 25 years ago. In 2016, some women politicians from local bodies who were also activists of the Mahila Rajsatta Andolan demanded that women from PRIs should get their share of power in the Vidhan Parishad (*Cable City Samachar*, 2016). However, no political party responded to this demand. In the Upper House, for many years the percentage of women members remained steady between 5 and 7 per cent. This figure includes both elected as well as nominated women members.

Members like Sanjivani Raykar (1988–2006) came to the Upper House from the Teachers' Constituency for three consecutive terms as an independent candidate. Vidya Chavan (2011–20) is a nominated member of the Nationalist Congress Party, while Neelam Gorhe, who is currently the

Table 10.4 Women members of the Maharashtra legislative council

Year	No. of Women in the Vidhan Parishad	Percentage
1952–58	10	13.89
1958–64	04	5.56
1962–68	03	3.85
1964–70	03	3.85
1968–74	02	2.56
1974–80	03	3.85
1978–84	05	6.41
1980–85	06	7.69
1987–92	04	5.13
1992–94	00	00
1994–96	07	8.97
1996–98	05	6.41
1998–2000	05	6.41
2000–2	05	6.41
2002–4	05	6.41
2004–6	06	7.69
2006–8	04	5.13
2008–10	04	5.13
2010–12	07	8.97
2012–14	07	8.97
2014–16	06	7.69
2016–18	04	5.13
2018–19	05	6.41

Source: Poonacha (2003) and the Maharashtra Vidhan Mandal Sachivalaya (2001, 2005, 2012, and 2019).

deputy chairperson of the Vidhan Parishad, has been elected to the House for four consecutive terms as a Shiv Sena candidate (Table 10.4).

The Vidhan Parishad has often provided space for political parties to save a possible faceoff with reference to their gender sensitivity. This House has also provided space for parties to accommodate women like Gorhe and Chavan who do not have a political lineage but who happen to be promising organizers, in addition to being articulate party spokespersons.

Women in Maharashtra's local bodies

Till the early 1990s the structural set-up of the local self-governing bodies provided little scope for women's inclusion. This meant that women's participation in local bodies was generally marginal barring some remarkable exceptions. These exceptions were outcomes of the special efforts made by various social movements due to which Maharashtra witnessed experiments of all-women gram panchayats. The oldest known all-women panchayat was in Nimbut village in the Baramati taluka of Pune district of Maharashtra (1963–68). This was an outcome of the initiative taken by Kamalabai who believed, 'If I can run a house, why not Panchayat?' (Datta, 1998, p. 2). More organized efforts were made with an initiative by Shetkari Sanghatana. In 1987, it held a four-day training camp for women at Ambethan near Pune where a strategy for women's participation at the zila parishad level was discussed (Omvedt, 1987). The Samagra Mahila Aghadi was formed to contest local bodies' elections. In the same year all-women panels contested gram panchayat elections and won in several places (Datta, 1998; also see Phadke and Parchure, 2016).

It was in this background that in 1990 the Congress government in Maharashtra headed by Sharad Pawar announced 33 per cent reservation of seats for women in the local governing bodies. Since 2011 Maharashtra has increased the reservation of seats for women from 33 to 50 per cent. There are 36 districts with 34 zila parishads, 351 panchayat samitis, and 27,870 gram panchayats in Maharashtra. The total number of elected representatives in these rural local bodies in 2018–19 was 240,122 of which 121,490 were women. In 2018–19, 50.60 per cent of the total elected representatives in the rural local bodies were women (Ministry of Panchayati Raj, 2019). For urban governance there are 27 municipal corporations, 241 municipal councils, and 128 nagar panchayats (State Election Commission of Maharashtra, 2019). The norm of 50 per cent reservation of seats for women is observed in the urban local bodies as well.

Maharashtra also witnessed early efforts in providing training and support to women members in local bodies. The P.V. Mandlik Trust, Mumbai (PVMT) with the aid of certain Gandhians and Socialist activists like Navanitbhai Shah, Prabhubhai Sanghavi, Rohini Gawankar, Neela Patwardhan, and Surekha Dalvi started organizing training camps for gram panchayat members in March 1993 (Patwardhan, n.d.). A training module was developed in collaboration with the Tata Institute of Social Sciences (Mumbai) and a series of training workshops were organized. PVMT also published a number of booklets with useful information on the responsibilities and functions of the gram panchayat and its members (Hatkar, 1994). In the latter half of the 1990s, a number of organizations for the training and support of the emerging women politicians were established in the state. The Alochana Documentation Resource Centre in Pune started conducting training workshops and documenting women politicians' narratives.

In March 2000, five divisional networks, the Marāṭhvāḍā Lokavikās Mañca, Vidarbha Lokavikās Mañca, Uttar Mahārāṣtra Lokavikās Mañca, Koṅkaṇvikās Samanvay Vyāspīṭh, and the Research and Support Centre for Development, organized a state-level workshop at Saygata village in Chandrapur district which gave birth to Mahilā Rajasattā Āndolan (MRA) (NCAS, 2002).

198

Table 10.5 No-confidence motions against women sarpanches (1999–2001)

District	No. of Women Sarpanches	No. of No-Confidence Motions
Thane	266	10
Ratnagiri	276	3
Sindhudurg	145	4
Nasik	414	11
Jalgaon	434	15
Ahmednagar	468	5
Pune	450	9
Satara	514	5
Sangali	248	10
Jalana	260	14
Parbhani	270	11
Buldhana	296	15
Akola	206	11
Washim	61	19
Yavatmal	440	18
Bhandara	228	28
	4,976	188

Source: Patwardhan and Gupte (2004, p. 310).

MRA has done systematic and sustained work in training and supporting women representatives in local bodies across the state and has also published certain insightful reports on women in PRIs. These reports challenge the myth of women being mere puppets or proxies of male members from their households. These studies also bring out the issues faced by able and active women representatives. Their fellow male party workers at times in an extremely patronizing way try to keep women away from the decision-making process by offering to provide assistance. If a woman participant still insists on participating then she is not nominated for a second term.

One of the most noteworthy problems that women representatives in local bodies, particularly women sarpanches, face is that of no-confidence motions from opposing male members (Table 10.5).

While women in the local bodies are facing a challenge of survival despite reservations, there are some women politicians in the state who have had long careers in politics. Their career graphs when juxtaposed with the realities of the women in the local bodies give an insightful understanding of how the dominant structures of power operate in the context of women.

The journeys of eminent women politicians of Maharashtra

Though women's representation in the state assembly has been small in Maharashtra, there have been some women politicians who have had/

have long innings. They include Ahilya Rangnekar (1922–2009), Mrinal Gore (1928–2012), Pramila Dandavate (1927–2001), Kesharbai Kshirsagar (1930–2006), Premalatai Chavan (1918–2003), Prabha Rao (1935–2010), Jayawantiben Mehta (1938–2016), Pratibha Devisingh Patil (1934–), Saroj Khaparde (1941–), Shobhatai Fadnavis (1942–), Suryakanta Patil (1948–), Fauzia Khan (1957–), Supriya Sule (1969–), Varsha Gaikwad (1975–), Pankaja Munde (1979–), and Praniti Shinde (1980–).

Ahilya Rangnekar was a freedom fighter who later became a long-standing member of the Communist Party of India (Marxist). She contested her first civic elections for the Bombay Municipal Corporation as a party candidate in 1963 and was elected for a number of consecutive terms for 19 years. In 1977, she won the North Mumbai Lok Sabha seat as a CPI(M) candidate (Katakam, 2008, p. 23). She was closely associated with women's organizations throughout her life. Along with her colleagues Mrinal Gore and Pramila Dandavate she took up a number of issues concerning women, urban dwellers, and workers.

Mrinal Gore was also a freedom fighter. She was a Socialist who started her political career while working with women on issues related to health, family planning, skill development training, employment, and marital counselling. Her association with local women brought her closer to civic issues emanating from speedy urbanization in the rural areas adjacent to Mumbai. Her untiring efforts in the mid-1950s to make drinking water available to the northern suburbs made her famous as *pāṇivālībāī* (woman who brought water). She took up the cause of urban housing, accessibility to clean public toilets, and availability of food grains in government's fair price shops. Her connect with the people developed her into an able legislator. She was elected as a member of the Goregaon gram panchayat (before it was merged in the Mumbai metropolitan region) in 1953, to Brihanmumbai Municipal Corporation (BMC) in 1961, to the Maharashtra legislative assembly (1972–77) and (1985–90), and to the Lok Sabha (1978–80) (Gawankar, 2003).

Pramila Dandavate had an illustrious career as a parliamentarian and graduated from the local to the national level. She was a member of the Mumbai Municipal Corporation (1968–73) and member of the Lok Sabha (1980–84). As a Member of Parliament, she made significant contributions in highlighting the evils of the dowry system and in the formulation of the Dowry Prohibition (Amendment) Act. She was an active member of the Praja Socialist Party and later of the Janata Party. She played a crucial role in party organization, in parliamentary politics, in the women's movement, as well as in various other avenues of non-party democratic politics (Surana, 2010, pp. 33–35). She was actively involved in the Samyukta Maharashtra movement, the Land Liberation movement, the anti-price rise movement, and the Malvan Port facilities movement. She co-founded Mahila Dakshata Samiti and was one of the organizers of the Rashtra Seva Dal – a Socialist youth organization. She was the founder member of the Samajwadi Mahila Sabha, Maharashtra, and played a crucial role in the party organization of the Socialist Party in its various avatars. She was joint secretary of the Socialist Party in 1974–75. During the Emergency she was detained under MISA for 18 months.

Kesharbai Kshirsagar (Beed), Premalatai Chavan (Karad), Prabha Rao (Wardha), and Saroj Khaparde were from the Congress. They played important roles in party organization and in the House they were elected to. Premalatai Chavan won consecutive elections to the Lok Sabha after the demise of her husband. She was part of numerous Lok Sabha legislative committees during her tenure (Lok Sabha Secretariat, 2020). Prabha Rao worked as the general secretary of the Maharashtra Pradesh Congress Committee for a sustained period and was an eminent party worker. Pratibha Devisingh Patil came from a family of freedom fighters. She was elected to the Maharashtra state assembly in 1962 and the Lok Sabha in 1968, 1985 (Jalgaon), and 1991 (Amaravati). She was a member of the Rajya Sabha from 1985 to 1990. She was the first woman President of India elected in 2007.

Saroj Khaparde had a very long political career. She represented the state in the Rajya Sabha for five terms, from 1972 to 2000. Khaparde introduced 28 private members' bills in the House. She was instrumental in introducing a bill for paying wages and a weekly holiday for housewives and for amending an act related to the indecent representation of women. She served on numerous committees of the House including the House Committee, Committee on Government Assurances, and the Subordinate Legislation Committee. She was union minister of state, holding portfolios of health and family welfare and textiles (1986–89). She also served as the vice Chairman of Rajya Sabha (1994–2000) and Chairman of the Rajya Sabha in 1996 (Kumar et al., 2019).

Shalinitai Patil is the wife of Vasantdada Patil, Chief Minister of Maharashtra. As a member of the state assembly she was instrumental in formally introducing the idea of reservations for Marathas on economic grounds (Patil, 2003). Suryakanta Patil hailed from Nanded and came from a political family. Her grandfather as well as her mother had been members of the Maharashtra legislative assembly. She started her career as a member of the Nanded Municipal Council. Later she worked in various capacities in the Congress Party organization as well as a member of the Maharashtra legislative assembly and the Rajya Sabha and Lok Sabha. She was a minister for state in UPA-I (Lok Sabha Secretariat, 2020). She joined the BJP in 2014.

Jayawantiben Mehta entered politics in 1962 and was elected as a municipal councillor of the Mumbai Municipal Corporation in 1968. Subsequently, she was re-elected and served as municipal councillor for ten years. During the Emergency (1975), she was imprisoned for 19 months. Jayawantiben was elected to the Maharashtra legislative assembly in 1978 and served two terms up to 1985. In 1980, she was made a member of the national executive of the BJP and in 1988, she was made the all-India secretary. In 1989, she was elected to the Lok Sabha. She was subsequently re-elected in 1996 and 1999 and was made a minister of state for power in the Vajpayee government from 1999 to 2004. Jayawantiben served as the president of the BJP Mahila Morcha from 1991 to 1995 and as vice president of the Bharatiya Janata Party from 1993 to 1995 (Lok Sabha Secretariat, 2020).

Neelam Gorhe started her career as a women's rights activist. She was the founding member of the StrīĀdhār Kendra established in the 1980s. At present she is a member of Maharashtra legislative council from the Shiv Sena and also holds the office of the deputy chairperson of the Vidhan Parishad.

Some women, despite no political lineage, have become successful politicians. However, many others end up being party workers or at the most party spokespersons and a large number of aspiring women politicians remain excluded from power. It is difficult to advance generalized explanations for this situation. The cases need to be addressed individually to understand how women politicians have achieved what they have and what stops them from achieving for themselves as well as for other women. One possible explanation could be traced in the location of women's entry to politics and in the graph of their political activism.

Women who come from families of politicians have strong support of their families, clans, castes, or communities. Their durability in politics owes a lot to this lineage. For women politicians without any family lineage, it is their strong and sustained connect with the autonomous women's movement and other social movements. Pramila Dandavate, Mrinal Gore, Ahilya Rangnekar, and Neelam Gorhe who succeeded without any political lineage shared a deep connect with social movements. Simultaneously they were/are active members of political parties. Their anchorage in social movements provided a social base to their political power. This makes it necessary to rethink the relationship between social movements and political parties as it has always existed.

Autonomous women's movements

Since the formation of the state, a large number of women's movements have enriched the terrain of non-party democratic politics. These movements have addressed divergent issues including caste-based oppression and discrimination, urbanization, civil liberties, corruption, fair prices for agricultural produce, issues of unorganized labour, and the land rights of tribal people. Women were actively involved in almost all these social movements.

Women across the state were mobilized around the issue of dowry deaths and rape. A large number of women's organizations like Nārī Samatā Mañca, StrīĀdhār Kendra, Strī Mukti Saṅghaṭanā, Majlis, Mashwarā, and Mahilā Dakṣatā Samiti were formed. A significant contribution was made by activists like Chhaya Datar, Vidya Bal, Pushpa Bhave, Geeta Sane, Sharada Sathe, Jyoti Mhapsekar, Neelam Gorhe, Medha Kotwal-Lele, Flavia Agnes, and Vibhuti Patel to change women's consciousness about self and society's perceptions about women. Women's magazines like *Bāyzā* and *Miḷūn Sāryazaṇī* played a crucial role in providing a platform for expression to the women who were challenging the structures of patriarchy. These also contributed in generating support and a sense of sisterhood among the educated middle-class Marathi women.

A sizeable number of activists including Pratima Pardeshi, Sulabha Patole, Pratibha Shinde, and Nutan Malvi who shared intellectual affiliations with Sharad Patil's writings had been emphasizing the need to understand the nexus between Brahminism and patriarchy. An extension of this position can be found later in the 1990s when Satyaśodhak Mahilā Āghāḍī was formed. Sharad Joshi's Shetkarī Saṅghaṭanā is equally significant in this context at least for two reasons. Firstly, when the autonomous women's movement was at its peak in the early 1980s, it endeavoured to redefine women's liberation by bringing the experiences of rural women in focus. Secondly, at a time when the women's movement had kept itself away from electoral politics, its women's wing – Lakṣmī Mukti Saṅghaṭanā – decided to contest elections for the zila parishad and other rural local bodies (Omvedt, 1990, pp. 1687–1690).

This awareness about the intersectionality can be seen in the movements for alternative development as well. For instance, the movements against Enron and Sardar Sarovar –Narmadā Āndolan – atomic energy projects like Jaitapur, hill stations at Lavasa, and against special economic zones in Raigad had been emphasizing the caste, gender, and ethnic dimensions of the developmental projects. Some activists from these movements including Medha Patkar, Sanjay Sangwai, Lata P.M., Surekha Dalvi, Ulka Mahajan, and Suniti Su R. consistently critiqued the mainstream model of economic development and emphasized the need to explore alternate models of development which were socially just and ecologically sustainable.

Addressing intersectionality

Developments within the social movements in the state and emerging awareness about intersectionality placed many autonomous women's organizations in an introspective mode. The long debate between Gopal Guru (Guru, 1995), Sharmila Rege (Rege, 1998), and Chhaya Datar (Datar, 1999) in the *Economic & Political Weekly* in the mid-1990s over the issue of theorization of Dalit women's voices in a way echoed the concerns and dilemmas faced by the women's movement in Maharashtra. In June 1996 Alochana, Documentation and Research Centre for Women, convened a seminar in Pune to address the issues of intersectionality between caste, class, and gender. The seminar reflected on integrating the agendas of the different shades of women's movements while facing the challenges emerging from rampant communalization in the post-liberalization era. Eminent activists from Dalit women's organizations like Kumud Pawade, Usha Wagh, and Lata Bhise contributed in this seminar (Sathe and Kulkarni, 1999). Though this meeting could not result in any organizational alliance, it did contribute in acknowledging the latent sensitivity about intersectionality of caste–class–gender as the foundation on which the future women's movement must proceed. This explains how the plea for reserving a quota for OBC and Muslim women in the Women's Reservation Bill could fetch support from a large number of women's organizations from Maharashtra.

Non-party democratic activism

Most of the social movements preferred to stay away from electoral politics and from party affiliations. In certain cases, individual members, with the approval of their organizations, did contest elections. But as organizations most of them consciously chose to confine themselves to non-party democratic politics. In certain cases, despite a close connect between the party and social organization, the latter avoided identifying itself as the front organization of a political party (Redkar, 2005; Vaidya, 1985). The power dynamics in political parties had made them sceptical of the efficacy of parliamentary politics. Some of them found it risky to put the social movement's activism at stake for entering the corridors of power. Activist Shiraz Balsara has articulated the dilemma that the non-party activism faced in the wake of the 33 per cent reservation for women. She writes:

> Should non-party political formations [...] field candidates for elections? If yes, mobilizing for elections as a process at best neutralizes all that one worked for in mobilizing for a struggle. If you contest, you must win; people want to win. If not, the elections will take place anyway and the field will be laid bare for all kinds of unscrupulous political parties to play havoc.
>
> (Balsara, 1997, pp. 143–144)

An acknowledgement of such dilemmas provides a chance to understand why the vitality of non-party democratic activism did not get transmitted to electoral politics. The trend of separation of electoral politics and other forms of democratic politics rarely contributed in strengthening women's role in political parties. Political parties continued to remain under the control of the dominant caste–class–gender interests (Datar and Ghotale, 2013). In recent times, politics has got increasingly criminalized and elections have become highly expensive.

The groups active in non-party democratic politics are still not prepared or are under-prepared to contest elections. This disjunct makes it difficult firstly to build pressure on the political parties to nominate more women or more able women as party candidates for elections. A study of the candidates contesting elections for the Kalyan-Dombivli Municipal Corporation showed that women candidates rarely had any motivation to contest elections as compared to their male counterparts. It was a compulsion arising out of the provision of reservations that the male members from their households made them contest elections (Patil, 2016). As against this there is a long list of able, efficient, articulate women at all the three levels of government who do not get nominations from their parties for a second term. The articulate women spokespersons of the parties continue in the same position, while the wives, daughters, and daughters-in-law of established politicians get immediate access to power. Of course, this phenomenon is not specifically true only for women. But in the case of women, it has more deep and lasting implications.

Secondly and most importantly, it desists the possibility of redefining the meaning of politics. It has been observed that in rare cases when social activists who have generally stayed away from elections decide to contest elections, they have rarely been able to win. The classic case is that of Medha Patkar who contested in the 2014 general elections from Mumbai North East constituency as an Aam Aadmi Party candidate and could not secure even 1 lakh votes.

One of the main reasons for this lies in the way power is perceived. The experiences of all-women gram panchayats formed by the Lakshmi Mukti Sanghatana are very educative in this regard. Women's work from this panchayat for village development and for building roads and schools was seen as 'social work' and not as politics (Datta, 1998). The association of the idea of power with nuisance value needs to be changed to a more positive definition. Social movements have an important role to play in this regard. They need to rethink about how they can develop their ties with political parties and strengthen able politicians of all genders to move closer to the centre of power.

Emerging dilemmas and challenges

New challenges and dilemmas emerge from the way the dominant interests are using the state while approaching the issue of women's political participation. The state manages to appear extremely accommodative and responsive to the demands of women and their movements but marginalization does not really end. Some scholars have seen this as the state's strategy to hijack the agenda of the women's movement and co-opt feminism (Guru, 1994). Two cases from Maharashtra substantiate this argument. Firstly, the Policy for Women introduced in 1994 by the Government of Maharashtra. The policy document was written in a feminist language and there was liberal use of progressive and developmental terms. It addressed a wide range of issues from health to violence, to common ownership of houses to sex workers. The policy had promises of women's economic empowerment, changing legal infrastructure to facilitate the issues of Muslim and Christian women in the state. The women's rights activists and academicians, however, did not find much promise in this document. Some also saw this as an attempt to use women's aspirations for catering to the requirements of the labour market emerging after globalization (Ghotaskar et al., 1994). By becoming more accommodative does the state hijack women's agenda without giving them any substantial share in power? Frequent changes in the legal infrastructure for governing urban and rural local bodies make this question more critical.

In 2011, the reservation for women in civic bodies was increased from 33 to 50 per cent, but this was coupled with frequent changes in the Bombay Provincial Municipal Corporations Act, 1949; the Maharashtra Municipal Councils, Nagar Panchayats and Industrial Townships Act, 1965; and the Maharashtra Gram Panchayat Act, 1958. In some municipal corporations the number of members representing a ward of the civic body was increased from one to two members, again back to one member, then to multi-members, and again back to one member in less than ten years. Similarly, there have been frequent changes in the system for the election of sarpanches. The BJP-led government in the state introduced the provision for direct elections of sarpanches in 2016 (Government of Maharashtra, 2018). The then Chief Minister Devendra Fadnavis had expressed his plan to introduce the system of direct elections of mayors in C and D type municipal corporations as well (*The New Indian Express*, 2017).

This was justified in the name of securing tenure for women sarpanches and saving them the frequent use of no-confidence motions against them. Women's organizations did not see in it any guarantee for tenure. Instead, they saw this as a centralizing tendency increasing the vulnerability of women sarpanches in the face of interference from the state-level leadership. After coming to power in 2019, the Shiv Sena–NCP–Congress Maha Vikas Aghadi amended this act and cancelled the provision for the direct elections of sarpanches.

Conclusion

The examples discussed in this chapter make it evident that the struggle for women's right to political participation and self-representation is becoming more and more complex. The provisions for reservation of seats, acknowledgement of intersectionality by providing quotas within quotas, and support and training for women representatives are essential conditions but need not be seen as sufficient conditions to break the dominant structures of power and to engender the entire political culture. The journey is long and requires social movements, researchers, and women politicians to work hand in hand to make it more effective and meaningful.

Bibliography

Balsara, S. (1997). 'The Panchayati Raj and the Rhetoric of Women's Empowerment: The Dilemma before Non-Party Feminist Groups', in V. Poonacha (ed.), *Women, Empowerment, and Political Participation*. Mumbai: Research Centre for Women's Studies, SNDT Women's University.

City Cable Samachar (2016, April 30). [In Hindi] 'Mahila Rajasatta Andolan ki patraparishad', Available at: https://www.youtube.com/watch?app=desktop&v =n9cvYB7bsgA, accessed on August 6, 2019.

Datar, A. and V. Ghotale (2013). 'Maharashtra Cabinets: Social and Regional Profile, 1960–2010', *Economic and Political Weekly*, 48(36), September 7, 37–42.

Datar, C. (1999). 'Non-Brahmin Renderings of Feminism in Maharashtra: Is it a More Emancipatory Force?', *Economic and Political Weekly*, 34(41), 2964–2968.

Datta, B. (ed.), (1998). *'And Who Will Make the Chapatis?': A Study of All- Women Panchayats in Maharashtra*. Calcutta: Stree for Alochana.

Dere, G. (2016). Rashtrawadi Congress Paksh: VisheshSandarbhPashchim Maharashtra, 1999–2012. Unpublished PhD thesis. Pune: University of Pune, pp 138–139. Available at: http://hdl.handle.net/10603/243733 accessed on August 6, 2020.

Election Commission of India (2020). 'Election Results Statistical Reports.' Available at: https://eci.gov.in/statistical-report/statistical-reports/#collapseTwo, accessed on October 31, 2021.

Gawankar, R. (2003). *[In Marathi]. PāṇivālīBāī*. Mumbai: SPARROW.

Ghunnar, P. P. and A. B. Hakhu (2018). 'The Aftermath of Farmer Suicides in Survivor Families of Maharashtra', *Economic and Political Weekly*, 53(5), 47–53.

Gupte, M., S. Bandewar, and H. Pisal (1997). Abortion Needs of Women in India: A Case Study of Rural Maharashtra. *Reproductive Health Matters*, 5 (9).

Guru, G. (1994). 'Maharashtra's Women's Policy: Co-opting Feminism', *Economic and Political Weekly*, 29(32), 2063–2065.

——— (1995). 'Dalit Women Talk Differently', *Economic and Political Weekly*, 30(41–42), 2548–2550.

Gothoskar, S., N. Gandhi, and N. Shah (1994). 'Maharashtra's Policy for Women', *Economic and Political Weekly*, 29(48), 3019–3022.

Hatkar, N. (1994). *Functions of Gram Panchayat (Pictorial booklet)*. Mumbai: P. V. Mandlik Trust.

India Today (2019a). 'AAP finishes pole race behind NOTA, set to lose all seats in Haryana, Maharashtra.' Available at: https://www.indiatoday.in/elections /story/aap-finishes-poll-race-behind-nota-set-to-lose-in-all-seats-in-haryana -maharashtra-1612649-2019-10-24, accessed on February 2, 2020.

——— (2019b). 'Inside story: Why Priyanka Chaturvedi left Congress and joined Shiv Sena.' Available at: https://www.indiatoday.in/elections/lok-sabha-2019 /story/why-priyanka-chaturvedi-left-congress-and-joined-shiv-sena-1505925 -2019-04-19, accessed on February 2, 2020.

Katakam, A. (2008). 'The Pioneers: Ahilya Ranganekar', *Frontline*, 6 June.

Kota, N. (2018). 'Widows of Farmer Suicide Victims in Vidarbha: Differential Dependence in Early and Later Cases', *Economic and Political Weekly*, 53(26–27), 24–31.

Lele, J. (1990). 'Caste, Class and Dominance: Political Mobilization in Maharashtra', in F. Frankel and MSA Rao (eds), *Dominance and State Power in Modern India: Decline of a Social Order*. Vol II (pp. 115–121). New Delhi: Oxford University Press.

Lok Sabha Secretariat (2020). 'All Members of Lok Sabha (Since 1952).' Available at: http://loksabhaph.nic.in/Members/lokprev.aspx, accessed on February 2, 2020.

Maharashtra Government Gazette (2018). *Maharashtra Act no. LIV of 2018*. August 13. Available at: https://www.maharashtra.gov.in/Site/Upload/Acts%20Rules/Marathi/Notification%20for%20Appointing%20of%20Sarpanch.pdf, accessed on January 16, 2020.

Maharashtra Vidhan Parishad (2001, 2005, 2012, 2019). *Sadasyāncā Saṅkṣipta jīvanparicay*. Mumbai: Maharashtra Vidhan Mandal Sachivalaya.

Ministry of Panchayati Raj, Government of India (2019). *Basic Statistics of Panchayati Raj Institutions*. New Delhi: Ministry of Panchayati Raj. Available at: https://www.panchayat.gov.in/documents/20126/0/Statistical+handbook_MoPR+02082019.pdf/4988ca1b-4971-1f3b-54e7-980228eb47f9?t=1564729098415, accessed on February 4, 2020.

Ministry of Statistics and Programme Implementation, Government of India (2018). *Report - Principal Characteristics by Major States in ASI 2017–2018*. (Annual Survey of Industries). Available at: http://mospi.nic.in/asi-summary-results/844, accessed on January 16, 2020.

Mitra, S. and S. Shroff (2007). 'Farmers' Suicides in Maharashtra', *Economic and Political Weekly*, 42(49), 73–77.

National Centre for Advocacy Studies & Research and Support Centre for Development [NCAS] (2002). *Report – Sangamnerte Aurangabad: Mahila Rajsatta Andolanachi Vatchal*. New Mumbai: National Centre for Advocacy Studies & Research and Support Centre for Development.

National Centre for Advocacy Studies & Research and Support Centre for Development [NCAS] (2017). *Madam Sarpanch: Stories of the undaunted women Sarpanch in MahilaRajasattaAndolan in Maharashtra*. Navi Mumbai: National Centre for Advocacy Studies & Research and Support Centre for Development.

Omvedt, G. (1987). 'Women and Maharashtra Zilha Parishad Elections', *Economic and Political Weekly*, 22(47), 1991–1993.

——— (1990). 'Women, Zilla Parishads and Panchayat Raj: Chandwad to Vitner', *Economic and Political Weekly*, 25(31), 1687, 1689–1690.

Palshikar, S. (1998). *[In Marathi] Zātva Mahārāṣṭrāce Rājakāraṇ*. Pune: Sugawa.

——— (2014). 'Maharashtra Assembly Elections: Farewell to Maratha Politics?' *Economic and Political Weekly*, 49(43–44), 10–13.

Palshikar, S. and R. Deshpande (1999). 'Electoral Competition and Structures of Domination in Maharashtra', *Economic and Political Weekly*, 34(34–35), 2409–2422.

Patel, V. (2020). *Advocate Varsha Deshpande Her Fight to Save the Girl Child*. Available at: http://oneindiaonepeople.com/advocate-varsha-deshpande-her-fight-to-save-the-girl-child/, accessed on February 2, 2020.

Patil, S. (2003). *[In Marathi] Swayamsiddhā: Rajkāraṇātīl 50 varṣe.* Satara: Chandrakant Patil Pratishthan.

———— (2016). *Contesting Municipal Elections: Motivations & Strategies - A Study of Kalyan-Dombivali Municipal Corporation Election 2015.* Mumbai: Institute for Democracy and Election Management, State Election Commission of Maharashtra.

Patwardhan, N. (n.d.). *Report – Dr P.V. Mandlik Trust Gram Panchayat Mahila Sadasya Prashikshan Prakalpa (1993–94).* Mumbai: PV Mandlik Trust Publication.

Patwatdhan, N. and P. Gupte (2004). [In Marathi] 'Panchayati Raj ani MahilaSahbhag: 73vi ghatanadurusti', in *Swādhār [In Marathi] Shodh Bai ManasachyaJeenyacha [An Anthology].* Mumbai: Akṣar.

Phadke, Y. D. (1979). *Language and Politics.* Mumbai: Himalaya.

Phadke, M. and R. Parchure (2016). *A Tale of Three Villages with All-Mahila Gram Panchayats.* Mumbai: Institute of Democracy & Election Management, State Election Commission of Maharashtra.

Poonacha, V. (2003). *Maharashtra: Gender Profile – Report submitted to National Commission for Women.* New Delhi: National Women's Commission. Available at: http://ncwapps.nic.in/pdfReports/Gender_Profile_Maharashtra.pdf, accessed on February 2, 2020.

Prasanna Kumar D. S., V. Singh, A. Singh, M. S. Ali, and M. Saleem (2019). *Rajya Sabha Members Biographical Sketches 1952–2019 (Corrected up to October 2019).* New Delhi: Rajya Sabha Secretariat.

Rai, P. (2011). 'Electoral Participation of Women in India: Key Barriers and Determinants', *Economic and Political Weekly,* 46 (3), 47–55.

Redkar, C. (2005). 'Samajwadi Parighatil Jan Sanghatana', in P. Bal (ed.), *Samajvādālā Āvhān Ekvisāvyā Śatakāche* (pp. 62–88). Mumbai: Rashtra Seva Dal.

Rege, S. (1998). 'Dalit Women Talk Differently: A Critique of 'Difference' and Towards a Dalit Feminist Standpoint Position', *Economic and Political Weekly,* 33(44), WS 39–WS46.

Sakal (2019). *[In Marathi], patīlā trapmadhūn soḍavṇyāsāṭhī citrā vāgh bhājapāt? [Chitra Wagh joins BJP to rescue her husband].* Available at: https://www.esakal .com/maharashtra/ncp-women-wing-president-chitra-wagh-enters-bjp-202559, accessed on February 4, 2020.

Sathe, N. and V. Kulkarni (eds) (1999). *[In Marathi] Dalit Strīasmitecā āviṣkār va diśā [Seminar Proceedings].* Pune: Alochana.

Spary, C. (2014). 'Women Candidates and Party Nomination Trends in India – Evidence from the 2009 General Election', *Commonwealth and Comparative Politics,* 52(1), 109–138.

State Election Commission of Maharashtra (2019). *Local Bodies in the State at a Glance.* Mumbai: State Election Commission of Maharashtra. Available at: https://mahasec.maharashtra.gov.in/Site/1383/Local-Bodies-Statistics-at-a -Glance-and-Maps, accessed on September 23, 2019.

Surana, P. (2010). *[In Marathi] Bulandāwaz Bāicā.* Pune: Sadhana.

The Economic Times (2014). 'Former Mumbai Mayor Shubha Raul of Shiv Sena is now MNS Nominee', September 17. Available at: https://economictimes .indiatimes.com/news/politics-and-nation/former-mumbai-mayor-shubha-raul-of

-shiv-sena-is-now-mns-nominee/articleshow/43617995.cms, accessed on January 20, 2020.

The Economic Times (2016). 'Uproar in Maharashtra Assembly over Shreehari Aney's Demand for Separate Marathwada State', March 21. Available at: https://economictimes.indiatimes.com/news/politics-and-nation/uproar-in-maharashtra-assembly-over-shreehari-aneys-demand-for-separate-marathwada-state/articleshow/51493396.cms?from=mdr, accessed on January 20, 2020.

The Indian Express (2019). 'Clarify Whether VBA is B-team of BJP: Ambedkar to Cong-NCP', June 4. Available at: Clarify whether VBA is B-team of BJP: Ambedkar to Cong-NCP | India News, The Indian Express, accessed on January 20, 2020.

The New Indian Express (2017). 'Maharashtra Mulls for Direct Election of Mayor', September 10. Available at: Maharashtra mulls for direct election of mayor- The New Indian Express, accessed on January 20, 2020.

The Times of India (2002). 'Cong Leader Withdraws Allegations of Sexual Harassment', January 22. Available at: https://timesofindia.indiatimes.com/city/mumbai/Cong-leader-withdraws-allegations-of-sexual-harassment/articleshow/870172750.cms, accessed on January 20, 2020.

——— (2019). 'Maharashtra Assembly Elections: Of over 100 Seats, MNS Pockets Only One', October 25. Available at: Maharashtra assembly elections: Of over 100 seats, MNS pockets only one | Thane News - Times of India (indiatimes.com), accessed on January 20, 2020.

Vaidya, S. (1985). *[In Marathi] Hind Mazdūr Sabhā: 1949–1989*. Mumbai: Maniben Kara Institute.

Zee 24 Taas (2017). 'Mumbai Shiv Sena Shubha Raul and Sheetal Mhatre on Abhishek Ghosalkar', Available at: https://www.youtube.com/watch?v=pGHii_dryho, accessed on January 20, 2020.

11

WOMEN AND POLITICS IN GUJARAT

Kalpana Shah

Introduction

The present state of Gujarat in western India came into existence in the 1960s as a result of the bifurcation of the erstwhile Bombay state. On the basis of its historical and socio-cultural heritage as well as its physiological features, the present state can be broadly divided into two sub-regions: mainland Gujarat and peninsular Gujarat consisting of Kathiawar, known as the Saurashtra and Kutch regions. Under colonial rule mainland Gujarat was a part of Bombay Presidency and had the *ryotwari* land tenure system with individual land ownership whereas peninsular Gujarat with as many as 499 autocratic politico-administrative units had a 'feudalistic' land tenure system. Being a part of the colonial regime, mainland Gujarat had a western administrative and educational system. Along with changes in the agrarian structure, the British also brought about industrial development with modern technology to mainland Gujarat.

Gujarat has 6 per cent of the total area of India. According to Census (2011), its 60 million population consists of 52 per cent males and 48 per cent females. Of them, 88.5 per cent are Hindus, 9.8 per cent Muslims, 0.9 per cent Jains, and the rest are Christians, Buddhists, and Sikhs. All these communities are governed by a patriarchal system in varying degrees, with women having a subordinate position to men. The population is also divided into different social groups popularly called jatis.

Social reform movements in the state

In the nineteenth century, the first generation of upper-caste western-educated males in mainland Gujarat launched social reform movements, primarily confined to their castes. Upliftment of their women was on the agenda. Their activities were mainly confined to widow remarriages, raising the age for marriage, and providing formal education to girls. In the early twentieth century, some women's organizations run for and by women came into existence. Their activities included several welfare

DOI: 10.4324/9781003374862-12

211

programmes such as facilitating interactions among women of elite classes–castes for their recreation, teaching them etiquette, starting shelter homes for widows and deserted women, providing counselling in case of disputes between husbands and wives to 'save the family', skill development for supplementing family incomes, and also spreading education among girls.

With this perspective, leading social reformers and litterateurs launched a journal, *Stribodh* (teaching women), in 1857. During India's freedom movement and also in the post-independence period, several journals including those sponsored by castes and sects were published advocating women's welfare (Mehta, 2009). Essays, poems, stories, and novels written by both women and men advocating improving women's education and social life also came up. However, a few isolated voices like Jamnabai Pandita in the early twentieth century raised the question: 'Is women's education the answer for *woman's independence*? Why people do not think that *male dominance is the root cause of women's subjugation*?' (Mehta, 2009, p. 395, emphasis added).

But one hardly finds such voices in Gujarati mainstream literature in the subsequent period till the early 1970s (Desai, 1987; Pathak, 1997). The thrust of girls' education till the 1960s remained on equipping girls to 'perform' their roles as women looking after their families. This approach of the government policy was, however, overtly put on the back burner in the 1980s thanks to a rising feminist voice.

A few social reformers encouraged women to participate in public life. However, all of them including Gandhi advocated women's freedom within the framework of the patriarchal system which invariably subordinates women's position vis-à-vis men (Mehta, 2009; Shah, 1984).

Gender profile

Gujarat has had an adverse sex ratio for females since the turn of the nineteenth century. The gap in the sex ratio at birth has increased over time. In 1961, there were 940 females per 1,000 males which declined to 919 in 2011. The difference is more glaring among children in the age group of 0–6 years.

A preference for a boy over a girl leading to female infanticide has a long tradition among a few upper castes like the Patidars and Rajputs. It has become widespread in the last three decades with a market-driven healthcare system and technological inventions. The sex ratio among tribals, Dalits, OBCs, and Muslims has gradually started following the hegemonic culture of the dominant castes. Women have themselves imbibed patriarchal values and males' superiority over them; hence, many of them prefer having a son instead of a daughter. There is widespread belief that a girl will go away to her in-law's house after marriage, whereas a son will stay with his parents and is expected to look after them in their old age and when needed. The dowry system contributes to females' vulnerability (Visariya, 2005).

More often than not, the decision to abort a female foetus is 'almost entirely that of the husband and/or mother-in-law'. Women cannot take the decision to abort on their own. At the same time, they do not express or convey any remorse about aborting a female foetus. Moreover, because of a scarcity of girls in endogamous circles, the dominant castes have started bringing brides from tribal communities. Such married women do not enjoy the social status and traditional rights available in the caste system. As a result, tribal women who traditionally enjoyed a relatively better position than caste-Hindu women in their community are losing this position.

It is a matter of concern that the sex ratio decreased to 854 in 2013–15 from 907 in 2012–14. However, the child sex ratio came up to 890 in 2011 from 883 in 2001 as per the 2011 Census.

The maternal mortality rate in Gujarat gradually declined from 160 in 2004 to 113 in 2015–16. The state is ranked eighth in child and maternal malnourishment. Enrolment of girls and boys at the primary school level has almost reached 100 per cent. Gross enrolment ratios of both boys and girls, however, declined from primary to secondary and further to the higher education levels (Figure 11.1).

The textbooks, by and large, reproduce prevailing gender stereotypes, subordinating women in the patriarchal system. Notwithstanding such a situation in the education system, education per se and modern exposure to a larger world do play a catalytic role in developing individualism, aspirations, and a sense of rights among a section of the women. A number of

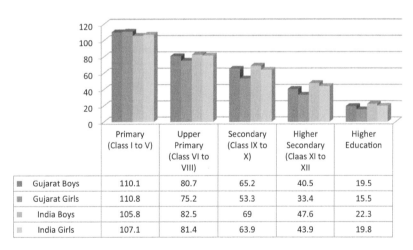

Figure 11.1 Gross enrolment ratio. Source: For schools (GoI 2014), for higher education (AISHE, 2017).

women journalists and writers as well as activists articulate feminist perspectives on several issues.

A woman is discouraged to complain against a male. The average incidents of crime against women were 8,420 per year as reported to the police between 2017 and 2019. Table 11.1 shows that over the years on an average more than one rape was recorded every day by the police. Gujarat ranks 15th in crimes against women and conviction rates for crimes against women are very low.

Gujarat, an industrialized state in the mid-1980s, attained the third position in terms of the number of industries and net value added in production. The process of industrialization accelerated further under a neo-liberal economy since the early 1990s (Parekh, 2014). Economic growth has also opened up opportunities for women to participate in the economic sphere. However, this has not ensured equal opportunities for women.

Almost as a norm, a woman is engaged in cooking, household chores, child raising, looking after old family members and domestic animals, and sharing farm and non-farm work in self-employed households. These are unpaid jobs. Besides domestic responsibilities, most of the women, particularly those from lower economic classes, are engaged in full- or part-time paid work whenever and whatever is available. Only 37 per cent of the women as against 84 per cent men in the age group of 15–49 years were employed in 2015–16. Among employed women, 82 per cent earned cash and 16 per cent were not paid. Most men who were employed earned cash (96 per cent) and only 3 per cent were not paid. Fifty-two per cent of the employed women worked in non-agricultural occupations, compared to 67 per cent employed men (NFHS, 2017, p. 26).

According to the 2011 Census, 32 per cent and 11.4 per cent women in rural and urban Gujarat, respectively, participated in main and marginal work in the market. Their work participation in urban areas has increased over the years. It, however, declined between 2001 and 2011 in the rural sector. Increased mechanization of agriculture replaced more female workers.

Table 11.1 Major crimes against women under the Indian Penal Code (IPC)

Major Crime	2017	2018	2019
Rape	477	572	529
Kidnapping and abduction	1,270	553	624
Dowry death	9	9	9
Cruelty by husband and relatives	2,678	2,928	3,629
Molestation	1,095	1,033	1,048
Sexual harassment	130	130	388
Assault	1,064	1,213	1,055

Source: National Crime Record Bureau reports (various years).

Most of the males as well as females are self-employed and/or casual workers. The proportion of women in these categories is higher than men. Economic growth did not evenly benefit female and male workers in the last decade. Moreover, women workers are paid lower wages as compared to their male counterparts for similar work in several farm and non-farm informal sectors.

According to a Tata Trust (2019) report, there are only 7.2 per cent women in the police and 5.5 per cent in prison staff. Unlike several states, Gujarat does not have reservations for women in the lower judiciary. Only 15 judges at the lower judiciary level are women.

Gender equality in the labour market is a concern in the state. Women's work participation rates are lower than the average recorded for India. Despite Gujarat being an industrially advanced state, the high proportion of women workers in agriculture reflects lack of appropriate and adequate opportunities for women in non-agricultural sectors (State-wise Trends: Gujarat, 2020, p. 4).

Since the early 1970s women social activists like Ela Bhatt have formed cooperative societies for women working in the informal sectors as vendors, embroidery and craft workers, mid-wives, patch workers, rag pickers, and child care workers. SEWA (Self-employed Women's Association) also has a women's cooperative bank which provides credit to women self-employed workers/entrepreneurs. There are also a few women cooperatives engaged in the milk sector as well as in making snacks and other edible items. A handful of women entrepreneurs from the middle class are visible. Several NGOs with support from the government, the National Bank for Agriculture and Rural Development (NABARD), and donors are engaged in self-help groups providing credit to women workers. Gujarati women are relatively better placed than women in the country as a whole in this sector.

Several states including Gujarat, under pressure from civil society groups, granted exemption or reduction in stamp duty/registration fees to women. With this and the efforts of women activists, the number of properties registered exclusively in the names of women has steadily increased since 2009 (Vasavada et al., 2015).

Women voters

Women have exercised their voting rights in different proportions for local government bodies as well as for the state assembly and Lok Sabha elections. Voter turnout among both women and men at local as well as higher levels varies from less than 50 per cent to above 70 per cent. Women's voter turnout in local government bodies, as well as in elections to the state assembly and the Lok Sabha, has been lower than the male voter turnout. The gap between the two declined from 11 per cent in 1985 to 3 per cent in 2012 (Figure 11.2).

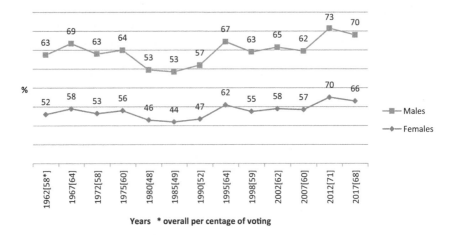

Figure 11.2 Voting patterns in the state assembly (1962–2017). Source: Compiled by the author based on 'Election Commission of India: Statistical Reports of Gujarat legislative elections' for different years.

There are no micro- or macro-level systematic studies of women's voting behaviour in Gujarat. There is only anecdotal evidence. According to Banerjee (2014), for some women, voting is associated with a cultural process as they see it as a tradition; for many, the process of voting is an outlet for the creation of one's identity. These answers do not tell us about the influence of male family members on women's voting preferences.

Women in the state assembly

In Gujarat, the number of state legislative assembly members increased from 154 in 1962 to 181 in 1975 and then 182 in 1980. In the last 13 assembly elections from 1962 to 2017, on an average only 52 women (4 per cent) as against 1,197 men contested the elections. Though the number of women candidates increased from 52 or less till 1990 to 94 in 1995, it again declined in the two subsequent elections, and again increased from 2007 reaching above 100 in 2017 (Figure 11.3).

Of the candidates who contested in the state assembly elections in the last five decades, on average only 4 per cent women got elected. Their proportion in the assembly varies from 2 per cent in 1975, 1990, and 1998 to 9 per cent in 2012, and 8 per cent in the first assembly in 1962. The very low proportion of women candidates indicates that they do not have aspirations or have no encouragement and networks of support to contest elections. This also reveals the marginalization of women in public life in the state.

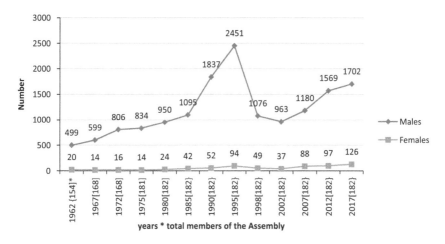

Figure 11.3 Male and female candidates in state assembly elections (1962–2017).
Source: Compiled by the author based on 'Election Commission of India: Statistical Reports of Gujarat legislative elections' (various years).

Since 1962, the Gujarat Vidhan Sabha has had 113 women MLAs and some of them have been elected more than once. In 2017, the Congress and the BJP together fielded 22 women, 13 of whom won. Out of these women candidates, 7 were incumbent MLAs while 13 were first-time contestants. Though the parties are not enthusiastic about giving tickets to women, as they think women are weak candidates, the victory margins, both in 2012 and in 2017, showed that women outperformed men in both the parties. Women getting tickets either from the BJP or Congress have better chances of winning (Basim-u-Nissa and Verniers, 2017).

In the Gujarat assembly elections in 2017, political parties indulged in tokenism when it came to selecting women candidates and foregrounding a mandate for women's development. Largely, the women who have contested elections have been supported by their families. Till now, only a few women MLAs like Neema Acharya (elected for the fourth time from Kutch district), Anandiben Patel (four-term MLA), Vibhavariben Dave (three-time MLA from Bhavnagar city), and the late Bhavnaben Chikhalia have been known to contest elections in their individual capacity.

These MLAs worked for political parties' cadres and rose through the ranks. Despite only a few women in active politics, the number of women casting their votes in elections has gradually increased from 1962. Social media platforms, especially Twitter and the Modi app, have contributed significantly to the mobilization of women. Initiatives like Sakhi Mandal Sammelans (conferences of women's small saving and microfinance groups), the Swachh Bharat Mission, building toilets, and Samras Yojana in Panchayati Raj are also to be noted in this context (Bhagat-Ganguly, 2017).

It is important to note that Kamla Beniwal and Sharda Mukherjee were Governors of the state (Figure 11.4).

Elected women representatives have been from major political parties like the BJP, Congress, and the Janata Dal. Most of the representatives belong to upper or middle castes. A few are from OBCs. There have been some exceptions of women representatives belonging to SCs or STs who got elected from reserved seats. Many of them are members of political families (Sanghavi, 1996). However, the parties have occasionally picked up women like Santokben Jadeja, a strong woman, and Dipika Topiwala (Chikhalia), who did the role of Sita in TV serial *Ramayan*. The former was elected in the assembly elections in 1990 as a Janata Dal candidate. However, a few women representatives have developed their own public stature like Anandiben Patel.

So far, the state has been ruled by 16 chief ministers for different lengths of time. Of them, only one woman, Anandiben Patel, was the Chief Minister for more than two years. She joined the BJP in 1987 and became the president of Bhartiya Mahila Morcha (BMM). In her ministry two women, including herself, were ministers. So far, the maximum number of women ministers has been three during 1989–90. Except for a few, most of the women ministers did not have a cabinet rank. In 2005, the State Commission for Women was set up as an advisory body 'to present the views of women to government'. During Anandiben's tenure, a 'gender budget' was introduced for the first time as a part of the government's annual budget clubbing all women centric provisions under one head. It is important to note that Gujarat

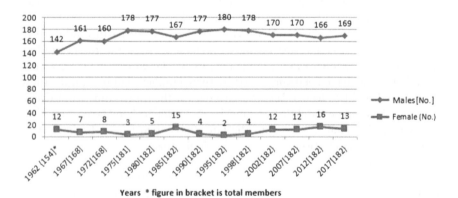

Figure 11.4 Number of male and female members in the Gujarat assembly. Source: Compiled by the author based on 'Election Commission of India: Statistical Reports of Gujarat legislative elections' (various years).

has granted the status of a cabinet minister to the chairperson of the State Commission for Women.

The elected representatives function as per their parties' political ideology and structure. Most of the political parties, by and large, are not much different in their views on the issue of patriarchy. After the 1970s, the parties talked about 'development' replacing the earlier 'welfare' of women. The rhetoric of 'empowerment' of women has now gained currency. However, their notion of empowering women has been limited to giving them education and/or income-generating activities.

Women's wings

Since the 1980s, the constitutions of the BJP and Congress provide reservation for women at all levels of the organization in their executive committees. They have formed their women's wings to mobilize women in political programmes during and between election campaigns. Congress has the Mahila Congress (MC) and BJP, the BMM. They function within the parties' ideological frameworks focusing on improving women's status.

BJP is connected with other women's organisations like the Rashtra Sevika Samiti and Durga Vahini. These organizations inculcate values like upholding womanhood/motherhood among women as glorified in their notion of Hindu culture (Basu, 1998; Menon, 2012).

Women's representation in Parliament

In 1962, Gujarat had 24 seats in the Lok Sabha; now the number is 26. Of them, three are reserved for STs and SCs. Of the total 395 members elected from the state between 1962 and 2019, 361 were men and only 34 were women. The highest number of female MPs was six in 2019. There was no female MP in 1980 and 1989 (Figure 11.5). Kumudben Joshi and Smriti Irani, who reached the positions of ministers at the Centre, have been members of the Rajya Sabha from Gujarat. Besides them, Ela Bhatt was a nominated member in 1981. Like in the state assembly, only a few women have contested in the Lok Sabha elections. In 2019, only six women of the total 26 seats got elected to the Lok Sabha. All of them were BJP candidates. This was the highest number of women MPs since the formation of the state.

Some women from Gujarat have been elected to the Lok Sabha more than once. Among them are Maniben Patel (Congress and then Janata Party) (Sardar Patel's daughter) and Bhavna Chikhalia (BJP) – both were elected four times. Jayaben Shah (Congress), Nisha Amarsinh Choudhary (INC), and Darshana Vikram Jardosh (BJP) were elected thrice, and Jayshreeben Patel (BJP), Ranjanben D. Bhatt (BJP), and Poonamben H. Maadam (BJP) were elected twice. Amee Yajnik (INC) and Ramilaben B. Bara (BJP) are members of the Rajya Sabha. Earlier Maniben Patel was also a member of the

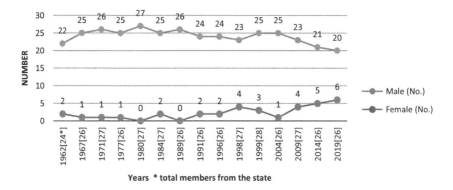

Figure 11.5 Number of male and female Lok Sabha members from Gujarat. Source: Compiled by the author based on 'Election Commission of India: Statistical Reports of Lok Sabha elections' (for various years).

Rajya Sabha. There are a few cases of upward mobility. Some women from the state have made it to decision-making bodies at the Centre after gaining experience at the state level like Bharatiben D. Shiyal and Poonamben H. Maadam, who are former MLAs. Gitaben V. Rathva, a member of the Lok Sabha at present, was a member of the district panchayat in Chhota Udepur for five terms. Bhavna Kardam Dave (BJP) elected to the 12th Lok Sabha was Mayor, Municipal Corporation, Ahmedabad.

Even though women MLAs and MPs speak across party lines on women's issues related to their welfare and violence against them, generally, they toe the party line. Their voice on increasing incidents of violence against women and women's trafficking is raised once in a while, but not very effectively.

They did not question the government when the financial allocation for women and child development was reduced from 1.35 per cent in 2015–16 to 1.27 per cent of the total budget in 2018–19 (Sahaj, 2018). Also, they did not build pressure on their parties in demanding women's reservation in legislatures.

Ela Bhatt's contribution as a nominated member of the Rajya Sabha has been distinctively notable in raising her voice for improving women's conditions among informal sector workers. She asserted the rights of informal women workers in Parliament. In 1987, the government appointed a commission under her leadership to enquire about the condition of women workers in the informal sector. Her report, *Shram Shakti* (1989), highlighted inadequate infrastructure, official insensitivity, and the innate resilience of these women.

Women in decision-making bodies at the local level

The Committee on the Status of Women in India (CSWI) recommended reservation for women in local governments. Moreover, two of its members in their dissenting note demanded reservation for women in Parliament. This demand, however, has not been accepted till today.

However, 33 per cent reservation for women in local government institutions was introduced with the 73rd and 74th Constitutional Amendments in 1992. It also provided headship to women in local government bodies at all levels by rotation. In 2018, like several other states, Gujarat too increased reservations for women to 50 per cent in local government bodies. Gujarat has 13,819 village panchayats with 112,552 members, 225 taluka (block) panchayats with 4,161 members, and 26 district panchayats with 819 members. The state has 159 municipalities and 7 municipal corporations.

The provision of reservations has provided significant opportunities for women to participate in public life. A study conducted in 1997 observed that 50 per cent women members in the village, taluka, and district level government bodies belonged to upper and middle castes and 36 per cent were from OBCs. Representation of women belonging to minority communities and Muslims was almost negligible. The proportion of SCs and STs was lower than their population which is 7 and 15 per cent, respectively (Shah, 1998).

Panchayat being a source of power, male power-seekers motivate and manipulate the system so that their women family members get the positions uncontested. Despite this, as many as 59 per cent women, though nominated by political parties or dominant political coteries, have contested elections. Once they were pushed in the power game, these women willy-nilly began learning the art of politics. However, most of them remain puppets in the hands of their husbands and/or powerful males of the community.

At the same time, one gets several cases where elected women have carved out their independent positions. In the course of time, they have learned administrative rules and how to exercise authority. They have gained confidence in dealing with the bureaucracy independently for getting their work done successfully. Women's presence in offices facilitates women's organizations to use the 'middle space' for empowering women. For instance, with their pressure, the government waived off the registration fee for women-owned properties (Vasavada et al., 2015).

However, women have yet to emerge as independent political leaders to assert prioritizing issues affecting women. This is not because they lack competency but because of constraints of time and the distance that they have to travel with dual and sometimes triple responsibilities. They work in male-dominated political parties. They are also not free from patriarchal values, which are reinforced in contemporary politics.

Though women do have an impact on everyday issues like those related to water, fuel, health, and education at the local level, they are not able to make an impact on, what Bishakha Datta (1998) calls, 'strategic needs'. These needs are rooted in the patriarchal structure of power relationships and include opposing forced abortions for a male child, challenging incidences of domestic violence, violence deriving from the dowry system, equal wages, and preventing rape incidents (Banerjee, 2007).

Local women representatives are also not united on women's common causes. A sense of sisterhood has not developed and they are divided along caste and religious lines. A recent study observes that around 85 per cent of the Dalit women were pushed into panchayat politics primarily by dominant castes or their husbands, the former often working through the women's husbands. Dominant castes also, for the most part, sought to directly engineer elections by consensus, thereby making the reservation policy redundant. The primary tool for this and the most significant factor drawn from this research was *benami* or proxy politics. The effective use of proxy candidatures provided legitimized political space for primarily dominant caste men and secondarily Dalit men to exploit Dalit women and reinforce their own interests and the suppression of these women. As one Dalit village head says:

> In the patriarchal system, there are lots of struggles for women to win the election. And within the system, Dalit women have to struggle more than other women. It is very difficult for them to win the election because nobody believes that they have the ability to carry out Panchayat works. Everyone plays politics with them and against them just because they – dominant castes and men – never want Dalit women to control the Panchayat administration ... Men never accept women's leadership.
>
> (Mangubhai et al., 2009, p. 3)

However, increased participation in public life has generated more confidence in several women. They have also gained greater freedom of speech in their families as well as in public spaces. While holding an office, quite a few of them effectively argue their positions and get things done effectively. However, though their space in family decision-making has increased, their position as equals with male members in all matters of personal, family, and social life continues to remain by and large unchanged. Moreover, most of them do not have their own financial resources and have to depend on male members who hesitate in accepting the notion of equality in their everyday socioeconomic lives.

Municipal corporations and municipalities have more women members mainly due to the reservation policy. Women mayors can be noticed in cities like Ahmedabad, Rajkot, Vadodara, and Gandhinagar. However, local factors and political parties play an important role in elections to urban local bodies. Of the 181 corporators in the Ahmedabad Municipal Corporation 91 are women, the Rajkot Municipal Corporation has 36 women, Vadodara 38, and Gandhinagar 16 (*Ahmedabad Mirror*, 2020). It is interesting to note that Aneesa Begum Mirza was the first Muslim woman to become a mayor in Ahmedabad, elected soon after the Godhra riots. She had been continuously elected long before reservations for women were implemented (Ashraya Maria, 2019).

Women in non-formal politics

The process of formation of voluntary (non-government) organizations for the welfare of women that started during the social reform and freedom movements accelerated in the early 1950s. Nearly 11 per cent of the NGOs in Gujarat work for women's welfare. Some of them have been started by women. Women social activists are also engaged with NGOs working for rural development, water, health, sanitation, skill development, and urban and rural labourers. One-fourth of the office holders including members of executive committees of the NGOs are women. However, most of these members belong to the upper and middle castes (Shah and Das, 1988). Except a few, these organizations rarely question the issue of gender equality. They provide training to women in child care, health, and skill development for income-generating programmes.

The report of the CSWI (1974), *Towards Equality*, coinciding with women's international year in 1975, was a turning point in the nature of the discourse on gender equality and women's movement. The report emphasized that the process of improving women's socioeconomic status needed to be coupled with gender equality. Though welfare-oriented organizations have continued, women's rights-based organizations asking for justice and equality for women have also started occupying a visible place in Gujarat's public life. The Mathura rape case (1972) resulted in countrywide protests by women activists. They demanded not only reforms in rape laws but also asserted that the state should take responsibility for crimes committed by its agents (police).

In urban Gujarat, women activists formed a forum against rape. Issues related to domestic violence including dowry deaths were also raised. In the 1980s, AWAG (Ahmadabad Women's Action Group), Sahiyar, Chingari, Olakh, and Astitva were formed which assert women's rights and equality. They mobilize women and evolve strategies to conscientize them for demanding equality, socioeconomic and political empowerment, and fighting against violence against them. These organizations are building an alliance with other organizations working on deprived communities' civil and political rights including religious minorities. Some of them also provide counselling to women victims of domestic violence. While doing so, their emphasis is on woman's dignity and rights rather than protecting the family (Shah, 2016). Besides them, a few women's NGOs concerned with gender equality are building pressure on the government for undertaking and implementing women-centric programmes for their empowerment. They have formed a network, the Gujarat Mahila Morcha/forum. The focus of their activities is on health, nutrition, food security, skill development, land rights, and security. The social base of these organizations, however, has so far been limited.

Women's participation in collective action with their male counterparts for preserving and asserting their real or imagined cultural identity and economic issues affecting their everyday lives has always been there though not recognized or recorded by mainstream historians. Some women also sporadically protest and rebel against perceived injustices. During the freedom struggle, thanks to Mahatma Gandhi's efforts, women, particularly from the upper and middle social strata, participated in various satyagrahas. During these struggles, some women were detained and also jailed. Women like Kasturba Gandhi and Maniben Patel were active in Gujarat during the freedom struggle.

In the 1950s, urban women participated in the Maha-Gujarat movement demanding a separate state for Gujarat. Urban middle-class women led an agitation in the early 1960s against price rise of essential commodities. They also actively participated in the 1974 students' movement against price rise and corruption (Bhagat-Ganguly, 2015). Middle-class women also participated in the 1985 anti-reservation as well as the Ram Janmabhoomi agitation. At the same time, urban and rural poor women peasants, agriculture labourers, fisher-folk, and industrial workers collectively struggled for land rights, wages, water, and other amenities. They actively participated in the agitations against the acquisition of their land and habitat for industries and irrigation projects (Bhagat-Ganguly, 2015).

Like men, women too got divided on communal lines during various communal riots (Shah et al., 1993). However, there were a few women, men, and organizations that not only registered their protest against violence against women but also provided protection to Muslim women and men (Dhruv, 2016).

A striking difference with the past is that women have now launched campaigns and struggles for gender equality around the issues affecting them as women. Though the scale of such struggles is small, the state and dominant classes cannot afford to ignore their voices.

Conclusion

Women's representation in the Gujarat state legislative assembly and Parliament has increased but it is still minuscule. These representatives are not effective in raising their voice for women. They are divided according to their party's ideology. All major political parties talk about gender equality as proclaimed by the Constitution but their promises are hardly translated into actions. Male members of the parties and the bureaucracy dominate the decision-making process. Women members cutting across party lines do raise their voices on issues related to violence against women.

The elected women representatives, including in local governments, did not join hands across party lines in building enough pressure on their parties' leaders when civil society demanded reservation for women in Parliament and state assemblies. Women have imbibed patriarchal values thanks to their socialization and they are divided along caste, religion, region, and class lines. However, notwithstanding the structural constraints, the constitutional commitment to equality and the growth of modern institutions, though deformed, have raised women's aspirations and determination to go ahead.

Bibliography

AISHE (2017). *All India Survey of Higher Education (2016–17)*.New Delhi: Ministry of Human Resource Development, Government of India.

Ashraya Maria (2019). 'How 7 Women Mayors Transformed Their Cities', Feminism in India, February 6. Available at https://feminisminindia.com/2019/02/06/7-women-mayors-transform-cities/#:~:text=3.,violent%20Godhra%20riots%20in%20Gujarat, accessed on February 1, 2022.

Banerjee, Mukulika (2014). *Why India Votes?* New Delhi: Routledge.

Banerjee, Sikata (2007). 'Chaste like Sita, Fierce Like Durga: Indian Women in Politics', in Ramashray Roy and Wallce Paul (eds), *India's 2004 Elections*. New Delhi: Sage Publications.

Basim-u-Nissa and Gilles Verniers (2017). 'Gujarat elected only 13 female MLAs – continuing a nationwide trend of low representation for women', Scroll.in December 2017. Available at https://scroll.in/article/862626/gujarat-elected-13-female-mlas-continuing-a-nationwide-trend-of-low-representation-for-women, accessed on February 1, 2022.

Basu, Amrita (1998). 'Hindu Women's Activism in India and the Questions it Raises', in Jeffery Paricia and Basu Amrita (eds), *Appropriating Gender: Women's Activism and Politicized Religion in South Asia*. New York: Routledge.

Bhagat-Ganguly, Varsha (2015). *Protest Movements and Citizens' Rights in Gujarat (1970–2010)*. Shimla: Indian Institute of Advanced Study.

———— (2017). 'Tokenistic 'Vikas' for Women in Gujarat', *Economic and Political Weekly, (Engage)*, 52 (52), December 30. Available at: https://www.epw.in/engage/article/tokenistic-vikas-women-gujarat, accessed on October 8, 2021.

Bhatt, Ela (1989). *Shramshakti*. Ahmedabad: SEWA.

CSWI (1974). *Towards Equality: Report of the Committee on the Status of Women in India*. New Delhi: Ministry of Education and Social Welfare, Government of India.

Datta, Bishakha (1998). *'And Who Will Make the Chapatties?' A Study of All Women Panchayats in Maharashtra*. Kolkata: Stree.

Desai, Anjna (1987).'Gujarati Navalkathman Adhunik Narinu Nirupan', in Kalpana Shah and Vibhuti Patel (eds), *Sri Samanata: Prashnoane Padkaro* (Gujarati). Surat: Centre for Social Studies.

Dhruv, Sarup (2016). *Ansar Kyank AAshano (Gujarati)*. Baroda: Yagnya Prakashan.

Government of India (2014). *Statistics of School Education 2011–12*. New Delhi: Ministry of Human Resources.

—— (2018). *Female Employment Rate*. New Delhi: Press Information Bureau, Ministry of Labour & Employment.

GSIDBS (Gujarat Social Infrastructure Development Board Society) (2012). *Socio-economic and Demographic Status of Women in Gujarat*. Gandhinagar: GSIDBS.

Hirway, Indira and Mahadevia Darshini (2004). *Gujarat Human Development Report*. Ahmedabad: Mahatma Gandhi Labour Institute.

Labour Bureau (2016). *Report on Fifth Annual Employment - Unemployment Survey 2015–16*. Chandigarh: Labour Bureau.

Mangubhai, Jayshree, Irudayam Aloysius, and Sydenham Emma (2009). *Dalit Women's Right to Political Participation in Rural Panchayati Raj : A study of Gujarat and Tamil Nadu: Executive Summary*. IDEAS, The Netherlands: Justitia et Pax. Available at: http://idsn.org/wp-content/uploads/user_folder/pdf/New_files/Key_Issues/Dalit_Women/India_Dalitwomen_PolParticipation_RuralPanchayati.pdf, accessed on October 8, 2020.

Manjrekar, Nandini, Trupti Shah, Lokhande Johanna, and Chaudhary Nitesh (2010). *Gujarat: Text Book Regimes*. Delhi: Nirantar.

Mehta, Shirin (2009). *Gujaratman Narichetna*(Gujarati). Ahmedabad: Darshakitihas Nidhi.

Menon, Kalyani Devaki (2012). *Everyday Nationalism: Women of the Hindu Right in India*. Philadelphia: University of Pennsylvania Press.

National Family Health Survey,(NFHS-4) 2015-16 (2017). Mumbai: International Institute for Population Studies.

Pandey, Saroj (1996).'Curriculum and Gender Question: Indian Experience', *Social Action*, 46, 340–347.

Parekh, Sunil (2014). 'Some Facets of Industrialization in Gujarat (1999–2009)', in Hirvey Indira, Shah Amita, and Shah Ghanshyam (eds), *Growth or Development: Which Way Gujarat is Going?* Delhi: Oxford University Press.

Ahmedabad Mirror, (2020), Patel, Lakshmi (2020). 'Women Mayors have all-men cricket teams', March 7. Available at https://ahmedabadmirror.com/women-mayors-have-all-men-cricket-teams/74520243.html accessed on December 9, 2020

Pathak, Ila (1997). 'Gujarati Navalkathaman Sfutthto Lekhakono Nari Pratye Abhigam', in Kalpana Shah (ed.), *Sahityaman Nari Chetna (Gujarati)*. Surat: Centre for Social Studies.

Sanghavi, Nagindas (1996). *Gujarat: A Political Analysis*. Surat: Centre for Social Studies.

Sahaj (2018). *Monitoring the Progress of Sustainable Development Goals in Gujarat: Situation Analysis for Selected Targets from SDG3 and SDG5*. Vadodara: Sahaj.

Shah, Ghanshyam and Biswaroop Das (1988). *Voluntary Organisations in Gujarat*. Surat: Centre for Social Studies.

Shah, Kalpana (1984). *Women's Liberation and Voluntary Action*. Delhi: Ajanta Publications.

—— (1998). *Women in Panchayati Raj Institutions*. Surat: Centre for Social Studies.

—— (2016). *Struggle for Equality*. Ahmedabad: AWAG.

Shah, Kalpana, Smita Shah, and Neha Shah (1993). 'The Nightmare of Surat', *Manushi*, 74–75, 50–59.

Shanley, Mary Lyndon (1993). '"Surrogate Mothering" and Women's Freedom: A Critique of Contracts for Human Reproduction', *Signs*, 18 (3), 618–639.

Tata Trusts (2019). *India Justice Report*. New Delhi: Tata Trusts.

Vasavada, Shilpa, Meena Rajgor, and Varsha Ganguly (2015). 'Panchayati Raj Institutions and Women's Land Ownership: Learning from Gujarat', *Journal of Land and Rural Studies*, 3 (2), 274–283.

Visaria, Leela (2005). *Sex Selective Abortion in India: Some Empirical Evidence from Gujarat and Haryana States*. Princeton Education papers. Available at: https://iussp2005.princeton.edu/papers/51652, accessed on October 8, 2020.

12

WOMEN AND POLITICS IN MAHARASHTRA

Bharati Patil

Introduction

Maharashtra, one of the most developed and progressive states in India, is also one of India's major commercial and industrial hubs. With a population of 11.24 crore (Census, 2011) and with a geographical area of about 3.08 lakh sq. km the state ranks second by population and third in terms of geographical area. The state is highly urbanized with 45.2 per cent of the population living in towns (Economic Survey of Maharashtra, 2020).

The birthplace of many social reforms and progressive movements, Maharashtra was at the forefront of the freedom struggle. Based on a demand for the linguistic reorganization of provinces it was created on May 1, 1960, by splitting the bilingual Bombay into Maharashtra (with a majority of Marathi-speaking people) and Gujarat (with a majority of Gujarati-speaking people). Since then, the state has witnessed increased urbanization and industries and migration from other states. Its capital, Mumbai, the city that never sleeps, has emerged as the nerve centre of finance, commerce, and trade at the national and international levels. The flourishing media and film industry casts its spell on the people from all over. The state, however, cannot be treated as one homogeneous entity. It comprises broad regions like Marathwada, Vidarbha, Western Maharashtra, and Konkan, each with varying cultural nuances, diverse natural features, and different levels of economic and social development.

It is assumed that women in the state are equal to men and get equal opportunities for their development. However, the reality is different. To begin with, the sex ratio according to the last Census was 929 (Economic Survey of Maharashtra, 2020, p. 18).

On the positive side, the literacy rate in the state is high. As per the National Sample Survey on 'Household Social Consumption: Education' conducted by the National Sample Survey Office during July 2017 and June 2018, the literacy rate in the state was 79.4 per cent in rural and 91.7 per cent in urban areas. Female literacy rate in rural areas was 71.4 per cent; it

228   DOI: 10.4324/9781003374862-13

was 87.6 per cent in urban areas, whereas male literacy in rural and urban areas was 87 per cent and 95.3 per cent respectively (Economic Survey of Maharashtra, 2020, p. 189).

However, despite having the highest gross state domestic product (GSDP) among all the states, in terms of gender, Maharashtra ranks low as compared to the other states (IWWAGE, 2020). It is a matter of grave concern that women in Maharashtra are victims of violence. There were 35,497 cases of crime against women (IPC+SLL) in 2018 (Crimes in India-2019, 2020, p. 195).

Women in the public sphere

Unlike some other states, the light of renaissance touched the lives of the women in Bombay Presidency early in the pre-independence era and motivated some of them to expand their scope of activities beyond their private spheres. Women like Tarabai Shinde, Anandibai Joshi, Rukhmabai Raut, Kashibai Kanitkar, and Pandita Ramabai were trendsetters. The rising political consciousness among women was expressed in their demand for the right to vote. A delegation of women led by Sarojini Naidu met Montagu and Chelmsford (Forbes, 1998). This delegation included women like Ramabai Ranade, Sarlabai Naik, and Dalvi (Karve, 2015).

Influenced by Mahatma Gandhi, many women in Maharashtra as in other parts of India, joined the Swadeshi movement and organized *prabhat pheris* (morning processions), picketing, and meetings. Poona and Mumbai were the centres of such activities. The Civil Disobedience movement of 1930–33 was a major landmark in women's political activities. Sarojini Naidu, Bachubai Lotwala, and Avantikabai Gokhale were members of the Bombay Municipal Corporation in 1923. Anasuyabai Kale was the first woman to be nominated as a member of Central Provinces and the Berar legislative council, Nagpur, in 1928, and she was the Deputy Speaker, Central Provinces legislative assembly, 1937.

During this period, Dr Babasaheb Ambedkar's movement for Dalit liberation was gaining momentum. At the Mahad Satyagraha the *Manusmriti* (Hindu scripture) was burnt; more than 50 women participated in the demonstrations. Later in July 1942, the All India Depressed Classes' Women Conference was organized in Nagpur which was attended by 25,000 women and chaired by Sulochanabai Dongre.

The Quit India Movement in 1942, the last mass struggle in the freedom movement, attracted women in huge numbers. One of the important developments during the Quit India Movement was the movement for parallel government, popularly known as *Patri Sarkar* in the districts of Satara and Sangli. An interesting feature of the parallel government was the involvement of women, both directly and indirectly. The most impressive contribution was by Lila Patil (captain in the Toofan Sena), Laxmibai Naikwadi,

Indutai Nikam-Patankar, Rajmati Patil Birnale, and others (Nalawade, 1989).

Social and political consciousness among women in Maharashtra continued increasing in post-independence times and was expressed in women's activities in the public sphere and in women's movements, demonstrations, and protests. Over the years several women's organizations have come into existence in different parts of Maharashtra.

Women from Maharashtra in the Parliament

Not many women from Maharashtra have been elected to the Lok Sabha. However, a few women were attracted to politics and their experience and involvement makes them winners in electoral politics. We have examples of veterans who have been elected to the Lok Sabha more than once like Premalabai Dajisaheb Chavan (Congress-I, four times), Jayawantiben Mehta (BJP, three times), Bhavana Gawali (Patil) (Shiv Sena, five times), Supriya Sule (NCP, three times), Priya Dutt (INC), Pritam Gopinath Rao Munde, and Poonam (Mahajan) Vajendla Rao (both from BJP) twice.

There have been some one-time winners as well: Maharani Vijayamala Rajaram Chhatrapati Bhonsle (Peasants and Workers' Party of India), Tara Sapre (Congress), Roza Deshpande (CPI), Mrinal Gore (Janata Party), Ahilya Rangnekar (CPI M), Pramila Dandavate (Janata Party), Shalini V Patil (Congress-I), Pratibha Devisingh Patil (Congress-I), Rajani Patil (BJP), Prabha Rau (INC), Kalpana Ramesh Narhire (Shiv Sena), and Bharati Pawar (BJP). Interestingly Navneet Ravi Rana won as an independent in the 17th Lok Sabha. The present Lok Sabha has eight women members from Maharashtra, the highest number of women from the state so far (loksabhaph.nic.in).

Representation of women from Maharashtra in the Rajya Sabha has remained very low (Table 12.1). Till date only 16 women from the state have been members of the Rajya Sabha in addition to two nominated members.

Despite their small numbers, women from Maharashtra in Parliament have been visible and the performance of many of them has been notable. Some women have been in both the Houses, and, in addition, some have been in the assembly as well. Some of them have followed the logic of upward mobility from the local to the national level. It is useful to take a look at the political profiles of some of these women.

Pratibha Patil is a prominent politician from the state. Elected to the assembly at the young age of 27 years from Jalgaon constituency and thereafter from Edlabad constituency four times, she efficiently handled various ministries. Thereafter she entered Rajya Sabha and was its Deputy Chairperson. She was also elected to the tenth Lok Sabha and was later appointed the Governor of Rajasthan. The culmination of her political career was her election to the highest office in India. She was the President

WOMEN AND POLITICS IN MAHARASHTRA

Table 12.1 Women from Maharashtra in the Rajya Sabha

Sr. No.	Period	Name
1.	1962–68	Tara Sathe (Congress)
2.	1967–72	Vimal Panjabrao Deshmukh (Congress)
3.	1968–74	Sarojini Babar (Congress)
4.	1971–72	Sushila Adivarekar (Congress)
	1972–78	Sushila Adivarekar (Congress) Sushila Adivarekar
	1978–84	(Congress-I)
5.	1980–86	Premala Chavan (Congress-I)
6.	1985–90	Pratibha Patil (Congress-I)
7.	1986–92	Suryakanta Patil (Congress-I)
8.	1980–86	Najma Heptullah (Congress-I)
	1986–92	
	1992–98	
	1998–2004	
9.	1984–90	Sudha Joshi (Congress-I)
10.	1972–74	Saroj Khaparde (INC)
	1976–82	
	1982–88	
	1988–94	
11.	1990–96	Chandrika Jain (Keniya) Congress-I
12.	2006–12	Supriya Sule (NCP)
13.	2013–18	Rajani Patil (INC)
14.	2012–18	Vandana Chavan (NCP)
	2018–24	
15.	2020–26	Fauzia Khan (NCP)
16.	2020–26	Priyanka Chaturvedi (Shiv Sena)
		Nominated Members
1.	1964–70	Shakuntala Paranjpe
2.	1997–2003	Shabana Azmi

Source: rajyasabha.nic.in/Members/AlphabeticalFormerMember, accessed on June 20, 2022.

of India from 2007 to 2012, the only woman president so far. Premalabai Dajisaheb Chavan had a notable political career as a four-time member of the Lok Sabha as well as a member of the Rajya Sabha.

Jayawantiben Mehta was elected to the Bombay Municipal Corporation and thereafter to the state assembly. She was elected thrice to the Lok Sabha and was the union minister of state for power.

Kesarbai Kshirsagar entered the political field as the sarpanch of the gram panchayat in village Rajuri and was elected to the assembly in 1967 and then to the Lok Sabha.

Prabha Rao, six times member of the assembly, was an efficient minister looking after various departments at the state level. She also reached the central level by being elected to the Lok Sabha. In 2008 she was appointed the Governor of Himachal Pradesh, and in 2009 was given the additional charge of Governor of Rajasthan. Sharda Subroto Mukherjee, twice elected to the Lok Sabha, was later appointed the Governor of Andhra Pradesh and Gujarat.

Supriya Sule with her experience of working in both the Houses of Parliament has emerged as a politician with her distinct way of handling difficult political situations. She has taken keen interest in issues like education, healthcare, women's development, and self-help groups.

Sushila Adivarekar, a competent member of the Rajya Sabha, was a well-known social worker associated with various organizations involved in the welfare of women and children.

Najma Heptullah has a long record of being in the Rajya Sabha for six terms and towards the end of her political life as Governor of Manipur. She was elected from Maharashtra for the first four terms. She was also the Deputy Chairperson of the Rajya Sabha. She was a prominent member of INC, but switched over to the BJP in 2004 and was the union minister of minority affairs and a vice president of BJP and a member of the party's national executive. Saroj Khaparde too had a meaningful record of being in the Rajya Sabha for five terms and had experience as the Deputy Chairperson of the Rajya Sabha.

Kalpana R. Narhire (Shiv Sena) was elected twice to the state assembly (1995–2004) and to the 14th Lok Sabha. Fauzia Tahseen Khan (NCP), one of the very few Muslim women in politics, is a member of the Rajya Sabha. She had two terms in the Maharashtra legislative council and was a minister of state in the state cabinet.

Some women retained their activist spirit despite being in the political arena. Mrinal Gore, Pramila Dandavate, and Ahilya Rangnekar carved out a niche in politics because of their concern for the people and their dauntless activism on issues of women's empowerment. They belonged to a special set of women leaders for whom women's rights, civil rights, and people's welfare were of utmost importance.

Initially a member of the Goregaon gram panchayat, Mrinal Gore emerged as a respected and effective member of the Bombay Municipal Corporation, and subsequently of the state assembly and Lok Sabha. She strived relentlessly to make essential needs like water, shelter, urban housing, and food grains available to the people at fair prices. She was affectionately called *paniwali bai* for her efforts in bringing water to Goregaon, a suburb in Mumbai. She was deeply involved in movements like Samyukta Maharashtra and was a leader in the anti-price rise movement.

Pramila Dandavate also remained an activist motivated by socialist ideas with deep empathy for the deprived. Starting her political work as a member of the Bombay Municipal Corporation, she worked tirelessly for the people and was elected to the Lok Sabha. She made significant contributions in highlighting the evils of the dowry system and in the formulation of the Dowry Prohibition (Amendment) Act. Her genuine concern for the downtrodden and zeal for women's emancipation were vibrant throughout her life. She was very active in movements like the Samyukta Maharashtra movement, the anti-price rise movement, and the consumers' resistance movement. She was founder member of Samajwadi Mahila Sabha and one of the founders and secretary of the Mahila Dakshta Samiti.

Ahilya Rangnekar remained a people's leader till the end of her life. She participated in the freedom struggle in 1942. She held an impressive record as a member of the Bombay Municipal Corporation for a little less than two decades and was an active member of the Lok Sabha. On the forefront of agitations against oppression and injustice, she was closely connected with various women's organizations, trade unions, and movements like Samyukta Maharashtra and anti-price rise. The Parel Mahila Sangh, an organization founded by her and her colleagues, evolved and then affiliated itself with the All India Democratic Women's Association. She was the secretary of the state unit of the CPI(M) and of the party's central committee.

Women as voters

As women in independent India readied themselves for their new role, they realized that the first step in political participation in a democracy was voting. Taboos and inhibitions in taking decisions independently were entrenched in social norms and age-old traditions, and it took women a lot of effort to come out of them. The percentage of women voters in Maharashtra trails a little behind male voters (Table 12.2).

Unfortunately, the enthusiasm of women voters has not resulted in an increased number of women in decision-making bodies. There have only been a few women in the Maharashtra legislative assembly (Table 12.3).

Women's representation in the Maharashtra assembly has remained below 7 per cent with exceptions of 7.4 per cent in 1972 and 8.3 per cent in 2019. The changing economic scenario and a not-so-welcoming political stage seem to have discouraged spirited women from joining politics and instead preferring to join women's organizations and devoting their time and energy to social work.

Politics in Maharashtra has gone through rough weather and has also experienced some smooth times. Like their male colleagues, women politicians are contained, thrown, and accommodated in the political vortex of state politics with changes in electoral politics. It is interesting to have a bird's eye view of the state politics and women politicians in the state.

In the first phase (1960–77) the Congress dominated. In all the elections of 1962, 1967, and 1972, the Congress secured the majority. Its impact can be seen on women's representation also. In 1962 all the elected women were from the Congress. In the governments of three chief ministers (Yashwantrao Chavan, Marotrao Kannamwar, and Vasantrao Naik)

Table 12.2 Voting percentage of women voters

Elections	Actual voters	Percentage of male voters	Percentage of female voters
1962	11706674	52.2	47.8
1967	14359577	51.22	48.78
1972	25869383	51.09	48.91
1978	20964045	51.2	48.8
1980	17946372	51.24	48.76
1985	22356632	51.43	48.57
1990	30213238	52.04	47.96
1995	39498861	51.82	48.18
1999	34663833	52.14	47.86
2004	41845710	52.11	47.89
2009	45337945	52.46	47.54
2014	52937040	52.82	47.18
2019	55149929	52.35	47.64

Source: eci.gov.in/statistical-report/statistical report, accessed on June 20, 2022.

Table 12.3 Number of women in the state legislative assembly

Year of election	Strength of the legislative assembly	No. of elected women	Percentage of elected women
1962	264	13	4.92
1967	270	9	3.33
1972	270	20	7.40
1978	288	8	2.77
1980	288	19	6.59
1985	288	16	5.55
1990	288	6	2.80
1995	288	11	3.81
1999	288	12	4.16
2004	288	12	4.16
2009	288	11	3.80
2014	288	20	6.90
2019	288	24	8.30

Source: eci.gov.in/statistical-report/statistical report, accessed on June 20, 2022.

Nirmala Raje Vijaysinh Bhosale was in the ministry. She belonged to a royal family and was elected from Akkalkot constituency. She remained the only woman minister up to 1967. In the 1967 elections also all the nine women elected to the assembly were from the Congress Party, and newly elected member Pratibha Patil became state minister. In 1972 all elected women except one (Mrinal Gore from the Samyukta Socialist Party) were from the Congress. Pratibha D. Patil and Prabha Rao from the Congress, who were then emerging women politicians, became cabinet ministers.

The second phase (1978–90) was a period of political changes and accommodations in the state. Elections after the Emergency witnessed a decline in Congress' dominant position in Maharashtra. There were eight elected women in the House – five from Janata Party, two from Congress (I), and one from Congress. Major opposition political parties came together in 1978 and supported Sharad Pawar, a leader who carved out his position of power. They put together a coalition government of the Progressive Democratic Front (PDF), the first non-Congress government in the state. This government had two women ministers, Pramila Tople (a member of the Vidhan Parishad) and Shanti Narayan Naik, both from the Janata Party. During this period, the Congress (I) was the opposition party and Prabha Rao and Pratibha D. Patil were effective leaders of opposition.

The elections in 1980 gave a thumping majority to Congress (I). Barring two women members, Kusum Abhyankar and Jayawantiben Mehta (both from the BJP), all the other women members were from Congress (I). In Chief Minister A.R. Antulay's cabinet, there were four women ministers: Shalinitai Patil (cabinet), Pramilaben Bhagunkar (cabinet, MLC member), Prabha Rao (cabinet), and Tarabai Vartak (state minister) (Pawar, 2012).

In Babasaheb Bhosale's cabinet Sharadchandrika Patil (cabinet minister) and Rajani Satav (deputy minister) were the only women. In Vasantdada Patil's cabinet there were two women state ministers, Celine D'Silva and Rajani Satav.

In the 1985 assembly, most of the women members were from Congress (I). Mrinal Gore won on a Janata Party ticket and Vinita Datta Samant, the wife of an important trade union leader Datta Samant, won as an independent. Celine D'Silva and Rajani Satav were state ministers in the ministry of Shivajirao Patil Nilangekar. Chandrika Kenia and Rajani Satav were state ministers in Shankarrao Chavan's cabinet.

Sharad Pawar became the Chief Minister in 1988 and remained in office till the 1990 elections. He appointed Prabha Rao as a cabinet minister and Rajani Satav and Pushpatai Hiray as state ministers.

The third phase (1990–99) can be characterized as the emergence of a multi-party system in Maharashtra. BJP and Shiv Sena emerged as major opposition parties for the first time. In the elections in 1990 only six women were elected, the lowest number in Maharashtra's history, three women were from BJP (Chandrakanta Goyal, Shobhatai Phadnavis, and Vimal N. Munada), two from Congress (Pushpatai Hiray and Shalini Borse), and Saroj Kashikar from the Janata Dal. In Sharad Pawar's cabinet there was only one woman, Pushapatai Hiray, as a cabinet minister. In Sudhakarrao Naik's cabinet, Pushpatai Hiray continued and Vasudha Deshmukh was appointed as a state minister.

After the 1995 elections, the SS-BJP alliance formed the government. Important women elected to the assembly were: Meenakshi Patil (PWP), Chandrakanta Goyal, Shobhatai Phadnavis, Vimlatai N. Mundada (BJP),

Manisha Nimkar, Kalpana Narhire (SS), Pushpatai Hiray, and Prabha Rao (INC). In Manohar Joshi's cabinet, Shobhatai Phadanvis of the BJP was the only woman minister. After him, in Narayan Rane's cabinet Shobhatai Phadanvis continued and Manisha Nimkar was added as a state minister.

During the fourth phase (1999–2020), political equations in Maharashtra politics changed considerably with the establishment of the Nationalist Congress Party (NCP) in 1999 under the leadership of Sharad Pawar. Twelve women were elected to the assembly in 1999: three from the BJP, four from the Shiv Sena, two from NCP, one each from INC and PWP, and Sulekha Kumbhare from RPI. In the cabinets of Vilasrao Deshmukh and Sushilkumar Shinde, Vasudha Deshmukh (INC), Vimal Mundada (NCP), Sulekha Kumbhare (RPI), and Meenakshi Patil (PWPI) were state ministers.

The INC-NCP coalition government was reinstated with Vilasrao Deshmukh as the Chief Minister after the elections in 2004. Twelve women were elected: four from INC (including Varsha E. Gaikwad), four from NCP (including Vimal Mundada and Shalini Patil), two from the BJP (Shobhatai Phadanvis and Rekha Khedkar), and two from the Shiv Sena (including Manisha Nimkar). In the Deshmukh cabinet Vimal Mundada was the only woman cabinet minister. Ashok Chavan replaced Vilasrao Deshmukh as the Chief Minister in December 2008 and remained in office till the 2009 elections. In his cabinet along with Vimal Mundada, Varsha Gaikwad (INC) and Fauzia Khan (NCP) also became ministers.

Consequent to the 2009 elections, the Congress and NCP continued their alliance in the formation of the government. Ashok Chavan became the Chief Minister who was succeeded by Prithviraj Chavan. Out of the 11 women elected to the assembly, five were from INC, two each from the NCP and BJP, and one each from the Shiv Sena and PWPI. Varsha Gaikwad and Fauzia Khan were ministers in Ashok Chavan and Prithviraj Chavan's governments respectively.

After the 2014 elections, Devendra Fadnavis (BJP) formed a coalition government with the Shiv Sena. A high number of 20 elected women members was an encouraging trend in these elections. Twelve were elected from the BJP, five from the Congress, and three from NCP. No woman from the Shiv Sena was elected. In the Fadnavis government, Pankaja Munde (daughter of BJP leader Gopinath Munde) became cabinet minister and Vidya Thakur became a state minister. Both of them belonged to BJP.

In the 2019 assembly elections, the political equations changed, and in a strange political twist a coalition, Maha Agadi, was formed by Shiv Sena, Congress, and NCP joining hands, and keeping BJP, the largest party in the House, at a distance. Uddhav Thackeray (Shiv Sena) became the Chief Minister after many dramatic developments. In this election 24 women were elected, the highest number till date. Among them 12 belong to the BJP, three belong to the NCP, five to the Congress, and two to the Shiv Sena. An interesting feature of these elections was that two women who contested as independents got elected: Geeta Jain and Manjula Tulshiram Gavit. Thackeray included Varsha Gaikwad (INC) and Yoshomati Thakur (INC) as cabinet ministers and Aditi Tatkare (NCP) as a state minister.

Attempts at women's development

There have been some important policies and initiatives taken by the government for women's development. In 1993 the Maharashtra government, under the leadership of Sharad Pawar, formed the State Women's Commission to improve the status of women in the state. In 1994 the Maharashtra government adopted the Women's Policy in the state. Maharashtra was the first state to adopt such a policy. The policy was aimed at improving the quality of women's lives, eliminating economic, political, and social constraints on them, and treating them as productive members of society. It was criticized by some activists and academicians. However, this policy document provided a strong platform for future government initiatives for women's empowerment. In 2013 the Prithviraj Chavan government and in 2014 the Fadnavis government took the initiative of formulating a new Women's Policy to provide protection to women, especially on the social media platform. But unfortunately, the new Women's Policy was lost in the corridors of power politics.

In December 2020 the government tabled two bills, the Maharashtra Shakti Criminal Law (Maharashtra Amendment) Act, 2020, and the Special Court and Machinery for implementation of Maharashtra Shakti Criminal Law, 2020, to curb crimes against women and children; there is a provision for severe punishment including the death penalty for the offenders. Key amendments in the Maharashtra Shakti Criminal Law Bill (2020) were passed in 2022. Some women's organizations and activists were critical of the move.

Women in the party hierarchy

In Maharashtra, the Congress, BJP, and NCP being national parties have national as well as provincial committees. Women like Pratibha Patil, Prabha Rao, Rajani Patil, and Suryakanta Patil have worked for the All India Congress Committee. Pratibha Patil and Prabha Rao were also the chairpersons of the Maharashtra Pradesh Congress Committee.

Similarly, Jayawantiben Mehta worked in the BJP Central Parliamentary Board and was vice president of the party during 1993–95. At the pradesh level women like Pankaja Munde, Poonam Mahajan, Vijaya Rahatkar, and Shobhatai Phadanvis have worked for the party. NCP's national executive has three women – Supriya Sule, Fauzia Khan, and Vandana Chavan. At the state level Vidya Chavan, Vasudha Deshmukh, and Usha Darade are working as vice presidents of pradesh committees. In the Shiv Sena Neelam Gorhe and Priyanka Chaturvedi are on the Central Executive Committee of the party. Neelam Gorhe is also the deputy chairperson of the Maharashtra legislative council and the spokesperson for the Shiv Sena.

Every political party in Maharashtra has a women's wing, which addresses women's issues and mobilizes them for expanding the party's mass base. The women's wing of the Nationalist Congress Party is the strongest and has been headed by women leaders like Nivedita Mane, Chitra Wagh, and Rupali Chakankar. Supriya Sule was instrumental in establishing the Rashtravadi Yuvati Congress, which provided a platform for young girls. She raised many issues such as female infanticide, LGBTs, and women's security and empowerment. BJP's Maharashtra Mahila Morcha is equally active and is headed by Vijaya Rahatkar. Charulata Tokas is the chairperson of the Maharashtra Pradesh Mahila Congress. The Shiv Sena Mahila Agadi consists of many 'women warriors' guided by leaders like Neelam Gorhe. Although women's wings of political parties have raised women's issues, it is the strong women's movement in Maharashtra which has brought women's issues to the forefront and which has fought political battles for justice for women.

Like their male colleagues, a few women politicians have defected from one party and joined another like Shalinitai Patil, Chandrika Kenia, and Priyanka Chaturvedi.

An overview of women leaders in Maharashtra presents three trends. Firstly, a few women leaders like Ahilya Ranganekar, Mrinal Gore, and Pramila Dandavate preferred to be closely associated with mass movements. Secondly, there are a few women leaders who were self-made and worked efficiently as elected representatives. Kesharbai Kshirsagar, Rajani Satav, Prabha Rao, Pratibha Patil, Jaywantiben Mehta, Suryakanta Patil, Manda Mhatre, Vandana Chavan, Rajani Patil, Shobhatai Phadnavis, and Neelam Gorhe can be included in this category. Thirdly, most of the women leaders entered politics because of their political backgrounds. Premala Chavan, Varsha Gaikwad, Poonam Mahajan, Priya Dutt, Pankaja Munde, Preetam Munde, Praniti Shinde, and Supriya Sule are a few examples of such women.

The Vidhan Parishad is primarily used for accommodating party workers in the power structure to appease them. Primarily men fit in this category, hence there are very few women in the Vidhan Parishad. In the entire history of the Vidhan Parishad hardly 20 women have been its members. Women like Shakuntala Paranjpe and Sarojini Babar, both eminent writers were nominated to the Vidhan Parishad. Political activists such as Sudha Joshi, Alka Desai, Pramila Tople, Vidya Chavan, and Fauzia Khan were nominated to the Vidhan Parishad. A few other members elected by the members of the legislative assembly include Shobhatai Phadanvis (BJP: 2010–16), Vandana Chavan (NCP: 2010–12), Neelam Gorhe (Shiv Sena: 2002 till date), Fauzia Khan (NCP: 2008–14), and Smita Wagh (BJP: 2014–20). There is hardly any women's representation from teachers, graduates, and local bodies.

Currently, there are two women in the Vidhan Parishad, Neelam Gorhe and Manisha Kayande, both from the Shiv Sena. Neelam Gorhe is a capable deputy chairperson of Vidhan Parishad.

Women in local-level politics

After the implementation of the 73rd and 74th Constitutional Amendments more than 1,20,000 women have been elected in Maharashtra at the local level. Though many of the elected women are wives/sisters/mothers of sitting male members in the local bodies, a silent change is taking place. There have also been a few instances of strong and independent women, which is heartening. Mangala Arolkar of Mukhai gram panchayat fought for closing down liquor shops and helped women become self-sufficient. The Mayor of Mumbai, Nirmala Samant Prabhavalkar launched the Nirbhay Mumbai Niramal Mumbai in the context of terrorist attacks. Kunda Vijaykar, Mayor of Nagpur, provided Rs 1 lakh as development fund to all-women corporators. Charu Rao, the Wardha Zila Parishad chairperson worked relentlessly and bagged the 'Best Zila Parishad Award' given by the Maharashtra government.

All-women panchayats are not new in Maharashtra. They were formed in villages like Brahman Ghar (Bhor taluka), Bitargao (Osmanabad), Vitner (Chopda taluka), Yenora and Metikheda. The women in these panchayats banned liquor shops, started gobar gas plants and smokeless cooking stoves, launched water schemes, worked in school committees, used barren land for cultivation of *bor* (jujube) trees, and made efforts to start schools and hospitals in their villages. The sarpanch of Vitner, Indirabai Patil, an activist of Shetkari Sanghatana launched the Laxmi Mukti programme, whereby cultivable land was transferred to women (Patil, 2014). Such instances show that women can work efficiently and effectively. However, it is a matter of grave concern that motions of no-confidence are brought against efficient and sincere women sarpanches usually on technical grounds.

Fortunately, now some steps are being taken to modify the rules to avert such situations.

In April 2011 during the tenure of Prithviraj Chavan as the Chief Minister, the Maharashtra legislative assembly took a unanimous decision of increasing reservations for women up to 50 per cent in local self-government. Consequently, the number of elected women members and the number of women office bearers increased considerably. At present, the strength of women office bearers in Maharashtra is: zila parishads: 17, panchayat samitis: 175, sarpanches: 13,641, mayors: 13, and nagar adhyakshas: 184. This means that approximately 14,030 women are heading/leading local self-government institutions in Maharashtra.

Interestingly, some more positive signs of change are now visible. A transgender person is the sarpanch of a small village called Tarangfal in

Solapur district. Dnyaneshwar Kamble, known as Mauli, was elected as the sarpanch defeating a male candidate in 2017. Moreover, some all-women panchayats were also elected in 2015. These panchayats were formed in three villages – Bubnal (Kolhapur district), Neerawagaj (Baramati taluka), and Wakrul (Pen taluka). Elected members of these villages are taking various initiatives for water conservation, purification of water, construction of roads using funds effectively, and maintaining accounts. They have changed their profiles from being homemakers to being public figures (Phadke-Parchure, 2016). The Mahila Rajsatta Andolan, the P.V. Mandlik Trust, and institutes like YASHADA play an important role in catalysing the role of elected women at the grassroots.

Reservations have provided space for women in elected bodies. However, reservations by themselves are not enough. A study of women councillors in the four mega-cities of Delhi, Kolkata, Mumbai, and Chennai offers a critical view of the functioning of the municipal corporations, with emphasis on women's roles and opportunities to participate and perform. The study reveals that 'working on issues specific to women's development is not a major concern for elected women, even though they are aware of the problems faced by women in their localities ... Women are not a special constituency for women councilors despite the fact that they are aware of women's issues' (Ghosh and Lama-Rewal, 2005, pp. 120-121).

Women in movements

Women in Maharashtra have been on the forefront of agitations and movements that include the movement demanding a separate state of Maharashtra, the anti-price movement, and protests against the evils that haunt women's lives such as dowry and rape.

The movement for Samyukt Maharashtra, launched on February 6, 1956, attracted many women. In Mumbai, the Samyukt Maharashtravadi Mahila Parishad, chaired by Sumati Gore, was organized in which 15,000 women took part. In the late 1960s and early 1970s, an energetic wave of feminism touched many parts of India including Maharashtra.

The drought in Maharashtra in 1970–73 and the scarcity of food grains/ essential commodities were the trigger points for the emergence of the women's movement in the state. In September 1972, representatives of about 70 women's organizations came together and formed the Anti-Price Rise Women's United Front to fight rising prices and also to bring prices down. Many activists like Mrinal Gore, Ahilya Ranganekar, Kamal Desai, Malti Bedekar, and Krushnabai Mote spearheaded the movement. The movement succeeded 'in exploding the myth that women, because of their social conditioning, do not participate in or reflect on politics as men do. In fact, the women actually widened the narrow meaning of politics' (Mehta and Thakkar, 1992, p. 87).

Rural Maharashtra suffered as much and a spark of the women's movement was ignited at Shahada. Furious Adivasis, especially women played a militant role in the movement. They led demonstrations, shouted militant slogans, sang revolutionary songs, and mobilized masses (Kumar, 1993). The anti-alcohol agitation which started in late 1972 continued in 1973 (Savara and Gothoskar, 1984).

The report *Towards Equality* stimulated the formation of various women's organizations. Many groups and organizations such as Stree Mukti Sanghatna, Nari Samata Manch, Purogami Mahila Sanghatna, Karantikari Mahila Sanghatna, Sarvahara Mahila Sanghatna, Stree Adhar Kendra, and the Stree Mukti Sangharash Chalval were established in rural and urban Maharashtra. Women's groups and mahila mandals provided a platform for women to interact. Women's organizations of Left parties such as Akhil Bharatiya Mahila Federation, Samajwadi Mahila Sabha, and the Janwadi Mahila Sanghatna became more vigorous in their efforts. To make women self-sufficient, groups such as SEWA and Annapurna Mahila Mandal were established (Sharma, 2003).

The women's movement in Maharashtra got momentum when the United Nations declared 1975–85 as the women's decade. Many women activists from Maharashtra attended various international conferences during this decade in Mexico, Copenhagen, and Nairobi and interacted with women from different countries (Patil, 2014).

During 1979–80 the segregated women's movement got an opportunity to come together on the issue of a judgement acquitting the culprits of the Mathura rape case. Women's organizations demanded a review of the judgement. The Forum Against Oppression of Women (FAOW) was formed in Mumbai which sought changes pertaining to laws including custodial rape. The issues of dowry deaths, sex selection abortions, and discriminatory family laws gave rise to a strong women's movement and groups in Maharashtra.

The anti-arrack/alcohol movement led by women is significant. The first such protest was launched by the tribal women of Shahada. Women's determination and courage stimulated outbursts against alcohol in 1992–93, 1996–98, and 2011–12 in different parts of Maharashtra. For example, in Kolhapur district, Parvatibai Mali led the movement in 1996–98 and in 2009 an effective movement was led by Swati Kshirsagar (Patil, 2009).

In the 1980s and 1990s, the women's movement started recognizing issues surrounding caste. This was a marked change in the women's movement. Around this time autobiographies of Dalit women started being published (Rege, 1998). These writings revealed that Dalit women were not only subjugated by patriarchy but also by the caste hierarchy. Some women's organizations such as Krantikari Mahila Sanghatana, Dalit Mahila Sanghatana, Vanchit Bahujan Mahila Aghadi, and Dalit Asmita Mahila Manch were established. Many ideological streams – Ambedkar, Dalit Bahujan, Satyashodhak, Satyashodhak-Marxist – can be seen in this movement.

Feminist scholars, centres for women's studies, and women's magazines (in Marathi) such as *Stree, Milun Saryajani, Bayaja,* and *Prerak Lalkari* have made a significant contribution in stimulating awareness about gender equality in Marathi society. Alochana in Pune is engaged in documenting the women's movement.

Conclusion

Politics is still a male domain. Obstacles such as patriarchy, financial dependency, household responsibilities, and character assassination are hampering development of women's leadership in Maharashtra as well as in India. A capable politician like Pramila Dandavate was often seen as the wife of Madhu Dandavate and her own political work was sidelined. Pointing out prevailing male chauvinism, Ahilya Rangnekar maintained that a woman has to slog to get recognition (Gawankar, 1995). Nonetheless, women are not dampened, they have started their journey on the way to equality in a determined way.

Bibliography

Crime in India 2019, Statistics Volume-1, National Crime Records Bureau, Ministry of Home Affairs, Government of India, New Delhi (2020). Available at: https://ncrb.gov.in/sites/default/files/CII%202019%20Volume%201.pdf, accessed on June 20, 2022.

Economic Survey of Maharashtra 2019-20 (2020). *Directorate of Economics and Statistics, Planning Department,* Mumbai: Government of Maharashtra.

Forbes, Geraldine (1998). *Women in Modern India.(The New Cambridge History of India, IV.2).* Cambridge: Cambridge University Press.

Gawankar, Rohini (1986). *Marathi Stree Shaktiche Rajkarni Rup* (Marathi). Pune: Aditya Prakashan.

——— (1995). 'Political Leadership of Women in Maharashtra', in Usha Thakkar and Mangesh Kulkarni (eds), *Politics in Maharashtra.* Bombay: Himalaya Publishing House.

Ghosh, Archana and Stephanie Tawa Lama-Rewal (2005). *Democratization In Progress: Women and Local Politics in Urban India.* New Delhi: Tulika Books.

Guru, Gopal (1994).'Maharashtra's Women's Policy: Co-opting Feminism', *Economic and Political Weekly,* 29 (32), 2063–2065.

IWWAGE, Maharashtra, (2020). Available at: https://iwwage.org/wp-content/uploads/2020/11/Maharashtra-Factsheet-upd.pdf, accessed on June 9, 2022.

Kantak, Prema (1940). *Satyagrahi Maharashtra* (Marathi). Pune: Sulabh Rashtriya Granthmala.

Karve, Swati (2015). *Stree Parishadancha Itihas* (Marathi). Pune: Abhijit Prakashan.

Kosambi, Meera (1988).'Women, Emancipation and Equality: Pandita Ramabai's contribution to Women's Cause', *Economic and Political Weekly,* 23 (44), WS-38–WS-49.

Kumar, Radha (1993). *History of Doing.* New Delhi: Zubaan.

Mehta, Usha and Usha Thakkar (1992). 'Anti-Price Rise Movement in Bombay', *Canadian Woman Studies*, 13 (1), 85–87.

Nalawade, Damayanti (1989). 'Pratisarkar chalvalimadhil streeyanche yogdan', unpublished MPhil dissertation submitted to Shivaji University.

Patil, Bharati (2009). *Daru vikri bandisathi nikarachi zunj: Stree samarthyache anokhe darshan* (Marathi). Ichalkaranji: Prabodhan Prakashan Jyoti, August.

——— (2014). *Streeya: Samaj ani Rajkaran* (Marathi). Pune: Harmis Publications.

Pawar, Vaishali (2012). *Mahilanchya Sattasangharshacha Alekh* (Marathi). Pune: Diamond Publications.

Phadke, Manasi and Parchure Rajas (2016). *A Tale of Three Villages with All Mahila Gram Panchayats*. Mumbai: State Election Commission.

Phadke, Shilpa (2003).'Thirty years on: Women's Studies Reflects on the Women's Movement', *Economic and Political Weekly*, 38 (43), 4567–4576.

Phadke, Y.D. (1979). *Politics and Language*. Bombay: Himalaya Publishing House.

——— (1993). *Visavya Shatakatil Maharashtra*, Vol. 4 (Marathi). Pune: Shree Vidya Prakashan.

——— (2007). *Visavya Shatakatil Maharashtra*, Vol. 7 (Marathi). Pune: Shree Vidya Prakashan.

Rath, Nilkanth and V.M. Dandekar (1971a). 'Poverty in India-I: Dimensions and Trends', *Economic and Political Weekly*, 6 (1), 25–48.

——— (1971b). 'Poverty in India-II: Policies and Programmes', *Economic and Political Weekly*, 6 (2), 106–146.

Rai, Usha (1986).'Abuse of Sex Determination Tests', *The Times of India*, October 29.

Rege, Sharmila (1998). 'Dalit Women Talk Differently: A Critique of Difference and Towards a Dalit Feminist Standpoint Position', *Economic and Political Weekly*, 33 (44), 39–46.

Savara, Mira and Sujata Gothoskar (1984).'An Assertion of Women Power', in Madhu Kishwar and Vanita Ruth (eds), *In Search of Answers: Indian Women's Voices from Manushi*. London: Zed Books.

Sharma, Kumud (2003). 'Institutionalizing Feminist agenda(s)', *Economic and Political Weekly*, 38 (43), 4564–4566.

13
WOMEN IN MADHYA PRADESH STATE POLITICS

An analysis

Rashmi Shrivastava

Introduction

Though women in India constitute nearly half of the electorate, their role and representation in elected bodies of Parliament and state legislative assemblies have always been negligible. This imbalance is also found in political parties, where women members are hardly more than 10 per cent (Rai, 2011) and their nominations as candidates for contesting elections are even fewer. The case is similar regarding women's participation in Madhya Pradesh's politics.

Madhya Pradesh is a state located in the central part of India. Under the provisions of the Reorganization Act 1956, the state of Madhya Pradesh (MP) was formed on November 1, 1956, by combining the existing states of Madhya Bharat, Bundelkhand, Bhopal, Mahakaushal, and other regions. At that time, Madhya Pradesh was the largest state in the Union of India (Surjan, 1991). On November 1, 2000, with the division of Chhattisgarh from Madhya Pradesh, it became the second largest state in India. MP is surrounded by Uttar Pradesh in the north, Chhattisgarh in the east, Rajasthan and Gujarat in the west, and Maharashtra in the south. MP is very rich in mineral resources, and different minerals are mined in the state.

MP's population is 84.5 million, making it the fifth-largest state by population. Madhya Pradesh is also known for its tribal population which is about 20 per cent of the total population of the state. In urban and rural local bodies seats are reserved for members of Scheduled Castes (SCs), Scheduled Tribes (STs), and Other Backward Castes (OBCs). Women from these categories also have seats reserved for them. The sex ratio in the state is 930 females per 1,000 males. The literacy rate is 70.60 per cent. MP's economy is primarily agriculture based. Nearly 75 per cent of the population lives in villages. Over 50 per cent of the land area is cultivable. MP is the third biggest food grain–producing state in the country. It is also called the soyabean state (Shrivastava, 1994). In the recent past, MP has also entered the area

244

DOI: 10.4324/9781003374862-14

of hi-tech industries, and it has taken a lead in cement production. Several major public sector industries are also located in the state where Hindi is the official language and also the most widely spoken language.

There are 10 commissionaires, 51 districts, and 89 tribal development divisions in Madhya Pradesh. There are 29 Lok Sabha seats in the state and 11 seats in the Rajya Sabha. The state legislative assembly has a strength of 230 members. The state has 476 cities, where nagar nigams, nagar palikas, and nagar panchayats are elected bodies. In rural areas, the three-tier Panchayati Raj system exists of gram panchayats, janpad panchayats, and zila panchayats which too are elected bodies (Shrivastava, 2008). Madhya Pradesh was the first state in the country where panchayat elections were held accordingly to the Constitution Amendment Act, 1993, with one-third reservation for women in the panchayats. The state voluntarily extended reservations for women to 50 per cent in panchayats and in some other rural-urban local bodies. A report rightly points out that the PRIs are to be viewed as institutions of local self-governance, not as mere implementers of centrally determined development programmes. Bottom-up planning, based on micro-planning, is to be the basis of self-governance as against bottom-down plans, which rarely take into account the actual grassroots requirements (Society of Tribal Women for Development, 2004).

The political scenario

Congress and BJP have been prominent parties in the state's politics, while the other political parties have not been significant as out of the 15 general elections to the Vidhan Sabha, Congress formed the government nine times and the Janata Party/BJP six times. MP also got a taste of a coalition government for a short time after the fourth general elections. In December 1992, the state came under the president's rule for the third time. Under Article 356 of the Constitution of India, the MP government was dismissed three times in 1977, 1980, and 1992. In all the mid-term polls for the assembly, the people of MP supported the ruling party at the Centre.

A challenging environment for women

Women in the state face a number of challenges when it comes to political leadership whether at the level of political parties or in municipalities and panchayats or even in administrative posts and the state assembly. No adequate attention is paid to their health and education, and crime rates against them are high. The disparities in women's education start right at the primary school level for social, political, and economic reasons. Girls' future is not prioritized because boys are seen as a support in parents' old age.

Madhya Pradesh faces huge challenges like infant and maternal mortality, women's poor health, and violence against women. It has been identified by the National Health Mission as a high-focus state. It is one of the Empowered Action Group states of the National Health Mission. These states have struggled to contain their population growth rates at manageable levels and have poorer quality of life indicators as compared to the other states in the country. Madhya Pradesh struggles with health problems that contribute to high maternal and child mortality rates (Health India, 2016).

Commissions established in the state for social justice and development mainly have men in positions of power. Out of the 11 commissions that have been set up by the Madhya Pradesh government, the Women's Commission is the only one which is headed by a woman. Though Madhya Pradesh has a Human Rights Commission for protection of human rights, it is one of the three states where violations of women's rights are the most. This commission has always been headed by a male. Similarly, the Madhya Pradesh State Schedule Castes and Tribes Commission has always been headed by a male chairperson. The Madhya Pradesh Public Service Commission is the only commission besides the Women's State Commission which has a woman member.

Women outnumbered by men

Reservations have secured seats for women in local bodies, but in the state assembly and Parliament they are still outnumbered by men. In the 2018 assembly elections, only 18 women members were elected to the assembly. In Lok Sabha, out of 29 seats, there were six women in 2009, five in 2014, and four in 2019. The reason for this is that the political mindset is not willing to give more seats to women.

Table 13.1 gives a glimpse of the state of affairs regarding women in different government decision-making institutions in Madhya Pradesh.

Participation in polity is said to be essential for human development. It is pointed out by some reports that priorities for women are different from men; hence their reasons for entering politics too are different. A sizeable

Table 13.1 Women in various institutions (2018)

Institution	Total Posts	Female	Per cent of Women
Cooperatives	8	0	0
Corporations Ltd.	6	0	0
Board/Mandal	5	0	0
Commissions	11	1	9
State Assembly	230	18	7.82
Lok Sabha	29	4	12.00
Rajya Sabha	11	3	27.27

Source: Jain.

number of women enter politics because of an interest in social service and not necessarily via the party politics route. Men control political and economic systems. In Madhya Pradesh, the typical male-dominated mindset is clearly reflected in the gender-wise distribution of authority and power. Women get fewer opportunities to reach higher positions in the political arena. The representation of women in the Madhya Pradesh Vidhan Sabha is low (Table 13.2).

Notwithstanding their tall claims of empowering women, political parties in Madhya Pradesh let them down in nominations for the 2018 state assembly polls. Both the main political parties, the BJP and the Congress, which have been advocating 33 per cent reservation for women in the Lok Sabha and state assemblies, have been miserly in fielding women. Before the distribution of tickets for the 2018 elections, the BJP Mahila Morcha president Lata Ailkar had demanded that 25 per cent (56 candidates) of the tickets be allotted to women as against 12 per cent (28) of the women candidates fielded in the 2013 assembly elections. However, the party ended up giving tickets to only 24 women candidates (*News Click,* 2018).

BJP, whose election manifesto promised 33 per cent seats in the Lok Sabha and state legislative assemblies to women, is now silent on this promise. Most of the political parties claim to firmly support the Women's Reservation Bill and have included it in their election manifestos (Chouhan and Singh, 2018). But the representation of women in the Lok Sabha and Rajya Sabha does not present an impressive picture. The parties headed by women like Mayawati and Sonia Gandhi have also given very few tickets to women.

Table 13.2 Number of women MLAs in the state assembly

Year	Seats	Women	Percentage
1957	288	11	3.81
1962	288	34	11.80
1967	296	08	2.70
1972	296	11	3.71
1977	320	08	2.50
1980	320	10	3.12
1985	320	03	0.93
1990	320	32	10.00
1993	320	22	6.87
1998	320	22	6.87
2003	230	18	7.82
2008	230	25	10.86
2013	230	30	13.04
2018	230	18	7.82

Source: Data up to 2008 from Shrivastava (2008) and the rest collected by the author from various sources including Chief Electoral Officer, Madhya Pradesh, https://ceomadhyapradesh .nic.in/History.aspx, accessed on accessed on August 27, 2020.

Table 13.3 Party-wise number of women candidates who contested in the last three assembly elections in Madhya Pradesh

	2008	2013	2018
BJP	25	28	24
Congress	37	23	29
BSP	26	22	13
Other	67	74	30
Independents	66	53	124

Source: *The Times of India* (Bhopal, October 15, 2018).

Table 13.4 Women candidates who won the elections out of the total number of women candidates who contested the elections

Year	Contested	Won (per cent)
2008	221	25 (11.3)
2013	200	30 (15)
2018	220	18 (8.2)

Source: *The Times of India* (Bhopal, October 15, 2018).

Glib talk by political parties on the Women's Reservation Bill apart, none of the parties practice what they preach. The number of candidates fielded by various parties in the last three assembly elections in the state is given in Table 13.3 while the winners are given in Table 13.4.

Despite women candidates' high winnability, when it comes to giving tickets to women, parties have barely given 10 per cent tickets to them. The entire electoral scenario is yet to evolve so as to make conditions conducive for women to contest elections. Many male politicians believe that reservations for women would mean a loss of political power for them. However, overcoming all the obstacles some women in Madhya Pradesh have made their presence felt.

MP's women in national politics

Some women from Madhya Pradesh have played an important role in national politics. Sumitra Mahajan has been a prominent member of BJP who is recognized as a sober and strong leader who has established her prestige in political circles. She was the Speaker of the sixteenth Lok Sabha from 2014 to 2019, the second woman after Meira Kumar to be elected to this post. She was elected eight times from the ninth to the sixteenth Lok Sabhas without a break from the same constituency (Indore) and on the same party's ticket. During her long political career, Mahajan occupied important positions such as union minister of state, ministry of human resource development; union minister of state, ministry of communication and information technology; and union minister of state, ministry of petroleum and natural gas. It is interesting to note that she started her political career as Deputy Mayor, Municipal Corporation Indore.

Sushma Swaraj (BJP) was an excellent parliamentarian, a great orator, and an able administrator. She was elected from the Vidisha constituency in MP in 2009 and 2014. She was a member of the Haryana legislative assembly in 1977 and 1987 and was also a cabinet minister in the state assembly. She was also an impressive member of the Rajya Sabha elected in 1990 (Haryana), 2000 (Uttarakhand), and 2006 (from Madhya Pradesh). She was also the Chief Minister of NCT of Delhi very briefly in 1998. She was elected to the eleventh and twelfth Lok Sabhas (from NCT of Delhi) and the fifteenth and sixteenth Lok Sabhas from Madhya Pradesh. She was the union cabinet minister, information and broadcasting; union cabinet minister, health and family welfare and parliamentary affairs; and union minister of external affairs. She was also the leader of the BJP parliamentary party, Lok Sabha, and the leader of the opposition in the Lok Sabha.

Madhya Pradesh has also had tribal women leaders from the grassroots. Jamuna Devi was a veteran leader of the Indian National Congress from MP. She was a member of the third Lok Sabha and later of the Rajya Sabha. She was elected to the state assembly six times and was the deputy Chief Minister (the first woman to occupy this post) in the eleventh assembly. In the twelfth and thirteenth assemblies she was the leader of opposition. She occupied key positions in her long political career.

Sahodrabai Devi Rai (INC) was elected to the second, third, fifth, and seventh Lok Sabhas. She worked for people's welfare and brought issues of the villages and their people to the surface. Vidyawati Chaturvedi (INC), an old-timer, was a member of the undivided Madhya Pradesh legislative assembly and a member of the seventh and eighth Lok Sabhas and a member of the Rajya Sabha for two terms.

Some women from the state from a privileged background too have entered politics. Vijaya Raje Scindia came to the forefront of the BJP leadership in the 1980s when she was made one of its vice presidents. She played a key role in propagating the party's Ram Janmabhumi agenda and was considered a hardliner. She was popularly known as the Rajmata of Gwalior and was a prominent Indian political personality having won elections to the legislative assembly and the Lok Sabha. In the days of British rule, as the consort of the last ruling Maharaja of Gwalior, Jivajirao Scindia, she ranked among the highest royal figures of the land. In later life, she became a politician of considerable influence and was elected repeatedly to both the Houses of Parliament. She was also an active member of the Jan Sangh and thereafter of the BJP for many decades. She was an active member of the second and third Lok Sabhas as a member of the Congress Party, the fourth Lok Sabha as a member of the Swatantra Party, and the ninth, tenth, eleventh, and twelfth Lok Sabhas as a member of the BJP. She was also a member of the Rajya Sabha for two terms. Her daughter, Yashodhara Raje Scindia (BJP), also decided to join politics and was elected to the fourteenth and fifteenth Lok Sabhas. She was elected to the eleventh and fourteenth state assemblies and worked as a minister and is now a member of the current fifteenth state assembly.

Women with a strong agenda of Hindu politics are visible in Madhya Pradesh. Uma Bharti (BJP), a 'fiery OBC sanyasin' has had a tumultuous political career. She was elected to the Lok Sabha six times to the ninth, tenth, eleventh, twelfth, and thirteenth Lok Sabhas from Madhya Pradesh and to sixteenth Lok Sabha from Uttar Pradesh. She held various portfolios in the ministry of youth affairs and sports, ministry of mines, ministry of water resources, river development and Ganga rejuvenation, and ministry of drinking water and sanitation. She was among the leaders in the controversial Ram Janmabhumi movement in the 1980s and 1990s and was present at the demolition of the Babri Masjid. She was the first woman Chief Minister of Madhya Pradesh elected in December 2003. She led the party to a sweeping victory based on her reputation as a Hindutva firebrand. She resigned from the post of Chief Minister in August 2004. Thereafter she floated her own political party, the Bhartiya Janshakti Party for a while before returning to the BJP fold in 2011. She caused ripples in political and feminist circles by demanding caste-based quotas in the Women's Reservation Bill. Her politics and life have attracted the attention of scholars.

Pragya Singh Thakur (BJP) contested the Lok Sabha elections from the Bhopal constituency and defeated Digvijaya Singh of the Indian National Congress and a former Chief Minister of Madhya Pradesh in the last elections to the Lok Sabha in 2019. According to political scientist Christophe Jaffrelot, she became the 'symbol' of the 2019 elections, in which nebulous fringe elements of the Hindutva ideology were mainstreamed (*The Indian Express*, 2019). During her college days, Thakur was an active member of the Akhil Bhartiya Vidyarthi Parishad (ABVP). She later joined various affiliate organizations of the Rashtriya Swayamsevak Sangh (RSS).

Like male politicians changing political parties, it is not unusual for women politicians too to change parties. Himadri Singh was elected to the Lok Sabha from Shahdol (ST) in 2019 as a BJP candidate. In a major blow to the ruling Congress ahead of the Lok Sabha elections she joined the BJP. A royal scion among the tribals in the Vindhya region, Himadri is the daughter of a three-term former MP, union minister from the Congress, Dalbir Singh and Rajesh Nandini Singh, a Congress MP from Shahdol elected in 2009. She had been the party's popular tribal face in the Vindhya region.

Role of family dynamics

Family dynamics also play a role in politics both for men and women politicians. Veena Singh, the daughter of Arjun Singh (a Congress leader, former Chief Minister of Madhya Pradesh and union HRD minister) has ruffled the feathers of many in state politics. The differences and tensions in the family surfaced when Veena Singh staked her claim to her father's political legacy. In the elections to the fifteenth Lok Sabha she decided to contest from Sidhi constituency as an independent. While Ajay Singh (Arjun Singh's son) campaigned for the Congress candidate Inderjit Patel, Veena's mother, Saroj Singh, canvassed for Veena Singh. In the end, both Veena Singh and Inderjit Patel lost the elections and BJP's Govind Prasad Mishra won.

There are important linkages between state and national politics. Some women politicians have been elected to the assembly as well as the Parliament. Jayshree Banerjee (BJP), a member of thirteenth Lok Sabha, was also elected to the Madhya Pradesh legislative assembly in 1977, 1990, and 1993. She served as cabinet minister (local self-government, social welfare, sports, and jail) in 1977. Sandhya Ray (BJP) was elected to the seventeenth Lok Sabha from Bhind (SC). Earlier she was a member of the state assembly in 2003 and a member, Madhya Pradesh State Women's Commission (2017–19). Riti Pathak (BJP) was elected to the sixteenth Lok Sabha and is now a member of the seventeenth Lok Sabha.

She was introduced to politics when she contested elections for the zila panchayat adyaksha.

Vijaylaxmi Sadho (INC) came to the limelight as a Congress youth leader. She has been elected as a member of the assembly five times. She was a minister till recently. She was also elected to the Rajya Sabha in 2010. Maya Singh (BJP) was a member of the fourteenth assembly and also a minister. She was a member of the Rajya Sabha for two terms.

Archana Chitnis (BJP) was a member of the twelfth and thirteenth legislative assemblies, a minister who started the Swayamsidhi Bank for women. Ranjana Baghel (BJP) was also a minister who was elected to the thirteenth legislative assembly. Hina Kawre (INC) was elected to the fourteenth and fifteenth assemblies and was also the Deputy Speaker of the assembly for some time.

Imarti Devi (earlier from INC, now BJP) was a member of zila panchayat, Gwalior. Thereafter she was elected to the thirteenth and fourteenth assemblies and was also a minister. However, in 2020 she supported senior Congress leader Jyotiraditya Scindia and was one of the 22 MLAs who resigned from the state assembly. The by-elections in Madhya Pradesh were held on November 3, 2020, and Imarti Devi lost the elections. Sampatiya Uikey (BJP) started her political career as a sarpanch of Tikarwada gram panchayat and has now been elected to the Rajya Sabha as a BJP candidate from Madhya Pradesh.

At present, there are 17 women in the fifteenth assembly – ten from the BJP, six from INC, and one from BSP. There are three women ministers: Yashodhara Raje Scindia, Meena Singh Mandve, and Usha Thakur in the 34-member council of ministers.

It is important to note that in Madhya Pradesh Muslims have a marginal presence when it comes to contesting elections and winning them. In the 2018 elections, 14 Muslims were nominated – one by the BJP, three by the Congress, nine by the BSP, and one by CPI. BSP's Muslim candidate did not win. CPI's Muslim candidate won in 1962, 1967, and 1972, but has been drawing a blank since then. Congress and BJP want to field winnable candidates. This time BJP gave a ticket to Faima Rasool 'Gudiya', well-known Congress leader Ahmed Rasool Siddiqui's daughter. She fought against five-time Congress MLA Arif Aqeel for the Bhopal North assembly seat, from where her father had won in 1980 and 1985. She lost the elections. Masarrat Shahid, the only woman candidate from the Congress too lost the elections. Only two Muslim MLAs got elected this time (Osama, 2019).

We find a qualitative change in women's representation in the seventeenth Lok Sabha. At 29 and 30 years of age respectively, Nusrat Jahan and Mimi Chakraborty are among the five youngest members to be sworn to the Lok Sabha. They gave the Trinamool Congress much bigger victory margins than in the last elections and are part of the biggest female contingent in Parliament today. Their choice of work wear – jeans and a white button-down shirt for Mimi and a wine-coloured suit for Nusrat – on their first day in Parliament raised many eyebrows. The two MPs took to their social media handles to share their excitement and showed off their IDs. Many people wrote against their jeans and shirts. But they bravely rejected the adverse comments and replied firmly which made them even stronger. Mimi said that what Nusrat and she wore was not indecent in any way and that they did not think that they had failed to maintain the decorum of the House (*The Times of India*, 2019).

Women in local-level politics

In Madhya Pradesh, there have been reservations for women in local bodies for more than 25 years, and it has been felt that women are capable of holding different posts and exercising their powers effectively. In urban areas in particular, where women's literacy rates are higher and traditional social restrictions are lesser in comparison to rural areas, women have successfully proved their efficiency in local bodies. For example, the Indore nagar nigam which is headed by a woman Mayor, Malini Gaur (2015–20), has been declared the cleanest and smartest city in India for the last two years. Similarly, the Ujjain nagar nigam, which is headed by a woman Mayor, Meena Jonwal (2015–20), has also been rated quite high in the national ranking of clean cities. These women mayors have shown that they are efficient in carrying out their duties. It is not surprising that they can be found inspecting different wards in their cities early in the morning. It has also been reported that they can sometimes be quite strict with their subordinates if they show slackness in their duties.

Elected women's work in panchayats in Madhya Pradesh shows that they are capable of leadership. It is worth noting that while the male panchayat representatives' priorities are construction work, employment, and social prestige, women representatives give importance to health, education, and other activities for social development. However, women representatives have to face many problems. There is no dearth of people who try to create hurdles in their way. Some examples are important in this context. Kamla Bai is the sarpanch of Rampur village in Baghelan tehsil in Satna district. For a year, she could not get work done for the Sampurna Gram Rozgar Guarantee Yojana (SGRGY) because the village secretary did not allow her to do so. The issue was taken to the chief executive officer of the local janpad panchayat several times, but no solution was found. The Dalit woman sarpanch in Ashta tehsil in Sehore district was stoned in public for organizing a gram sabha on January 26, but the police did not register an FIR. In Petlavad tehsil in Jhabua district several anganwadis remain closed because the anganwadi workers had to come from another village. Despite several complaints by the Dalit woman sarpanch, the women and child development officer did not take any action. (Jain)

As compared to rural women in politics, urban women have more opportunities to take part in politics due to their higher literacy levels and a more open society. In the rural areas, illiteracy, a rigid and conservative attitude of the villagers, and a compulsory veil system for women hinder their participation in politics. Hence, even though women have 50 per cent reservation in panchayats, it is mostly their male counterparts who wield the power and women *panchs*/sarpanches only sign the official papers. For example, the post of the president of the janpad panchayat, Ujjain, is reserved for a woman, but when the collector visited one of its meetings, he found a male on the seat and on enquiry he was informed that the person was the woman president's husband.

He further came to know that the husband presided over the meetings instead of the lady every time and the lady just sat there wearing a veil. The collector ordered that this would not be allowed and the husband had to go out of the meeting.

For women's empowerment it is very essential that the veil system is removed for women in rural areas. Education and training of elected women representatives must be arranged so that they can understand the importance and use of their power.

In most places, Dalit women sarpanches and *panchs* complain that district and janpad level officials openly ask for commissions for disbursing amounts meant for government schemes, but senior officials have not found any solution to this problem. The court orders are openly violated in the public distribution system shops and as a crude estimate only 17 to 20 kg of food grains are being given instead of the 35 kg that is due. In panchayats which have women as sarpanches, the officials do not even listen to the problems, let alone finding solutions. The middle-level and rural-based administrative officials reportedly find it difficult to communicate with the women leaders. Probably, they doubt their competence and abilities and thus the problems continue year after year. If some empowered, educated, and financially well-off woman decides to participate in the self-governance process by accepting the leadership challenges then too there is conspiracy to somehow remove the woman from the leadership. In Madhya Pradesh women get power only up to the level where they have to follow fixed policies and programmes without any discussion or argument. Policies and programmes are implemented without their participation.

A long road ahead

Mahatma Gandhi said that in the fight for social justice, where the weapons are peace and truth, women are the natural leaders. SEWA (Self Employed Women's Association), started in 1972 in Ahmedabad, has grown in size and today it has members in seven states in India including in Madhya Pradesh. SEWA MP has its headquarters in Indore. It is working in 16 districts of the state and has more than six lakh members (SEWA Madhya Pradesh, 2022).

There are many NGOs in Madhya Pradesh working for women's welfare. For example, the Manav Vikas Sewa Sangh, Sagar, and the Pahal Jan Sahyog Vikas Sansthan, Indore, are resource agencies working on gender equality and women's rights. Adivasi SC Utthan Samiti, Sheopur, and the Avadh Narayan Shukla Samiti, Gwalior, are also working for women's development and empowerment.

The state government has been trying to bring positive changes in women's lives by implementing schemes for their health and nutrition and also their education and employment including the Beti Bachao Abhiyan, Ladli Laxmi Yojana (keeping an amount for a girl), Lado campaign (for discouraging and preventing child marriages), creation of Shaurya Dals to create a women-friendly atmosphere, Mangal Diwas Yojana in anganwadis for adolescent girls, Gaon ki Beti Yojana, and the Balika Shiksha Protsahan. The first gender-based budget in the country was also made in MP.

The Shah Bano case in Madhya Pradesh evoked a strong response from women and concerned citizens, and the Supreme Court's judgement had a deep impact on Indian politics. The Narmada water issue also became an issue of national importance bringing issues of displacement and development to the national level. Medha Patkar and her Narmada Bachao Andolan (NBA) were at the forefront of the movement. Very recently it was reported that the COVID-19-induced lockdown negatively impacted nutritional availability for women workers in Madhya Pradesh (*The Hindu*, 2020).

Conclusion

Women still have a long road to travel before they reach equality. Reservations for women at the local levels have resulted in a gradual positive change in society's attitude towards women. Reservations of seats for them in the state assemblies and the Lok Sabha will further contribute to women's empowerment. It is hoped that women will change the nature of power, and as a result all members of society – men and women – will benefit.

Bibliography

Chouhan, Rajeev and Sagat Singh (2018). 'Politics of Women's Reservation in India: Some Observations', in Kanta Kataria and Mahesh Parihar (eds), *Women's Political Participation in India*. Jodhpur: JNV University.

Dhavan, Nandita Banerjee (2017). 'From 'fire-brand' to 'water-brand': The Caste Politics of Uma Bharati', *Asian Journal of Women's Studies*, 23 (4), 498–517.

Health India (2016). *Madhya Pradesh Health System Assessment Report-Prepared for the Department for International Development*.

Jain, Sachin Kumar, 'Women Leadership in Madhya Pradesh', Available at: http://www.mediaforrights.org/infopack/english-infopack/39, accessed on February 16, 2021.

Komenda, Katherine Jane (2001). 'Sojourn Through Saffron: The Life of Sadhavi Uma Shri Bharati and the Feminine Heart of Hindutva Religion and Politics in India', PhD dissertation, University of California, Santa Barbara.

National Family Health Survey-4 (2015–16). *State Fact Sheet, Madhya Pradesh*. Mumbai: International Institute for Population Sciences.

News Click (2018). 'Madhya Pradesh Polls-congress-bjp Show Little Faith in Women Candidates', November 14. Available at: https://www.newsclick.in/madhya-pradesh-polls-congress-bjp-show-little-faith-women-candidates, accessed on February 16, 2021.

Osama, Mohd. (2019). 'Madhya Pradesh and Its 'missing' Muslim Legislators', The Hindu Centre for Politics and Public Policy, January 14. Available at: https://www.thehinducentre.com/the-arena/current-issues/article25991277.ece, accessed on June 13, 2021.

Rai, P. (2011). 'Electoral Participation of Women in India: Key Determinants and Barriers', *Economic and Political Weekly*, 46(3), 47–55.

Surjan, Mayaram (1991). *Chief Ministers of Madhya Pradesh*. New Delhi: Radhakrishna Publications.

SEWA Madhya Pradesh (2022). Available at: https://www.facebook.com/SEWAMPofficial/community/?ref=page_internal, accessed on June 13, 2022.

Shrivastava, Rashmi (1994). 'Madhya Pradesh Politics', *The Indian Journal of Political Science*, LV (3), 261–270.

———— (2008). *Madhya Pradesh Government and Politics* (in Hindi). Jaipur: College Book Depot.

Society of Tribal Women for Development (n.d.). 'Impact of bottom up planning under PRIs and women participation therein in the States of Madhya Pradesh, Orissa, Chhattisgarh, Gujarat, Jharkhand and Maharashtra', Report commissioned by the Planning Commission. New Delhi: Government of India. Available at: https://niti.gov.in/planningcommission.gov.in/docs/reports/sereport /ser/ser_pri1102.pdf; http://ww.stwfd.org, accessed on June 11, 2022.

The Hindu (2020). 'Coronavirus | Lockdown Hits Nutrition of Women Workers in M.P.: Survey', August 24. Available at: https://www.thehindu.com/news/national /other-states/coronavirus-lockdown-hits-nutrition-of-women-workers-in-mp -survey/article32431113.ece, accessed on June 13, 2022.

The Indian Express (2019). Christophe Jaffrelot, 'Election Results Invite Questions For Liberals. Worldwide, They Lack Their Rivals' Discipline', May 24. Available at: https://indianexpress.com/article/opinion/columns/narendra-modi-vikas-lok -sabha-elections-5745364/, accessed on June 12, 2022.

The Times of India (2018). 'Where Are the Women in Madhya Pradesh Politics?', October 15. Available at: https://timesofindia.indiatimes.com/city/bhopal/ where-are-the-women-in-madhya-pradesh-politics/articleshow/66211011.cms, accessed on June 12, 2022.

———— (2019). 'So What's Wrong with Nusrat Jahan and Mimi Chakraborty's Parliament Wardrobe, Exactly? Hint: Nothing!', May 30. Available at: https:// timesofindia.indiatimes.com/life-style/fashion/buzz/so-whats-wrong-with-nusrat -jahan-and-mimi-chakrabortys-parliament-wardrobe-exactly/articleshow /69563479.cms, accessed on June 13, 2022.

14

WOMEN LEGISLATORS IN RAJASTHAN

A paradoxical scenario

Asha Kaushik

Introduction

Gender equality, as a tenet, is enshrined in the Indian Constitution in its Preamble, Fundamental Rights, and Directive Principles. The state is also particularly empowered to adopt measures of positive discrimination in favour of women (Article 15 (3)). Yet, gender equality and equity remain a major concern in Rajasthan, as elsewhere in the country. This chapter discusses the paradoxical scenario in Rajasthan, wherein the predominantly conservative, patriarchal, inequitable socioeconomic set-up notwithstanding, the state is acclaimed for highest representation of women in the legislative assembly.

With deeply embedded feudal and patriarchal norms in the social structure, Rajasthan has, for long, been a state where women's low status is a norm, rather than an exception. Albeit, the state has made strides in several spheres, women's share in the benefits of development has not been equitable. An analysis of gender-disaggregated human development indicators highlights the discrimination that women in the state experience at every stage of their lives, with differential access to quality healthcare, nutrition, education, and other basic services.

The vicious circle of poverty, patriarchy, and low access to opportunities and resources has resulted in a notable exclusion of women from power and entitlements, generally speaking. Yet, combating the formidable feudal, patriarchal socio-political challenges, the political journey of women in Rajasthan has been steady, though uneven. This scenario reflects the feudal, patriarchal socio-political ethos of the state.

Rajasthan has a population of about 6.86 crore of which approximately 3.30 crore are women. A look at Rajasthan's profile clearly brings out the multiple dimensions of gender disparities and inequalities in the state such as a gender gap in the child sex ratio (*Business Standard*, 2019; Census of

DOI: 10.4324/9781003374862-15

257

India, 2011), continued neglect of the girl child during infancy and early childhood (Census of India, 2011), a high maternal mortality ratio (MMR)

(Rajasthan, National Family Health Survey, Round 4 - 2015-16), a high percentage of child marriages (Census of India, 2011), the lowest female literacy rate and decline in workforce participation (Census of India, 2011), increasing graph of crimes against women (NCRB, 2019), and low female participation in household decisions (NFHS-3, 2005-06).

Persistence of customary laws and regressive social practices such as sati, dowry, child marriages, polygamy, polyandry, *atta-satta, nata-system, kukadi,* and even witch hunting (despite the Rajasthan Prevention of Witch Hunting Act 2015) control and subjugate women further. Caste- and community-based *jati panchayats* and *khap panchayats* pronounce regressive diktats that continue violating women's right to choice and agency.

Women in the state assembly

It is paradoxical that a predominantly conservative, hierarchical, and patriarchal social set-up notwithstanding, Rajasthan is among the few states with the highest representation of women in its state assembly. The number of women candidates in the 2018 polls surely, though marginally, went up to 189 from 166 in the 2013 elections, but even this was a meagre 8.3 per cent of the total contestants in the fray. The total number of voters in Rajasthan is 4.74 crore, of which 2.27 crore are women. In a state with 22 million women voters, this translates into an abysmal ratio of one woman candidate for every 1.16 lakh women voters. This is so, despite the fact that the state has had the distinction of having a woman Chief Minister, not once, but twice – in 2003–08 and 2013–18. Rajasthan also witnessed a drop in the number of women MLAs from 27 in 2013 to 24 in 2018, although female voter turnout (74.6 per cent) was higher than the male voter turnout (73.80 per cent) in the state. There was an overall drop in the female voter turnout also from 2013 (75.23 per cent) as per the State Election Commission's statistics. This uneven trend is visible in the comparative account of all 15 assemblies till date.

Despite claims by the Congress and BJP of giving increasingly more representation to women in politics, the past record of both the parties in Rajasthan reveals facts to the contrary. On an average in the last three assembly polls – in 2003, 2008, and 2013 – BJP gave 13 per cent tickets to women and Congress gave 11 per cent. In the 2003 elections, BJP gave tickets to 22 women and Congress to 18. The BJP formed the government and Vasundhara Raje became the first woman Chief Minister of the state. However, in her council of ministers, she included only one woman minister as minister of state.

In 2008, polls, BJP gave tickets to 32 women and Congress to 23. Congress formed the government. Chief Minister Ashok Gehlot's council of ministers included four women ministers, one with cabinet rank. In 2013, BJP gave 26 women tickets and Congress 24. Vasundhara Raje was returned to power. Her council of ministers this time included four women, including one cabinet minister, Kiran Maheshwari. Political parties' decisions of fielding women candidates, more often than not, are based on (false!) notions that women make weaker candidates, whereas analyses of their vote share and success rate show that the facts are quite different.

Frequent re-elections of sitting women MLAs – more than two dozen at different points of time – also confirm this. This is further vindicated by the fact that re-elections have thrown strong women leaders in Rajasthan such as Sumitra Singh (nine times elected member), Kamla Beniwal, Ujla Arora, Vidya Pathak, Pushpa Jain, Gauri Poonia, Madan Kaur, Prabha Misra, Laxmi Kumari Chundawat, and Bina Kak. Proven merit notwithstanding, a small number of women in the elected legislature is a clear mismatch with the greater involvement of women in elections as voters and even as campaigners. The situation is worrisome, as the persistent reaction of political parties to increased competitiveness is reducing the already small space that women politicians occupy.

In 2008, 28 women were elected to the assembly (14 per cent) – the highest percentage of women legislators in the country along with Bihar and Haryana. The 2013 elections saw 27 women being elected to the state assembly (13.5 per cent) one seat less than the previous elections. In 2018, only 24 women politicians were able to make it to the assembly, inclusive of one bye-election win (12 per cent), showing a continuous decline, though marginal, from 2008 to 2018.

The process of uneven representation of women in the assembly needs to be placed in a historico–comparative context. It is true that from the first assembly elections in the state in 1952, the number of women candidates contesting and winning assembly seats has been increasing, although slowly and unevenly.

The first Rajasthan assembly elections for 160 seats in 1952 witnessed 757 contestants out of which the number of women contestants was merely four, none of whom won. In a subsequent bye-election in November 1953 for the Banswara assembly seat, Yashoda Devi of the Praja Socialist Party was elected, breaking the ceiling in the overwhelmingly feudal-patriarchal disposition of Rajasthan. In another bye-election in June 1954 for Amber-'A' constituency another woman, Kamla Beniwal from the Congress, got elected, taking the number of women legislators to two in the first legislative assembly. It is notable that in Chief Minister Sukhadia's council of ministers, Kamla Beniwal was included as a deputy minister (November 13, 1954–April 10, 1957). These beginnings, however small, were surely significant as a solid stepping stone in women's political journey in the state.

In the second assembly elections in 1957, 21 women contested of whom nine got elected. Seven out of these nine elected members belonged to the Congress and two were independents. No woman was included in Sukhadia's second council of ministers.

A lesser number compared to the previous assembly – 15 women – contested for the third assembly in 1962 and only eight (one less) – all from the Congress – were returned to office.

In 1967, for the fourth assembly, only six women legislators – again all from the Congress – got elected out of 19 contestants. One more woman politician was returned to the assembly later on in a bye-election in July 1967. It might be recalled that the period 1967–71 witnessed a big, 'somewhat baffling' transition in Indian politics, resulting in a major re-alignment of political forces in the country, including in Rajasthan. The Congress lost its hold over eight states. A political upheaval of sorts was visible, defections becoming commonplace and political mood swinging between extremes of hope and pessimism (Narain, 1972). In the fourth Sukhadia council of ministers only one woman legislator was included as a minister of state and another as a deputy minister.

Following the mid-term Lok Sabha polls in 1971, Sukhadia was replaced by Baraktullah Khan as Chief Minister of Rajasthan. During his brief tenure, no woman legislator found a place in his council of ministers. The fourth assembly was seen as a theatre of political drama in public perception as reported in the local press at that time.

The number of women legislators rose to 13 in the fifth assembly elections in 1972, all belonging to what came to be known as Congress (N). This was the first de-linked election (separate elections for Parliament and state assemblies) in India. The Indian National Congress was split. The election scene was, however, dominated by Congress (N). Riding on the so-called Indira wave, Prime Minister Indira Gandhi had dramatically transformed the political ethos, mores, and equations in the country. This had a visible impact on the dynamics of state politics as well. The fifth Rajasthan assembly saw five women politicians re-elected. Women were getting a foothold in politics in the state against all odds. In Khan's council of ministers, one woman legislator was included as a minister of state.

Following the untimely demise of Baraktullah Khan on October 11, 1973, Haridev Joshi was sworn in as the next Chief Minister. Kamla Beniwal was re-sworn as minister of state in Joshi's council of ministers. Eight women legislators got elected out of 31 contestants to the sixth Rajasthan assembly (1977–80), showing a decline in numbers. Six of these, belonging to Janata Party, were new entrants. Although they were new entrants to the formal political space of the legislative assembly, it was public knowledge that they had been active participants in the informal public space and the social and political movements for a decade or so (Jain and Sharma, 2018; Kaushik, 1982). It was given out that they had been involved in the JP movement, preceding the Emergency in 1975. The 1977 polls resulted in a historic win for the Janata Party in Rajasthan, as elsewhere in the country – with 150 seats in a House of 200. Bhairon Singh Shekhawat formed the first non-Congress government in the state. His council of ministers included just one woman legislator as a minister of state.

It is evident that a feudal-patriarchal social ethos was reflected in the continuing small number of women legislators in the state. However, even these small numbers did not deter the active performance of confident women legislators in the House.

The seventh assembly (1980–85) recorded the number of women contestants at 31 and winning legislators at 10. Chief Minister Jagannath Paharia's council of ministers included two women legislators.

The seventh assembly was ridden by political conflicts. Chief Minister Paharia resigned in July 1981. Shiv Charan Mathur was sworn in as the new Chief Minister, with one cabinet rank and one deputy minister rank for women. At the beginning of 1985, there was another change in leadership, with Heeralal Devpura as the incoming Chief Minister. In his brief tenure (February 23, 1985, to March 10, 1985) both women retained their positions.

In the eighth legislative assembly (1985–90) the number of women legislators rose to 17. Of these, 15 were elected in the main elections and two joined through bye-elections. Haridev Joshi's council of ministers included three women legislators, one as cabinet minister and two as deputy ministers. Following Haridev Joshi's resignation, Shiv Charan Mathur was sworn in again as Chief Minister on January 20, 1988. His council of ministers included three women ministers of state. The parliamentary secretary was also a woman.

The next Vidhan Sabha (1990–93) saw a decline in the number of women representatives in the House from 17 to 11. Bhairon Singh Shekhawat formed the government and included four women politicians in his council of ministers. Two of them resigned when Janta Dal withdrew from the government in October 1990.

In the tenth assembly (1993–98) only ten women representatives – one less than in the previous one – were returned to office. Bhairon Singh Shekhawat was again sworn in as the Chief Minister of the state. Shekhawat's team of ministers included three women ministers, while one woman legislator was appointed Vidhan Sabha's vice-chairperson – the first instance of such an appointment, adding one more feather to women politicians' cap.

The eleventh assembly (1998–2003) once again saw an increase in the number of women legislators to 15; 69 women contested in 1998 and 14 succeeded at the hustings. One more woman joined the assembly in February 2000 by winning a bye-election. Ashok Gehlot was sworn in as Chief Minister. His council of ministers included two women legislators as cabinet ministers and two more as ministers of state. In May 2003, the ministers of state were removed, leaving only two women ministers in the power team. However, on the same day (May 13, 2003) two other women legislators were appointed parliamentary secretaries. Cabinet minister Kamla Beniwal was elevated to the office of deputy Chief Minister – an honour and a distinction in women's journey towards sharing power by occupying higher political positions.

In the twelfth Vidhan Sabha (2003–08) the number of women representatives went down to 12 out of 118 contestants, although following the 2003 polls, the state got its first woman Chief Minister, Vasundhara Raje – a valuable milestone in women's political journey to the highest office in the state. However, it was ironic that no other woman was included in her council of ministers. At a later stage, Usha Poonia was added as a minister of state. Out of the 17 permanent committees of the House, women were confined to just two in a lopsided manner, with one legislator in a 12-member committee on Question and Reference and nine women in one 9-member committee on Women and Children Welfare. In January 2004 Sumitra Singh was unanimously elected the Speaker of the Vidhan Sabha, which was another milestone in women's rise to power in the state.

Rajasthan witnessed an unprecedented presence of three women in the highest positions of power – Governor, Chief Minister, and Speaker of the Vidhan Sabha in 2003–08. Pratibha Patil, Vasundhara Raje, and Sumitra Singh occupied these high offices in the state respectively.

The thirteenth assembly (2008–13) holds the distinction of the highest ever number of women legislators in the House. The highest number of women – 154 – had contested and the highest number – 28 – was returned to the assembly. But only two women, one as cabinet minister and another as minister of state – could find a place in Chief Minister Ashok Gehlot's council of ministers.

In the fourteenth assembly (2013–18), 27 of the 166 women who contested the elections, won. The female voter turnout was acclaimed as 'encouraging' at 75.52 per cent, which was 10 per cent more, compared to 65.31 per cent in 2008 (*The Times of India*, 2013). Vasundhara Raje was sworn in as Chief Minister once again. Her council of ministers included one woman legislator as a cabinet minister and two legislators as ministers of state (independent charge). It is notable that women legislators have been regularly and actively engaged in the functioning of various committees of the House in all these decades.

Polls to the current, fifteenth assembly in 2018 witnessed the highest number of women – 189 – ever to contest for the assembly in the state. Even this was a mere 8.23 per cent share held by women in the candidates' list. However, the tally of successful women candidates came down from 27 in the previous assembly to 23 this time. One more woman legislator was added through a subsequent bye-election bringing the tally to 24 at present. The current Ashok Gehlot council of ministers has only one woman as minister of state.

Women as voters and contestants

A comparative analysis of the percentage of women as voters, contestants, and winners across legislative assemblies from 1952 to 2018 is useful for a holistic view of women's political journey in Rajasthan.

It is heartening to note that women voters' participation stood at 74.66 per cent in the Vidhan Sabha polls in 2018, as per data released by the Election Commission, although, comparatively speaking, 74.66 per cent was a minimal dip from the previous assembly polls in 2013, which recorded the highest ever female turnout at 75.57 per cent. However, women's voter percentage (74.66 per cent) was higher than male voter percentage (73.80 per cent) in a total turnout of 74.21 per cent. This is heartening because the trend continues the 2013 pathbreaking reversal of gender gap in voting percentage. The desert state has traditionally recorded a high voting percentage. A comparative look at the voting percentage of women and men across various assembly polls puts women's participation as voters in perspective (Table 14.1).

As indicated in Table 14.1, the percentage of female voting has been gradually increasing in assembly polls over the preceding decades, with the exception of 1977 and 1980 when women's voting percentage dwindled from 50.02 per cent in 1972 to 48.72 per cent in 1977 and 45.96 per cent in 1980. Subsequent elections saw a persistent and gradual increase in their participation. In the 1985 and 1990 assembly polls the female voting percentage was at 48.40 per cent and 51.54 per cent respectively. This rose to 55.23 per cent in 1993 and to 58.96 per cent in 1998. In 2003, women's voting percentage rose further to 64.21 and to 65.42 in 2008.

However, all these elections also show a persistent gender gap in voting patterns. Notably, the increasing women voter percentage was parallel to

Table 14.1 Voting patterns in Rajasthan's Vidhan Sabha elections

Year	Men	Women	Gender gap
1972	65.03%	50.02%	15.01%
1977	59.77%	48.72%	11.05%
1980	57.99%	45.96%	12.03%
1985	60.91%	48.40%	11.51%
1990	62.00%	51.54%	10.46%
1993	65.44%	55.23%	10.21%
1998	67.56%	58.96%	8.6%
2003	69.91%	64.21%	5.7%
2008	67.31%	65.42%	1.89%
2013	74.92%	75.57%	0.65% (Reverse trend: 0.65% more female voting)
2018	73.80%	74.66%	0.86% (Reverse trend : 0.86% more female voting)

Source: Election Department, Rajasthan.

an increase in the percentage of male voters. It is interesting to note that in the 1977 and 1980 elections both male and female voting registered a decline to 59.77 per cent (1977) from 65.03 per cent (1972) for males and to 48.72 per cent (1977) from 50.02 per cent (1972) for females and further declined in 1980 to 57.99 per cent and 45.96 per cent for males and females respectively. The gender gap in the 1972, 1977, and 1980 polls was registered at 15 per cent, 11.05 per cent, and 12.03 per cent respectively. This gender gap started narrowing from 1980 onwards. In 1985 it came down to 11.51 per cent and slid further down to 10.46 per cent in 1990; 1993 saw a marginal change with male voting percentage going up (after 1972) to 65.44 per cent and female voting percentage to 55.23 per cent. Further, the 1998, 2003, and 2008 elections showed encouraging trends in narrowing the gender gap from 8.6 per cent in 1998 to 5.7 per cent in 2003 and 1.89 per cent in 2008.

The highest women voter percentage was recorded in 2013 at 75.23 per cent surpassing the male voting percentage (74.92 per cent) by 0.65 per cent. This reversal in the gender gap continued in 2018 as well. Women's voting percentage at 74.66 per cent (slightly lower than 2013) surpassed the male voting percentage (73.80 per cent – also slightly lower than the previous assembly polls) by 0.86 per cent. This is a notable trend.

It is also notable that since 1972 the electoral sex ratio in Rajasthan has improved. This is to state that women voters per 1,000 men voters have increased: 723 (1972), 763 (1971), 744 (1980), 728 (1985), 736 (1990), 755 (1993), 786 (1998), 841 (2003), 874 (2008), 899 (2013), and 919 (2018). The trend has generally been interpreted as electorally significant on several counts. In Bihar, when women outvoted men in 2015, Nitish Kumar rode the wave on the back of his policies like prohibition, as highlighted by the Centre for the Study of Developing Societies (CSDS) in its report on the Bihar elections (Lokniti-CSDS, 2015). Overwhelming support by women also helped AIADMK beat anti-incumbency in the 2016 Tamil Nadu assembly elections. In Rajasthan, high female voting went in favour of the winning party – BJP in 2013 and Congress in 2018. The trend may need further probing in terms of other co-related factors. However, generally speaking, it does hold water.

The overall high voter turnout percentage since 2013 was attributed by the state bureaucracy to efforts by various agencies, especially the Election Commission to increase electoral awareness among the masses. The Election Commission initiated a special Systematic Voters Education and Electoral Participation (SVEEP) programme across the state. It was further reported that young voters in large numbers got their names added to the voters' list (*The Times of India*, 2018).

Pande and Deanna Ford (2011) brought out that growing women's representation in local-level governance has fuelled an increase in women's voting share in elections. Political parties have not been particularly proactive in fielding women candidates, thereby attracting women voters. Claims of political parties having a pivotal role in this respect, therefore, are misplaced.

However, it is evident that there is no co-relation between women voter turnout and the number of women candidates in the field. Also, high women voting percentages do not get translated into increased women's representation (Table 14.2). Multiple factors intervene in the process.

A comparative view of Tables 14.1 and 14.2 confirms this assertion. For instance, in 1998, women's voting percentage was 58.96 per cent, whereas the number of female contestants was just 69, a mere 4.79 per cent of the total candidates (1,439) in the electoral fray. In contrast, male contestants' percentage was 95.2 per cent. In 2003, the women voting percentage was 64.21 per cent but the percentage of women candidates was only 7.65 per cent of the total number of candidates in the race (1,514). In 2008, the number of candidates rose from 118 (in 2003) to 154 but a proportional increase in the percentage of female candidates was not visible. It came down from 7.64 (in 2003) to 7.01 in 2008.

One probable reason for this sliding percentage was the increase in the total number of candidates in the fray – 2,194 – of which the number of male candidates was 2,040 (92.9 per cent). The Vidhan Sabha elections of 2013 were historic in the sense that a reverse trend, of women outvoting men with the highest ever voter turnout at 75.57 per cent, was witnessed. Even this huge voting percentage could not raise the number of women contestants beyond 166, a mere 7.92 per cent of the total number of contestants (2,096).

The trend of increasing voting turnout and number of women contestants continued in the 2018 polls. Female voting percentage at 74.66 per cent outshone that of their male counterparts (73.80 per cent), but with 2,873 candidates in the fray, the percentage of women candidates did not cross 8.23 per cent. However, it is satisfactory to note that from the first assembly polls in 1952, when the number of women contestants was just four, the increase, albeit with variations, was 50-fold in 2018. It is certainly not a healthy political process where an over 74–75 per cent voting turnout is mismatched with an abysmal low percentage of candidates, not reaching even a double-digit mark. The reasons for this dismal percentage are structural as well as electoral.

Political parties to blame

Serious rethinking on the issue is warranted on the part of political parties. Tall claims apart, on an average in the last three elections – 2003, 2008, and 2013 – even the two big national parties' tally of tickets to women candidates did not move beyond 13 per cent in case of the BJP and 11 per cent in the case of the Congress. At this rate, commentator Hasan M. Kamal maintains, it will take another 90 years to reach 20 per cent and 315 years

Table 14.2 Contestants in the Vidhan Sabha elections

Year	Total contestants	Male contestants	Percentage	Female contestants	Percentage	Lost	Won
1952	757	753	99.47	4	0.52	4	0
1957	653	632	96.78	21	3.21	12	9
1962	890	875	98.31	15	1.68	7	8
1967	892	783	97.63	19	2.36	13	6
1972	875	853	97.63	17	1.94	4	13
1977	1146	1115	97.29	31	2.70	23	8
1980	1406	1375	97.79	31	2.20	13	10
1985	1485	1440	96.96	45	3.30	28	17
1990	3088	2995	96.98	93	3.01	82	11
1993	2438	2341	96.02	97	3.97	87	10
1998	1439	1370	95.20	69	4.79	55	14
2003	1514	1423	92.34	118	7.65	106	12
2008	2194	2040	92.98	154	7.01	126	28
2013	2096	1930	92.08	166	7.92	139	27
2018	2873	2684	93.42	189	8.23	165	24

Source: Election Department, Rajasthan.

to reach a stage where the number of women candidates is equal to male candidates (*The Hindustan Times*, 2018).

A small number of candidates results in a smaller representation for women. Women make up less than 9 per cent of the legislators across all state assemblies in the country (*The Economic Survey*, 2017-18). Rajasthan's case is illustrated in Table 14.3.

As shown in Table 14.3, the political journey of women representatives in the Rajasthan assembly has been steady, notwithstanding the challenges that they have had to face. The journey of women's representation in the state began with two legislators in the first Vidhan Sabha.

It was a beginning with a mere 1.25 per cent representation in a House of 160 members. This figure moved up to 5.11 per cent in a House of 176 in 1957, 4.54 in 1962, 3.80 in a House of increased strength of 184 seats in 1967, 7.06 per cent in 1972, to a dismal 4 per cent in the expanded assembly of 200 in 1977, 5 per cent in 1980, and 8.50 per cent in 1985.

Hopes were raised only to be belied by the results of the subsequent ninth, tenth, eleventh, and twelfth assemblies: 1990–93, 1993–98, 1998–2003, and 2003–08, showing a diminishing representation of women at 5.50 per cent, 5 per cent, 7.50 per cent, and 6.50 per cent respectively.

It was in the thirteenth assembly (2008–13) that women legislators' percentage reached double digits. With 28 women legislators (14 per cent), Rajasthan topped the chart of women's representation in state assemblies in the country. The fourteenth assembly (2013–18) registered a marginal decline from 14 per cent to 13.50 per cent representation.

Table 14.3 Women legislators in the Rajasthan assembly

Year	Total seats/number of legislators	Women legislators	Percentage of women legislators
1952	160	2	1.25
1957	176	9	5.11
1962	176	8	4.54
1967	184	7	3.80
1972	184	13	7.06
1977	200	8	4.00
1980	200	10	5.00
1985	200	17	8.50
1990	200	11	5.50
1993	200	10	5.00
1998	200	15	7.50
2003	200	13	6.50
2008	200	28	14.00
2013	200	27	13.50
2018	200	24	12.00

Source: Election Department, Rajasthan.

The 2018 polls, for the current assembly, resulted in a further decline, bringing down the number of women leaders to 24 (23 through the main elections and one through a bye-election). That closed the tally at 12 per cent.

This account demonstrates the uneven and imbalanced nature of women's representation in the Rajasthan Vidhan Sabha. Surely, it is a reflection of politics outside – at the state and national levels. In all, the total number of women legislators spanning 15 legislative assemblies in Rajasthan has been a mere 202.

Lack of sharing of power with women

The situation is worse at the level of distribution and sharing of power. Certainly, Rajasthan has had the distinction of having a woman Chief Minister, not once but twice, who is acknowledged as a strong and capable leader, her critics notwithstanding. But this feeling of pride evaporates when we look at women's position in the power hierarchy in the assembly (Table 14.4).

As shown in Table 14.4, in all the 15 state assemblies in the last 66 years, a minimal number of women have been part of the power-sharing experience. Only 10 times have women leaders been able to reach the cabinet rank, 16 times the rank of minister of state, eight times the rank of a deputy minister, and three times as parliamentary secretaries. Only one woman has been the Speaker of the House and one woman a vice-chairperson. One woman legislator has been a deputy Chief Minister once. Surely, one big thing of pride for Rajasthan has been the much-acclaimed fact of having been governed by a woman Chief Minister – Vasundhara Raje – twice – in 2003–08 and 2013–18, though one may have a difference of opinion regarding the political and ideological fallout of her two tenures. All in all, not more than 42 times have women legislators occupied important positions of power in the last six and a half decades, spanning 15 legislative assemblies in the state. This amounts to a virtual exclusion of a large segment of women from power. It is a scenario of a highly imbalanced political arrangement. It needs to change. It must change.

Need for a change

The need to change the existing scenario is being felt. It is encouraging to note that the Economic Survey for 2017–18 tabled in Parliament in January 2019 underlined the fact that 'out of the total 4,118 MLAs across the country only 9 per cent were women' (as in October, 2016). Expressing concern about low political participation of women, the survey reaffirmed factors such as domestic responsibilities, prevailing cultural attitudes regarding role of women in society, and lack of support from family as the main reasons

Table 14.4 Women in the council of ministers and in other high positions in the assembly

Sl. no.	Year	Chief minister/deputy chief minister	Cabinet minister	Minister of state	Deputy minister	Speaker/parliamentary secretary/vice-chairperson	Total
1	1952	–	–	–	1	–	1
2	1957	–	–	–	–	–	–
3	1962	–	–	–	2	–	2
4	1967	–	–	1	1	–	2
5	1972	–	–	1	–	–	1
6	1977	–	–	1	–	–	1
7	1980	–	1	–	2	–	3
8	1985	–	1	3	2	1	7
9	1990	–	4	–	–	–	4
10	1993	–	–	3	–	1	4
11	1998	1 (Deputy CM)	2	2	–	2	7
12	2003	1 (Chief minister)	–	1	–	1	3
13	2008	–	1	1	–	–	2
14	2013	1 (Chief minister)	1	2	–	–	4
15	2018	–	–	1	–	–	1
Total	66 years	Chief minister twice, 1 deputy CM= 03	10	16	08	05	42

Source: Election Department, Rajasthan.

that prevented women from entering politics. The Economic Survey called for an increased political participation of women: 'Recognizing the significance of role of women in decision-making process in the society, is critical to strengthen women's agencies for building a progressive society with equality of opportunities among all citizens' (*The Economic Survey*, 2017-18). Although there has been substantial representation of women at the local government levels, lack of it at the state and national levels needs to be addressed.

In Rajasthan, it has been rightly appreciated in political quarters that in spite of the predominantly patriarchal, hierarchical, and feudal social structure and mindset, the state is part of the 'exclusive club of states' having the highest representation of women in the legislature. The appreciation is justified, as it places Rajasthan on 'the scale of the states' in the country and is based on a comparative statistical assessment. However, as argued in this chapter, women's representation in the Rajasthan state assembly has never crossed 14 till now and is far from being adequate given women's political potential in the public space in the state. If judged on the anvil of gender equality and gender justice, this scenario demands a serious reassessment. The women's movement needs to address the issue with utmost rigour.

Impediments to women entering politics have been identified by numerous studies, as emanating from the patriarchal structures and attitudes governing the political parties, financial facilitators, and the entire socio-cultural edifice of society. This holds true for Rajasthan, as elsewhere (Burns et al., 2001). Criminalization of politics, violence against women, and women's lower mobility are additional barriers. At the root is an overwhelming gender stereotyping based on a patriarchal gender construct. This scenario restricts the number of women entering politics – mostly perceived as a dirty game of money and muscle power. The argument put forward largely in the 1990s (Kishwar, 1996) unfortunately remains relevant even today in Rajasthan. Moreover, those who enter the political arena have a limited impact on policy matters, broadly speaking (exceptions apart), owing to their negligible numbers.

Conclusion

In the electoral field, the most visible and directly relevant political player is the political party. As discussed earlier, political parties have been distributing a dismal number of tickets to women. It has also been pointed out that women's numerical strength in political parties is not large enough to impact decision-making even within the political parties. For instance, during a conversation when asked about the poor representation of women in the BJP, the curt and quick reply was that the party constitution has already been amended to give 33 per cent reservation to women in its organizational structure. On the ground, the facts are different. The Congress, or any other political party for that matter, is no better. This situation may become better, if political parties are directed and legally bound to give minimum 33 per cent tickets to women in elections at all levels. We would like to endorse the view recommended in many political quarters that through amending India's Representation of the People's Act of 1951, political parties be mandated to allocate at least one third of tickets to women (Kishwar,1996).

Another potent strategy, already successfully tested in several countries and in India at the local governance level with positive results, is statutory reservation of 33 per cent seats for women to ensure the much-needed 'critical mass' to impact policy and decision-making. The Women's Reservation Bill (WRB) passed by Rajya Sabha way back in 2010 still looks like a distant goal, except of course, in the election manifestos of political parties. Unfortunately, it remains simmering in the crucible of the political class, fiercely guarding their own politico-patriarchal interests.

In the present scenario, an effective intervention by the women's movement, along with other civil, political, and human rights movements is called for. As for women's own collective initiatives in Rajasthan, their struggles for legitimate space and share in power on an equal footing continue in both formal and informal spaces.

Bibliography

Aery, Raj Rani (1966). 'Women Legislators in Rajasthan – 1952–1962', unpublished Dissertation, Department of Political Science, University of Rajasthan, Jaipur.

Burns, Nancy, Kay Lehman Scholzman, and SidneyVerba (2001). *The Private Roots of Public Action: Gender, Equality and Political Participation.* Cambridge: Harvard University Press.

Press Trust of India, Gender ratio at birth up by four points in Rajasthan, Business Standard, July 4, 2019, https://www.business-standard.com/article/pti-stories /gender-ratio-at-birth-up-by-four-points-in-rajasthan-119070400791_1.html accessed on October 20, 2021.

Census of India (2011) *Office of the Registrar General and Census Commissioner, Ministry of Home Affairs,*New Delhi: Government of India.

The Economic Survey (2017–18). *Department of Economic Affairs, Ministry of Finance,* New Delhi: Government of India.

Election Commission of India (n.d.) *Highlights on Rajasthan.* Available at: eci.gov .in/files/category/88-rajasthan, accessed on October 30, 2021.

Jain, Pratibha and Sangeeta Sharma (2018). *Women's Struggles in Rajasthan.* Jaipur: Centre for Rajasthan Studies, University of Rajasthan.

Kaushik, Asha (1982). 'Legislative Elite and Social Change: A study of Women Legislators in the Rajasthan Assembly', *Journal of Constitutional And Parliamentary Studies,* 16 (1–2), 140–152.

Kishwar, Madhu (1996). 'Women and Politics: Beyond Quotas', *Economic and Political Weekly,* 31 (43), 2867–2874.

Lokniti-CSDS (2015). *Bihar Post-poll 2015 Survey Findings.* Available at: www .lokniti.org>media>pdf 1536304574 and www.lokniti.org>state-election studies, accessed on October 20, 2021.

Narain, Iqbal (1972). *Twilight or Dawn- Political Change in India (1967–71).* Agra: Shiv Lal Agarwala & Co.

National Crime Records Bureau (n.d.). Ministry of Home Affairs, Government of India.

National Family and Health Survey (NFHS) (n.d.). *Rajasthan, Ministry of Health & Family Welfare.* Mumbai: International Institute of Population Sciences and the Government of India.

Official website of the Chief Electoral Officer, Jaipur: Election Department Rajasthan.

Pande, Rohini and Deanna Ford (2011). 'Gender Quotas and Female Leadership: A Review', Background paper for the World Development Report on Gender, Harvard University.

Rajasthan Legislative Assembly Portal (n.d.). Rajasthan Legislative Assembly Secretariat, Jaipur.

The Hindustan Times, December 10, 2018.

The Times of India, December 11, 2013.

———— December 9, 2018.

Varma, Sudhir (2004). *A Situational Analysis of Women and Girls in Rajasthan.* New Delhi: National Commission for Women.

15

WOMEN IN STATE POLITICS IN WEST BENGAL

Kaberi Chakrabarti

Introduction

Engendering governance, as a proactive strategy of the UN 2030 Agenda for Sustainable Development is understood as revisiting the normative focus of governance and the creation of a more accessible, violence-free, and capable environment for women. This means scrutinizing the sources of gender inequalities in institutions and beyond the institutional spaces of governance and acting towards gender-sensitive transformations.

At the core of this transformative politics lies the urgency of reframing notions like rights, access, and ownership in institutionalizing gender equality and challenging the culture of exclusion. Women's access and engagement in political spaces through participation in decision-making processes and leadership, both institutional and non-institutional, is a crucial indicator of achieving gender equality in governance. In the context of achieving gender equality goals under SDG 5, a UN report on India observed that despite 'achieving gender parity at the primary education level and efforts to extend it at all education levels', the proportion of seats in Parliament and local governments held by women is quite low in the country (United Nations in India, SDG 5: Gender Equality). At present, women hold 14.39 per cent of the seats in the Lok Sabha and 10.66 per cent in the Rajya Sabha.

Despite the focus of successive governments to prioritize gender equality programmes, women's access to resources and their share in political-economic processes is abysmally low in India. Experts see the wide diversity in women's positions at the global, national, and local levels as a challenge in fulfilling basic minimum goals of sustainable development. It is, therefore, important to understand the variations in experiences and multiplicity of conditions in which women live for framing strategies for achieving a broad-based vision like SDG 5 instead of homogenizing the context of marginalization and representation.

DOI: 10.4324/9781003374862-16

273

States: new sites of power

In India, development politics is increasingly evolving in federal units. Scholars are interested in understanding the political dynamics of social welfare with federal provinces shaping social policies and the modes of governing welfare (Tillin et al., 2015). States are, therefore, emerging as new sites of power in meeting development goals and strategies in a cooperative turned competitive federalism vis-á-vis the national government. These changing dynamics of federal politics in India have prompted greater roles of provincial governments in (re)shaping the scope of the politics of development and representation. In this respect engendering governance suggests incorporating the regional context in realizing the scope of common goals and strategies. 'Region' may allow us to understand the dynamics of participation and representation with its 'inclusions' and 'exclusions' in a historical context.

As reflected in the NITI Aayog Baseline Report (2019–20), in terms of the SDG 5 Index score, West Bengal featured in the aspirant category with a score of 38. A brief look at the overall position of women in West Bengal in terms of some basic social and economic indicators will help contextualize the political participation of women in the state. According to Census (2011) the sex ratio in West Bengal was favourably higher for women at 950 compared to the Indian average of 940. NFHS-5 (2019–20) data shows an improved sex ratio at birth for children born in the last five years at 973. However, there are wide variations in district-wise data on the sex ratio with some of the northern districts showing a higher ratio compared to a declining sex ratio in southern districts like South 24 Parganas.

NFHS-5 (2019–20) shows that 24.7 and 22.5 per cent urban and rural women respectively owned a house or land (alone or jointly with others). Contrary to women's marginal economic position in terms of ownership of basic assets, women are increasingly integrated into banking facilities in the state. A significant feature of women's status in the family is reflected in women's voices in family matters. NFHS-5 (2019–20) data shows that 96.1 per cent urban married women and 85.8 per cent rural married women in West Bengal could take part in household decisions about healthcare for themselves, major household purchases, and visiting their families or relatives. However, there has been a slight decline in respect of rural women which showed these figures as 89.9 per cent for rural married women (NFHS-4, 2015–16). The female literacy rate in the state is 76.1 per cent (NFHS-5, 2019–20).

However, on the flip side, West Bengal ranks higher in the list of states with violence against women. The National Crime Records data (2018) shows that the state had 8 per cent of India's reported crimes against women, ranking third on the national list (National Crime Records Bureau, 2018). In another survey, 36 per cent married women aged 15–49 years faced spousal violence in the state (SDG 5 India Index, 2019-20). These figures indicate that women's increasing share in decision-making in their families does not mean a greater share for them in socioeconomic processes which could help reduce their oppression in private and public spheres. It is in this context that women's political representation is analysed in contemporary West Bengal.

Women's political representation

Bengal has a rich legacy of the social reform movements on the 'women's question' that emerged as the core of public debates in the nineteenth century on issues like abolition of 'sati', widow remarriages, and age of consent. Scholars like Partha Chatterjee (2006, p. 252) argue that the grand narrative of nationalism subsequently settled the question of women's emancipation in the sphere of home, setting up a 'new patriarchy' that facilitated the 'false essentialisms of home/world, spiritual/material, feminine/masculine propagated by nationalist ideology'. This corresponded with an increasing gendering of social roles which rendered women's political participation and their visibility in the public sphere problematic.

An interesting anecdote about women's socio-political roles can be added here from the archives of vernacular literature, particularly the popular genre of *battala*, known for its barbed satirical content. One such lesser-known tract, *Meye Parliament* (Parliament of Women), written by an anonymous writer, depicted a utopian narrative of a Parliament led only by women in the *bhaginirajtantra* (Republic of Sisters). Reflecting on this piece, Samita Sen showed how the satirical tract portrayed a reversal of gender roles. To cite one example, 'the women ran the country and the men looked after the household' (Sen, 2012, p.138).

Despite social anxiety about gender roles and limited scope of nationalist projects in terms of women's freedom and equality, a large number of women participated in historic movements like Swadeshi and satyagraha and other revolutionary activities in Bengal. In the 1930s, leaders like Shanti Ghosh, Suniti Chowdhury, Pritilata Waddedar, and Bina Das played historic roles in military action against the British rule along with their male counterparts. Women leaders like Renuka Ray and Phulrenu Guha contributed extensively to the Gandhian movement and integrated social work like famine relief and communal harmony during riots with their core political activism. Women from peasant families fought battles against zamindars and *jotedars* in the Tebhaga movement.

Gendering of social roles in Bengal took a critical turn in the backdrop of the socio-political developments following the Partition that brought the women's struggle for basic livelihoods into the broader space of refugee movements. The engagement of women from different sections of society in these movements in the pre-independence period set the tone for a vibrant and active agency for women in political spaces. Women leaders from communist parties and liberal, independent women formed the Mahila Atmarokkha Samiti in 1942 which played an instrumental role in mobilizing women in relief work, against price rise and black marketing, and more importantly, in the movement demanding release of political prisoners in the 1940s. Four Mahila Atmarokkha Samiti women leaders were martyred on April 27, 1949, in the movement demanding the release of political prisoners. From the very beginning, the influence of communist ideology and leadership was noticed in the dominant spaces of women's political movement in West Bengal along with a Gandhian influence.

Women organizers from Left-wing parties contributed to the food movement, refugee rehabilitation, transport, and primary teachers' movements in the state. Many well-known women revolutionaries like Suhasini Ganguly, Ujjala Rakshit, Manikuntala Sen, and Kalpana Dutta joined the Communist Party after independence and also had successful political careers. Manikuntala Sen, representing the CPI, was elected twice to the state assembly as a lone woman candidate in the 1950s. Leaders like Shanti Das, Bina Das, and Kamala Mukherjee joined the Congress Party and played important roles in forming the Congress Mahila Sangha.

Women leaders from Bengal also played an instrumental role in parliamentary affairs as ministers and members. Renuka Ray, a veteran Gandhian social activist, led the movement for legal reforms for women in India as the legal secretary of the All India Women's Conference. She served as a member of the Constituent Assembly and the provisional Parliament and became the minister of rehabilitation and relief in the West Bengal assembly in 1952–57. Phulrenu Guha, one of the leading faces of the Congress Party, was the social welfare minister in the union cabinet in the 1960s. She played a leading role in preparing the *Towards Equality* report in 1974 as the chairperson of the Committee on the Status of Women in India and contributed greatly as the first chairperson of the Centre for Women's Development Studies with Vina Mazumdar as the director. Phulrenu Guha, along with other women leaders like Prativa Bose, Sudha Sen, and Maitreyi Basu led movements for women's financial autonomy and social health.

In the first general elections to the Lok Sabha in 1952, two women MPs from the state – CPI's Renu Chakravarty and Ila Palchaudhuri from the Congress Party – were elected, and they served three terms. Geeta Mukherjee, another veteran CPI leader and well-known face of the women's movement in the country, was elected to the West Bengal legislative assembly four times and represented her constituency Panskura in Midnapore district for seven terms as MP till her death in 2000. She was the first woman secretariat member of any communist party in India. Geeta Mukherjee was one of the chief architects of the movement for women's reservation and the chairperson of Parliament's Joint Select Committee on the women's reservation bill that was tabled in Parliament in September 1996.

In the 1960s, tribal and peasant women fought gallantly with male revolutionaries in the Naxalbari movement. However, women's agency in these movements was comparatively shadowed by their personal suffering of being victims, or narratives of individual heroism and limited by 'patriarchal prejudices' of their male co-workers.

The split in the communist movement in 1964 had a profound impact on women's organizational activities with fragmentation of the movement leading to the formation of different mass organizations. The Paschimbanga Mahila Samiti, an inheritor of the Mahila Atmarokkha Samiti, was affiliated to the Communist Party of India which disintegrated as a result of the division of the Communist Party with the new faction sympathetic to the CPI(M), emerging as the Paschim Banga Ganatantrik Mohila Samiti (PBGMS). Partisan affiliations also created increasing distance between independent women's movements and party-led women's organizations that were eventually reduced to front politics.

The front governments played an instrumental role in empowering women through radical decentralization with land reform legislations, securing joint *pattas* in favour of women or implementation of the 50 per cent reservations for women in the panchayats, and organizing female literacy programmes. In the panchayat elections held in 1993, an all-women gram panchayat, the first of its kind in West Bengal, was formed in Kultikari, a tribal-dominated village in Midnapore district. Women panchayat members in Kultikari exemplified leadership potential in governance at the grassroots level. During the Left Front rule, Paschim Banga Ganatantrik Mohila Samiti established itself as the largest women's organization in the state. Front-affiliated women's organizations played crucial roles in government's redistributive reform programmes and women's participation. With their efforts, the first Women's Commission was established in 1992 in the state with Bela Dutta Gupta as its first chairperson. However, over the years, their programmatic focus shifted to enhancing the Front government's support base, and in the process, they assumed a more catalytic role in the Front's electoral politics instead of radicalizing the scope of the women's liberation movement.

Women's electoral mobilization by these organizations played a significant role in substantially increasing their participation in electoral processes, thereby enhancing their visibility in suffrage politics. However, this was not proportionately translated into enlarging the base of their political representation at all levels of decision-making – not only to select but also to be selected. The dismal figures of women in the highest bodies of power, especially in the assembly and state cabinet till today, shows a wide gender gap in the crucial space of decision-making despite a rich legacy of women's political activism in the state.

Women's under-representation in decision-making

Women's under-representation in institutional spaces of political decision-making reflects the challenges before the women's movement in creating empowered women. A recent study on electoral participation in West Bengal revealed that women constitute only 10 per cent of the total contestants in parliamentary or state assembly elections (ADR and West Bengal Election Watch, 2021). The highest percentage of women MLAs elected to the state assembly since independence till 2015 was 13.60 per cent with 40 women elected in the 294-seat House in the 2006 elections. On average, since the 1970s, the share of women members in the West Bengal assembly has been 7 to 8 per cent of the total MLAs elected. Their share started increasing from 2001 with more women members contesting and winning elections. The total number of women candidates was 199 in the 2016 elections reflecting a 10 per cent share of the total candidates.

The number of women voters is also increasing gradually with a favourable gender ratio. In the last assembly elections (2021), women voters constituted 49.01 per cent of the total voters enrolled.

The number of elected women assembly members is slowly increasing in the state. The previous assembly, elected in 2016, had 40 women MLAs. A brief look at the candidates' profiles from some of the major political parties in the assembly elections in 2016 (Table 15.1) shows the broad nature of a gender bias in the selection and performance of women candidates in the state.

Table 15.1 Performance of women candidates in the 2016 assembly elections

Name of the political party	Total contested 2016	Total candidates/ seats elected 2016	No. of female candidates contested 2016	No. of female candidates elected 2016
AITC	293	211	43	29
CPM	148	26	20	6
INC	92	44	6	4
BJP	291	3	30	0
CPI	11	1	0	0
AIFB	25	2	2	0
RSP	19	3	1	0
SUCI	182	0	18	0
GJM (incl. all factions)	3	3	1	1

Source: Election Commission of India, West Bengal General Legislative Election (2016). Available at: https://eci.gov.in/files/file/3469-west-bangal-general-legislative-election-2016/, accessed April 2, 2019.

WOMEN IN STATE POLITICS IN WEST BENGAL

Data shows a discouraging trend in a very low share of votes polled in favour of women with 118 candidates' deposits being forfeited (Election Commission of India, 2016).

The current assembly, elected in May 2021, also has 40 women MLAs reflecting 14 per cent of the total elected MLAs. It is a polarized picture with 33 women MLAs representing the All India Trinamool Congress (TMC) and 7 the BJP. The TMC nominated 49 women candidates (16.83 per cent of its total candidates) out of which 33 women won. The BJP gave tickets to 32 women candidates (a share of 10.92 per cent of its total tickets) of which seven got elected. The Left Front and the INC nominated 19 and seven women candidates respectively, none of whom could win. A major constituent of the Left Front, the CPI(M) nominated about 11.67 per cent women candidates, increasing their share from 10.81 per cent in the previous elections (2016).

A number of young and leading female members of the student and youth fronts of the left parties contested in these elections with a new genre of political campaigning attracting wide public attention. The ruling TMC nominated the highest number of women candidates in these elections. One interesting feature of the assembly elections is the increasing number of women candidates contesting as independents. Besides the three major contesting political alliances, about 70 women candidates were nominated by the smaller parties and 40 women contested as independents. However, these parties in general and their women candidates in particular could hardly show any performance in the state electoral politics and mostly forfeited their deposits.

A dominant trend over the years also reflects that a large number of women candidates are nominated by their parties because of patronage/lineage of male members of their families or party leaders. They are often given tickets to seats previously held by their male family members. A number of elected women candidates in the previous assembly were part of the high-strung politics of defection in the state before the assembly elections in 2021 with even the ruling TMC and the BJP following their immediate male mentors in the party.

This trend of paternal politics is more evident in seats reserved for women. Firoza Bibi, a 'martyr's mother', whose son was killed in police firing in Nandigram in 2007 in the anti-land acquisition movement got elected by a huge margin from Nandigram constituency in 2011. In the next assembly elections in 2016, she was shifted to a distant seat in Panskura to accommodate young leader, Subhendu Adhikary, the then MP, in the 'safer' seat of Nandigram as the TMC supremo wished to induct him in her cabinet.

Swati Khandoker was elected from a constituency in Hooghly previously contested by her late husband. Deepa Dasmunshi, wife of well-known Congress leader late Priyaranjan Dasmunshi, also contested from Raigunj constituency after her husband failed to contest due to illness.

These examples show the fragility of women's candidature as independent leaders. Such instances are comparatively rare in regimented parties like the left parties and BJP which have structured organizations.

The problem of under-representation of female members in the state assembly in terms of numerical strength is often conjoined with the lack of social diversity among women members. In the last two assembly elections (2016 and 2021), out of the 40 female members elected, 14 and 11 were elected from constituencies reserved for the Scheduled Castes respectively and two each in both the elections from constituencies reserved for Scheduled Tribes. Women from religious minority communities were elected in eight and six constituencies respectively. Though the share of women from SC, ST, and religious minority communities in electoral politics in the state is increasing, it is still dominated by the presence of upper- and middle-caste Hindu women, limiting the agency of socially marginalized women in decision-making processes.

Women in Panchayati Raj institutions

The Left Front regime initiated reservations for women for one-third of the panchayat seats. Since 1993, the share of women members in panchayats has crossed the 33 per cent reservation figure, implying women's greater engagement in grassroots-level governance. The proportion of women elected to PRIs increased to 36 per cent after the 1993 elections (Chattopadhyay and Dufflo, 2003). Reservations for women for office bearers' posts at the panchayat level were ensured in 1998 to help increase their share in decision-making spaces. All-women panchayats were also formed in West Bengal following this reform.

Many researchers have found that women members took significant initiatives in implementing basic developmental issues like literacy programmes, sanitation, and drinking water to change the social profile of PRIs in favour of the marginalized population. However, women's entry at the grassroots panchayat level was not translated proportionately in promoting women's leadership in higher political-administrative bodies in the state like zila parishads or the state administration.

Women's representation in Parliament and the ministries

Women's under-representation is more evident in the elections of female members to Parliamentary seats from the state. In the first general elections in 1952, only two women members were elected to the Lok Sabha out of 39 members from the state. This number increased to three in the fourth general election. Since 1952, the highest number of women MPs elected to the Lok Sabha from the state is 15 in 2014 (35.71 per cent of the total Lok Sabha representation from the state). In the last general elections in May

2019, 11 women were elected out of 42 MPs from the state. The ruling TMC fielded 17 women candidates providing a significant 41.6 per cent share to women this time. In the current Rajya Sabha, two women members have been elected from the state out of 16 members. The figures in the Lok Sabha show a more significant picture of women's political participation as they are elected through direct contests reflecting the level of women's capabilities as political leaders in their parties and in the public sphere.

Gender-based discrimination is reflected in political parties' reluctance to induct women members in the highest decision-making bodies like the cabinet or high-level committees of the parties. The previous TMC cabinet formed in 2016 had only six female members including Chief Minister Mamata Banerjee in a House of 41 (11.76 per cent of the cabinet berths). This was only 8.8 per cent in the previous cabinet in a government run by a woman Chief Minister for the first time in Bengal's history.

The present cabinet formed in 2021 has nine female members and 16 male members. The cabinet is headed by Chief Minister Mamata Banerjee who holds six departments. Only one woman member, Shashi Panja has been made minister-in-charge of women and child development and social welfare. Three others act as independent ministers and four as ministers of state. Unfortunately, the Front regime in the state was also marked by a feeble presence of women members in the state cabinet. The highest share of female members holding ministerial positions in the Front government was in 2001 with five women inducted into a cabinet of 48 members. Women members' nominal presence in the cabinet was often supplemented by narrow sex-linked roles assigned to them in terms of ministerial responsibilities, substantiating gender stereotyping in their political roles.

Since 2011, Chief Minister Mamata Banerjee has been in charge of most ministries in successive cabinets as the indisputable leader of her party. TMC runs on Mamata Banerjee's personality as the supreme power in the organizational structure of the party and government. It often creates a powerful replication of a paternalistic political culture in the ruling regime based on individualization of leadership. Other female members in her cabinet are ministers of state with the exception of only two ministers with independent charge. Interestingly, her women colleagues in the cabinet are given 'soft' ministries like fisheries, backward classes' welfare, health and family welfare, women and child development, and social welfare while crucial portfolios like industry, finance, and education are given to male members. Even in the Front governments women were not preferred with independent charge of ministries and their roles were limited to portfolios like relief, social welfare, backward classes' welfare, and forests.

The situation is replicated in the executive powers of the local bodies like corporations and municipalities. There are seven municipal corporations in the state in which very few women are serving as members of the highest body of power, the Mayor-in-council. The Bidhannagore Municipal

Corporation is headed by Krishna Chakraborty, the only woman mayor in the state. Two women leaders served as deputy mayors in the last body of the Mayor-in-council in Asansol and Durgapur Municipal Corporations. In the last board elected, the Kolkata Municipal Corporation had only one woman member; 58 women have been elected as councillors (a 40 per cent share). The last elected Siliguri corporation did not have a single woman member in the Mayor-in-council. The present Kolkata Municipal Corporation is run by a board of administrators in which only one female member has been inducted into a board of 14. Only three women councillors have served as borough chairpersons in 16 borough committees.

This proves that the fulcrum of power still revolves around males in institutional spaces of governance and the fight for gender-just governance is yet to materialize in higher seats of power. These examples vindicate the argument of a section of scholars that women's mere visibility in democratic public institutions and electoral politics does not necessarily bring their agency as political leaders. The socio-political culture of exclusion and sex stereotyping in public roles create an unfavourable environment for women legislators in many cases.

Women in party organizations

Marginalization of women in political decision-making is more evident in party structures with only a handful of women becoming members of the highest bodies in most of the mainstream party organizations in the state. The ruling TMC banks on the popularity of its leader Mamata Banerjee who played a significant role as opposition leader in the state before coming to power in 2011. Banerjee rose to power as a youth leader and parliamentarian in the Indian National Congress but then broke away from the party to form TMC in 1998 protesting against the functioning of the then provincial leadership of the Congress Party. Under her firebrand leadership TMC emerged as the main opposition party against the entrenched rule of the Front government, displacing the traditional electoral and political base of the Congress Party to a great extent. She became the first woman Chief Minister of the state defeating the 34-year-long Left Front rule by leading a massive political-cultural coalition against the Front government.

Ranabir Samaddar termed her 'the unsettling politician of West Bengal' (Samaddar, 2013, p. xvii) whose political career exemplifies challenges for women without a known familial or wealthy background in sustaining themselves in leadership positions.

Over the years, Banerjee has evolved with a very personalized (fondly referred to as 'didi' – the elder sister), often spontaneous style of functioning, imbued with an anti-elite, colloquial language and idioms of politics as against political-ideological scaffolding of the Left or BJP in the state and the historical legacy of the Congress Party. Her political style as a 'street-fighter' (as she calls herself) and strategy as the 'voice of dissent' reached a zenith in the latest assembly elections in 2021 in a high-pitched electoral battle against the newly emerging political opposition, the BJP, in the state. She could win one of her biggest political victories in 2021 fighting against a consolidated national force like the BJP with her unique appeal to ethno-cultural emotions as *banglar meye* (daughter of Bengal) or *didi ke bolo* (Talk to Didi) programmes as against *bohiragoto* (the outsiders). Mamata Banerjee lost the prestigious battle in Nandigram to one of her previously close aides and presently BJP member, Subhendu Adhikary, despite a huge victory in the state. She could draw support from a wider section of the people notwithstanding strong anti-incumbency, joblessness, and corruption in a highly polarized electoral battle.

A poll analysis covering years reflects Banerjee's personal popularity and support base among women, particularly the marginalized sections. She makes consistent appeals to women power in her fiery speeches and promises women's empowerment through different programmes with women as beneficiaries. However, over her two terms in power, she has been subjected to strong criticism from different quarters for gradually moving towards an 'authoritarian' masculine model of governance and political style with strong centralization of power.

It is interesting to note that since its inception, TMC has inducted only three female members including the Chief Minister and founder of the party Mamata Banerjee in its highest body –the national working council, consisting of 22 members. Left parties like the CPI(M) have only one woman member in their highest bodies, the state secretariat. At present, only one woman represents the national council of the CPI from the state. As mentioned earlier, Geeta Mukherjee served as the first woman member in the CPI secretariat. In the last West Bengal Pradesh Congress Committee, Deepa Das Munshi was the sole female member as working president along with her three male colleagues. Women's leadership in decision-making spaces is more evident in the mass front organizations of political parties than in their formal parental bodies. Patriarchal norms pervade party functioning beyond ideology and substantiate a political culture of exclusion and narrow sexism.

Celebrity politics

An interesting addendum can be provided in an example of star campaigners enrolled with the Election Commission by the parties during the state assembly elections. The Indian National Congress and CPI(M) enrolled seven female leaders each out of a total of 40 leaders in the 2016 elections. For both the parties, most of these campaigners were known party workers. The ruling TMC enrolled 31 leaders of which nine were women including Mamata Banerjee. Six of these female star campaigners were popular actresses of the Bengali film industry with no prior political organizational experience. The BJP enrolled 40 star campaigners of whom eight were women. Six of them represented the central leadership of the party and two from the state are well-known Bengali actresses who were inducted into the organizational leadership later. In the last assembly elections (2021), both the TMC and BJP nominated a number of celebrity women members representing the Bengali film and television industry and music world, some of whom joined the parties only before the elections.

This shows an increasing trend of celebrity politics in Bengal with the parties capitalizing on an appeal to glamour in electoral mobilization and a considerable reliance on male political leaders in drawing popular support in terms of political mobilization. It is interesting to note that none of the female celebrity members could gain a berth in the cabinet.

However, the gendering of 'selection' for public roles often gets supplemented by strong reservations about the 'eligibility' of the women candidates reflected in subtle threats, abusive comments in public forums, and coverage of women leaders in sexist terms in the media. In the last parliamentary elections in 2019, two of the women candidates from TMC, known faces of the Bengali film industry, faced sexist trolling in social media that targeted their outfits, social behaviour, and personal lives. The Left women candidates, leading faces of the national students' movements, or women celebrity figures of the BJP experienced the same kind of trolling and sarcasm in the recent assembly elections. Mainstream media substantiates this gendering of roles by its subtlety in representing women candidates with individualized narratives, personal profiling based on their private lives thus segregating them from their organizational profiles.

The last assembly elections (2021) witnessed an allegation of competitive sexist barbs in political campaigns by political leaders, often targeted at Mamata Banerjee and other female contestants. Women's rights activists strongly objected to this kind of stereotyping and sexist politics.

Women's organizations

Women's claim to power and socioeconomic entitlements are emerging as key issues in the political battle and increasingly being integrated with the tension zones of regional and federal politics. Following the growth of autonomous women's organizations throughout India since the 1980s, a number of women's organizations and women's rights-based NGOs have been formed in West Bengal as well. These organizations have played an instrumental role in mobilizing campaigns for gender equality, especially with respect to violence against women perpetrated in private and public spheres along with rights-based activities. Women's non-partisan networks have extended the basis of furthering women's political role in the state through these organizations. For instance, the Nari Nirjatan Pratirodh

Manch joined the *Bandimuktiandolon* (movement for release of political prisoners), especially against the torture of Left-wing leader Archana Guha in prison during the 1970s.

Women's organizations put up collective protests in rape cases in Bantala, Kamdunior, and Park Street, which were met with widespread outrage during the Front government and the TMC regime respectively. In the mid-1990s this networking was further extended by the formation of Maitrias, a broad platform of women's organizations to fight for gender justice. In recent years, state politics has witnessed the participation and leadership of a large section of women from across religious, class, and educational backgrounds in the anti-CAA movement. The movement started in Park Circus in Kolkata and gradually spread to some other parts of the state demanding right to citizenship.

Women's vulnerability in the politics of citizenship provided an important dimension to the movement empowering them to leadership roles. These movements supplemented women's political roles by increasing the visibility of their participation and leadership in social issues.

In the contemporary period, women's issues are taking centre stage in state politics with increasing cases of violence against women in the state and new hype zones of federal politics. The launching of state-funded projects like Swablamban, Kanyashree, and Rupashree for girls and women and the rhetorical war around these projects validate this point. One important dimension of this battle is that the essence of empowering and transformative politics is often getting swayed by the exigencies of political power play provoked by the potential of a rhetorical war. To combat the crucial problems of girls' dropout rates and trafficking in the state, the West Bengal government has launched the Kanyashreeprokolpo to incentivize girls' education through a direct cash transfer scheme. It has initiated programmes like Muktir Aloy and Swabalamban to rehabilitate victims or rescued girls with skill-based training with NGO support networks and advocacy groups.

Kolkata Police has been supporting the Swayamsiddha programme and engaging rescued girls in awareness generation against trafficking. Independent women's organizations and advocacy groups also supplement these efforts. These programmes emerge as important issues in the electoral politics and claims and counterclaims of federal politics.

Besides, in the spree of populist welfare politics, programmes like Rupashree (for supporting poor girls above 18 years of age with one-time funding for marriage) that sustain sexist norms and vindicate the stereotyping of girls' roles in society, with inherent symbolism of beauty and marriage, often get promoted by the government and the party leadership. Recently, the government launched a project for women cab drivers (pink taxi) with the help of NGO Azad Foundation. These projects uphold de-stereotyping of women's roles in public services, especially in male-dominated spaces, thereby challenging discriminatory social norms. However, on occasions such projects fail to challenge the subtlety of stereotyping by conceding to the promotion of 'feminine' skills in government welfare programmes or commercializing traits of womanhood.

'Sexist' bias is occasionally reflected in the responses of the ruling regime to atrocities against women and the socio-political movements against them. In a way, these examples demonstrate the puzzled nature of engendering governance with nuances of reformative politics and electoral gains.

Agnihotri and Mazumdar (1995) argue that the women's movement makes the 'reassertion of citizen's claim to participate as equals in the political and development process'. However, women's role in the political arena as equals is deeply thwarted by endemic violence in private spaces and state politics, especially electoral violence. West Bengal is one of the frontrunners in the index of violence against women. Incidents of widespread political violence in the last few years, particularly during the election period, have impacted the daily livelihood of women in rural and semi-urban areas in the state. Women have been victims of rapes, threats of rape and intimidation, and displacement from their homes and livelihoods due to political violence and confrontational politics. While, on the one hand, this has prompted women's active agency in resisting violence in their neighbourhood spaces in the absence or near-absence of male members, on the other hand, this endemic violence creates a sense of political disengagement for ordinary women.

It can be noted here that independent women's associations in the state, barring a few exceptions, have not been very vocal about this political/electoral violence against women, which has been taken up mostly by the parties and their mass fronts.

Conclusion

Historically, there has been a disjunction in networking by independent women's organizations with party-sympathetic women's groups in mobilizing women's participation in public spaces in the state. Independent women's organizations have been more interested in social transformative politics, socioeconomic violence being one of the core agendas of that politics. On the other hand, party-based women's organizations are appropriated for electoral battles for power with agendas of competitive and mass front politics. The absence of an integrated space for a women's movement may lead to the danger of diluting the struggle for connecting the demand for political entitlements to the creation of a violence-free environment in the state. In the recently held assembly elections, both the party-based women's organizations and independent women's movements, on occasion, came close to strongly criticize sexist political comments by well-known political leaders.

In this situation, engendering governance faces the challenges of overcoming the disconnection between socio-cultural politics and electoral politics.

Women's representation in contemporary state politics in West Bengal has to be understood in the context of the emerging scope, nuances, and interface of both federal/regional politics and emancipatory politics.

Bibliography

ADR and West Bengal Election Watch (2021). Available at: https://adrindia.org/research-and-reports/state-assemblies/west-bengal, accessed on May 5, 2021.

Agnihotri, Indu and Vina Mazumdar (1995).'Changing Terms of Political Discourse: Women's Movements in India, 1970s-1990s', *Economic and Political Weekly*, 30 (29), 1869–1878.

Census of India (2011). Available at: https://www.census2011.co.in/census/state/west+bengal.html, accessed on February 1, 2019.

Chatterjee, Partha (2006).'The Nationalist Resolution of the Women's Question', in K. Sangari and S. Vaid (eds), *Recasting Women: Essays in Colonial History*. New Delhi: Zubaan.

Chattopadhyay, R. and E. Duflo (2003). 'The Impact of Reservation in the Panchayati Raj: Evidence from a Nationwide Randomized Experiment.' Available at: https://economics.mit.edu/files/769, accessed on June 10, 2019.

Election Commission of India (2016). *West Bengal General Legislative Election, 2016.* Available at: https://eci.gov.in/files/file/3469-west-bangal-general-legislative-election-2016/, accessed on April 2, 2019.

Members: Lok Sabha. Available at: loksabhaph.nic.in/Members/women.aspx, accessed on April 10, 2020.

Members: Rajya Sabha. Available at: rajyasabha.nic.in/rsnew/members_site/women.aspx, accessed on April 27, 2020.

National Crime Records Bureau (2018a). *Crime in India: Statistics*, Vol. I, Government of India, p. 195. Available at: https://ncrb.gov.in/sites/default/files/Crime%20in%20India%202017%20-%20Volume%201.pdf, accessed on April 9, 2020.

National Crime Records Bureau (2018b). *Crime in India: Statistics*, Vol. III, Government of India, pp. 973–974. Available at: https://ncrb.gov.in/sites/default/files/Crime%20in%20India%202017%20-%20Volume%203.pdf, accessed on April 9, 2020.

National Family Health Survey –3 (2005–06). State Fact Sheet, West Bengal. Available at: http://rchiips.org/nfhs/pdf/NFHS4/WB_FactSheet.pdf, accessed on February 3, 2019.

National Family Health Survey –4, (2015–16). State Fact Sheet, West Bengal. Available at: http://rchiips.org/nfhs/pdf/NFHS4/WB_FactSheet.pdf, accessed on February 3, 2019.

National Family Health Survey –5, (2019–20). State Fact Sheet, West Bengal. Available at: http://rchiips.org/nfhs/pdf/NFHS4/WB_FactSheet.pdf, accessed on May 6, 2021.

Samaddar, Ranabir (2013). *Passive Revolution in West Bengal: 1977–2011*. New Delhi: Sage Publications India Pvt. Ltd.

SDG India Index (2019). *Baseline Report 2019–20*. Available at: https://www.niti.gov.in/writereaddata/files, accessed on May 6, 2021.

SDG 5: Gender Equality (n.d.). *Sustainable Development Goals*. United Nations in India. Available at: https://in.one.un.org/page/sustainable-development-goals/sdg-5/, accessed on April 10, 2020.

Sen, Samita (2012). 'A Parliament of Women: Dystopia in Nineteenth-century Bengali Imagination', in B. Bagchi (ed.), *The Politics of the (Im)Possible: Utopia and Dystopia Reconsidered*. New Delhi: Sage Publications India Pvt. Ltd.

Tillin, L., R. Deshpande, and K. K. Kailash (2015). *Politics of Welfare: Comparisons across Indian States*. New Delhi: Oxford University Press.

16

ENGENDERING BIHAR POLITICS
Myth or Reality?

Shefali Roy

Introduction

India as a union of states leaves little space for state sovereignty, so for years the states did not have the tradition of autonomy and remained neglected and least studied. However, the democratic processes have strengthened the assertion of state identity politics amidst the dominance of national politics. This has led to states becoming prime actors where politics, economy, and culture blend harmoniously.

There has been a growing realization that it is at the state level that the 'future analyses of Indian politics must concentrate' (Chibber and Nooruddin, 1999, p. 53). New states have emerged as dominant players in games of power structures thus breaking the hinges of the central government. Voting behaviour after India's independence was primarily influenced by national interests, but gradually we have entered an era of conflicting regional interests which are specific to local issues in different states. Regional parties were formed to counteract the dominance of the one-party system. Issues of caste, community, gender, and deprivation became the foundation of regional political parties.

In Bihar, the Rashtriya Janata Dal (RJD), the Janata Dal United (JDU), the Lok Janshakti Party (LJP), the Hindustani Awam Morcha (HAM), the Rashtriya Lok Samta Party (RLSP), the Jan Adhikar Party (JAP), and Vikassheel Insaan Party (VIP) have pushed the Bhartiya Janata Party (BJP) to the backstage so much so that the BJP was forced to align with state parties to contest the last state assembly elections. This was also quite evident in the 2014 and 2019 Lok Sabha elections.

The evolution of Panchayati Raj Institutions (PRIs) has further mobilized local politics. Political space has also been created for grassroots activities.

Over the years, participation has gone up both in terms of electoral turnouts and in election-related political activities. The degree of this varies from state to state. Bihar records lower political participation as compared to the other states, but this does not mean that voters in the state are apathetic to

DOI: 10.4324/9781003374862-17

289

their political engagements. The expansion of democracy in Bihar takes the form of protests, insurgencies, and political movements.

At another level, Bihar is a part of the BIMARU states and lags much behind the mainstream states in all parameters. Being an agrarian state with a semi-feudal outlook, Bihar has failed to form an egalitarian society. The state has also seen a sea change in the behaviour of political leaders with criminal moorings, and a visible change in people's voting behaviour, where caste-community considerations are more pronounced.

In the 1990s, power in the state shifted from dominant castes to intermediaries with the amelioration of Dalits through Sanskritization. However, the Dalits still remain a hapless lot. The Muslim-Yadav ('MY') chemistry is relevant in Bihar despite the development agenda projected by various political parties. Social engineering is the cardinal principle in Bihar politics rather than a developmental agenda.

Glancing at the state's history, till 1912 Bihar was a part of the Bengal Presidency under the British rule along with Odisha but later both of them were separated. By the Government of India Act of 1935, Bihar became an independent province on March 22, 1936. It became a part of the Republic of India with independence in 1947. In 1950 Bihar got statehood and in 1956 with the reorganization of states, Purulia was separated from Bihar. A setback came on November 15, 2000, when South Bihar became a new state called 'Jharkhand' truncating Bihar; all industries, resources, and modes of production were owned by Jharkhand. The people of Bihar had to fight

Table 16.1 Bihar's demographic status

Total area	*94,163.00 sq. km*
Divisions	9
Districts	38
Number of Police Districts	44
Number of Subdivisions	101
Number of Towns	Total: 199
	Statutory Towns: 139
	Non-statutory Towns: 60
Number of Police Stations	853
Blocks	534
Panchayats	8,406
Number of Revenue Villages	45,103
Total Population	10,40,99,452
Male Population	54278157
Female Population	49821295
Literacy	61.80%
Male Literacy	71.20%
Female Literacy	51.50%

Source: Census (2011). Available at: https://state.bihar.gov.in/main/Content.html?links&page =Bihar%20State%20Profile. accessed on June 21, 2022.

for survival as floods and droughts were regular features along with poverty, illiteracy, and unemployment. However, Bihar survived, despite odds (Figure 16.1).

Women invisible in public spaces

Bihar has seen and survived many upheavals and political instability. Once regarded as the best governed state (Appleby, 1953), it came to be known as a 'Jungle Raj' state as observed by the Patna High Court (*Business Standard*, 2013). The state lost its credibility because of the prevailing political anarchy. The state with the potential of creating a revolution witnessed a steady downfall of democratic ethos. The people of Bihar were disgruntled and the women suffered a lot. Even at present, Bihar is at a critical juncture. According to a NITI Aayog report, in terms of development Bihar is at the last rung (Bhuyan, 2019).

Bihar is grappling with emerging crises, but the condition of women demands immediate attention. Gender disparities are socially conditioned and socially engineered. According to Thelma (1981, p. 16), 'Sexual inequality in social, economic and political life is worldwide.' Over the last few decades, a lot has been said about women's status and their problems, but even today women remain socially weak, economically dependent, and politically powerless. This situation is worse in Bihar where women face discrimination and violence is inflicted on them by different quarters. Women remain victims of social orthodoxies and self-inhibitions.

Women have been recipients of change, but the welfare society we are living in does not aspire to make them an instrument of change. Can we ever imagine an egalitarian society where women are at par with men? That is still a distant dream, and this period of their taking off is very long and cumbersome (Roy, 2011).

Soon after independence, women in Bihar played a reasonable role in party politics, but it did not continue for long. Those who actively participated were mainly from political families. Krishna Devi was elected to the Vidhan Sabha in 1952, Shakuntala Devi and Shanti Devi were nominated to the state assembly. Ram Dulari Sinha became a Member of Parliament, a union minister, and later the Governor of Kerala. Tarkeshwari Sinha, an activist and a freedom fighter, entered the first Lok Sabha at the age of 26 years. Four times MP, she became the first deputy finance minister in Nehru's cabinet. Krishna Shahi, Uma Pandey, and Prabhawati Gupta were actively involved in state politics. However, they all belonged to renowned political families. Meira Kumar, a parliamentarian from Bihar became the first woman Speaker of the Lok Sabha in 2009; she too is carrying the legacy of her father Babu Jagjivan Ram.

At the time of its formation, Bihar's women were reeling under practices such as purdah, early marriages, widowhood, and illiteracy. Even today women from Scheduled Castes, Scheduled Tribes, and Other Backward Castes suffer atrocities. For these women, access to political decision-making is limited. Though the state government is trying to increase women's political participation in the state, the impact is not visible because of criminalization of politics, violence, and caste rivalries. These social ills have been accelerated by political high handedness (Verma, 1986). Hence, women are invisible on the political scene nationally and at the state level. In Bihar, in particular, their problems are inherent and deep rooted.

Lack of women's political participation

Political participation means citizens acting with the intention of knowing who governs them and how. Women have family responsibilities that prevent their full participation in politics. On the other hand, Mill (1989) claims that if men are allowed to exercise their suffrage, then there is no justification for not allowing women to do so as well. Huntington and Nelson (1976) regard political participation as an activity by private citizens designed to influence governmental decision-making. But a question arises here: Does involvement or activity include mere behavioural patterns or also understanding the political system in taking decisions? In pre-independence India, political participation was aligned with the national movement which uniformly involved women from different castes, classes, and communities, but after independence women wanted freedom from male domination, which many nationalists were not willing to concede to. Women's activities were checked and controlled because they appeared to be a threat to men's privileges (Chaturvedi, 1985). In India, feminism and nationalism went hand in hand (Asthana, 1974).

In the post-independence period, a new trajectory of political participation emerged emphasizing power sharing. An analysis of the Indian electoral process makes it evident that women's political participation is very less. Even if they participate, it is involuntary. It is mainly influenced by the male members in their families. Women show less interest in politics, so it has become a masculine affair. In Bihar, family influence on women is huge, and it is one of the important agencies that shapes and transforms women voters' actions in a significant way (Shukla, 1988). Voting is an extended family process, but of late women are becoming viable voters as the 2015 assembly elections in the state showed when women voters outnumbered men which led to JDU's win on a development agenda.

However, it would also not be incorrect to say women were swayed by emotions which remained quite transitory. Women's political participation is at a basic stage and is not reflected in their electoral behaviour. At times, women are forced to step into the political arena despite their unwillingness or lack of general interest in politics. For example, Rabri Devi became the first woman Chief Minister of Bihar in 1997 after her husband Lalu Yadav was convicted in the fodder scam (Dasgupta, 1997). This was an awkward development in the political history of Bihar.

We know that political participation is also an outcome of education and social status. Since women are less educated and have a poor social status as compared to men, they are kept out of power.

Women in PRIs

Women were forced to contest elections for PRIs by their family members on reserved seats which earlier belonged to men. This promoted proxy rule and concepts of *mukhiya patis* (MPs) and sarpanch *patis* (SPs) ridiculing women in the political arena. Women became representatives but lacked political experience and training and remained *goongi gudias*.

However, over the years, women have learnt the art of governance and have become vocal in expressing their demands. Since democracy can flourish only when there is citizens' political participation, women's active political participation is highly desirable. Reservations for women have added to their empowerment at the panchayat level, but they have failed to cross 15 per cent representation in state and national bodies in the absence of any reservations at these levels.

Poor voluntary participation

There is no doubt that women voters' turnout has increased, but their voluntary participation in the electoral process is still poor. Figure 16.1 shows the trends in women's voting behaviour since 1967. It shows women's apathy

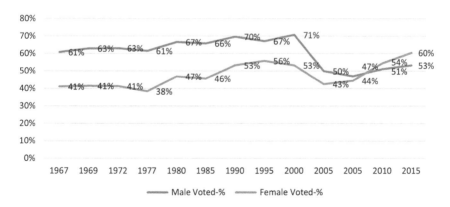

Figure 16.1 Male versus female voting behaviour in assembly elections (percentage).
Source: https://eci.gov.in/assembly-election/assembly-election/, accessed on June 21, 2022.

towards politics as the percentage of women voting as compared to men is considerably low. However, after 2005 the number of women voting in the state has increased.

As can be seen in Figure 16.1, the percentage of women voters in the assembly elections is low, and the number of women contestants too is abysmally low as compared to male contestants. Women are not accepted as winning candidates by the political parties. Several explanations are offered for women's low participation in politics. One explanation is that men keenly and deliberately try to keep women away from politics to protect their privileged positions and domination. Some change has taken place, but it is more symbolic than substantive. The harsh reality is that women are far from achieving gender parity in public life. Figure 16.2 shows the percentage of female contestants in assembly elections.

The number of elected women in the assembly has been low as seen in Table 16.2. The number of elected women varies from 1 to 15 over the years, which is insignificant in proportion to women's population in the state.

There are five women members in the Bihar legislative council out of 75 members. Surprisingly there is no woman from the BJP, though it has good strength in the council. Three women are from JDU, one from RJD (Rabri Devi), and one from LJP, Nutan Singh (who has now joined the BJP).

Since 2002 Bihar has been sending 16 members to the Rajya Sabha. This number was earlier 22, but after the creation of Jharkhand in 2000 the number was reduced to 16. Table 16.3 shows that women's representation in the Rajya Sabha from Bihar is marginal. Initially, the ratio was good as

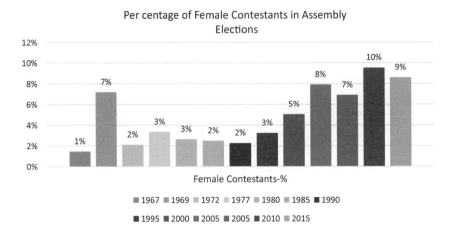

Figure 16.2 Percentage of female contestants in assembly elections. Source: Election Commission https://eci.gov.in/assembly-election/assembly-election/, accessed on March 12, 2021.

ENGENDERING BIHAR POLITICS

Table 16.2 Elected women representatives in the Bihar assembly

Year	Number of seats	Number of female elected representatives	%
1952–57	318	13	4
1957–62	318	34	11
1962–67	318	25	8
1967–69	318	10	3
1969–72	318	4	1
1972–77	324	13	4
1977–80	324	13	4
1980–85	324	14	4
1985–90	324	15	5
1990–95	324	13	4
1995–2000	324	12	4
2000–05	243	14	7
2005–05	243	23	9
2005–10	243	25	10
2010–15	243	37	15
2015–20	243	29	12

Source: https://vidhansabha.bih.nic.in/former_women_mla.html, accessed on June 30, 2020 and June 21, 2022.

Table 16.3 Women members in the Rajya Sabha from Bihar since 1952

Sl. no	Name	Term	Year
1	Tiga Angelina	1	1952–54
2	Lakshmi N Menon	3	1952–54, 1954–60, & 1960–66
3	Vijaya Raje Kunwarani	1	1952–57
4	Pratibha Singh	4	1970–76, 1976–82, 1982–88, & 1988–1992
5	Aziza Imam	2	1973–76 &1976–82
6	Manorama Pandey	2	1980–86 & 1986–92
7	Jahanara Jaipal Singh	3	1958–64, 1964–70, & 1970–1976
8	Kamla Sinha	2	1990–94 & 1994–2000
9	Saroj Dubey	1	1998–2004
10	Kumkum Rai	1	2000–06
11	Kahakashan Perween	1	2014–2000
12	Misa Bharti	1	2016–2022

Source: https://rajyasabha.nic.in/Members/AlphabeticalFormerMember, accessed on June 21, 2022.

three women came to the Rajya Sabha during 1952–57. But their numbers reduced gradually. Those who were nominated to the Rajya Sabha mostly belonged to elitist families. Lakshmi N. Menon was the wife of Professor V.K.N. Menon, first head of the Department of Political Science and founder of the Institute of Public Administration, and former vice chancellor of

Patna University. Pratibha Singh, Kamala Sinha, Manorama Pandey, and Aziza Imam all came from affluent families in Bihar. This was not a truly democratic representation. At present, there is only one woman in the Rajya Sabha from Bihar. Misa Bharti needs no introduction as she is Lalu Prasad Yadav's daughter.

Women voters

Table 16.4 shows that more women are voting, and there was a remarkable increase in their numbers in the 2014 Lok Sabha elections when the state's women voted for Narendra Modi; this trend continued with more fervour in the 2019 general elections taking the women's voting percentage to an all-time high at 60 per cent. The paradigm shift to Hindutva and nationalism attracted women voters.

Table 16.5 shows women elected to the Lok Sabha from Bihar. In 1962 a large number of women won the Lok Sabha elections from Bihar after which there was a steep fall in 1967 and in 1977 when there was an anti-Indira Gandhi wave all over Bihar and no woman won the elections though this period saw enough women's involvement in the JP movement. However, in 1984 with Indira Gandhi's assassination, 56 per cent of the women who contested the Lok Sabha elections won. It can, therefore, be deduced that women's victory in elections depends on the existing situation and is not based on their merit or political efficacy. Political parties give very few tickets to women because their chances of winning are bleak.

Table 16.4 Number of women voters in the Lok Sabha elections in Bihar

Year	Female electors	Female voted	%
1962	10311504	3388688	33
1967	13154137	5358422	41
1971	14748369	5423203	37
1977	16606983	8430387	51
1980	18699066	8211228	44
1984	20583040	10124680	49
1989	24299104	12210700	50
1991	23509637	11623760	49
1996	27425781	13822823	50
1998	27624272	14961661	54
1999	27627286	14732844	53
2004	23506264	12134913	52
2009	25284439	10775241	43
2014	29676576	17124395	58
2019	33532797	19980370	60

Source: https://loksabha.nic.in/officiallinks.aspx
https://eci.gov.in/statistical-report/statistical-reports, accessed on April 7, 2021.

Table 16.5 Women representatives in the Lok Sabha from Bihar

Year	Women contestants	Women winners	%
1951	7	2	29
1957	9	4	56
1962	8	6	88
1967	12	4	33
1971	16	1	6
1977	9	0	0
1980	19	5	26
1984	16	9	56
1989	17	2	12
1991	35	3	9
1996	41	3	7
1998	22	4	18
1999	20	5	25
2004	14	3	21
2009	46	4	9
2014	47	3	6
2019	56	3	5

Source: http://loksabhaph.nic.in/Members/womenar.aspx?lsno=1&tab=15, accessed on June 21, 2022.

Hence, reservation of seats for women at the assembly and Parliament level is the only viable solution for increasing their participation in political decision-making.

Reservations for women

Coming to reservation of seats for women in panchayats, which has shown a tremendous impact in the state, it can be seen that women have started making rigorous demands as political actors at this level of governance. The Bihar Panchayati Raj Act was passed in 1993 and extensively revised in 2006. There were no elections even after the passing of the Bihar Panchayati Raj Act in 1993. It was after a period of eight years that panchayat elections were held in 2001 which had 33 per cent of the seats reserved for women while single posts like that of a mukhiya or pramukh were not reserved for them. However, the 2006 amendments created ripples in local governance as the state government took a historic decision to give 50 per cent reservation to women in PRIs including chair seats. Bihar became the first state to take this initiative. It was hailed by the Centre and other states. The most significant gain of these reservations for women in panchayats is the emergence of women power in rural Bihar (Table 16.6).

Urban local bodies also have 50 per cent seats reserved for women. Urban local bodies are divided into three: 12 municipal corporations comprising

Table 16.6 Elected women representatives in PRIs

Sl. no.	Local rural bodies	Number of women representative
1	Gram Panchayat	51998
2	Block Panchayats	5341
3	District Panchayats	548
4	Total	57,887

Source: https://www.panchayat.gov.in/reservation-of-women-in-pris, https://state.bihar.gov.in/biharprd/CitizenHome.html http://nrcddp.org/file_upload/Status%20of%20Panchayati%20Raj,%20Bihar.pdf, accessed on June 30, 2020 and April 7, 2021.
Note: The total number of elected representatives in PRIs is 1,27,391. Women's share is 45.44 per cent.

593 wards, 49 municipal councils comprising 1,388 wards, and 82 municipal panchayats comprising 1,396 wards. Currently women representatives are heading 88 of the 139 municipal bodies (approximately 64 per cent). This affirms that reservation of seats for women infuses a spirit of confidence among them which eventually leads to their active political participation.

Empowerment of women, particularly in Bihar is very significant. Rural Bihar presents a classic case of subjugation of women at all levels, and women in urban areas too are discriminated against. They have remained victims of male dominance in every walk of life from religious to social, economic, and political.

Political dynasties

As elsewhere in the country, political dynasties exist in Bihar too. For example, RJD supremo Lalu Prasad did not miss any chance to promote the women in his family. His daughter Misa Bharti is a member of the Rajya Sabha and his wife is a member of the state legislative council. He also patronized Kanti Singh who became a Member of Parliament (1999–2009) twice. She was also the minister for women and child development at the Centre.

It is interesting to note that Kumari Manju Verma, minister for social welfare, Government of Bihar, had to quit because of her husband's involvement in a shelter home controversy in Muzaffarpur in 2018. Even then she was given a ticket by JDU to contest for the Bihar assembly elections in 2020. However, she lost.

Women's entry into politics is not easy, but their survival is even more difficult and the enhancement of their political careers demands being part of political circles. Bima Bharti (JDU), minister for sugarcane industries, was the only woman minister in the last Nitish Kumar government but with no significant role. In the current ministry, Renu Devi is the Deputy Chief Minister along with a male counterpart. The other two women ministers,

Sheela Kumari Mandal and Leshi Singh, have been given transport and food and consumer protection ministries, respectively.

The situation seems to be changing with women putting pressure on the state government for welfare schemes and trying to make their presence felt in decision-making. Bihar is testimony to the fact that *goongi gudias* have become vocal and assertive and have given a setback to proxy rule.

Protests and movements

Bihar was privileged to launch a democratic non-cooperation movement in 1917 from Champaran under Mahatma Gandhi. Women like Prabhawati Devi (daughter of Braj Kishore Prasad and wife of Jay Prakash Narayan), Rajbansi Devi (wife of Rajendra Prasad), and Bhagwati Devi initiated protests against the purdah system, untouchability, and illiteracy simultaneously which prompted women's entry in the freedom struggle. In 1930, the Civil Disobedience movement had a strong impact on women in Bihar. Lady Shami Imam took out processions and marches against the use of foreign goods. She delivered motivating speeches among college girls and gained their support. In Gaya, Chandrawati Devi was arrested for vocally condemning the *chowkidari* tax. The chairman of the Hazaribagh District Congress Committee, Saraswati Devi and Sadhana Devi, were the first two women in Bihar who got arrested for protesting. The Peasants' movement popularly known as the Kisan Andolan of 1934 was launched by Swami Shahjanand Saraswati against landlords (zamindars) and princely states who had possession of 90 per cent of the land while the rest of the population was landless labourers working as serfs and beggars.

Women actively participated in Shahjanand Saraswati's Kisan Andolan. By the end of 1938, this movement had spread to the whole of Bihar and had a large number of women participating. Swami Shahjanand gave all the credit to Brahmin women who fought the battle under the leadership of Jadunandan Sharma. On August 9, 1942, Bhagwati Devi, Ram Pyari Devi, Sundari Devi, Shakuntala Devi, Jambati Devi, Shanti Devi, Prema Devi, and many others were put behind bars for organizing meetings and delivering nationalist speeches. After independence, many women in Bihar continued participating in public and political life.

Lok Nayak Jay Prakash Narayan spearheaded 'Total Revolution' in 1975 against political corruption.

Women's involvement in this crusade was commendable. Leadership was provided by educated women who had long been engaged in political work through unions, political parties, social service agencies, and research institutes. Women worked on multiple fronts, not only at the state level but also at the local community level. They actively participated in the Bodh Gaya Land movement of 1974 for their land rights. In this decade-long movement women relentlessly fought against feudal attitudes and deprivation of their rights. Women organized *shivirs* (camps) to discuss their concerns, especially independent land rights for them (Agarwal, 2002). They were attacked by different segments of society. They organized protests against wife beating, alcoholism, child marriages, and also for social equality and right to land and other resources with the Chatra Yuva Sangharsh Vahini. They were successful in socially mobilizing downtrodden Dalit women. In 1982, it was decided that women would get ownership of land and the villagers succumbed to the pressure and approved this. This was a significant achievement for the women's leadership in the state.

One of the major protagonists of this movement claimed that women raised questions regarding land ownership and compelled their spouses to register land in their names. There were many success stories, but they have not been registered or reported or legitimized. Women's movements were a result of an ardent desire to break from servility propagated by the state and patriarchy.

Surprisingly women also jumped into the violent Naxal movement in Bihar. Many organizations like the Jaanvadi Mahila Manch and the Pragatishil Mahila Manch were formed, and many women sacrificed their lives in the movement including Dhaneshwari Devi, Sorubala Burman, Sonamoti Singha, and Phulomati Singha. Some women deserve special mention like Kunti Devi, an unassuming personality who rigorously fought for women's liberation from feudal atrocities.

Analysing the participation of Dalit women in the Naxalite movement in Bihar, Srivastava states that, 'The act of resistance at the individual level and organized collective movement often reinforce each other. The women like Lahri (party name), Sonamati (party name Agni), Sheela Chateijee (Tutu), Manju Devi and Jharo Devi who died became the foci of songs and resistance' (2007, p. 37).

Today, many women are working as social activists with INGOs and CSOs like the Mahila Jagran Kendra, Koshish, Action Aid, Oxfam, Centre for Catalysing Change (C3), Equity Foundation, Bihar Gender Network, and SPSDC. They are playing a vital role in influencing government policies and generating awareness among women. Unfortunately, with the weakening of the movements, women were relegated to subordinate positions and they failed to create a permanent space for themselves in the democratic order.

Elections in the pandemic

Bihar became the first state to go for elections amidst fears of COVID-19. The migrant labourers coming back to the state in huge numbers were dissatisfied with the Bihar government's apathetic attitude towards them. When opposition parties in Bihar came to their rescue, Nitish Kumar finally saw them as a vote bank in the assembly elections in 2020 and started appeasing them with some benefits and quarantine wards.

It is often asserted that Nitish Kumar won the 2015 assembly elections because women voted for him. Women were a 'silent force', but in the 2020 assembly elections, Nitish Kumar's rule was under the scanner. Though there was an increase in polling percentages, rhetoric to attract women failed to show tangible results in these assembly elections.

Out of 26 women winners in the most recent assembly elections, 18 winners had higher percentage of women voters' turnout in their constituencies. As per the updated draft of Electoral Rolls total numbers of electors were 71,822,450 out of which 37,912,127 were males and 33,907,979 were females, and 2,344 were from the third gender.

In the 2020 assembly elections, 84 women out of the total 371 women candidates contested on party tickets. Twenty-six were able to make it to the assembly. Almost all political parties had been reluctant to give tickets to women candidates. BJP fought on 110 seats but gave tickets to only 13 women candidates of which nine could win. Congress gave tickets only to seven women candidates out of its 70 candidates; out of them only two could win. Only JDU gave 22 tickets to women candidates, that is 19 per cent of the seats contested by the party; unfortunately, only six women candidates could win. RJD fought on 144 seats but gave tickets to only 16 women candidates, out of whom seven won. Small parties like HAM and VIP gave only one ticket each to woman candidates and they both won the elections. LJP also gave tickets to 22 women candidates, but none of them could win. The number of women legislators was 34 in 2010 (14 per cent). In 2015 it reduced to 28 (11.5 per cent), and in 2020 it was 26 (10.69 per cent).

This data becomes more interesting if it is compared with women voters' turnout which was more than men's. Women voters' turnout was 59.7 per cent as against that of men voters' at 54.7 per cent.

As per the Election Commission of India data, in over 140 of the 243 Bihar assembly constituencies, women's polling percentages were more than 60 per cent. But they did not get their share in power. The three-phase elections showed that the voting percentage of women had increased, but the number of women winners had decreased. Throughout the campaign women remained silent, so it became difficult for political analysts to judge the situation. The results were the opposite of exit polls. There were factors like anti-incumbency and migrant labourers' plight, but the women were reminded of 'Jungle Raj' which scared them. The arrival of Prime Minister Modi in the second phase of the elections with his aggressive campaigning strategy and resounding slogans 'double engine' and 'Jungle Raj Ka Yuvraj' compelled women to feel more connected with NDA. It was observed that wherever there was more percentage of women voting, NDA, particularly BJP came out with flying colours in contrast to expectations.

Conclusion

Bihar presents a picture of contrasts notwithstanding many of its handicaps – political, social, and attitudinal; it has had immense potential to resurrect herself over the years, from erratic flux to a participatory democracy (Roy, 2009). In Bihar, women actively participated in the pre-independence phase, with the clarion call given by Mahatma Gandhi. In the post-independence phase women actively joined the land reforms movement, total revolution, and Naxal movements, but they always remained followers. A few came to the forefront, but they remained unsung heroes. Some even sacrificed their lives but are not fondly remembered today. Coming to electoral politics women became almost invisible in assembly politics.

All the parties in the Bihar assembly elections in 2020 failed to address the gender gap in their manifestoes. The commitments made in their manifestoes appeared to be an eyewash as they were not fulfilled by any party. Women who had a political legacy were in the electoral fray. Common women felt deprived and voters did not recognize the potential of independent women candidates. Plurals Party of Pushpam Priya Choudhary tried to initiate women-centric politics but faced a debacle because women voters were not impressed with its elitist electoral strategy.

Till the reservation bill is finally passed, all political parties should give mandatorily 33 per cent tickets to women candidates. We are living in the twenty-first century, which demands gender equality in a democratic structure. The shackles of bondage should be broken and the cause of human freedom should be championed. Women should become torchbearers of a political empowerment movement and demand equal share in power structures which will become a panacea for myriad evils prevailing in the political process in Bihar.

Bibliography

Agarwal, Bina. (2002). *Are We Not Peasants Too? Land Rights and Women's Claims in India, SEEDS*. Available at: https://www.binaagarwal.com/downloads/apapers/are_we_not_peasants_too.pdf, accessed on June 20, 2022.

Appleby, Paul H. (1953). *Public Administration in India: Report of a Survey*. Delhi: Cabinet Secretariat, Government of India.

Asthama, Pratima (1974). *Women's Movement in India*. New Delhi: Vikas Publishing House Pvt. Ltd.

Bhuyan Anoo (2019). *Bihar, UP Rank Lowest Yet Once Again in Government's Latest Health Index*, The Wire, 26 June. Available at: https://thewire.in/health/bihar-up-rank-niti-aayog-health-data, accessed on June 20, 2022.

Business Standard, (2013). 'Jungle Raj in Bihar, Says Patna HC', February 26. Available at: https://www.business-standard.com/article/economy-policy/jungle-raj-in-bihar-says-patna-hc-197080601166_1.html, accessed on July 1, 2020.

Chaturvedi, Geeta (1985). *Attitude Towards Social Change*. Jaipur: RBSA Publishers.

Chibber, Pradeep K. and Irfan Nooruddin (1999). 'Party Competition and Fragmentation in India', in Ramashray Roy and Paul Wallace (eds), *Indian Politics and the 1998 Elections: Regionalism, Hindutva and State Politics*. Delhi: Orient Longman.

Dasgupta, Swapan and Farzand Ahmed (1997). 'Fodder Scam: Politics Unmakes Bihar Chief Minister and Messiah Laloo Prasad Yadav', *India Today*, June 9. Available at: https://www.indiatoday.in/magazine/cover-story/story/19970531 -fodder-scam-politics-unmakes-bihar-chief-minister-and-messiah-laloo-prasad -yadav-831479-1997-06-09, accessed on June 16, 2022.

Election Commission of India. Available at: https://eci.gov.in/statistical-report/ statistical-reports/, accessed on June 28, 2020 and March 12, 2021.

Government of Bihar. Available at: https://state.bihar.gov.in/main/Content.html ?links&page=Bihar%20State%20Profile, accessed on April 22, 2020.

Huntington, Samuel and Joan M. Nelson (1976). *No Easy Choice: Political Participation in Developing Countries*. Harvard: Harvard University Press.

Mallapur, Chaitanya (2020). 'Bihar Election 2020 Results: 26 Women Triumph in State Polls', *Money Control*, November 11. Available at: https://www.moneycontrol .com/news/politics/bihar-election-2020-results-26-women-triumph-in-state-polls -will-form-11-of-the-assembly-strength, accessed on November 13, 2020.

Mill, John Stuart. (1989), *On Liberty with The Subjection of Women And Chapters on Socialism* Stefan, Collini. (ed.), Cambridge, Cambridge University Press.

Ministry of Panchayati Raj, Basic Statistics of Panchayati Raj Institutions, Government of India (2019). Available at: https://www.panchayat.gov.in/ documents/20126/0/Statistical+handbook_MoPR+02082019.pdf/4988ca1b -4971-1f3b-54e7-980228eb47f9?t=1564729098415, accessed on June 30, 2020 and July 4, 2021.

Roy, Shefali, (2009). 'Democracy- In a State of Flux in Bihar', *Review of Politics*, 17 (1), pp. 42–52.

——— (2011). *Empowerment Status of Women Representatives*. Patna: Novelty & Co.

Salomi, Vithika (2015). 'Bihar Election Results 2015: Women MLAs Number Comes Down by 6 Comes to 26', *The Times of India*, November 10. Available at: https://timesofindia.indiatimes.com/elections/bihar-elections-2015/news/ Bihar-election-results-2015-Women-MLAs-number-comes-down-by-6-to-28/ articleshow/49730479.cms, accessed on June 28, 2020.

Shukla, D.M. (1988). *Political Socialization and Women Voters*. New Delhi: Janaki Publishers.

Srivastava, Sunit S. (2007). 'Violence and Dalit Women's Resistance in Rural Bihar', *Indian Anthropologist*, 37(2), 31–44.

Thelma, Mccorna (1981). *Development with Equity for Women*. New Delhi: Sage Publications.

Verma, V.P. (1986). 'Assembly Elections in Bihar 1985', *Democracy: A Journal of Jagjivan Ram Institute of Parliamentary studies and Political Research*, 6, 1–4.

Verniers Gilles and Samridhi Hooda (2020). 'Bihar Assembly Election 2020: More Women Candidates but Fewer Winners', *Hindustan Times*, November 12, https://www.hindustantimes.com/bihar-election/bihar-assembly-election-2020 -more-women-candidates-but-fewer-winners-in-bihar-polls/story-Z46mZ5D bKvZqIWnUq7iTbJ.html, accessed on November 13, 2020.

Vidhan Sabha, Bihar. Available at: http://vidhansabha.bih.nic.in/index.html, accessed on June 30, 2020 and June 21, 2022.

Yadav, J.P. (2007). 'Kidnapping Raj Flourishing in FLOODED BIHAR', *The Indian Express*, August 17. Available at: http://archive.indianexpress.com/news /kidnapping-raj-flourishing-in-flooded-bihar/210804/, accessed on September 9, 2020.

17

WOMEN'S REPRESENTATION IN STATE POLITICS IN SIKKIM

Nancy Choden Lhasungpa

Introduction

Sikkim, which became the twenty-second state of India on May 16, 1975, is located on the foothills of the Eastern Himalayas. It is the least populous and second smallest state in the country after Goa (Census, 2011). The total population of Sikkim is 610,577, and its total area is 7,096 sq. km. It is bordered on the north and the northeast by the Tibet Autonomous Region (TAR) of China, on the southeast by Bhutan, by Nepal on the west, and by Darjeeling district of West Bengal on the south.

Sikkimese society is an amalgamation of various communities and religions. The three main ethnic groups in the state are Lepchas, Bhutias, and Nepalese. Lepchas, also known as *Rongkup* or children of god, are aboriginal inhabitants of Sikkim. It is believed that Sikkim was *Rong-Lyang*, the waiting place for Lepchas going to Tibet for salt. With time, the people of *Rong-Lyang* came to be known as *Rongs* (Nirash, 1982). The Lepchas are nature worshippers and practise subsistence agriculture as one of their main occupations.

In 2005, they were accorded the status of a Primitive Tribe (PT). Today, this tribe inhabits the northern and central areas of the state. The Bhutias are believed to have migrated from Chumbi valley and Kham district in Tibet in the fourteenth century. They brought with them the Tibetan way of life including its culture, religion, language, and economic system which was a combination of pastoralism and semi-settled agriculture (Mukherjee, 1995). Together these two ethnic groups comprise less than 20 per cent of the total population of Sikkim (Census, 2011).

The Nepalese are the largest ethnic community with a conglomeration of caste groups and diverse sub-groups. While a majority are Hindus, a few follow Christianity, Buddhism, and other traditional forms of worship. From being hunters and gatherers to practising settled agriculture and domesticating animals to joining the service and business sectors, changes have been steady in this community. Other minority communities like the

DOI: 10.4324/9781003374862-18

Biharis and Marwaris are engaged in trade and commerce, and they mostly live in the urban areas of east and south Sikkim.

Religion plays an important role in the everyday lives of the Sikkimese people. The two major religions in the state are Hinduism and Buddhism. The former has been the main religion since the arrival of Nepalese migrants. Buddhism is practised by the Bhutias, Lepchas (apart from nature worship and Christianity), and the Tamang, Sherpa, and Gurung communities. It was brought to Sikkim through Tibet by Guru Padma Sambhava in the eighth century (Bhutia and Mishra, 2014). Christians have a 9.91 per cent share of the population in the state. Most of the Christians are converts from the Lepcha community who were converted by British missionaries in the late nineteenth century.

In recent times, religious conversions have seen an upward trend among the Rai community as well. Other religious minorities include Muslims, Jains, and Sikhs. Nepali language, which was recognized as a scheduled language in 1992, is the lingua franca of Sikkim.

A brief historical context

The concept of planned development in Sikkim was introduced decades before its merger with India in 1954 (Lama, 2011, p. 182). Pre-merger Sikkim was characterized by a predominantly agrarian economy with rice, maize, wheat, finger millet, buckwheat, pulses, and cash crops (cardamom, ginger, and oranges) as the major crops. Post-merger with the Indian Union in 1975, the manufacturing and construction sectors contributed the largest share towards the state economy, followed by the service sector.

At the time of India's independence, Sikkim was ruled by Maharaja Tashi Namgyal. In December 1950 the Indo-Sikkim Treaty was signed. Sikkim was granted the status of a protectorate of India while handing over control of defence, territorial integrity, external affairs, and communication to the Indian government (Tenzing, 2011). In December 1963, the Maharaja passed away. In the following year, Pandit Nehru passed away in New Delhi. The post-Nehru era was marked by uncertainty. Despite Chogyal's repeated efforts to emphasize the need for a 'Sikkimese' identity, a tripartite agreement was formally signed in May 1973 between the Durbar (represented by Chogyal Palden Thondup Namgyal), the Government of India (represented by foreign secretary Kewal Singh), and the people of Sikkim (represented by the Sikkim Janata Congress, the Sikkim National Congress, and the Sikkim National Party) (*Sikkim Chronicle*, 2020). One of the core agreements was the Indian government's direct involvement in the internal administration of the kingdom. This agreement signalled the end of monarchy. In July 1974, a new constitution was promulgated, and in the ensuing few months Sikkim was given status as an Associate State of India. Finally, with the passing of the 36th Amendment to the Indian Constitution, monarchy was formally abolished in May 1975 and Sikkim joined the Indian Union as its twenty-second state.

Gender disparities, a living reality

In Sikkim, gender disparities are a reality. The sex ratio, the work participation rate (WPR) in both the organized and unorganized public/private sectors, and access to education, property, and political representation are some of the core indicators of such inequalities. Women constituted 47 per cent of the total population of Sikkim in 2011. The National Family Health Survey (NFHS)-4 data shows the sex ratio at 942 in 2015–16. Based on the projected population figures for 2016–19, the sex ratio is still not in favour of females.

In terms of literacy, Sikkim registered an outstanding increase from a 34.1 per cent literacy rate in 1981 to 82.2 per cent in 2011. This figure was stated to be approximately 90 per cent in 2015 (Qrius, 2018). The female literacy rate rose from 22.2 per cent in 1981 to 76.4 per cent in 2011 while the national average was 65.5 per cent (Census, 2011). The gender gap in the literacy rate fell from 21.8 per cent (1981) to 10.9 per cent (2011) in the state. Nationally, the figure stood at 16.5 per cent. The gross enrolment ratio (GER) in Sikkim, in keeping with the national trend, showed a steady rise from 28.2 per cent in 2011–12 to 53.9 per cent in 2018–19.

Female GER increased from 27.4 per cent in 2011–12 to 53.9 per cent in 2018-19 which is almost at par with the male GER at 54 per cent in 2018–19 (AISHE, 2018-19). In the area of reproductive health, around 99.1 per cent of expecting mothers had registered pregnancies for which they received mother and child protection (MCP) cards (NFHS-4, 2015-16); 94.7 per cent of the deliveries were institutional births (NFHS-4, 2015-16). Perhaps improvements in ante-natal and post-natal care helped reduce the MMR from 540 (per 100,000 live births) in 2001 to 8 per 100,000 live births in 2018 (DESM&E, 2018). The infant mortality rate (IMR) also decreased from 49/1,000 live births (2000) to 30/1,000 live births in 2015–16 (NFHS-4, 2015-16).

Apart from participation in non-remunerative household work, Sikkimese women engage in agricultural activities (livestock, poultry farming, and animal husbandry), administration, and trade. The worker population ratio for females aged 15 years and above in Sikkim rose from 39.5 per cent in 2012–13 to 48.2 per cent as against the all-India figure of 25.8 per cent in 2015–16 (NSSO, 2018). In the primary sector, female participation was higher at 85.1 per cent as against 60.8 per cent for males (Samantroy, 2017, p. 29). It is argued that women are preferred as they can be employed for low wages and manipulated due to their subservient nature owing to low levels of education and awareness. In contemporary times, there has been a fundamental transformation in gender relations with the propelling forces of education, women entering paid employment avenues, and enjoying representation in decision-making and polity.

Women's employment in the government sector is more than that of men. This could be attributed to the state government's provision of 30 per cent reservations for women from Sikkimese communities in posts and services to be filled by direct recruitment which has benefitted educated women in gaining socioeconomic empowerment.

However, it is imperative to highlight here that women supersede men in total numbers in Class C and D categories. Within Class A and B cadres, which form the decision-making and higher end of the bureaucracy, it is found that the state is far short of the gender equality goals. A good example of this can be observed from the fact that out of the present 60 heads of departments, only 13 (21.6 per cent) are women (GoS, official website, 2021). It can be asserted that direct recruitments to these posts are based on a higher educational qualification and expertise. Given that men have held an undue advantage for decades with the pool of deserving male candidates being larger owing to preferential treatment and better opportunities, only a few women have managed to break into this circle. Women bureaucrats who do fall in the A and B cadres mostly tend to come from a more privileged background, so this does not truly reflect an overall social change.

Encouraging trend

However, an encouraging trend in the last two decades has been the increase in total female candidates selected for gazette posts through the State Public Service Commission (SPSC) examinations. This is an indication of there being gender balance within the workforce in the future.

A look at gender status in Sikkim highlights that 85 per cent women in the state enjoy freedom of movement, including to the market, health facility, and places outside the village or community (NFHS-4, 2015–16), and 95.3 per cent of all currently married women in Sikkim participate in household decisions as against the national average of 84 per cent. On the socioeconomic front, 63.5 per cent Sikkimese women operate their own bank accounts and approximately 19.9 per cent women who worked in the year before the NHFS-4 survey had been paid in cash. Women are generally not secluded, and instances of female infanticide and foeticide are rarely reported in the state. The presence of social customs like bride price among certain communities gives importance to the girl child.

Despite such figures, a patriarchal social structure, social conditioning, and ignorance coupled with lack of women's participation at the policy level make gender disparities a social reality in Sikkim as much as elsewhere in the country. The National Crime Records Bureau (NCRB) in its publication 'Crime in India, 2018' shows an upward trend in crimes against women in Sikkim (NCRB, 2018). The ongoing COVID-19 pandemic, while emphasizing social distancing and quarantine, has also led to a spike in domestic violence cases. In Sikkim, the Sikkim State Commission for Women (SSCW) confirmed six cases of domestic violence between March 28 and April 6, 2020.

Since independence, the country has had only one woman as president and one woman as prime minister and very few women governors and women chief ministers. No woman has occupied the position of Chairman of the Finance Commission or the Attorney General of India. Even the states have no women advocate generals. So far, there has been only one woman Chief Election Commissioner and only a few members of the Union Public Service Commission (UPSC) have been women. Even an institution like the Reserve Bank of India (RBI) has never appointed a woman as its Governor.

Women and political participation

1975 was a watershed in Sikkim's history. Although council elections were held regularly in Sikkim in 1953, 1958, 1967, and 1970, the fifth election in April 1974 decided the actual shift of power from monarchy to democracy. The central objective of democracy is to enable every person to have a say in deciding about the greater good. In India, democratic institutions were not thrust upon the Indian people in one stroke (Vora and Palshikar, 2004). The scenario in Sikkim was no different. With high illiteracy and poverty, development was one of the fundamental factors that gave impetus to the pro-merger movement. The participation of women in Sikkim politics reflects a larger trend which has kept women in the background, continuing to be under-represented and denied the right to participate fully in democratic governance.

At the time of its merger, the Sikkim National Congress headed by Kazi Lhendup Dorji as the president and K.C. Pradhan as the vice president took over the reins of administration of the newly formed state. The former served as the first Chief Minister of Sikkim from May 1975 to August 1979. A unicameral legislature and a parliamentary form of government were adopted. A look at the list of members of the legislative assembly (MLAs) shows that out of the 32 seats, only one was represented by a woman. Hemlata Chettri, the lone woman contestant, won from Gyalshing constituency (Sikkim Assembly Archives). The 1979 elections resulted in an all-male legislative assembly. It also heralded the candidature of Nar Bahadur Bhandari, a leader of Sikkim Sangram Parishad (SSP), as the second longest-serving Chief Minister of Sikkim. The elections in 1985 also witnessed continuity of the same trend even though seven women fought for seats from various constituencies. The total voter percentage stood at 62.9 per cent with women voters having a 43.4 per cent share (Election Commission of India, 1985).

In the 1989 elections, the SSP once again emerged victorious with a total sweep in all the 32 constituencies in the state. Out of the 139,227 persons who voted, 62,353 were women voters (44.78 per cent) (Election Commission of India, 1989). The list of newly elected MLAs also featured a successful woman candidate, Chong Lhamu Bhutia from Rinchenpong constituency, a seat earmarked for a contender specifically from the Bhutia Lepcha (BL) community. That year three other women candidates unsuccessfully contested the elections – Ram Maya Chettriand Dawa Lhamu of INC and Mandodra Sharma of the Rising Sun Party (RIS).

The 1994 state elections are remembered as being historic as they announced the arrival of the Sikkim Democratic Front (SDF), a rival political party started by defected MLA Pawan Kumar Chamling who went on to become the longest-serving Chief Minister in the country with a rule of 25 years (1994–2019). The new party won 19 seats, while the SSP managed to win only 10 seats. Out of the 178,023 persons who voted, 82,317 (46.23 per cent) were women (Election Commission of India, 1994). Nine women candidates contested, but only one of them was victorious. The winning woman candidate was Rinzing Ongmu of the SSP who contested from Ranka (ST) constituency.

The elections in 1999 helped SDF further solidify its base by increasing its winning margin to 24 of the 31 seats contested (Election Commission of India, 1999). Its rival, the SSP, managed to win only seven seats.

The Sangha seat, which is a unique reservation policy wherein only monks and nuns from registered monasteries in Sikkim are allowed to vote for a political representative from amongst themselves, was won by Palden Lama, an independent candidate (Election Commission of India, 1999). Once again only one of the six women candidates managed to win. Kalawati Subba, the lone female MLA, won from Yuksam constituency with a slim margin of 52.80 per cent of the total votes polled (Election Commission of India, 1999). In this election, 208,989 persons voted (81.83 per cent) with the female voter percentage at 46.47 per cent.

For the first time in the electoral history of the state, three women candidates were elected to the legislative assembly in the 2004 elections. That year six female candidates contested the state elections with Kalawati Subba, Manita Thapa, and Nimthit Lepcha of the SDF winning from their respective constituencies of Yuksam, Losing Pachekhani, and Ranka (BL). Once again, the incumbent SDF government emerged victorious, winning 31 of the 32 seats. The lone opposition came from the Sangha seat, with the winner representing the Indian National Congress (INC). The total voter turnout was approximately 79.23 per cent with the female voting share being 46.77 per cent (Election Commission of India, 2004). SDF secured a 100 per cent victory in the 2009 elections. Fifteen women contested in these elections with four women candidates emerging victorious – Chandra Maya Subba from Maneybung Dentam, Tulshi Devi Rai from Melli, Tilu Gurung from Namthang Rateypani, and Neeru Sewa from West Pendam (SC) constituencies respectively (Table 17.1). The total

WOMEN'S REPRESENTATION IN STATE POLITICS IN SIKKIM

Table 17.1 Female representation in Sikkim's legislative assembly (1974–2019)

Sl. no.	Election year	Total MLAs	Winning male candidates	Female contesting candidates	Winning female candidates
1	1974	32	31	N.A.	01
2	1979	32	32	11	00
3	1985	32	32	11	00
4	1989	32	31	4	01
5	1994	32	31	9	01
6	1999	32	31	6	01
7	2004	32	29	6	03
8	2009	32	28	15	04
9	2014	32	30	11	03
10	2019	32	29	16	03
	Total	320	304	89	17

Source: The Election Commission of India (various years).

female voter percentage stood at 46.93 per cent (Election Commission of India, 2009).

The 2014 elections witnessed a repeat of what had happened in 1994 in Sikkim politics. It marked the entry of a new party, the Sikkim Krantikari Morcha (SKM), which was floated by a rebel SDF MLA, Prem Singh Tamang (Golay), who was a trusted Chamling aide from the latter's initial days of defection from the then Bhandari government. The SKM wave was a result of growing sentiments against the ruling party and its leader. Eleven women contested in the elections, but only three women candidates, Tulshi Devi Rai, Tilu Gurung, and Chandra Maya Limboo (Subba) of SDF, won. Of the total votes polled, the female voters share was 47.13 per cent (Election Commission of India, 2014).

In 2019, SKM was able to topple the SDF government which had been in power for the last 25 years. It won 17 seats which was enough for it to emerge victorious. The total female vote share, excluding postal votes, stood at 48.89 per cent (Election Commission of India, 2019). Out of the 16 female candidates who contested the elections, three won – Raj Kumari Thapa (SDF), Farwanti Tamang (SDF), and Sunita Gajmer (SKM). In an unprecedented twist, the subsequent by-elections resulted in the ruling national party, the BJP, which had had no presence in Sikkim politics so far, becoming the main opposition party in the state assembly. This was possible after 13 MLAs from SDF defected to join the BJP at its headquarters in New Delhi. The remaining two MLAs from the SDF defected to join SKM. With this move, ex-Chief Minister, Pawan Kumar Chamling, was left as the sole representative of the once indomitable SDF in the state assembly.

311

Women's poor representation in the state assembly

The dismal presence of women in the state assembly can be seen in Table 17.1. The party manifestoes of the two political giants, SDF and SKM, for the 2019 state elections in Sikkim highlighted a similar focus on addressing political, socioeconomic, and youth-centric issues. However, there was a deafening silence on women's representation in the upper echelons of the political arena. With low visibility in state politics, the few women who have managed to become MLAs find a dismal representation in the council of ministers in the state. In the absence of any available data, it is estimated that less than five women were given ministerial berths during 1974–2019. Women ministers are yet to be assigned prominent portfolios such as finance, home, and power. Most of the women MLAs have been accommodated as chairpersons of various government departments or public sector undertakings. In a historic decision, Kalawati Subba was elected as the first and only woman Speaker of the legislative assembly in 1999.

Women in national-level politics

At the national level, Sikkim has one seat each in the Rajya Sabha and Lok Sabha. Here too women's participation in policymaking is negated. An internal political arrangement within the state means that the nomination of candidates to the Lok Sabha and Rajya Sabha is divided as – Rajya Sabha (BL seat) and Lok Sabha (General seat). Leonard Soloman Saring was the first MP to be nominated by the INC to represent Sikkim in the Rajya Sabha. Since then, 10 MPs have been nominated to the Upper House with no representation of women. Till 2019, 13 MPs had been elected to the Lok Sabha from the state. Dil Kumari Bhandari of SSP is the lone woman MP from Sikkim who was elected twice to the Lok Sabha in 1985 and 1991 (Lok Sabha Archives). This could be credited to the fact that as the wife of the then Chief Minister, Nar Bahadur Bhandari, her nomination was accepted by all party members. A significant contribution during her tenure was the inclusion of the Nepali language in the Eighth Schedule of the Indian Constitution in August 1992.

Women in local self-governance

At the level of local self-governance, Sikkim increased women's reservation to 50 per cent through the Sikkim Panchayat Amendment Act, 2007. The state is divided into four zilas or districts, with traditional institutions (*dzumsas*) in Lachen and Lachung being deemed to be gram panchayat units (GPUs) (Sikkim Panchayat Act, 1993). When compared to their representation at the national and state levels, Sikkimese women seem to be enjoying a near-equal platform at the level of PRIs. In 2012, Sikkim had

113 zila panchayats (ZPs) and 176 GPUs comprising 987 wards. In the same year, of the 987 elected functionaries, 493 were women (49.94 per cent) (GoS, 2012). In 2017, the total number of GPUs increased to 183 (east-53/west-61/south-48/north-21) taking the total number of gram panchayat wards to 1,040. Women accounted for 50 per cent of the elected representatives with many being assigned the position of ZPs (Sikkim Police, 2017).

Most of these elected functionaries were affiliated to the then ruling political party, SDF. These women were actively involved in the women's wing of the party before being given an opportunity to contest in panchayat elections. With adequate support from family and community members, entry into village politics seems to have brought some effective changes in women's lives in terms of empowering them in their social, political, and economic well-being (Sinha, 2008). However, much is left to be desired still.

Many women are first-time panchayat members whose political journeys will end here. Independent decision-making is absent, and most of the work at the village level is based on the directives of the party high command. Nevertheless, reservations have given an impetus to the mass entry of women in politics, even if it is at the provincial level. This has been significant in addressing many social myths about the induction of women in roles of power that require decision-making abilities and an authoritative temperament.

Some firsts

Over the years, there have been a series of firsts for the women of Sikkim. Santosh Nirash was the first female journalist in Sikkim. Hemlata Chettri was the first woman to be elected to the state legislative assembly in 1974. Kalawati Subba was the first woman Speaker. Rinzing Ongmu was the first woman Cabinet Minister in the state assembly during SDF's rule. Rinchen Ongmu, a 1979 batch IAS officer, was elevated to the post of the first woman Chief Secretary of the state, the highest bureaucratic position, in March 2013. B.M. Singh, IAS (Retired), was appointed the first woman Chairperson of the State Public Service Commission in 2000 for two years (SPSC Archives). Another notable achievement is of Tilu Gurung, who served as minister of the buildings and housing departments in the 2009–14 SDF government. She was awarded the best legislator award for 2017–18.

Sikkim has many policies in place which provide a platform for women. However, the guidelines are yet to take full effect. SSCW was constituted to protect the rights of women and for delivering justice to them. The state government also implemented the Protection of Women from Domestic Violence Act, 2005, in 2007 to provide speedy resolution to victims of domestic violence by involving protection officers and voluntary organizations as service providers. In terms of property rights, all three dominant communities follow patriarchal norms. In the past, the old laws of Sikkim gave no inheritance rights to daughters (Gazetteer of Sikkim, 1894, p. 66).

Today, the Sikkim Succession Act, 2008, gives unmarried daughters the right to a share of their fathers' property in equal proportion along with his son(s) and wives giving a sense of some sort of gender equality. At the same time, the act disqualifies any female heir who marries a person not in possession of a valid Sikkim Subject Certificate (COI) or who has acquired foreign citizenship. In this regard, the 'Daughters of the Soil' petition, which was submitted to the then Chief Minister, Pawan Chamling, more than a decade ago highlighted the feudal nature of the act. The petitioners raised questions about the existing gender bias that affected a significant percentage of the female population. The petition demanded equitable inheritance rights to property for women which were at par with their male counterparts irrespective of their marital status. Later, a High Court ruling in 2017 quashed this act. At present, the state government is yet to frame new rules vis-à-vis the act.

Challenges faced

The National Institute for Transforming India (NITI) Aayog ranked Sikkim, along with Kerala, among the states in the performers category in 2018 (*Down to Earth*, 2018). However, Sikkim has many things to worry about such as creating employment avenues for the youth, improving the quality of education, better preparatory measures to handle natural disasters, and higher political representation for women. Even the TFR is well below the replacement level of 2.1 (NFHS-4, 2015–16). The political vote-bank trajectory has highlighted the fact that even though women continue to contribute more than 45 per cent share of the voter strength on average, even exceeding the male vote bank in certain constituencies, the overall female participation as candidates in the state elections has been dismal at less than 15 per cent over the years.

The challenges and obstacles faced by women in the political arena cannot be listed in a few bullet points. Traditionally, Sikkimese society has been a patriarchal society with men occupying positions of authority for generations. Misogynistic mindsets have confined women to the domestic sphere. Over the years, there has been a sort of continuity and change in the way society operates. With the advent of globalization and information technology, more women are stepping outside their comfort zones. At the same time, there is a categorization of careers considered to be women-centric or appropriate for women. An overarching observation of the previous generation of working women was their viewpoint regarding professional growth which was never the focus of attention; rather it was an activity to break the monotony of domestic life.

In contemporary times, this is no longer the case. In the political field, contenders are required to be vocal, unapologetic, and extroverts which are not always traits imbibed by women due to the socialization process at play. Further, it is not necessarily men who are against the idea of women entering the political field. Women too are less likely to vote for female candidates or have faith in a female leader because of low experience, less power, and incapability to take on male-oriented responsibilities.

Many times, family responsibilities are seen as the biggest impediment to a woman's political growth which leaves men with a better shot at leadership positions. Strengthening capacity gaps are expected to help women overcome educational, public resources, and other barriers in becoming effective leaders. In Sikkim, this is something that is already in process given that women in the twenty-first century have been provided with near-equal access to education, work opportunities, and freedom. But such freedom has not necessarily generated large-scale awareness of the inequality at play. In June 2020, Sikkim lost two advocates of the feminist movement in the state – Santosh Nirash and Hemlata Chettri. While their deaths were covered by the local dailies, in this age of social networking where a #MeToo or a #BlackLivesMatter trend is instantly caught on by the present generation, it is upsetting to see no one pay homage to these individuals who paved the way for the women's movement in the state.

Conclusion

Women's political journey in the Sikkimese context has been a combination of highs and lows. Initially, political participation in Sikkim was witnessed in the form of voting in local and national elections. However, over the years, one can see a surge in people's interest in the political field. In contemporary times, citizens are actively involved in the campaigning process, political rallies, party meetings, and other activities. Every party has a dedicated *cheli morcha* (women's wing) which plays a dynamic role in the parties. Despite this, power still seems to be a privilege for men alone. Efforts must now be made to provide support to women's political participation through a series of programmes aimed at building the capacity of the supposedly 'weaker sex' to play effective roles as political actors and improving the overall gender responsiveness of governance structures.

Bibliography

Bhutia, Zigmee W. and P. K. Mishra (2014). 'Bhutia Tribe in Sikkim: A Sociological Study', *International Journal of Innovative Research and Development*, 3(11), 322–326.

Department of Economic Affairs, Ministry of Finance (2020). *Economic Survey:2019–20, Volume 2*. New Delhi: Ministry of Finance.

Department of Health & Family Welfare, Government of Sikkim. *Demographic Indicators*. Available at: https://sikkim.gov.in/DepartmentsMenu/health-family

-welfare-department/State%20Heath%20Profile/demographic-indicators, accessed on April 23, 2020.

DESM&E, Government of Sikkim (2018). *Sikkim at a Glance: 2018.* Available at: http://www.desme.in/page/10, accessed on August 4, 2019.

Down to Earth (2018). 'Almost All States in Red Zone on Gender Equality: NITI Aayog', Available at: https://.downtoearth.org.in/news/governance/almost-all -states-in-red-zone-on- gender-equality-niti-aayog-62592, accessed on May 5, 2020.

Election Commission of India. Available at: https://eci.gov.in/files/file/3358-sikkim -1985/, accessed on April 30, 2020.

Election Commission of India. Available at: https://eci.gov.in/files/file/3358-sikkim -1989/, accessed on April 30, 2020.

Election Commission of India. Available at: https://eci.gov.in/files/file/3358-sikkim -1994/, accessed on April 30, 2020.

Election Commission of India. Available at: https://eci.gov.in/files/file/3358-sikkim -1999/, accessed on April 30, 2020.

Election Commission of India. Available at: https://eci.gov.in/files/file/3358-sikkim -2004/, accessed on May 1, 2020.

Election Commission of India. Available at:https://eci.gov.in/files/file/3358-sikkim -2009/, accessed on May 1, 2020.

Election Commission of India. Available at: https://eci.gov.in/files/file/3358-sikkim -2014/, accessed on May 1, 2020.

Election Commission of India. Available at: https://eci.gov.in/files/file/3358-sikkim -2019/, accessed on May 1, 2020.

Government of Sikkim (2001). *Sikkim Human Development Report.* New Delhi: Social Science Press.

Government of Sikkim, FR&ED Department (2014). Available at: http://www .sikkimfred.gov.in/FRBM/Documents/2014-15/Final%20_Sikkim_MTFP_2014 -15.pdf, accessed on March 22, 2020.

Government of Sikkim, Heads of Departments. Available at: https://sikkim.gov .in/mygovernment/whos-who/head-of-departments, accessed on September 1, 2021.

Sikkim Police. *Counting Tally.* Available at: http://www.sikkimpolice.nic.in/Polling /Polling_2017_Zilla_Ward_Panchayat/Pancha yatPoll2017Counting.htm, accessed on July 21, 2020.

International Institute for Population Sciences(IIPS) and ICF (2017). *National Family Health Survey(NFHS-4), 2015–16: India.* Mumbai: IIPS.

Lama, Mahendra P. (2011). 'Development Trajectory', in S. Wangdi (ed.), *Sikkim's Raj Bhavan* (pp. 181–183). Gangtok: Department of Information and Public Relations, Government of Sikkim.

Lok Sabha Archives. Available at: http://164.100.47.194/loksabha/members/lokprev .aspx, accessed on May 12, 2020.

Ministry of Human Resource Development (2019). *All India Survey on Higher Education (AISHE):2018–19.* New Delhi: Department of Higher Education. Available at: http://aishe.nic.in/aishe/viewDocument.action?documentId=262, accessed on November 2, 2019.

Mukherjee, Bandana (1995). 'Some Aspect of Bhutia Culture in Sikkim: A Case Study', *Bulletin of Tibetology*, 31(1), 82–87. Available at: https://.repository.cam

.ac.uk/bitstream/id/636797/bot_1995_01_18.pdf/;jsessionid=BA8313412A2 81575CDA9DC6B9E12C72E, accessed on January 10, 2020.

National Crime Records Bureau (2016). *Crime in India*. New Delhi: Ministry of Home Affairs.

National Sample Survey Office (NSSO) (2018–19). *Annual Report of Periodic Labour Force Survey (PLFS)*. New Delhi: Ministry of Statistics and Programme Implementation.

News18Online (2013). 'Tripura Tops Literacy Rate with 94.65 Percent, Leaves Behind Kerala', Available at: https://.news18.com/news/india/tripura- tops-literacy-rate-with-with-94-65-per-cent-leaves-behind-kerala-637592.html, accessed on April 24, 2020.

———— (2018). 'The Curious Case of Missing Women in Indian Polity. Available at: https://.news18.com/news/india/count-metoo-the-curious- case-of-missing-women-in-indian-polity-1683031.html, accessed on April 28, 2020.

Nirash, N. (1982). *The Lepchas of Sikkim*. Available at: http://himalaya.socanth .cam.ac.uk/collections/journals/bot/pdf/bot_1982_02_03.pdf, accessed on January 12, 2020.

Qrius (2018). 'All You Need to Know About Sikkim's 100% Literacy Rate', Available at: https://qrius.com/all-you-need-to-know-about-sikkim-achieving -100-literacy/, accessed on April 24, 2020.

Rajya Sabha Archives. Available at: http://164.100.47.5/Newmembers/mpterms.asp x, accessed on May 12, 2020.

Samantroy, E. (2017). *Understanding Women's Work: Gendered Analysis of Women's Participation in Domestic Duties in North East India*. New Delhi: V. V. Giri National Labour Institute.

Sikkim Assembly. Available at: http://www.sikkimassembly.org.in/Members-of -Sikkim-Legislative-Assembly-since-1975, accessed on April 30, 2020.

Sikkim Chronicle (2019). '8th May Tripartite Agreement: Sikkim Congress Perspective', Available at: https://.thesikkimchronicle.com/8th-may-tripartite -agreement-sikkim-congress- perspective/, accessed on April 20, 2020.

Sikkim Public Service Commission. Available at: http://www.spscskm.gov.in/ Chairmen_Member.html, accessed on May 10, 2020.

Sinha, A. C. (2008). *Sikkim Feudal and Democratic*. New Delhi: Indus Publishing Company.

The Gazetteer of Sikkim (1894). *With an Introduction by H. H.* Risley: Bengal Secretariat Press.

Tenzing, P.C. (2011). 'Relationship of the Chogyals with the Government of India 1947–75', in S. Wangdi (ed.), *Sikkim's Raj Bhavan* (pp. 107–118). Gangtok: Department of Information and Public Relations,Government of Sikkim.

United Nations Development Programme (UNDP). (1995). *Human Development Report(HDR)*. Available at: http://hdr.undp.org/en/content/human-development -report-1995, accessed on September 23, 2019.

Vora, R. and S. Palshikar (eds) (2004). *Indian Democracy: Meanings and Practices*. New Delhi: Sage Publications.

Wangdi, Sonam (2011). 'The Chogyals Through the ChangingTimes', in S. Wangdi (ed.), *Sikkim's Raj Bhavan* (pp. 87–98). Gangtok: Department of Information and Public Relations, Government of Sikkim.

18

THE LANDSCAPE OF INADEQUATE ASSERTION

Women in Bihar politics

Narendra Kumar Arya

Introduction

Contemporary India is witnessing the onset of democratic processes reconfiguring its politics and economy. One of the most significant processes is the assertion of identity politics. The struggle to assert conflicting claims by identity groups is based on region, religion, language (even dialect), caste, and community. These struggles have found expression in a changed mode of electoral representation that has brought local/regional politics into focus with the hitherto politically dormant groups and regions finding a voice (Kumar, 2011). However, the issue of gender has not received adequate attention. Some national and regional parties have been controlled by women leaders for relatively long periods at the apex; still, it has not changed the general patriarchal structure and nature of political parties.

Demographic details

Bihar is the third most populous state in India. Out of the 10,40,99,452 people in the state as per Census 2011, 4,98,21,295 were women. The sex ratio in Bihar is 916 females per 1,000 males. Bihar's literacy rate is just 61.8 per cent – the lowest in the country – and only 51.5 per cent of the women in the state can read or write. Its female literacy rate is the second lowest in all Indian states (Census, 2011; Khushboo, 2017). The gap between women and men's literacy is around 20 per cent. The rate of rural women's literacy is even lower (Director of Census Operations, 2011).

Bihar has the lowest labour force participation rate among women (aged 15–59 years) in India at 4.4 per cent as compared to the male labour force participation rate (LFPR) of 71 per cent (aged 15–59 years). This signifies a combination of complex socio-cultural forces limiting women's opportunities to get work, earn money, and achieve economic independence. Most of the women in Bihar are engaged in the agricultural sector, but they own just

318

DOI: 10.4324/9781003374862-19

THE LANDSCAPE OF INADEQUATE ASSERTION

14 per cent of the agricultural landholdings and 92 per cent of these land-holdings are small and marginal (Government of Bihar); this is also noted in a UN report 'Gender Equality: Women's Economic Empowerment' (2018).

Due to traditional social norms as well as constraints in getting education and resources, women have not been able to emerge as a separate political constituency of any significance that can compel political parties and political leaders to take them seriously in the electoral process at various levels.

Women in the state assembly

The Bihar legislative assembly came into existence in 1937. It had 152 members of which there were only four women members (1.32 per cent). All these women belonged to the aristocratic or high upper-class stratum. In 1946 too, there were only four women members in the state assembly. Table 18.1 gives the number of women contestants and winners over seven decades in state politics in Bihar.

After independence, the provision of universal franchise provided women an opportunity to participate in the political process. In 1952, 13 women were elected to the state assembly including one member from the Scheduled Castes – Saraswati Chowdhary, the first Dalit woman to be elected to a position of power in Bihar. All elected members belonged to the Congress Party (Election Commission of India, 1957). There was a significant increase in the number of women who won in the next elections in 1957; 46 women contested in the elections of which 34 won (10.7 per cent). However, the winning percentage of women contestants was a whopping 73.9 per cent. This explains that only those women contested in the state assembly elections who had strong party support. In all 1,393 candidates fought in the elections in 1957 of which 46 were women (3.01 per cent). The total poll percentage stood at 41.32 per cent in 264 constituencies. All elected women MLAs belonged to the Congress while one belonged to the Praja Socialist Party. This also shows that only the most confident parties allowed women to contest on their tickets.

In the next elections in 1962, 1,483 men and 46 women contested. Of these 46 men and 25 women emerged victorious. There were 318 seats at stake. So, in comparison to the last elections, the share of women reduced from 10.7 per cent to 7.9 per cent. The social profile of these women shows that six belonged to SCs and two to STs while the rest belonged to the general category. Two women represented religious minorities, and like the elections in 1957, one woman (Elsie Augier, 1957–69) belonged to the nominated Anglo-Indian category (Election Commission of India, 1962). Sumitra Devi was first elected to the Bihar legislative assembly in 1952, and in 1963 she became the first woman cabinet minister in Bihar.

The elections held in 1967 proved detrimental to the cause of women's representation in the Bihar legislative assembly. Women constituted 41.09

Table 18.1 Women in assembly elections in Bihar (1952–2015)

Year	Total seats	Total contestants	Polling per centage male (%)	Polling per centage female (%)	Total polling per centage (%)	Avg. no. of contestants per seat	Female contestants	% of the female contestant to total contestant	Female won	% Of win to total seats	Total Dalit women	Total tribal women	Total minority women
1952	318	1594	NA	NA	39.51	5	NA	NA	13	4.1	1	0	1
1957	318	1393	NA	NA	41.32	4	46	3.30	34	10.7	3	0	0
1962	318	1529	54.94	32.47	44.47	5	46	3.01	25	7.9	6	2	1
1967	318	2025	60.82	41.09	51.51	6	29	1.43	11	3.5	2	0	3
1969	318	671	62.86	41.43	52.79	2	46	6.86	5	1.6	1	0	0
1972	318	2133	63.06	41.3	52.79	7	45	2.11	13	4.1	0	0	2
1977	318	2994	61.49	38.32	50.51	9	96	3.21	13	4.1	2	1	0
1980	318	3002	66.57	46.86	57.28	9	77	2.56	14	4.4	0	1	1
1985	324	3352	65.81	45.63	56.27	10	103	3.07	15	4.6	2	1	0
1990	324	6482	69.63	53.25	62.04	20	147	2.27	13	4.0	3	0	0
1995	324	8388	67.13	55.8	61.79	26	263	3.14	13	4.0	3	3	0
2000	324	3941	70.71	53.28	62.57	12	189	4.80	17	5.2	2	0	0
2005(Feb.	243	3193	51.02	42.1	46.51	13	234	7.33	23	9.5	3	0	0
2005(Oct.)	243	3193	50.89	40.8	45.85	13	138	4.32	27	11.1	5	0	0
2010	243	3523	51.12	54.49	52.67	14	307	8.71	36	14.8	4	0	1
2015	243	3450	53.32	60.48	56.66	14	273	7.91	28	11.5	7	1	0

Note: The list gives names of 10 women members (http://vidhansabha.bih.nic.in/pdf/ex%20mla/4.pdf).
The common list (all sexes) for the same period has 11 women members based on gender and cultural markers of name and a prefixed Hindi honorific word for women. The women specific list has missed the name of Susheela Kapoor at no.129 (common list) from Kishanganj constituency (http://vidhansabha.bih.nic.in/pdf/ex%20mla/4.pdf). Discrepancies exist for other years as well. We use the figures given in the common list.
Source: Election Commission Statistical Reports on the Bihar Assembly (the Bihar vidhansabhawebsite).

THE LANDSCAPE OF INADEQUATE ASSERTION

per cent of the electorate, but only 29 women contested when the total number of candidates was 2,025. Compared to the 1962 elections they could win only ten seats.

However, two were elected from parties other than the dominant Congress Party and one each was elected from the Samyukta (United) Socialist Party and the Praja Socialist Party. Minority women were absent from the assembly as were women from tribal and Dalit backgrounds (Election Commission of India, 1967). After the collapse of Chief Minister Bhola Paswan Shastri's government, mid-term elections were held in Bihar in 1969. However, enthusiasm among contestants had lessened as the number of contestants dropped to 671 compared to 2,025 in 1967. There were 46 women contestants of which only four won (Election Commission of India, 1969).

There were elections again in 1972. This time 45 women contested the elections (2,133 candidates). The maximum number of women contestants hovered around 45–46 despite changes in their demographic profile after two decades. The only exception was 1967 when 13 women made it to the state assembly. The elections in 1977 were a repeat for women as the number of women contestants who won remained the same. However, there was an almost 200 per cent increase in the number of women challenging their male counterparts (2,994). Women representatives from religious minorities despite their significant numbers in Bihar's population did not contest or win any seats, and one tribal and two Dalit women won the assembly elections (Election Commission of India, 1972).

In the assembly elections held in 1980, 77 women contested, which was a dramatic decrease in their numbers. Only 14 women won including in by-elections held for vacated seats. One noteworthy development was that for the first time an independent woman candidate became an MLA, Muktidani Sumbrai from Chaibasa (presently in Jharkhand).

In 1985 voting was held for 324 seats, 103 women were in the political fray but only 15 won. The period 1985–90 was full of upheavals, and 1990 became a historical year for the cause of social justice and socio-political transformation in the state. The elections shifted the pivot of power from upper-caste dominance to lower-caste leaders and Lalu Prasad Yadav – coming from a lower-caste background – became the Chief Minister for the first time. But social justice for women seemed a distant dream. The number of male power-seekers was 6,482 while women totalled just 147. From 1990 to 2000 there was a similar trend in terms of women's representation in the state assembly (10–15 MLAs).

In February 2005, the assembly was dissolved because of no clear mandate and elections were held again in October 2005. In February 2005, there were 234 women candidates (total 3,193 candidates or 7.33 per cent). More women won as compared to previous elections, but they were still far behind their earlier record of 34 MLAs in 1957. In a 243-strong assembly, women's share was around 10 per cent (Election Commission of India, 2005). In the next elections there were 3,523 contestants of which 307 were women. This was the highest percentage of women candidates so far.

In the 2010 elections, 36 women were elected breaking all previous records (more than 15 per cent women were victorious). Five Dalit women and two from minority communities won in the elections. Muslim males won 24 seats, while Muslim women candidates won only two seats (Election Commission of India, 2010).

In the assembly elections held in 2015 women surpassed men in the electorate in terms of percentages – 60.48 per cent (of total female votes) against just 53.32 per cent (of total male votes). This is exciting because women comprise just 87.39 per cent of the total male electorate in Bihar.

Women missing in parties' organizational structures

Women have not been able to penetrate intra-party organizational structures (Verma and Yadav,1996). Women as a monolithic identity have not been able to mobilize themselves enough to influence decision-making processes in the political parties to coerce them to allocate tickets to more women. It is noteworthy that they have been turning out in huge numbers to vote in Bihar since 2010 and are often hailed as the 'silent' force behind Chief Minister Nitish Kumar's re-election in the 2015 assembly elections. There were over 3 crore women voters in Bihar, forming 47 per cent of the voting population as per the Election Commission's data for the 2019 Lok Sabha elections. Currently, there are just three women MPs and only 28 MLAs in the 243-member state assembly.

In a very politically dynamic state, women are still under-represented as political representatives and candidates in state- and national-level elections. Female voters' turnout surpassed that of men in the last few elections for the Lok Sabha as well as the state assembly. While political parties have been wooing the women's vote bank with several schemes, they have failed to give proper political representation to women who constitute nearly half of the voting population in Bihar. Women are acting as voters and not victors.

In the 2015 state assembly elections major parties for which data is available allotted roughly 10 per cent of the seats to women and the winning percentage of women contestants stood at around 8 per cent. Women hardly seem to have any prospect of winning without mobilization provided by party banners. While having the largest number of seats among all the parties, BJP has the lowest winning percentages.

Table 18.2 gives the position of women candidates in various political parties in three assembly elections in the state between 2000 and 2010.

THE LANDSCAPE OF INADEQUATE ASSERTION

Table 18.2 Women candidates in state assembly elections (2000–10)

	BJP	INC	CPI	CPM	NCP	BSP	JDU	RJD	LJP	TOTAL
2000										
Total seats on which party contested	168	324	153	107	5	249	87	293	NA	1386
No. of women	9	24	5	7	1	11	2	17	NA	76
%	5.4	7.4	3.3	6.5	20	4.4	2.3	5.8	NA	6.1
2005										
Total seats on which party contested	102	36	35	10	8	212	139	175	203	920
No. of women	9	1	2	0	0	7	16	13	19	67
%	8.8	2.8	5.7	0	0	3.3	11.5	7.4	9.4	5.4
2010										
Total seats on which party contested	102	243	56	30	171	239	141	168	75	1225
No. of women	13	38	4	3	19	15	24	12	11	139
%	12.8	15.6	7.1	10	11.1	6.3	17	7.1	14.7	11.3

Source: Election Commission Statistical Reports on Bihar Assembly Elections and data from the VidhanSabhawebsite.

Criminalization of politics

Elections in Bihar are a very costly affair in which criminals have an edge. Emerging trends signify that Indian democracy is transforming into a plutocracy. Bihar politics is no exception, and women seem disadvantageous in this context. Plutocracy is intimately coupled with criminality. In February 2020, a Supreme Court judgement took note of the criminalization in Indian politics and held that, in 2004, 24 per cent of the Members of Parliament had criminal cases pending against them; in 2009, that went up to 30 per cent; in 2014 to 34 per cent; and in 2019 as many as 43 per cent of MPs had criminal cases pending against them (Sastry, 2020).

In the Bihar assembly elected in 2015, 140 elected MLAs had criminal charges against them. Of these, 34 belonged to the Rashtriya Janata Dal, 27 to the Janata Dal-United, 19 to the BJP, and 11 to the Congress (*The Statesman*, 2018). The Association for Democratic Reforms (ADR) in its report dated October 9, 2020, analysed financial and criminal charges against MPs/MLAs and candidates since 2005 (2005 to 2015 for Bihar assembly elections and 2005 to 2019 for the Bihar Lok Sabha elections) and found that 151 (19 per cent) of the 779 women candidates who contested elections in Bihar since 2005 declared criminal cases against them and 94 (12 per cent) declared serious cases against them. The figures for male candidates were 31 per cent and 21 per cent respectively (ADR/Bihar Election Watch, 2020a). The report further stated that candidates with a clean record had a 5 per cent chance of winning an election (without criminal charges declared) against 15 per cent chances of winning for those with criminal records.

The average assets of the candidates analysed since 2005 was Rs 1.09 crore, and the average assets of all MPs and MLAs analysed since 2005 was Rs 2.25 crore. Of the 240 sitting MLAs studied, 160 (67 per cent) were crorepatis. Of these, 51 (74 per cent) out of the 69 MLAs were from JD(U), 51 (64 per cent) of the 80 MLAs from RJD, 33 (61 per cent) of the 54 MLAs from BJP, 17 (68 per cent) of the 25 MLAs from INC, two (100 per cent) of two MLAs from LJP, one (100 per cent) of one MLA from the All India Majlis-e-Ittehadul Muslimeen, and five (100 per cent) of five MLAs were independents who declared their assets valued at more than Rs 1 crore (ADR/Bihar Election Watch (2020b).

ADR also observed that average assets of male contestants since 2005 were Rs 1.07 crore while for female candidates they were Rs 1.37 crore. Average assets of men MPs/MLAs since 2005 were Rs 2.17 crore, and the average assets of women MPs/MLAs were Rs 2.98 crore (ADR/Bihar Election Watch, 2020a).

In its report dated September 14, 2020, ADR said that in the 2015 assembly MLA Poonam Devi Yadav (from JD-U, Khagaria constituency) had the highest declared assets of Rs 41.34 crore. Two women MLAs were on the list of top 10 MLAs with the largest assets in the same assembly. Two women were also in the list of 10 MLAs with the lowest assets (ADR/Bihar Election Watch, 2020b).

Another interesting aspect is the co-relationship between money and winnability. Bihar Election Watch (BEW), ADR's state unit reported that in the Bihar assembly elections in 2015, 23 per cent or 56 of the 243 MLAs were those who declared the highest assets among the contesting candidates and their average assets were almost Rs 8 crore. Twenty per cent (60 seats) of the contestants with the second-highest declared assets won the elections and their average assets were Rs 2 crore. Further, about 33 per cent (79 MLAs) were those whose assets were at the third or fourth position among all the contesting candidates in their constituencies.

Another analysis points out that only 0.1 per cent of the candidates with assets less than Rs 10 lakh managed to win the elections (*The Times of India*, April 1, 2016). In Bihar's 2010 elections 214 crorepatis contested for the assembly seats with the Congress fielding 53, RJD 47, and JD-U 35 (*The Times of India*, November 17, 2010). This pattern compels one to make the point that the richest among the rich have an edge over other candidates and the probability of winning elections goes down as the assets declared fall.

Women achievers from Bihar

Meira Kumar hails from Bihar and contested on a Congress ticket in 1985 from the Bijnor Lok Sabha constituency and defeated two prominent leaders Ram Vilas Paswan (Janata Dal) and Mayawati (BSP). Apart from being an AICC general secretary in 1992, she became union minister for social justice and empowerment in 2009 and later minister for water resources. Kumar created history in India's Parliament when she was elected as the first woman Speaker of the Lok Sabha (2009–14).

Sumitra Devi, one of the most active women leaders in the freedom struggle in Bihar, belonged to the Indian National Congress; she is Meira Kumar's mother-in-law. She was first elected to the Bihar legislative assembly in 1952 from Tarapur constituency Munger and became the first woman cabinet minister in the Bihar assembly.

Tarkeshwari Sinha was one of the youngest MPs at 26 when she was elected to the first Lok Sabha and become the first female deputy finance minister in the union cabinet led by Jawaharlal Nehru in 1958–64. She started her political career as the president of the Bihar students Congress, turned a bitter critic of Indira Gandhi and supported the Congress Party's old guard. She retired from politics after suffering two successive defeats in 1977 from Begusarai and in November 1978 from Samastipur.

Ram Dulari Sinha was elected twice to the Bihar assembly and became a cabinet minister. She was elected to the third, seventh, and eighth Lok Sabhas and was a union minister of state holding various portfolios. She was elected the vice chairman of the International Labour Organization and was appointed the Governor of Kerala from 1988 to 1990. Her husband, Thakur Jugal Kishore Sinha, was known as the 'father of the cooperative movement' in India.

Kishori Sinha was elected to the seventh and eighth Lok Sabhas. She was married to the former Chief Minister of Bihar Satyendra Narayan Sinha. Krisha Shahi was elected to the seventh, eighth, and ninth Lok Sabhas. Before entering the Lok Sabha she was elected to the Bihar legislative assembly. She was minister of state holding various portfolios like human resource development, education and culture, and water resources.

Shyama Singh came from a political family and was elected to the thirteenth Lok Sabha. Her mother Madhuri Singh was also a two-term Member of Parliament from Purnea. Rama Devi was elected to the twelfth Lok Sabha on an RJD ticket and to the fifteenth, sixteenth, and seventeenth Lok Sabhas on a BJP ticket.

Some other women made a brief appearance on the political scene like Putul Kumari who was elected to the fifteenth Lok Sabha in a by-election as an independent and Lovely Anand (Samata Party) elected to the tenth Lok Sabha. Shahdun Nisha (CPI) was elected to the Bihar legislative assembly from Ramgarh in a 1973 by-poll. She is the widow of CPI leader Manjur Hassan Khan.

Rabri Devi became the first woman Chief Minister of Bihar on July 25, 1997, and has served three times as the Chief Minister of the state, all in all, for more than seven years. Despite her limitations of being less educated, she learnt the rules of the game and left her mark on state politics. It is interesting that while women in Bihar are voting more than men, Rabri Devi projects her son Tejaswi Yadav as the chief ministerial candidate of her party RJD.

Misa Bharti is a member of the Rajya Sabha. She is a dynastic scion and could be the only MP in India to have both parents as former chief ministers.

Women at the grassroots

While women in decision-making bodies at the state level are not very visible, women in the institutions of local government in rural Bihar have brought about significant changes. Provision of 50 per cent reservations for women in Bihar's Panchayati Raj Institutions (PRIs) introduced in 2006 has brought a silent revolution in the state. Bihar is at the top of the list of states in the country which has the highest number of women representatives in panchayats with women occupying more than 54 per cent of the positions in the 9,040 panchayats in the state. Out of the 130,091 elected panchayat representatives in 9,040 panchayats in Bihar, the number of women representatives was 70,400 or 54.12 per cent (NDTV, 2014).

The socio-cultural feudalist forces and the prevailing political atmosphere in Bihar in general and in rural areas in particular do not allow women to have an easy entry into politics. Caste has been an important factor for mobilizing political support in Bihar, and even during the freedom movement, caste played a key role in deciding the formation and features of political leadership in the state (Jha, 1967). Initially, the upper castes faced political rivalry among themselves (during those times, political rights were dependent on property and educational qualifications and people from non-upper castes were almost negligible to be of any influence in state politics), early Congress leadership consisted of anglicized Kayasthas (Chaudhary, 1964). Their dominance in the 1940s–1960s was challenged by Bhumihars and Rajputs.

The Congress leadership prominently reflected an upper-caste character till the 1967 elections to the state assembly. Vote bank politics and caste-based political polarization found new nectar in universal franchise. Middle and lower landed castes started taking advantage of the Green Revolution and education and formed alliances for the 'ethnicization' of backward castes (Jaffrelot, 2000). Land, caste, and power are the three interdependent variables through which we can understand the nature of dominance of a particular group or persons in Bihar's rural society. The influence of the dominant castes has pervaded Bihar's society.

Patriarchal values and a feudalistic approach are not in agreement with the ambitions of women and the other marginalized groups. Women in Bihar lack control over economic resources, wealth, and property and are dependent on male family and society members. On the other hand, elections in Bihar are a very costly affair. Due to lack of resources, the shadow of crime in politics and a mélange of various socio-cultural factors, women cannot freely participate in politics in the state. Reports and analyses of elections in Bihar by ADR and Bihar Election Watch give glimpses of the nexus between crime, wealth, and major political players in the state.

Chandra (2016) in her landmark study on dynastic tendencies in Indian politics both at the state and national levels demonstrates the impact of dynasts in assemblies and Parliament at around 25 per cent which increased to 30 per cent in the 2019 elections for the Lok Sabha. Some perceive a kind of resilience (Ghosh and Jha, 2019) in the dynastic phenomenon in Indian politics under the garb of democracy. Some, however, see an affirmative side of dynasties, paradoxically an inclusive role of making marginalized communities, 'backward castes and women' empowered (Deo and Chawla, 2017). It is also pointed out that women candidates are more 'dynastic' than male candidates. Parties tend to select their women candidates from within existing political families, as they still perceive that fielding women candidates constitutes a risk (Verniers and Jaffrelot, 2019). There are relatively discernible traits like 'cult worship', 'charisma', and 'celebrity over substance' prevailing since long in Indian politics.

In Bihar, the NDA won 39 of the 40 Lok Sabha seats in the seventeenth Lok Sabha in 2019. In more than 25 per cent of the seats, the NDA winners are either dynasts or belonged to political families where other family members had been MPs or MLAs (Table 18.3).

Table 18.3 gives the details of the extension of the political networks of dynastic families. This tendency pervades all parties and has given rise to many political families during the last seven decades of state politics.

When Lalu Prasad Yadav was the Chief Minister of Bihar, he insulated nepotism in state politics. His wife became Chief Minister and son the deputy Chief Minister. His brothers-in-law Subhash Yadav and Sadhu Yadav held powerful portfolios during his chief ministerial tenures (18.4).

Women are neglected in this complex mess called state politics. They can enter under the patronage of a leader as protégés. In the last parliamentary elections in 2019, NDA gave tickets to 13 women candidates from upper castes, 12 candidates from the OBC community, seven candidates from extremely Backward Castes, six from the SC/ST communities, and only one candidate from the Muslim community. The Congress-RJD Mahagathbandhan gave five tickets to women candidates.

Table 18.3 Dynastic trends in Bihar politics

S.no.	Name of MP	Patriarch/relative/matriarch	Party	Status
1	Chirag Paswan	Ram Vilas Paswan	LJP	Won
2	Ravi Shankar Prasad	Thakur Prasad	BJP	Won
3	Pashupati Kumar Paras	Ram Vilas Paswan	LJP	Won
4	Ram Chandra Paswan	Ram Vilas Paswan	LJP	Won
5	Veena Devi,	MLC Dinesh Singh	JD (U)	Won
6	Chandan Kumar	Surajbhan Singh	LJP	Won
7	Kavita Singh	Jagmato Devi	JD (U)	Won
8	Sushil Singh	Ram Naresh Singh	BJP	Won
9	Sanjay Jaiswal	Madan Jaiswal	BJP	Won
10	Ashok Yadav	Hukumdeo Narayan Yadav	BJP	Won
11	Ajay Nishad	Capt. Jai Narayan Nishad	BJP	Won
12	Misa Bharti	Lalu Prasad	RJD	Lost
13	Pappu Singh	Madhuri Singh	INC	Lost
14	Meira Kumar	Jagjivan Ram	INC	Lost

Source: Tabulated by the author from an article in *The Deccan Herald*.

Table 18.4 Dynastic trends in state politics

Patriarch	Name	Relationship	Other relations	Links within the state or with political dynasties out of state
Lalu Prasad Yadav	Tej Pratap Yadav	Elder son	Bihar's ex-CM Daroga Prasad Rai	Ex-Health Minister of Bihar [9]
	Tejaswi Yadav	Younger son		Ex-Deputy Chief Minister of Bihar
	Misa Bharti	1st daughter	Married a software engineer Shailesh Kumar in 1999 [10]	Misa Bharti, Rajya Sabha MP
	Rohini Acharya	2nd daughter	Rao Samaresh Singh	Rao Ranvijay Singh of Arwal
	Ragini Yadav	4th daughter	Jitendra Yadav in 2012	Jitendra is SP's MLC
	Hema Yadav	5th daughter	Vineet Yadav	
	Anushka Rao	6th daughter	Capt. Ajay Singh Yadav, INC	Ajay is ex Power Minister of Haryana SP's ex-Lok Sabha & the grand-nephew of Mulayam Singh Yadav
	Rajlaxmi Singh	7th daughter	Tej Pratap Singh Yadav	

Source: Compiled by the author from different sources (Biplab Majumder @MyInsights June 30, 2019; Ashraf, 2018; India Today Desk, 2019).

Women in non-formal politics

Women have participated enthusiastically in non-formal politics. Women in rural areas have protested against sexual exploitation by dominant-caste landholders and have been demanding the right to own land and minimum wages. In some areas of rural Bihar such as Bhojpur, Jehanabad, Gaya, and Patna districts, the Naxalite movement attracted women at the grassroots level. Women were very active in the struggle for land against the chief priest of the Bodh Gaya temple and in the JP movement. However, they did not get recognition despite their participation.

Women have also participated in activities of nationally recognized as well as locally formed trade unions and associations to protest against the state's unfair policies. Women form a large part of the MGNREGA workers' union, accredited social health (ASHA) workers, anganwadi workers, and mid-day meal workers' unions as members, workers, and activists besides being closely related to the All India Trade Union Congress (AITUC), the Centre of Indian Trade Union (CITU), the Indian National Union Congress (INTUC), the All India Central Council of Trade Unions (AICCTU), the Trade Union Coordination Centre (TUCC), and the Hind Mazdoor Sabha (HMS). Women have demanded 'worker' status in all schemes (central and state government). The All India Progressive Women's Association (AIPWA) is an active organization that brings women-related issues to the notice of wider civil society. It has played a key role in bringing to light the plight of girls in shelter homes in Muzaffarpur and other places.

The state government has introduced a seven-point (*saatnischay*) agenda for development, one of which is for women – Arakshit Rozgar Mahila ka Adhikar (reservation in employment is every woman's right). The Hunar programme (skill development programme) was launched in 2008 by the Government of Bihar and the National Institute of Open Schooling (NIOS) for enabling girls from minority and socially vulnerable groups in Bihar to develop skills for generating incomes, sustaining families, and self-reliance. The Mukhyamantri Balika Cycle Yojana is aimed at increasing the number of schoolgirls in educational institutions. The Mukhyamantri Kanya Utthan Yojana is an ambitious scheme. It makes provisions for a girl child's health and education. The government has also prohibited liquor and banned dowry as well as mass child marriages. The Kishori Balika scheme seeks to provide nutrition to non-school-going girls in the age group of 11–18 years.

Akshar Aanchal promotes literacy among women from the Mahadalit, minorities, and the extremely backward communities in the state. Mukhyamantri Kanya Vivah scheme provides financial assistance to poor families for the marriages of their daughters and encourages marriage registration, thwarting child marriages. The Mukhyamantri Girl Child Protection scheme aims to prevent foeticide and encourage the birth of girl children and birth registration. The objective of the Mukhyamantri Nari Shakti scheme is helping women who opt for inter-caste marriages.

Conclusion

Despite the progress made by the state and the initiatives taken by the state government, women in Bihar are far from experiencing gender equality. There are hindrances of casteism and social norms, electoral and political corruption, violence and muscle power in politics, gender discrimination, using female attendance as a proxy, and huge expenditure and unethical practices during elections. The under-representation of women in governance and decision-making bodies is a formidable obstacle in the working of democracy. Forward-looking policies or reservations will help in removing this obstacle to a great extent.

Bibliography

ADR/Bihar Election Watch (2020a, October 9). *Analysis of Criminal and Financial Background Details of Candidates and MPs/MLAs since 2005 in Bihar.* Available at: https://adrindia.org/download/file/fid/8283, accessed on January 13, 2021.

—— (2020b, September 14). *Bihar Assembly Election 2015 Analysis of Criminal Background, Financial, Education, Gender and other Details of Sitting MLAs.* Available at: https://adrindia.org/download/file/fid/8246, accessed on January 13, 2021.

Ashraf, A. (2018, November 20). *Why Tejashwi Yadav and Akhilesh Yadav Represent a New Trend in How Dynastic Politics Works in India.* Scroll.in. Available at: https://scroll.in/article/902433/why-tejashwi-yadav-and-akhilesh-yadav-represent-a-new-trend-in-how-dynastic-politics-works-in-india, accessed on January 13, 2020.

Bansal, Aanchal (2019). 'Leading the Way: In Bihar, Women form Majority in 25 of 40 LS Seats', *The Economic Times*, April 19. Available at: https://economictimes.indiatimes.com/news/politics-andnation/leading-the-way-in-bihar-women-form-majority-in-25-of-40-ls-seats/printarticle/68842215.cms, accessed on January 13, 2020.

Bihar Government (2019). 'Women & Girls in Bihar: Taking Stock, Looking Ahead, Gender Report Card – 2019'. Available at: http://www.c3india.org/uploads/news/Bihar_Gender_Report_Card_2019_28th_Jan_2020_FOR_WEB_FILE.pdf and https://www.ideasforindia.in/topics/human-development/can-double-fortified-salt-in-school-mid-day-meals-help-reduce-anaemia1.html, accessed on July 19, 2020.

Biplab Majumder @MyInsights (2019, June 30). Dynastic Politics and Indian Society. *Times of India Blog.* Available at: https://timesofindia.indiatimes.com/readersblog/myinsights/dynastic-politics-and-indian-society-4374/, accessed on March 17, 2020.

Census 2011.co. (n.d.). *Bihar Population Sex Ratio in Bihar Literacy rate data 2011–2020.* Available at: https://www.census2011.co.in/census/state/bihar.html, accessed on July 5, 2020.

Chandra, Kanchan (2016). *Democratic Dynasties: State, Party and Family in Contemporary Indian Politics.* New Delhi: Cambridge University Press.

Chaudhary, V. C. P. (1964). *The Creation of Modern Bihar.* Patna: Yogeshwar Press.

Deo, Neelam and Arjun Chawla (2017). *The Paradox of Dynastic Politics in India in Democracy under Threat.* New Delhi: Oxford University Press.

Election Commission of India (1957). *Statistical Report on General Election, 1957 To The Legislative Assembly Of Bihar Election,* https://eci.gov.in/files/file/3887 -bihar-1957/?do=download. accessed on July 15, 2020

Election Commission of India (1962). *Statistical Report on General Election, 1962 To The Legislative Assembly Of Bihar Election,* https://eci.gov.in/files/file/3888 -bihar-1962/?do=download. accessed on July 15, 2020

Election Commission of India (1967). *Statistical Report on General Election, 1967 To The Legislative Assembly Of Bihar Election,* https://eci.gov.in/files/file/3889 -bihar-1967/?do=download accessed on July 15, 2020

Election Commission of India (1969). *Statistical Report on General Election, 1969 To The Legislative Assembly Of Bihar Election,* https://eci.gov.in/files/file/3890 -bihar-1969/?do=download accessed on July 15, 2020

Election Commission of India (1972). *Statistical Report on General Election, 1972 To The Legislative Assembly Of Bihar Election,* https://eci.gov.in/files/file/3892 -bihar-1972/?do=download accessed on July 15, 2020

Election Commission of India (2010). *Statistical Report on General Election, 2010 To The Legislative Assembly Of Bihar Election,* https://eci.gov.in/files/file/3903 -bihar-2010/?do=download accessed on July 15, 2020

Election Commission of India (n.d.). *Statistical Report on General Election,2015 To The Legislative Assembly Of Bihar.* https://Ceobihar.Nic.In. Available at: https://ceobihar.nic.in/PDF/Stat_Assem_GE_Bihar_2015.pdf, accessed on June 11, 2020.

Ghosh, Ambar Kumar and Avishek Jha (2019). 'What Explains the Enduring Resilience of Political Dynasties in India?', *The Diplomat,* July 9. Available at: https://thediplomat.com/2019/07/what-explains-the-enduring-resilience-of -political-dynasties-in-india/, accessed on May 11, 2020.

Jaffrelot, Christophe (2000). 'Sanskritization vs. Ethnicization in India: Changing Identities and Caste Politics before Mandal', *Asian Survey,* 40 (5), 756–766.

Jha, Chetkar (1967).'Caste in Bihar Politics', in Iqbal Narain (ed.), *State Politics in India.* Meerut: Meenakshi Publication.

Khushboo Balani, Indiaspend.com (2017, January 6). *Bihar Has the Most Illiterate People in India, but Spends the Least Per Elementary School Student.* Scroll.in. Available at: https://scroll.in/article/825848/bihar-has-the-most-illiterate-people -in-india-but-spends-the-least-per-elementary-school-student, accessed on June 18, 2020.

Kumar, Ashutosh (ed.) (2011). *Rethinking State Politics in India: Regions within Regions.* New Delhi: Routledge.

Kumar, A. (2019). 'End of Dynastic Politics in Bihar? Not Really', *Deccan Herald,* May 26. Available at: https://www.deccanherald.com/lok-sabha-election-2019/

end-of-dynastic-politics-in-bihar-not-really-736234.html, accessed on June 16, 2020.

List of Honorable Members elected to Bihar Legislative Assembly (n.d.). Available at: http://vidhansabha.bih.nic.in/pdf/ex%20mla/1.pdf, accessed on June 8, 2020 and http://vidhansabha.bih.nic.in/pdf/ex%20mla/4.pdf, accessed June 7, 2020.

Mishra, M. (2015). 'Bihar Elections: Is the State's Crime-politics Nexus Cracking?' *Business Standard*, October 9. Available at: https://www.business-standard .com/article/elections/bihar-elections-is-the-state-s-crime-politics-nexus-cracking -115100900057_1.html, accessed on June 6, 2020.

NDTV (2014). 'Bihar ki Panchayato me Mahilaon ka Pratinidhitva Sarvadhik (Hindi)' *NDTV India*, 7 February. Available at: https://khabar.ndtv.com/news/ zara-hatke/bihar-panchyats-have-most-women-representatives-379918, accessed on May 11, 2020.

Office of the Director of Census Operations, Patna (2011). *Census of India 2011*. Available at: Https://Censusindia.Gov.In/. https://censusindia.gov.in/2011-prov -results/data_files/bihar/Provisional%20Population%20Totals%202011-Bihar .pdf, accessed July 5, 2020.

Office of the Registrar General & Census Commissioner, India (n.d.a). *Area And Population*. Census of India. Available at: https://censusindia.gov.in/census_and _you/area_and_population.aspx, accessed July 5, 2020.

Office of the Registrar General & Census Commissioner, India (n.d.b). *State of Literacy*. Available at: Https://Censusindia.Gov.In/, accessed on July 5, 2020 and https://censusindia.gov.in/2011-prov-results/data_files/india/Final_PPT_2011 _chapter6.pdf, accessed on May 11, 2020.

Pai, Sudha (2000). *State Politics: New Dimensions*. Delhi: Shipra.

Sastry, T. (2020). 'Owning up to Criminalisation in Politics', *The Hindu*, July 9. Available at: https://www.thehindu.com/opinion/lead/owning-up-to -criminalisation-in-politics/article32035186.ece, accessed on May 18, 2021.

Singh, M. P. (2012). 'State Politics in India', *Astha Bharti Dialogue*, 14.

The Hindu (2019, May 26). *43% Newly-elected Lok Sabha MPs Have Criminal Record: ADR*. Available at: https://www.thehindu.com/elections/lok-sabha-2019 /43-newly-elected-lok-sabha-mps-have-criminal-record-adr/article27253649.ece, accessed on July 11, 2020.

The Statesman (2018, September 27). *122% Rise in Candidates with Criminal Cases in Bihar*. Available at: https://www.thestatesman.com/cities/122-rise-in -candidates-with-criminal-cases-in-bihar-1502689740.html, accessed on June 19, 2020.

The Times of India (2010, November 17). *214 `crorepatis' in Poll Fray*. Available at: https://timesofindia.indiatimes.com/city/patna/214-crorepatis-in-poll-fray/ articleshowprint/6937897.cms, accessed on June 19, 2020.

——— (2016, April 1). *50% Bihar MLAs among Top 2 Richest Candidates*. Available at: https://timesofindia.indiatimes.com/city/patna/50-Bihar-MLAs -among-top-2-richest-candidates/articleshowprint/51641840.cms, accessed on June 11, 2020.

UN India (2018). *Gender Equality: Women's Economic Empowerment*. Available at: https://in.one.un.org/unibf/gender-equality/, accessed on June 18, 2020.

Verma, Ravindra Kumar and Gyanendra Kr. Yadav (1996). 'Women in Bihar Politics', *Economic and Political Weekly*, 31 (15), 935–937.

Verniers, Gilles and Christophe Jaffrelot (2019). 'Explained: Why So Many MPs Are Dynasts', *Indian Express*, May 27. Available at: https://indianexpress.com/article/explained/experts-explain-why-so-many-mps-are-dynasts-lok-sabha-election-bjp-congress-rahul-gandhi-5749570/, accessed on June 10, 2020.

19

GENDER DYNAMICS IN ELECTORAL POLITICS IN ASSAM

Pallabi Medhi and Sandhya Goswami

Introduction

Women's struggle to earn their space in Assam politics has not changed much even today despite their key role in the social life of the state over the years. What is presently seen is their increased participation as voters in the electoral process. Women voters have given a decisive edge to electoral outcomes in the state. This is evident from the fact that women voters surpassed their male counterparts by a margin of 0.3 per cent in the assembly elections in 2016. Even in the recent assembly elections in 2021, women's vote share was less by only 0.1 per cent as compared to the male vote share. With the growth of the multi-party system in the state, since the late 1980s political parties have increasingly sought women's electoral support. The popularity of welfare schemes can also be regarded as a key factor in explaining an increase in women voters. And yet women stand at the periphery of the democratic process in the state.

A new paradox

The state is faced with a paradox of a high rate of participation of women in the electoral process and poor representation in the legislative assembly and Parliament. This paradox raises some basic questions concerning why women continue to lack effective political power in the political process in the state. What are the structural obstacles which women fail to address for desired positions in politics? What is the relationship between women and political parties? How useful are quotas in increasing women's representation within parties as well as parties' commitment to eliminating gender inequalities?

The question of women's space in the public sphere (that is, the state assembly and Parliament) has to be seen in the backdrop of the socio-cultural diversity of the state. Diversity, which is more pronounced in the state, needs to be looked at more closely as women are not one homogeneous

DOI: 10.4324/9781003374862-20

335

group. Women are diverse in so far as their tribal and non-tribal identities are concerned. The state has displayed unity with respect to demands related to structural issues in the state. It is seen that when group-based identity like ethnic identity becomes a tool for pursuing various interests, including political ones, women are considered an important constituent not only for maintaining such identities but also for creating boundaries of such identities (Deka, 2019). Therefore, while recounting the gender relations between diverse ethnic communities, one needs to note the significant changes in the existing gender relations and women's position in the larger societal hierarchy in the state.

Women's cultural positioning continues to affect how they are treated in politics, in economic matters, and in educational institutions, all of which end up side-stepping women in social rankings. Culture as a people's way of life is the map through which women navigate social complexities. This phenomenon makes sense to us only within the context of culture such that the reality is always mediated, determined by the cultural worldview within which we operate (Uroh, 2003).

Major aspects of the cultures of various ethnic communities living in the state are biased against women. This symbolism is continued in the various processes of socialization, religious indoctrination, educational and economic institutions, and media and knowledge systems. Therefore, generalizations about women's higher positions in the state actually ignore women's relations to their communities based on norms and values specific to their society. These observations have been conditioned by a number of factors including the relative absence of the evils of dowry, child marriages, purdah, and bride burning along with the prevalence of matrilineality, a flexible marriage system, bride price, economic roles for women, and totem-based religious practices which contribute to the creation of a unique status for women in this region.

Women's status debatable

However, this kind of presentation is only one part of the interpretation, while the other part shows that women's status in these societies is a very debatable one, conditioned by the fact that women in the region face various other constraints. An exploration of the location of women in the ethnic discourse, by emphasizing on the notions of group rights and gender equality reflects women's limited access to the advantages generated by group-based rights if conceded to a demanding group. In fact, there is no denial of the responsibility of creating a more restrictive space for women channelized through provisions of such rights owing to the fact that the onus of maintaining community distinctiveness is largely seen as women's responsibility.

Women's crucial role in ethnic movements to give them a mass character and achieve collective rights remains severely restricted by the way the question of women's representation has been handled by political parties and institutions. Such a state of affairs makes the conflict between group rights and gender equality wide open (Deka, 2019).

Women in the state play a variety of economic roles such as planting, harvesting, carrying food grains home from the fields, fishing, collecting firewood and vegetables from the forest, and selling goods as vendors. These economic roles make them more visible in different spheres of life in their respective communities. Though women are seen as widely supporting subsistence and commercial agricultural activities alongside their male counterparts, decision-making is always a male prerogative. Customarily the role has been preserved for men among all the communities. Though tribal women are considered to be freer than their non-tribal counterparts, they are quite inexperienced in the empowerment domain. For example, the Karbis, a hill tribe of Assam excludes its female folk from the village administration. No society is more male dominated than that of the Karbis. The female occupies an inferior status. She has no share in administration (Bhattacharjee).

Community leadership of the various tribes is always in the hands of the men. The village communities are headed by a chief known differently by different tribes – such as *sar-the* by the Karbis, and this post is traditionally held by a man and not by a woman. The chief or the village headman is an influential person who is instrumental in taking community decisions. His aides are a coterie of men which means women are not allowed in the sphere of public life. As stated by Sir Charles Lyall (1972), 'Among the Karbis, the decision of disputes is the business of the village *me*, or council presided over by the *gaonburha (sar-the)*. The *me* is composed of all the male householders.' An identical practice exists among non-tribal communities where community decisions are taken by the village headman and his clique.

The multiple other communities living in Assam are tea tribes, immigrant Muslims and Hindus, and linguistic minorities who also customarily exclude women from the domain of community decision-making.

The tea tribe community in every tea estate of Assam is under the influence of a *sardar* (community leader) who plays a decisive role in shaping their opinions and choices. The immigrant communities mostly living in the *char* areas are guided by a *matabbar* (leader of the village) or *dewani* whose decisions on community issues are final. They are like feudal lords dominating the poor and illiterate masses and making them work according to their wishes (Hussain, 1997).

Each village in the *char* areas has one or more *matabbars* having their own followers. The political leaders usually approach these *matabbars* and *dewanis* during elections (Bokth, 2014).

Women's poor status in all spheres

This analysis is an indication of the patriarchal control of the political space where women are customarily excluded from the decision-making process in the state. Contrary to the popular belief of gender equality in Assam, the women actually enjoy a much lower status at all levels, micro, meso, and macro. Society is deeply ingrained with patriarchal values that get reflected in different crucial dimensions like sex ratio, literacy rate, employment opportunities, and violence against women.

The sex ratio has improved over the last decade in the state. It increased from 932/1,000 (2001 Census) to 958/1,000 (2011 Census). This improvement can partly be attributed to an improvement in female life expectancy. However, the child sex ratio has declined abysmally in the state over the last Census decade, and this is definitely going to have a telling effect on the sex ratio in the coming years. The child sex ratio which was 965 in 2001 declined to 962 in 2011. Among the Muslims, the child sex ratio is worse. According to the Human Development Report Assam (2014), it was 933 among Muslims which is much lower than the Hindus at 957. The low child sex ratio can be attributed to teenaged motherhood and high rate of maternal mortality.

Violence against women is on the rise in the state. According to the National Crime Records Bureau (NCRB) 2019, 'Assam has the highest crime rate against women, which is about three times more than the national figure' (*The Times of India*, 2020). As per the National Crime Records Bureau's Report on Crime in India (2019), out of the total 30,025 registered cases of crimes against women in Assam 1,773 were rape cases, 6,989 were kidnappings and abductions, 156 were dowry deaths (dowry is relatively a recent addition to the Assamese society), 4,619 were assaults with intent to outrage modesty, and 11,943 were cases of cruelty by husband and his relatives. Acts of violence against women are a key indicator of women's status in society.

Data presents a grim picture of the gender situation in the state if one goes through the status of women against the backdrop of the spatial and religious diversity in the state. Women in Assam are not a homogeneous unit. The picture of women belonging to the minorities, tea tribes, SCs, and *char* areas is a gloomy one compared to ethnic Assamese Hindu and indigenous Muslim women. The high rate of maternal mortality, teenaged motherhood, a plummeting child sex ratio, low literacy rates and educational attainments, and high rates of crimes against women are mostly witnessed by women from these spatial categories and minorities. Marriage in the age group of 7 to 10 years is not known, but in the adolescent age group of 12 to 16 years for girls and 16 to 20 for boys, it is widely prevalent. The Health and Family Welfare Department, Government of Assam (2018), shows that cases of underage marriages are mostly prevalent among the dwellers of

GENDER DYNAMICS IN ELECTORAL POLITICS IN ASSAM

char areas, tea belts, and some tribal areas (https://hfw.assam.gov.in), and as a direct side effect of this, the MMR is also very high, especially among the *char* and tea belt areas.

The location of women within the ethnic discourse in the state also reflects the limited access that they have to the advantages of group-based rights. Women's interests and gender justice are also undermined by the politics of ethnicity in the state.

Women and political parties

The national political parties in the state, mainly the BJP, Congress, and the Communist Party (Marxist), have approached women's issues in very different ways based on their ideological commitments. But these parties' ideologies have not determined their positions on gender inequalities. A regional party AGP and other ethnic parties' (Bodo People's Front and the All India Democratic Front) concern for gender equality is also no different. Political parties appear to be good at making promises to woo the women electorate because of their numerical strength. They are always seen fine-tuning their campaigns and policies to gain more women votes without caring to offer them a proportionate number of nominations. For example, in the recent assembly elections in 2021 only 74 (a mere 7.82 per cent) women candidates were in the fray out of the total 946 candidates. Party-wise nominations seemed to be biased against women candidates. Analysts, therefore, rightly point out that political parties are not making serious efforts to empower women.

Political parties continue to show prejudices against women not only in terms of seat allotments but also in their ranks and files and their decision-making collectives. Presence of a low percentage of women candidates in the institutions of governance clearly establishes the fact that most political parties only pay lip service to women's issues. Their commitment to gender justice stops far short of giving tickets to women candidates. Mobilization of women during the national movement by Gandhi partly shaped the backdrop against which mahila samitis were formed in Assam in 1915 which legitimized women's entry into the new public.

Hence, women remained active in the Congress-led nationalist movement in the state. During the Civil Disobedience movement in the 1930s, the founding secretary of the Assam Mahila Samiti (AMS) Chandra Prava Saikiani organized a mass uprising in Nowgong district of the state and asked women to respond to the call for freedom struggle. Although she and her friends were put behind bars, this did not fail to deter the spirit of the enthusiastic women from the state in participating in the movement for achieving freedom for the country. However, the decades after independence witnessed a remarkable decline in women's involvement in politics nationally and also in the state. This was at a time when there were outstanding women associated with experiences of the freedom movement in the state. Their long years of involvement in social and political work and experience in various fields (like providing relief to the victims during the 1950 Assam earthquake) would have made them suitable for taking responsible position in politics. But they were systematically ignored and bypassed by the political parties. There was no serious attempt to politically educate and bring women into active politics.

Political parties' apathy and indifference have resulted in fewer nominations of women candidates. No doubt, state-sponsored women's empowerment schemes, announcements of various policy packages for women, large-scale funding to non-governmental organizations working on women's issues by international agencies, establishment of women's study centres across the country (also in Assam), and more importantly, constitutional amendments extending reservations for women in local governments marked the sudden arrival of women in Indian politics (Deshpande, 2004).

A major change in the 2021 assembly elections saw the number of women contesting assembly elections dropping to 74 from 91 in 2016. The candidates who stood the highest chance of being elected were those nominated by major political parties. However, the number of women candidates nominated by the major parties in the state is markedly low. Party nominations matter a lot. But overall, the number of women candidates also matters (Rai and Spray, 2019, pp. 84-85). The nominations given to women candidates by national parties are significantly low in the state. The Congress Party's record in the initial period was not impressive. However, the party seems to have increased its tally to some extent in the later period. The BJP's record in the initial period was also significantly low; however, in subsequent assembly elections of 2006 and 2011 the numbers increased to some extent. But the number of women candidates came down in the 2016 and 2021 assembly elections (Tables 19.1A,B). The regional party AGP, despite having strong support of women in the historic Assam movement (1979–85) which eventually brought the party into power in the state in 1985 with a massive mandate, has failed to give due share to women.

The party offered merely four seats to women candidates in 1985 out of a total of 107, of which two women, Jyoshna Sonowal from Sadiya constituency and Rekha Rani Das Boro from Barama constituency won their seats. In the subsequent elections the party gave a similar raw deal to the women candidates. Other ethnic parties like the All India United Democratic Front (AIUDF) and Bodoland People's Front have also followed the same pattern.

Data shows that over time the number of women contesting elections has increased, but most of the candidates are still men. The number of women candidates nominated by the Congress is more than the BJP. On the other hand, other parties like AGP and the newly formed All India United Democratic Front (AIUDF) and BPF have a mixed record in nominating women candidates. In the 2011 assembly elections, 85 women candidates

Table 19.1(A) Women candidates nominated by major national political parties assembly elections (1952–2021)

Year	Party											
	INC		CPI		CPM		BJP		NCP		JNP	
	T.C.	F.C.	T.C.	F.C.	T.C.	F.C.	T.C.	F.C.	T.C.	F.C.	T.C.	F.C.
1952	92	4	18	0	–	–	–	–	–	–	–	–
1957	101	4	22	0	–	–	–	–	–	–	–	–
1962	103	4	31	0	–	–	–	–	–	–	–	–
1967	120	4	22	0	14	0	–	–	–	–	–	–
1972	114	8	28	0	20	0	–	–	–	–	–	–
1978	126	4	35	0	27	0	–	–	–	–	117	8
1983	109	2	25	0	24	0	–	–	–	–	–	–
1985	125	9	21	0	39	0	37	0	–	–	–	–
1991	125	7	37	0	29	0	48	2	–	–	–	–
1996	122	10	11	0	10	0	117	3	–	–	–	–
2001	126	15	19	1	22	1	46	1	62	4	–	–
2006	120	16	9	0	16	0	125	15	–	–	–	–
2011	126	20	17	0	17	1	120	12	35	6	–	–
2016	122	17	15	1	19	0	89	6	12	0	–	–
2021	92	9	–	–	–	–	91	7	–	–	–	–

Table 19.1(B) Women candidates nominated by major state political parties assembly elections (1985–2021)

Year	Party											
	AGP		BPF		AIUDF		AJP		Independent	Others		
	T. C.	F.C.	T.C.	F.C.	T.C.	F.C.	T.C.	F.C.	F.C.	F.C.		
1985	107	4	–	–	–	–	–	–	–	–		
1991	121	3	–	–	–	–	–	–	–	–		
1996	96	3	–	–	–	–	–	–	–	–		
2001	77	4	–	–	–	–	–	–	–	–		
2006	70	6	–	–	78	2	–	–	–	–		
2011	85	7	29	4	74	5	–	–	–	–		
2016	91	2	13	2	–	1	–	–	–	–		
2021	76	2	–	1	–	1	67	9	24	23		

Note: TC: Total contestants; FC: female contestants.
Source: Election Commission of India.

contested of which 14 got elected. The Congress put up 19 women, while the BJP had 12, AIUDF two, AGP seven, and BPPF only four.

In the 2016 assembly elections, 91 women candidates contested and eight got elected. The Congress put up 16 women candidates, the BJP only six. The Congress had a higher number of candidates, but over time BJP's number of women candidates has also increased slightly. On the other hand, AIUDF offered five seats to women and AGP and BPPF to two women candidates each. In the recent 2021 assembly elections in the state, the BJP had seven women candidates, the Congress nine, AGP two, AJP nine, AIUDF one, and BPPF one.

A major change in the 2021 elections was the decline in women representatives. Only six women (three from the BJP, two from the Congress, and one from AGP) made it as against eight in 2016 and 14 in 2011.

By looking at the growth of parties representing ethnic communities and intensification of political competition among parties one can safely say that politics in the state has become more competitive and democratic over the years, but very few have asked whether this trend has enabled opportunities for women's participation in the political process. Although women are increasingly being seen as a vote bank, this does not translate into their genuine political representation. Besides, political parties in the state continue to be more dole oriented and protectionist in their promises for women's rights.

Women and elections

Women's presence in the democratic process in the state has been consistent if we only look at their voting percentages. Women's voter turnout in the elections is one of the important dimensions to enquire about gender as an explanatory factor in electoral outcomes. Women's participation as voters has significantly increased in the state since the late 1980s. This reached an all-time high at 84.67 per cent in the 2016 assembly elections. Even in the latest assembly elections in 2021 it went up to 82.04 per cent. What is significant in these elections is that, not only did the gender gap reduce but women voters outnumbered men voters (Table 19.2).

Voter turnout patterns in the Lok Sabha elections in the state are different from those in the assembly elections. Gender gap in voters' turnout in Lok Sabha elections has reduced. During the six years period of the Assam movement (1978–85), women from all walks of life and of all age groups came out publicly in large numbers and enthusiastically participated in the movement. Mass participation and popular support by women made the movement historically significant. The main actors behind the Assam movement recast themselves into a new regional political party called the Asom Gana Parishad (AGP) two months after the signing of the Assam Accord. The party won a decisive victory in the 1985 state elections and formed the

Table 19.2 Voter turnout in assembly elections (1962–2021)

Year	Percentage of men voters	Percentage of women voters	Gap between men and women voters (%)
1952	–	–	–
1957	–	–	–
1962	58.39	42.05	16.34
1967	69.04	53.30	15.74
1972	66.02	54.8	11.4
1978	71.97	60.87	11.1
1983	35.84	29.20	6.64
1985	79.91	78.40	1.51
1991	75.37	73.86	1.51
1996	80.12	77.58	2.54
2001	77.68	72.19	5.49
2006	76.49	74.89	1.6
2011	76.85	74.94	1.91
2016	84.33	84.67	+0.3
2021	82.05	82.04	0.1

Source: Election Commission of India (ECI).

government in the state for the first time. The change in the nature of the party system in the state, with proliferation of ethnic-based parties contributed to an increase in women's turnout, as these parties made special efforts to mobilize their support base (Goswami, 2009).

Moreover, political parties have realized that woman voters have become a force and could influence elections. Hence the parties have changed their campaign strategies to woo and appease women voters. Besides, the number of state schemes and programmes that target women (like cash incentives for girl students scoring high marks and cycles for high school students, and scooties for college-going ones) has also increased in the state. The SHGs in the state have also contributed to a high percentage of political participation by women.

High-voltage election campaigns since the 2014 elections have shown a substantial increase in voter turnout. The role played by the media, women's groups, and civil society in creating awareness among women about their voting rights, the steps taken by the Election Commission to encourage and facilitate women's participation in voting, and mobilization of women voters by political parties have contributed to an increase in women's participation in the elections. Moreover, reservations in panchayats and women-centric development programmes (like the Mahatma Gandhi National Rural Employment Guarantee Scheme that offers equal wages to men and women) have given a boost to women's participation in the elections.

The Lokniti Post Poll Survey data for 2021 points out that while overall among women it was the BJP that led the *Mitrajut* (friendly grouping of

GENDER DYNAMICS IN ELECTORAL POLITICS IN ASSAM

parties) by 3 percentage points, among homemakers specifically (63 per cent of the women identified themselves as so), it was the Congress-led *Mahajot* (mega coalition of parties) that was ahead 47 per cent to 39 per cent (*The Hindu*, 2021).

Interestingly, however, none of the political parties in the state promote policies to ensure increased participation of women in their own party organizations or in the legislature.

Further, the plummeting gender gap in voter turnout in the last few assembly and Lok Sabha elections in the state is well marked by political parties. Almost all the political parties are now seen wooing women voters by promising different empowering schemes and policies. This has happened due to the realization of women emerging as a decisive force as voters not only in Assam but all over India. Thus, women are seen as being active in supporting democracy with their high turnout in the elections but are on the margins of public life in the state.

Selection of women candidates

Largely, the selection of women candidates in the state is based on political considerations rather than their contributions towards the socioeconomic development of the state. Factors like affiliation to the party hierarchy via family connections or elitist backgrounds are often considered at the time of selecting women candidates. Total women candidates in the assembly since the first elections till the last one in 2021 are only 96 as against 1,720 men. Out of the total women candidates (till the 2016 elections) 27 served for one term, nine for two terms, five for three terms, six for four terms, while one served for six terms. Of these, 28 members had familial political connections (58.3 per cent) and the remaining 20 (41.6 per cent) did not have such a background. On the other hand, 15 women candidates' husbands were former MLAs (31.2 per cent). Most of the women candidates were Hindus while only five were from the Muslim community. A reasonable number of these members entered the political arena as widow successors. Ajanta Neog of INC is the widow of late Nagen Neog who was a minister of state while her mother was an MLA. Renupoma Rajkhowa of the AGP is the wife of AGP minister late Lalit Chandra Rajkhowa.

On the other hand, a few like Puspalata Das, Renuka D Borkotoky, Amiya Gogoi, Jyotsna Sonowal, Pramila Rani Brahma, Rupam Kurmi, and Kamali Basumatary are known for their contributions in the socio-political field before coming into politics. However, in the 2016 assembly, out of eight women MLAs four had political connections while the remaining four came from elitist backgrounds. For example, in the 2016 assembly, Suman Haripriya of BJP was the daughter of former MP and union minister of state for water resources Bijoya Chakravarty. Angoorlota Deka of the BJP is a popular cinema actress in the state and Roselina Tirkey is the daughter of

Table 19.3 Assembly elections, Assam (gender-wise) (1952–2021)

Year	Men contestants	Men elected	Women contestants	Women elected	% of total (women representatives)
1952	449	124	6	2	1.6
1957	304	121	8	5	3.7
1962	402	122	6	4	3.2
1967	486	120	9	6	4.8
1972	496	118	12	8	6.3
1978	916	125	22	1	0.8
1983	472	124	3	2	1.5
1985	1124	121	29	4	3.9
1991	242	121	50	5	3.9
1996	1012	120	17	8	4.7
2001	861	116	53	10	7.9
2006	927	113	70	13	10.3
2011	896	112	85	14	11.1
2016	973	118	91	8	6.3
2021	872	120	74	6	4.7

Source: Statistical Reports on Assembly Elections, Election Commission of India.

ex-MLA of the state Sri Aklius Tirkey. Table 19.3 shows the low representation of women in the assembly.

Women members in the Parliament

The number of women members who have represented the state in the Rajya Sabha so far is 12. Puspalata Das was a member of the Rajya Sabha for two terms in 1952 and 1956. She played an effective role in every phase of the freedom movement, and in June 1940 she was entrusted with the task of organizing the women of Assam under the Congress' women's wing for their better participation in the movement. The BJP, on the other hand, has since its emergence in the state put up only one woman candidate. The elected women members usually have a dynastic lineage and/or elitist background.

There have been 19 women from the state in the Lok Sabha since the first elections. Members like Jyotshna Chanda, Ranee Narah, and Bijoya Chakravarty got elected for three terms each while Renuka Devi Borkotoky got elected twice. Bonily Khongmen, a member of a Scheduled Tribe, was the first woman member from Assam in the first Lok Sabha. Rani Manjula Devi and Begum Mofida Ahmed represented the state in 1957 (Table 19.4).

Although over time the number of women candidates contesting elections has increased in the state, men are still in a majority. Usually, politicians who stand the greatest chance of being elected are those nominated by major political parties. Women candidates failed to win any seat in the 1980, 1985, 1991, and 2004 elections. In the 1980 elections the Janata

GENDER DYNAMICS IN ELECTORAL POLITICS IN ASSAM

Table 19.4 Women contestants for the Lok Sabha (1952–2019)

Year	Women contested	Women elected	% of elected women
1952	2	1	
1957	2	2	3.7
1962	6	4	3.
1967	1	1	7.1
1971	3	1	7.1
1977	3	2	14.1
1980	2	0	0
1985	3	0	0
1991	8	0	0
1996	9	1	7.1
1999	9	2	14.2
2004	6	0	0
2009	11	2	14.3
2014	16	2	14.2
2019	14	1	7.1

Source: Statistical Reports on General Election, Election Commission of India.

Party had two women candidates while the Indian National Congress (U) had one but no woman was elected. Only three women candidates contested the elections in 1985 as independent candidates and no single political party offered any candidature to women. Surprisingly even under the AGP banner no woman candidate could win any seat in 1985 even though women had participated in the Assam movement in large numbers and had made their presence felt in different forums.

In the 1991 Lok Sabha elections, only eight women candidates contested the elections, of which six were independent candidates, while one was from the Janata Party, and one from the Assam Jatiyatabadi Dal. But none of them won. In the 2004 general elections, six women contested – one each from BJP, INC, and Samata Party and three contested as independents. But no one could win. In the 2009 elections, 11 women candidates fought the elections – Congress and BJP fielded one candidate each, while AGP and AIUDF did not put up any woman candidate. Bijoya Chakravarty from BJP and Ranee Narah from INC won the elections. Ranee Narah won from the same constituency (Lakhimpur) for three times in 1998, 1999, and 2009. In the 2014 general elections, 15 women contested of which two won –Bijoya Chakravorty from the BJP and Susmita Dev from the Congress. In 2019, only Queen Ozha, Mayor of Guwahati, won the elections on a BJP ticket. These numbers reveal a lopsided engagement of women in electoral politics in the state.

Women holding ministerial berths

Visibility of women members in Assam as ministers both at the state and central levels is limited. Women politicians who could make it to the higher tier of politics are mostly from established political families, although most of them lack experience of working at the grassroots level. Till now only 23 women have become ministers of which ten held a cabinet rank while the rest were either state or deputy ministers. Syeda Anwara Taimur, four times MLA, became the first and the only woman Chief Minister of Assam, though for a short time. Rupam Kurmi became the first woman cabinet minister from the tea community whose husband was the secretary of the Assam Chah Majdur Sangh, Margherita unit. She was the first graduate among the women of the tea community. Ajanta Neog was another capable woman cabinet minister who held the Public Works Department (PWD) portfolio. At present she holds the finance department, a privilege always enjoyed by male ministers.

Women ministers were mostly given portfolios like handlooms, sericulture, textiles, and cultural affairs, while the more important portfolios like home, finance, education, and health were not allotted to them. At the central level, only four women MPs from Assam got ministerial berths, mostly as state ministers. Women representatives' performance shows that they raised issues specific to the problems of their own constituency and issues related to the state as a whole. Women's welfare does not figure significantly during assembly and parliamentary sessions. Most of the women felt that women's issues were ignored because of poor representation of women at all levels of political power. Moreover, lack of initiatives and indifference of male legislators as well as the presence of only a few women members have led to 'women's issues' not being adequately addressed. Besides, very few women members are viewed as leaders with the capacity to deliver on issues related to women. It appears that women's representatives in the earlier period were more active and concerned about raising women-related issues like education, health, and security than women representatives today.

Winnability perception

An analysis of data for the assembly elections during 1952–2021 (Table 19.5) shows that the success rate of women candidates is higher than that for men – a striking feature of the electoral politics in the state that a higher percentage of women has a chance of winning as compared to men.

However, though in the 1978 and 2021 assembly elections women's winning percentage was lower as compared to men, compared to the number of contestants men's winning percentage was much lower. The average rate of winnability among all the contestants shows that while 21.4 per cent women were elected against 4.2 per cent women contestants, 17.5 per cent men won against 94.7 per cent male contestants. This clearly reflects that women could win at a higher rate in the seats allotted to them while men's winnability rate was lower.

Table 19.5 Winnability percentage in the assembly elections (1952–2021)

Year	Men contestants	Men elected	Winning %	Women contestants	Women elected	Winning %
1952	449	124	27.6	6	2	33.3
1957	304	121	39.8	8	5	62.5
1962	402	122	30.3	6	4	66.6
1967	486	120	24.6	9	6	66.6
1972	496	118	23.7	12	8	66.6
1978	916	125	13.6	22	1	4.5
1983	472	124	26.2	3	2	66.6
1985	1124	121	10.7	28	4	14.2
1991	242	121	50	50	5	10
1996	1012	120	11.8	45	8	13.3
2001	861	116	13.4	55	10	18.1
2006	927	113	12.1	70	13	18.5
2011	896	112	12.5	85	14	16.4
2016	973	118	12.1	91	8	8.7
2021	872	120	13.7	74	6	8.1
	Average men contestant=94.8 %	Average men elected=17.5%		Average women contestant=4.2%	Average women elected= 21.04 %	

Source: Statistical Reports on Assembly Election, Election Commission of India.

Women's participation in social movements

The women of Assam played an important role in the freedom movement, thereby contributing in the independence of the country. A sizeable number of women responded enthusiastically to Gandhiji's call for freedom from British rule. Women like Kanaklata and Bhogeswari Phukanani became martyrs and Chandra Prabha Saikiani fought for equal rights for women in society. Her sacrifice at the personal level, her leadership qualities, her organizational capabilities, and her struggle against patriarchal values and gender inequalities went largely unacknowledged during her lifetime. It is significant to note that Chandra Prabha was the first Assamese woman to establish herself as a powerful public speaker as early as 1919 when she stood on the dais of the Assam Chatra Sanmilan, a male-dominated student body.

However, history has not been very kind to women as no Assamese woman could achieve recognition as a leader at the national level. In the post-independence period, women have been gradually empowered through modern education and economic independence. These changes have been reflected in their increased participation in the political process and involvement in legitimate issues concerning the state. However, it appears that their experience has been systematically undermined and overlooked by the political parties operating at the national, state, and regional levels.

The Assam movement (1979–85) is an ideal example that highlights this exclusion. The movement was organized against 'foreign national issue' affecting the state. Women's large-scale participation was exemplary in this movement. In fact, at many crucial times when the male leadership was either in jail or being hunted by the armed forces, women came to the forefront of the movement. As in earlier movements like the refinery and language movements, women were excluded from the peace-making deal that resulted in the famous 'Assam Accord' of 1985. Rita Manchanda points out that as the peace table is set, women who had been so visible at the community level managing survival, building peace, and reconciliation are marginalized (Manchanda, 2005).

Leading women agitators of the Assam movement were completely ignored in the public space that they acquired momentarily during the movement. No single woman representative was there during the time of the signing of the Assam Accord. Women who participated in the Assam movement and later also supported the cause of the militant organization which subsequently emerged were mostly students or first-generation learners and they were comparatively better acquainted with the issues involved. But no woman could emerge as a leader of any organization. Women have had no significant role to play in resolving issues through political negotiations. They have not been a part of any peace initiative in Assam. Had they been included in such an initiative, perhaps their sincerity of purpose and willingness to see the truth without any complicated sophistry could have helped resolve the conflicts better and faster. Girl students had joined protests against the Citizenship (Amendment) Act, 2019 in the state. The spectacle of thousands of college girls in their uniforms leading the way together with the boys, breaking barricades, facing batons and bullets bravely on the streets of Guwahati on December 11, 2019, caught the attention of the entire country. The forceful voices of women are being heard as loudly and clearly as those of the men. They are emerging as the leaders of a new youth movement (*The Assam Tribune*, 2020).

Conclusion

While women's groups played a significant role during the active phases of social movements, there is often no continuity in the associational activities of the women after the conclusion or termination of such movements. As all these movements were on a specific issue, the efforts were fragmented and the mobilization at the local level was not consolidated at the national level. Since women's organizations and groups are not networked, participation or success is seen as individual achievements and has not generated the capital to sustain women's mobilization on interests common to women across different regions (Vijayalakshmi, 2005).

More importantly, the gap between women's assertion as voters and appalling record of political representation in the state is unsustainable. The political culture as it exists today is more discriminatory for women than perhaps any other area. It definitely needs urgent attention from all stakeholders. Gender prejudices are very deep rooted. More women in Assam are exercising their electoral rights today. Similarly, women's participation in election campaigns has also increased significantly, but this has not translated into their genuine political representation. It is clear that the political establishment and party personnel, apparatuses, and procedures are detrimental to women's interests. Schemes for girl students and women beneficiaries have only created a captive vote bank. Gender justice is always undermined by identity politics of ethnicity and religion in the state. Moreover, lack of political mobilization and effective sensitization among women appears to be a major area of inadequacy in feminist politics in the state.

This situation therefore warrants adequate reservations for women. Reservations for women is a gender issue, desirable for an equal society. It is necessary to initiate corrective measures to contest the marginalization of women from political institutions.

Bibliography

Assam Human Development Report (2014). *Managing Diversities, Achieving Human Development*. Available at https://transdev.assam.gov.in/sites/default/

files/swf_utility_folder/departments/pndd_medhassu_in_oid_2/portlet/level_1/
files/FINAL_Assam_HDR_2014.pdf accessed on August 17, 2021.

Basu, Amrita (2010). 'Gender and Politics', in Nirja Gopal Jayal and Pratap Bhanu Mehta (eds), *The Oxford Companion to Politics* (pp. 168–180). New Delhi: Oxford University Press.

Bhattacharjee, Tanmay (1986). '*Sociology of the Karbis*', New Delhi: B.R. Publishing Corporation.

Bokth, Humayun (2014). 'Social Life in Char Area: A Study of Neo Assamese Muslim Village in Brahmaputra Valley of Assam', *International Journal of Development Research*, 4 (12), 2843.

Chowdhuri, Rita (2021). *Mare Asom Jiye Kon (in Assamese)*. Guwahati: Jyoti Prakashan.

Dagar, Rainuka (2011). 'Gender Discourse in Elections: Constructing a Constituency?' in Paul Wallace and Ramashray Roy (eds), *India's 2009 Elections: Coalition Politics, Party Competition, and Congress Continuity*. Sage Publications India Pvt. Ltd.

Deka, Barasa (2019). 'Gender Equality and Group Rights in North East India', in J. K. Sarma (ed.), *Gender and Democracy in North East India: Politics of Inclusion and Empowerment* (pp. 57–67). Guwahati: Purbanchal Prakash.

Deshpande, Rajeshwari (2004). 'How Gendered was Women's Participation in Elections 2004', *Economic and Political Weekly*, 39 (51), 5431–5436.

Dutta, N. L. (1992). 'Political Status of Women in Assam Since Independence', in S. L. Baruah (ed.), *Status of Women in Assam.*New Delhi: Omsons Publications.

Goswami, Sandhya (2009). 'Assam: A Fractured Verdict', *Economic and Political Weekly*, 44 (39), 159–163.

——— (2020). *Assam Politics in Post Congress Era 1985 and Beyond* (Vol. 4, pp. 9–10). New Delhi: Sage Publication India.

Hussain, Ismail (1997). *Asomor Jatiya Jivon Aru Abhibhasi Asomiya Musalman'(in Assamese)*. Nalbari, Assam: Anamika Granthalaya.

Kishwar, Madhu (1998). 'Women's Marginal Role in Politics', in Subrata Mukherjee and Sushila Ramaswamy (eds), *Political Science Annual 1997* (pp. 354–374). New Delhi: Deep and Deep Publications Pvt. Ltd.

Kumari, Abhilasha and Sabina Kidwai (1998). *Crossing the Sacred Line, Women's search for Political Power*. New Delhi: Orient Longman.

Lyall, Sir Charles (ed.) (1972). *The Karbis*. Guwahati: Spectrum Publications.

Mahapatra, Richard (2013) 'Women Take the Lead Parties Follow', *Down To Earth*, December 9. Available at: https://www.downtoearth.org.in/news/women -take-the-lead-parties-follow-42924, accessed on February 20, 2020.

Manchanda, Rita (2005). 'Women's Agency in Peace Building: Gender Relations in Post-Conflict Reconstruction', *Economic and Political Weekly*, 40(44–45), 4737–4745.

Rai, Praveen (2011). 'Electoral Participation of Women in India, Key Determinants and Barriers', *Economic and Political Weekly*,46 (3), 47–55.

Rai, Shirin and Spray Carole (2019). *Performing Representation: Women Members in the Indian Parliament*. New Delhi: Oxford University Press.

The Assam Tribune, January 19, 2020. Editorial, *No Assamese Women Leaders yet*, interview of Tilottama Misra.

The Hindu (2021). 'Assam a Tale of Two Congress Guarantees: One Clicked, Another Did not', Sardesai, Shreyas and Nurul Hassan, May 7. Available at: https://www.thehindu.com/elections/assam-assembly/a-tale-of-two-congress-guarantees-one-clicked-another-did-not/article34508315.ece, accessed on August 17, 2021.

The Times of India (2019). 'Women Voters Outnumbered Men in 13 States and Union Territories', May 21. Available at: https://timesofindia.indiatimes.com/india/women-voters-outnumber-men-in-13-states-and-union-territories/articleshow/69419602.cms, accessed on March 10, 2020.

——— (2020). 'Crime Rate Against Women Highest in Assam: NCRB', October 3. Available at: https://timesofindia.indiatimes.com/city/guwahati/crime-rate-against-women-highest-in-assam-ncrb/articleshow/78460406.cms, accessed on February 4, 2021.

Uroh, C. (2003). 'Empowering the African Women: The Many Bumps Ahead', *Journal of Political Science*, 3, 21–31.

Vijayalakshmi, V. (2005). *Feminist Politics in India: Women and Civil Society Activism*, Working Paper 161. Bangalore: Institute for Social and Economic Change.

EPILOGUE

Glimpses of perspectives/experiences of four women active in politics and movements

Epilogue

This epilogue reflects experiences and insights of women in politics. Women, though in small numbers, have been entering the messy field of politics. Not always welcome and at times miserable, they have been defiant and willing to face challenges. They have to steer their way through the intricate cobwebs of power. Electoral battles in an environment insensitive, and at times even hostile to women, and with very few women role models and mentors are challenging.

The trajectory of each of them is fascinating and stimulating, though a lot remains submerged under the sea of politics. All of them present successes and failures, giving rich insights into politics. The tone and tenure of each of them is distinct and inviting. The experiences of the elected women representatives indicate the thrill and tension of working within the structure, while the encounters of women activists bring to the surface the impulses and challenges at the grassroots level. Both are equally interesting, inspiring and at times problematic/baffling/perplexing.

Glimpses of four perspectives/experiences are given below. Margaret Alva (a parliamentarian, a minister, and finally holding a gubernatorial post) and Neelam Gorhe (four times a member of the Upper House in Maharashtra and currently its Deputy Chairperson) are well-known and established leaders in politics, the former had successful political innings at the Centre and the latter at the state level. Ruth Manorama (a Dalit women's rights activist and a recipient of the Right to Livelihood award) and Sudha Varghese (a grassroots activist amidst the Musaharis, Mahadalits, and an awardee of Padmashri) are entrenched in movements and have still to find their moorings in politics.

Margaret Alva

Margaret Alva draws our attention to an important issue regarding voting by women. According to her, 'Though women vote in large numbers,

354   DOI: 10.4324/9781003374862-21

EPILOGUE

almost at par with men, unlike Dalits or OBCs or the minorities, they do not form a political constituency and have not been able to gain negotiating power on the basis of their vote. Rather than their gender, it is their caste or religion or community which determines their basic political identity.'

She adds, 'As recipients and beneficiaries of governance, women are the most marginalized, exploited and neglected majority, and within this marginalized section, are the further marginalized minority, Dalit, and Scheduled Tribes women. Instead of upgrading their capacities and skills, urban women at the grassroots are being offered the alternative of 5P technology – Papads, Pakoras, Pizzas, Parlors (Beauty) and Pre-school child services.'

She perceptively also observes, 'The challenges facing India can never be solved by top-down bureaucratic interventions. The needs of communities can only be met locally – through local planning responsibility and accountability. This truth and the Gandhian principle of Swaraj were recognized at the time of Independence, but were not institutionalized and never fully practiced.'

The situation is changing slowly with the entry of women in the Panchayati Raj Institutions. In Alva's opinion, 'Thanks to these elected women, women have started storming the otherwise "for men only" *chaupal*. Emphasis on down-up politics has created women supporters, women campaigners and vocal self-help groups with economic power, standing together and creating a powerful force of local leaders, demanding change and better governance. The civil society movements, especially in urban areas have brought women into focus.'

She acknowledges, 'There are state-specific issues which need greater study. Politics in the states is dominated by regional parties mostly off-shoots of national parties like the Congress, and personality dominated. Mamata Bannerjee's TMC in Bengal; Lalu Prasad Yadav's RJD in Bihar; the Thackeray family led Shiv Sena and the Pawar led NCP in Maharashtra; MGR-Jayalalitha's AIADMK, which was an off-shoot of the DMK dominated by the Karunanidhi family in Tamil Nadu; the Mulayam Singh Yadav family dominated SP; the Mayawati led BSP in Uttar Pradesh; the BJD led by Naveen Patnaik in Odisha, the TRS founded and dominated by the Chandrashekar Rao family in Telangana; the TDP dominated by the founding family of N.T. Rama Rao; the YSR Congress led by the Y.S. Rajasekhara Reddy family in Andhra Pradesh; and the PDP/National Conference dominated by the Mufti/Abdullah families in Jammu and Kashmir.'

'Their policies and programmes centre around state issues, family interests, guided by an inner circle of a trusted coterie loyal to the leadership. Issues of gender are of little consequence as they tend to be influenced by local customs, traditions, caste and community equations.'

Alva sees a path ahead for women who are unnerved by the obstacles in their way. She observes, 'As opinion makers women are becoming vocal

EPILOGUE

in the media, women's organizations, the civil society movements, NGO initiatives, and political parties and their campaigns. They are getting organized, trained and motivated, demanding a share and a place in the structures of social, economic and political power that operate the levers of government.'

Based on her long political experience, she comments, 'While no ideal environment currently exists to jumpstart the advancement of women's political participation, there are certain conditions that would make it easier:

- -Ensuring gender mainstreaming and women supporting policy reform for gender equality.
- -Support of male political leaders which is key to creating a political climate that encourages women's political participation. More women in politics is not fewer men in politics, but a more equitable society for everyone.
- -Transparency in the political and legislative processes that is critical for the advancement of women in political and civil society. Undemocratic internal processes are challenging for all newcomers.'

'The image of the ideal Indian woman as a "weak subjugated suffering – Sita" is now in transition to an empowered Durga. Women are becoming the change they want to see. They are influencing opinions and attempting to change traditional mind sets. There is no way the trend can be reversed. Women are being noticed, listened to and being presented in a positive way even in the press.'

'The journey is difficult but the fight must go on. We were pioneers who launched the initiative. It is for the younger generation to carry it to its inevitable victory. I believe that women will emerge, bold and empowered by 2030. We must and we will overcome.'

Dr Neelam Gorhe

According to Gorhe, 'The changing status of women and overall "change" in Maharashtra was backed by some leaders and workers from political and social fields. There was, however, no red carpet welcome for such changes and the supporting leaders and also the women taking a lead role in addressing women's issues had to suffer differences, negligence, struggle, negative propaganda, side-lining, threats, and so on. However, Maharashtra, which stands strong on the foundational work of progressive and constructive social reformers like Chatrapati Shivaji Maharaj, Mahatma Jyotiba Phule, Savitribai Phule, Gopal Ganesh Agarkar, Rajashri Shahu Chatrapati, Prabodhankar Thackeray, Ramabai Ranade, Dr Babasaheb Ambedkar, Dhondo Keshav Karve and other social reformists, slowly accepted the developmental changes happening in favour of women.'

EPILOGUE

Based on her vast experience in politics, Gorhe is aware of the obstacles women face in the political arena. 'There are some serious concerns also which restrict women's participation in mainstream political processes. This is due to the fact that despite all the opportunities for women's empowerment, the number of women in the state assembly is still very meagre barely 8 per cent to 10 per cent. Several factors attribute to this low representation at the level of state assembly. Some of the observed reasons are – character assassination, muscle power and money power. These factors inhibit aspiring and promising women to take an active political route. Thus many women prefer an "activist" role to demand rights and highlight social issues, rather than to be a part of active "politics." Further, those already in the political arena elected to various government bodies at the local level face another hurdle that leaves them disappointed and disheartened. Though reservation for women guarantees their participation in governance at local level, it is still wrought with challenges.'

'One of the challenges is the process of constituency reservation for three consecutive terms, after which the post will be reserved for other castes. Although all caste women get political representation through reservation, yet, this process has eroded the very basis of women's political movement because women will not get opportunities as per their calibre but as to how they fit politically into a reserved seat. This defeats the essence of "good governance" and "limits" the time available for the elected women to work effectively on that reservation. However, mention needs to be made here that the Mumbai BMC (Brihan Mahanagar Palika) under the Shiv Sena regime disregarded this Reservation Bill in consultations with women's organizations to appoint capable women (from other than reserved categories) disregarding caste considering calibre alone to the reserved posts for good governance. From 2009 the women representation in local bodies has been increased from 33 per cent to 50 per cent on proven merit alone.'

'2010 was used for analysing various bottlenecks faced by women in governance. Women in governance faced a backlash from own party workers. Elected women have a box type of participation in governance. An active and genuine women leader faces several challenges at the local level especially from elected male colleagues, who fear to face the challenge of women at the decision-making level. Hence decision-making is limited for women. How much space is given to women in governance depends on the policies of a particular party. Often women in governance, despite having capabilities, follow stereotyped functioning and refuse to venture into larger territories fearing inability to meet deadlines and handle issue-based politics, hence the box type limited functioning in local bodies.'

Gorhe remains connected to the grassroots. She indicates opportunities for women in politics citing her own work/example, 'Two organizations founded by me namely *Krantikari Mahila Sanghatna* and *Stree Aadhar Kendra* have been active for past 36 years advocating relevant policy changes on issues affecting women in Maharashtra. I have also drafted the agenda for policies for political parties to enable them to fulfil their duties as leaders. This is mentioned here to give a message that women need not be merely passive recipients of the political process but should also actively participate as representatives of the vibrant critical mass of women voters. Women's organizations have helped elected women create a space in the political arena for them.'

Gorhe encourages women to be active in politics, 'Good political governance calls for equal involvement of women.' Some of her suggestions/comments in this context are:

- '-Women need to work at decision-making levels and have a say in all related matters.
- -Women need guidance to move forward to better positions at the state level as they gain people's mandate to represent them.
- -It is necessary to have "women inclusive governance" at all levels with independent hold and infrastructure where they are answerable to the highest authority, interactive men and women's forums and quasi-judicial powers to take their own decisions.'

'Other areas that women leaders need to see opportunities for themselves are the 'Gender Responsive Budgeting' and the agenda for "Women's Security." Unfortunately, these are presently moving at a very slow pace. The SDGs have a component on women's empowerment where every goal is connected to the others through different ways and then connected to various processes to move towards the 2030 goals (for example, 50 per cent representation at all levels). However, the plans regarding this opportunity for women are neither clear nor transparent both at national and state levels. Surprisingly, very few elected women are aware of the SDGs.'

'Women as representatives of local government bodies are becoming proactive on environment issues. For example, cities like Mahabaleshwar and Panchgani (Maharashtra) are managed by 50 per cent women in local bodies, and they have become garbage and plastic free cities and efforts are on to make the rivers and lakes pollution free. All this was possible because of a ban on the use of plastic imposed by the state government which enabled women in governance to move ahead. So there is a resurgence of new women's movement. These newly elected women in governance after 2010 have taken up cudgels on behalf of different local issues like social security, health and SGDs. So the journey which started with price rise, dowry, and social security has moved towards local, national and on to global issues. In fact an activist woman's slogan crafted thoughtfully by women in Gadhchiroli district, reflects the prevalent mood of women in governance "*Delhi Mumbai mein hamari sarkar aur hamari goanmein ham hi Sarkar.*"'

She further states, 'I am glad to share that during the Budget session this year, on 6th March 2020, in both the houses of the state assembly and legislative council there were in-depth and entire day discussions on SDGs and obstacles in women's development and MLAs took keen interest in the subject.'

'Efforts are on to enable women to be a part of the governing system: they cannot remain outside the changing social political purview. They need not be termed as *becharis* (helpless): they have to be empowered women demanding their rights.'

Ruth Manorama

Political empowerment, holds Ruth Manorama, is a long march for women. 'Women in South India,' she points out, 'have better figures for the sex ratio, education, maternal mortality, infant mortality, female labour force participation yet Kerala and Karnataka have worst figures for elected women in the assembly and Lok Sabha levels. Better education and better quality of life for women have not translated into their better representation. Politics has remained a bastion for men in the south though there have been powerful women like Jayalalitha.'

Reflecting on why women's participation in election is low, Ruth Manorama joins other women politicians to say, 'Societal discrimination follows women in politics particularly in perceptions about money, muscle and party workers in election campaign. Male politicians have a good relationship with party workers: they eat and drink with them, stay in their houses till late in the night. There are limitations to women doing all this. For men, if this behaviour is a qualification, for women it is an immediate disqualification as rumours start to spread questioning their character.'

According to Ruth Manorama, 'Violence against women in politics (VAWP) is a major deterrent to women exercising their political rights. It undermines policy outcomes and the work of political institutions such as the Parliament or local governments. Women in politics who speak out the harassment they face often silenced by being reminded that they chose the job that comes with risks. Moreover, women do not have adequate resources to contest elections.'

Speaking for women from discriminated communities, Ruth Manorama highlights the difficulties that they face in exercising their right to vote, to contest, and to hold elected offices at the local and other levels. She points out, 'During the 2009 general elections, the National Dalit Election Watch reported several incidents of violence of which 32 per cent were threats / intimidation / violence by Dominant Caste groups, 20 per cent SCs were deliberately excluded from the voters lists.'

According to her, 'For democracy to prevail women's political participation is imperative and their participation shall lead to:

EPILOGUE

- -Opening the avenue to more inclusive and resilient democracies, balanced economies, and enhanced peace building processes (SDG 5).
- -Enabling women to break multiple barriers such as prevailing social norms and cultural attitudes.
- -Acknowledging women's role in the prevention and resolution of conflicts, in humanitarian responses and in post conflict reconstruction.
- -Women's politics to work for a society free of violence and where women's right to health, education and livelihood are guaranteed.
- -Enhance checking the growing violence, fundamentalism and criminalization of politics."

For women's effective and meaningful participation and representation, Ruth Manorama underlines some fundamentals:

- '-the need of role models who share their experiences and knowledge to help build local capacity.
- -women's wings within political parties / trade unions / people's movements as part of political party decision-making structures.
- -coalition of women's movements / NGOs to lobby for policy reforms with governments in support of gender equality and to commit to a debate on women in all the elections.
- -women's caucuses to provide structured support through capacity building through training programs and making working places more women friendly.
- -fund raising for women political candidates, working together with key political institutions.
- -and last but not the least media and social media training, advocacy and campaigning, establishing women leadership institutions as was done by NAWO, NFDW-India, and the Women's Democracy Network.'

On the basis of her experience of being a part of a political party, Ruth Manorama strongly feels that, 'Women need to enter politics in large numbers to change the system and challenge the patriarchal and misogynistic values that dominate the political system in our country. Women need to enlighten political parties in large numbers, especially women from the feminist movements. Women's role is to mainstream women's agenda in their political party's agenda and manifesto and occupying important offices in their parties to attack patriarchal values and leadership.'

In her opinion, there is a need to question and dismantle patriarchy at all levels by strengthening women's membership and active participation in all events in large numbers and claiming their rightful spaces in meetings. That is the only way, she argues to break the entry point of men's paradigm. Once the women appear in party meetings, automatically they will be given an opportunity to speak and also given space on the dais. Women to be

360

EPILOGUE

leaders in their own right, and enjoy positions and status in their parties, must give time to party work. They need to develop oratorical skills, must be articulate, and have an understanding of the socioeconomic and political issues and political realities. Political parties on the other hand must organize capacity-building programmes for their members to enable them to break the multiple barriers that they face.

On women's day in 2020, under her presidentship, the mahila wing of JD(S) passed a number of resolutions on crucial issues pertaining to women and it also passed a resolution in favour of Women's Reservation Bill. Power sharing, says Ruth Manorama, is most critical and women need to be given one-third of the positions in national committees, state committees, as well district committees by party bosses. More democratic values need to be inculcated; there should be equal involvement of women, men, youth, and marginalized communities at all decision-making levels.

Sudha Varghese

Commenting on the obstacles women in politics face, Sudha Varghese observes, 'There is an active role played by women in local politics, they understand the caste factor and they articulate the factors that affect the decisions made in the locality about matters that concern society and community. Women are very much aware of what is happening in the panchayats. Unless a panchayat is reserved for women it is almost impossible for a woman candidate to fight elections. There are so many lame reasons why women should not fight elections and there are very few people who like to let women have a chance to try their abilities in politics. Here I would like to share an experience of mine – how a young Dalit woman belonging to the most marginalized community, educated and capable, was ready to stand for elections to the panchayat president's position. The people in the area were quite happy with the decision she took with the support of her own community. They went on foot campaigning for her as they did not have much money. The atmosphere was very favourable for her and everyone was very sure of her winning the elections. On the day of the elections, some disturbance was created to stop people of that particular caste from voting but that was taken care of and peaceful voting went on. The opposition devised a way and they managed to remove the *swastik* sign from the stamp so the ballots stamped without the *swastik* sign were considered invalid. This was done in two booths where the particular community came to vote and thus the Dalit woman candidate was defeated.'

'In addition, women candidates feel the crunch of not having funds to spend on election campaigns. Unfortunately, today money power has become the yardstick for winning elections. Criminalization of politics has also kept women away from coming into politics. There is a need for change in the whole process of political competence and women have to be prepared to enter this competition and really fight the elections with democratic values in front and not money and power used through corrupted ways.'

'It's a challenge for women to enter politics on their own merit and to demand votes on merit and to prove themselves on their merit through their ability to speak up and stand for policies that will benefit children, women, Dalits, minorities, and vulnerable sections. A woman's efforts to develop her own constituency will speak for her, that she is a woman of her people, for her people, and with her people through thick and thin. Take the challenge! It's high time that we work towards pulling up the percentage of women in the assembly and in the Parliament to over 50 per cent.'

These enriching experiences of the women politicians and activists raise some fundamental questions: Is there a possibility of a better tomorrow? Do efforts made by women yield visible results? Or will they be trailblazers only to fade away? Or will such efforts continue with the changing times to keep the hope alive?

Answers to these questions are not easy in the foreseeable future; hence advocacy coupled with research in this critical area of seeking feminization of politics has to be a priority for realizing gender equality.

While the governments and political parties must translate their political obligation to advance gender parity in the political arena from local to national levels, it is time women too do not wait to be asked and be complacent with tokenism but claim their spaces to shatter the glass ceiling and be the agents of transformative politics.

INDEX

active politics 110, 187, 188, 217, 340
activism 32, 156
agitation 61–63, 66, 83, 90, 160, 166, 168–170, 224, 233
agitational politics 128–129
agriculture 83, 101, 117, 161, 214, 215, 244
Alva, Margaret 354–356
Amarnath agitation 61–63, 66
anti-arrack/alcohol movement 22, 161, 166–170, 241
anti-price movement 21, 240
armed militancy 57, 63–65, 67, 68
Assam 4, 6, 7, 9, 11, 337–340, 345–348, 350, 351; gender dynamics in electoral politics 335–351
assembly elections 3, 4, 11, 59–61, 78, 79, 121, 178–182, 279, 301, 321, 322, 340, 343
assembly polls 3, 5, 97, 258, 263
autonomous women's movements 202, 203

Banerjee, Mamata 9, 13, 19, 26, 34, 281, 283, 284
barriers 2, 3, 10, 14, 23, 24, 30, 35, 38, 44, 134, 139
Basu, A. 188
Beniwal, Kamla 14, 218, 259–260, 262
Beniwal, Vidya 135
Bhajan Lal-led Janata government 73
Bihar 3, 32, 289–292, 294, 296, 298–300, 302, 318, 319, 322, 324–328; assembly elections 19, 298, 302, 324, 325
Bihar Election Watch 324
Bihar politics, engendering 289–302

BJP 4, 18, 34, 76, 103, 106, 109, 123, 219, 230, 235, 236, 249–252, 258, 279, 284, 343
Bombay Municipal Corporation 200, 229, 231–233
by-elections 77, 78, 121, 123, 251, 311, 321, 326

careers 65, 201, 202, 314
caste 27, 102, 103, 113, 152, 156–158, 202–204, 211, 212, 327, 357; dynamics 72; politics 2, 153
CEDAW 36–39
celebrity politics 283–284
Chandra, Kanchan 327
Chavan, Vidya 196
Childs, Sarah 43
civil society 40, 68, 225, 330, 344, 356
communities 66, 67, 86, 111, 113, 128, 186, 211, 213, 305, 308, 336, 337, 355, 361
community identity 9, 22, 66, 67
conflict situation 55, 65, 66
Congress Party 13, 18, 72, 74, 80, 121, 123, 126, 276, 282, 319, 325
Constitutional Amendment Acts 119, 124, 127
contestants 58, 59, 136, 137, 259, 260, 262, 263, 265, 321, 322, 325, 348
council of ministers 77, 106, 108, 124, 126, 258–262, 312
criminalization of politics 8, 14, 129, 130, 270, 292, 324, 360, 361
CSW 41, 42

Dandavate, Pramila 12–13, 15, 20, 200, 202, 230, 232, 238, 242
Dang, Satyawati 126

INDEX

DasGupta, Sumona 69
Datta, B. 221
decision-making bodies 8, 12, 14, 18, 20, 22, 28, 35–38, 118, 220
democratic politics 191, 200, 202, 204
demographics 101, 318
development politics 274
Devi, Rabri 16, 17, 26, 292, 294, 326
Dikshit, Sheila 13
dilemmas 191, 203–205
disobedience movement 299
diversities 2, 10, 53, 273, 335
domestic space 65
domestic violence 22, 128, 166, 167, 222, 223, 309, 313
dominant castes 204, 212, 213, 222, 290, 327, 359
dynastic women politicians 14, 15
dynasties 14, 327

economic development 2, 71, 177, 203
economic recovery 41, 42
elected women members 6, 108, 163, 236, 239, 346
election campaigns 26, 80, 179, 219, 351, 359, 361
Election Commission of India 3, 136, 141, 279, 309–311, 319, 321, 322
election manifestos 31, 97, 247, 271
elections 7, 9, 57, 58, 80, 119, 135, 139, 184, 204, 235, 236, 309, 310, 319, 321, 322, 327, 343, 347
electoral mobilization 277, 284
electoral politics 19, 57, 187, 188, 203, 204, 277, 279, 280, 282, 285, 286, 337, 347, 348
empowerment 10, 42, 44, 55, 71, 81, 84, 97, 219, 223, 238
equality 20, 21, 25–30, 32, 36–38, 160, 161, 223
ethnic communities 66, 336, 343

Faludi, Susan 25
federal politics 274, 284, 285
female candidates 11, 58–60, 107, 111, 138, 310, 311, 315, 324
female contestants 58–60, 109, 111, 265, 284, 294
female literacy levels 86
female/women voters 3–6, 34, 57, 91, 103, 109, 119, 145, 172, 181, 233, 278, 292, 301, 310, 311, 322, 335

first assembly elections 127, 178, 259
formal politics 3, 11, 20, 21, 57, 60, 61, 90, 111, 128, 176
freedom movement 12, 20, 101, 118, 223, 229, 327, 340, 346, 350

Gandhi, Sonia 7, 12, 15, 19, 26, 105, 107, 112, 247
Garikipati, Supriya 41
gatekeepers 35, 182
gender: balance 35, 37, 38, 308; disparities 19, 257, 291, 307, 308; equality 27, 28, 40–44, 176, 177, 223, 224, 257, 273, 336, 337; gap 3, 41, 257, 263, 264, 277, 302, 307, 343; parity 35, 36, 40–42, 45, 273, 294, 362; politics 61, 65, 66, 68, 141, 152; profile 212
gender-based discrimination 281
General Assembly Resolutions 39, 42
general elections 91, 92, 123, 134, 141, 145, 170, 192, 205, 245, 347
Generation Equality Forum 43
Goa 3, 4, 8, 176–182, 184, 186–189; gender profile 177; politics 176, 177, 180, 181, 185, 187, 189
Gore, Mrinal 13, 20, 200, 202, 230, 232, 234–235, 238, 240
Gorhe, Neelam 13, 196, 202, 203, 238, 239, 354, 356–359
governance 2, 6, 90, 134, 273, 277, 282, 283, 293, 297, 355, 357, 358
grassroots 23, 99, 240, 249, 326, 355, 357
gross enrolment ratio (GER) 307

Haryana 7, 14, 15, 71, 72, 74, 80, 81, 134–139, 249; assembly 73, 75–79; assembly elections 76, 80, 136; politics 71, 73, 75, 77, 79, 81, 133–139
high-voltage election campaigns 344
Himachal Pradesh 91, 116–119, 121, 123, 124, 126–129, 131; assembly 121, 123, 126, 127; politics in 116–131
Hust, Evelin 133

inadequate assertion 319, 321, 325, 327, 331
independent candidates 7, 73, 172, 178, 184, 187, 196, 310, 347

364

INDEX

independent women candidates 7, 193, 302

Indian National Congress 95, 102, 105, 107, 109, 121, 191, 249, 250, 260, 282

Indian politics 1, 5, 15, 20, 33, 104, 254, 260, 324, 327, 328

informal politics 3, 11, 20, 21, 23

institutional spaces 278

International Covenant on Civil and Political Rights 36

intersectionality 203, 204, 206

Irani, Smriti 106, 112, 219

Jaitley, Arun 32

Jammu and Kashmir (J&K) 9, 11, 16, 21, 22, 53–57, 60–62, 65, 66; politics in 53–69

jati panchayats 258

Jayalalitha 19, 26, 27, 112, 359

Kakodkar, Shashikala 8, 16, 177, 180, 182

Kambhampati, Uma 41

Kashmiri identity 55–57

Kerala 9, 10, 86, 117, 141, 145, 150–158; model of development 141

khap panchayats 138, 258

Kriplani, Sucheta 12, 15, 104

Krook, Mona Lena 43

Kumar, Meira 105

Kumari, Chandresh 126

legislatures 9, 14, 18, 28, 42, 43, 59, 151, 172, 192, 220

local bodies 8, 10, 134, 139, 196–199, 238, 239, 252, 357, 358

local-level politics 239, 252

local politics 138, 361

local self-governance 245, 312

Lok Sabha 11–13, 15, 17, 31, 72, 104–106, 126, 135, 150, 171, 230–232, 249, 250, 312; elections 5, 6, 111, 112, 134–137, 180, 250, 296, 343, 345, 347

long political career 201, 248, 249

low participation 129, 294

Madhya Pradesh, state politics 244–255

Mahajan, Leela Devi 126

Mahajan, Sumitra 135

Maharashtra 191, 192, 197–199, 201, 203, 205, 228–230, 232, 233, 235, 237–241, 356; politics in 228–242

mainstream politics 2, 61, 66, 145, 151, 154, 157, 158

male members 107, 110–112, 199, 205, 222, 224, 279, 281, 286, 292

male politicians 9, 27, 160, 173, 248, 250, 359

Mandal Report 102

Manorama, Ruth 359–361

marginalization 89, 98, 164, 196, 205, 216, 273, 282, 351

mass movements 84, 89, 238

maternal mortality rate 86, 102, 213

Mayawati 7, 10, 11, 13, 19, 26, 103–105, 107, 112

Mazumdar, Vina 286

militancy 21, 53, 59, 63–65, 68, 69

ministerial berths 347, 348

Mishra, Garima 110

misogynistic mindsets 314

mobilization 62, 67, 152, 154, 155, 217, 322, 339, 344, 351

modern-day Telangana struggle 170–171

modern democracies 112, 139

money power 27, 184, 357, 361

movements 20, 21, 90, 113, 157, 160, 166, 168–171, 187, 203, 233, 240, 241, 276, 285, 300, 350

Mufti, Mehbooba 11, 16, 19, 60–61

Mukherjee, Geeta 12, 31, 276, 283

Muslim women politicians 11, 106

Narain, Iqbal 1

National Crime Records data 274

national-level politics 103, 312

national politics 2, 80, 104, 106, 248, 251, 289

Naxal movement 22, 90, 164, 166, 302

NITI Aayog Report 9, 10, 85, 117, 177, 274, 291

non-formal politics 223, 330

non-party democratic activism 8, 191, 204

Norris, P. 43, 44

Okin, Susan Moller 26

opposition parties 177, 235, 282, 300, 311

organizational structures 90, 95, 270, 281, 322

365

INDEX

Pais, C. S. 177
panchayat elections 137, 145, 184, 245, 277, 297, 313
Panchayati Raj Institutions (PRIs) 30, 80, 81, 109, 111, 119, 127, 128, 130, 145, 184, 196, 199, 280, 289, 293, 297, 355
Panchayat Regulations 184
Pande, Rohini 264
Pandit, Vijay Laxmi 104
parliamentary elections 4, 60, 72, 73, 75, 76, 79, 80, 180
parliamentary secretaries 77, 78, 124, 126, 261, 268
Parobo, P. 186
party hierarchies 124, 130, 237, 345
party organizations 196, 200, 201, 282, 345
Patel, Anandiben 8, 12, 109, 217–218
paternal politics 279
Patil, Pratibha 12–13, 230, 234, 237–238, 262
patriarchy 22, 25, 85, 151, 153, 155, 157, 160, 166, 203, 241, 242
political activities 25, 113, 118, 129, 130, 229
political agency 97–99
political career 13, 17, 63, 104, 106, 200, 249–251, 276, 282
political consciousness 55, 141, 150, 229, 230
political constituency 3, 66, 181, 188, 355
political culture 26, 156, 191, 206, 281, 283, 351
political discourse 55, 65, 66
political dynasties 14–16, 298
political empowerment 145, 223, 359
political families 13, 16, 74, 75, 77, 78, 95, 98, 182, 326, 328
political identity 22, 56, 57
political leaders 3, 10, 12, 60, 61, 153, 155, 281, 282, 284, 286, 290
political life 7, 36, 38, 42, 45, 129, 134, 138, 139, 291, 299
political mobilization 56, 60, 66, 284, 351
political movements 55, 68, 260, 276, 290, 357
political participation 2, 9, 10, 84, 102, 133, 134, 139, 178, 184, 205, 292, 293, 315, 356

political parties 5, 6, 17, 19, 34, 35, 95, 124, 130, 170–172, 182, 204, 265, 270, 271, 339, 340, 360
political power 20, 37, 98, 103, 150, 188, 202, 248, 285, 348, 356
political process 19, 84, 302, 319, 335, 343, 350, 357, 358
political representation 9, 36, 181, 275, 277, 307, 343, 351, 357
political rights 36, 118, 130, 223, 327, 359
political roles 63, 65, 112, 129, 281, 284, 285
political scenario 114, 160, 245
political significance, UP 101–102
political spaces 63, 111, 273, 276, 289, 338
political structures 23, 43, 111
political transformation 55
political work 1, 111, 232, 242, 299, 340
politicians 11, 12, 14, 16, 19, 26, 27, 60, 106, 173, 198, 199, 202, 205, 233, 250, 251, 259, 261, 359
politics 1, 2, 8, 14, 23, 26, 27, 56, 60, 110, 129, 130, 182, 185, 187, 270, 292, 354, 359, 361; in Gujarat 211–225; of Uttar Pradesh 7, 101–114
post-independence period 161, 162, 212, 292, 350
post-liberation Goa 176
powerful political leaders 16, 60, 79
power politics 129, 237
private spaces 65, 286
protest politics 61, 63, 64, 67
protests 18, 20, 21, 89, 90, 128, 129, 152, 157, 224, 230, 240, 241
public spaces 63–65, 155, 156, 163, 222, 270, 286, 291, 350
public sphere 15, 151–156, 158, 229, 230, 275, 281, 284
Punjab 3, 4, 15, 71, 83–86, 89–92, 95, 97, 98
Punjab politics 83–85, 91, 98, 99

Quit India Movement 89, 90, 126, 229
Quraishi, S.Y. 3

Rajasthan 8, 12–14, 16, 257–261, 263, 264, 268, 270, 271
Raje, Vasundhara 8, 16, 258–259, 262, 268

366

INDEX

Rajya Sabha 13, 32, 72, 73, 105, 106, 126, 135, 150, 192, 201, 219, 220, 230, 232, 249, 251, 294, 295, 312

Rangnekar, Ahilya 12–13, 200, 202, 230, 232–233, 242

Records Bureau's Report on Crime in India 338

representation: parliament 126, 128; state assembly 119–124

reservations 3, 28, 31, 33, 109, 127, 130, 198, 297–298

resilience 41, 327

responsibility 40, 75, 111, 184, 198, 223, 336

Roy, Prannoy 5, 6

Sabha, Vidhan 262

selection, women candidates 345–346

separatist politics 61, 64–66

The 73rd and 74th Constitutional Amendment Acts 127

sexist bias 286

sex ratio 81, 86, 97, 102, 137, 141, 212, 213, 274, 307, 338

sexual inequality 291

Shakti Criminal Law Bill 237

Sikkim 14, 16, 305–315; state politics in 305–315

Singh, Sumitra 12, 14, 259, 262

social anxiety 275

social capital 111

social movements 163, 197, 202–205, 350, 351

social reform movements 71, 81, 161, 162, 211, 275

socio-political movements 160, 286

Sopariwala, Dorab R. 5, 6

state assemblies 3, 10, 29–31, 106, 107, 119, 121, 123, 124, 127, 145, 215, 232, 249, 251, 258, 267, 319; elections 7, 9, 11, 103, 121, 145, 216, 278, 283, 319, 322

state legislatures 29, 60, 83, 91, 118, 121, 130, 192

State Women's Commission 251

Subba, Kalawati 14, 310, 312–313

Sundarayya, Putchalapalli 164

sustainable development goal 37

Swaraj, Sushma 135

Tata Trust 215

Telangana 9, 13, 17, 21, 160–164, 170–173; state politics 161, 163, 165, 167, 169, 171, 173

Telangana movement 162, 166, 170, 173

Thakur, Viplove 126

traditional patriarchal culture 65

traditional societies 62, 111, 157

underground movement 161, 164, 165

UN Fourth World Conference on Women 37

United Nations 35, 36, 42, 104, 241, 273

United Nations Convention on the Political Rights of Women 36

Uttar Pradesh state assembly 13, 105, 106

Varghese, Sudha 361–362

Vidhan Sabha elections 7, 135, 136, 265

violence against women 338

voluntary participation 293

voters 5, 6, 57, 118, 119, 130, 131, 136, 137, 181, 258, 259, 263, 264, 343

voting 3, 5, 6, 57, 58, 118, 119, 178, 181, 216, 263, 265, 292

'Wajib Ul Urj' 128

Weiner, Myron 1

West Bengal, state politics in 273–286

winnability perception 348

woman legislator 77, 260–262, 268

women achievers 325–326

women legislators 23, 24, 30, 32, 34, 97, 98, 136, 259–263, 267, 268

women members, parliament 346–347

women politicians 12, 13, 16, 26, 27, 60, 104–106, 199, 202, 233, 251, 259, 261

women's agency 67, 277

women's development 97, 217, 232, 237, 240, 254, 359

women's movements 185

women's organizations 6, 29, 30, 33, 65, 66, 138, 233, 240, 241, 284, 285, 356–358

INDEX

women's representation 7–10, 28, 37, 38, 76, 77, 119, 126, 135, 172, 233, 267

women's status 54, 160, 161, 274, 291, 336, 338

women's voices 65, 66, 187, 274

women's wings 17, 18, 182, 183, 189, 191, 192, 219, 238, 313, 315

women voters 3–6, 34, 91, 109, 145, 172, 181, 233, 278, 292, 301, 335

Yadav, Dimple 15, 26, 105